D1108554

Handbook of
Hindu Mythology

TITLES IN ABC-CLIO's
Handbooks of World Mythology

HANDBOOKS OF WORLD MYTHOLOGY

Handbook of Hindu Mythology

George M. Williams

A B C CLIO

Santa Barbara, California • Denver, Colorado • Oxford, England

Library of Congress Cataloging-in-Publication Data

Williams, George M., 1967–
    Handbook of Hindu mythology / George M. Williams.
        p. cm.—(Handbooks of world mythology)
    Includes bibliographical references and index.
    ISBN 1-57607-106-5 (hardcover : alk. paper) ISBN 1-85109-650-7 (e-book)
    1. Hinduism—Sacred books. 2. Mythology, Hindu. I. Series.
BL1111.4.W55 2003
294.5'13—dc22
                                2003017013

07 06 05 04 03   10 9 8 7 6 5 4 3 2 1

This book is also available on the World Wide Web as an e-book.
Visit http://www.abc-clio.com for details.

ABC-CLIO, Inc.
130 Cremona Drive, P.O. Box 1911
Santa Barbara, California 93116-1911

This book is printed on acid-free paper ⊗ .
Manufactured in the United States of America

CONTENTS

PREFACE

Writing the *Handbook of Hindu Mythology* proved to be a project that rounded out three decades of work as a historian of religion specializing in religion in India. I had sought out a colleague in India to fill in any gaps I might have in the nearly five thousand-year span of Hindu mythology, but in the end I needed to fill those gaps with new study and translations of materials I had previously ignored. Hindu mythology was once something I had looked down upon with an intellectual contempt that partial ignorance blesses. But now I look back with a bemused smile and hear the laughter of Hindu gods and goddesses at so rash a conceit. Just like the many reversals in Hindu myths, my colleague's withdrawal from the project allowed me to enter a magical landscape of complexity, reversals, and ambiguities that the more rational approaches of philosophy, theology, and history do not allow.

It is difficult to give up scholarly trappings. I have spent the last seven years preserving Sanskrit manuscripts, digitizing some myself and training archivists and librarians all over India to utilize these new tools. To be called a pioneer in anything leads to a little pride, but Indian culture humbles any Western scholar. To be invited twice to the Sir Ashutosh Mukerjee Chair as a visiting professor at the National Institute of Advanced Studies in Bangalore was a great honor, allowing access to some of the oldest surviving sacred texts. But the real fruit of comparative textual studies lies in the future when scholars will have an abundance of versions of the same text and will be freed by a notion of an inclusive text that encompasses all its versions. That all versions of a myth are necessary for a complete understanding of its richness can only be hinted at in a book of this size, but versions of each myth are selected to be representative of the variations over time and among even contemporary accounts.

For the *Handbook* there will be no attempt to surprise the reader with new interpretations. Rather, the intention of this study is to engage anyone interested in Hindu mythology in its variety, its richness, its reversals, and its play *(līlā)*. As a handbook for the general reader, a number of decisions have been made about the transliteration of Sanskrit, the sacred language of India, that will aid in better readability, pronunciation, and use in moving through the literature on a given topic. The Sanskritist will have no problem knowing a technical term when I use a more popular Romanization of a Hindu term or the name of a god or goddess. Conversely, it is the general reader who suffers when we use the most accurate transliteration of Sanskrit. I will use as few diacritics as possible to help the general reader in identifying precisely in Roman letters the term or name in question, but will resist making these spellings too foreboding. Consequently, I will use an ś for one of the three "s" consonants in Sanskrit, as in Śiva. It is too often spelled "Siva," which gives no help in pronunciation, or "Shiva," which helps in pronunciation but does not alert the beginner to the study of Sanskrit and hides the complexity of the multiple ways of spelling the name of this deity. Long vowels will be marked to help in pronunciation. Sanskrit vowels are pronounced much like Spanish or Latin vowels except for the short "a," which is pronounced as a short "u" (but). Aspirated consonants (such as "bh" or "dh") are best learned in oral practice from a teacher. "C" is pronounced as "ch" in "check" but there is also an aspirated "ch" that doubles the aspiration. The beginner should be alert to the fact that a word like *âcârya* might also be transliterated as "acharya" by some.

An old rule of thumb in a beginning Sanskrit class to try to learn the rhythm or cadence of the language is to give a consonant one count, a short vowel two counts, and a long vowel three counts. Thus, diacritics will be used for long vowels to help the general reader's pronunciation and to avoid some hidden pitfalls. Thus, *"brâhmin"* (priest) is pronounced with the first syllable twice as long as the second. And the use of *brâhmin* for priest instead of *brâhmana*, or its often shortened version, *brâhman*, chooses a later spelling rather than its more ancient form so that the reader will not confuse *brâhmin* with *Brahman*, the Absolute. Both words for priest, *brâhmin* and *brâhman*, have a long vowel in the first syllable and omitting the diacritical mark leaves one with no distinction in the written word between a priest and the Absolute—a confusion that priests have not minded, but one that needs to be avoided nonetheless.

This text will follow the academic custom of not capitalizing the words *god* and *demon*. This can be justified from most Hindu perspectives as well, since the Absolute, the Supreme Being, is not being referred to as a whole. When the Absolute, or the entirety of the Godhead, is indicated, then God will be capitalized. There is no theological truth intended, even though almost all capitalization has disappeared from current English prose. This choice will not seem scholarly enough for some and may seem too Western for others. Hopefully, the reader should accept this practice for its face value as a modern attempt to avoid too much capitalization while respecting a tradition.

The "n" used for neuter endings will be not used in instances where another term is more common in English. Such words as *karma* and *dharma* will be used instead of the older neuter forms *karman* and *dharman*. *Karma* and *dharma* will be italicized when they are concepts but when they are personified as *devas* (gods), such as Dharma, they will be capitalized and not italicized.

Another aspect of transliterating Sanskrit involves the lack of spaces between words. Thus, any use of spaces is a concession to other languages used in its transliteration. The same can be said concerning hyphenation. Since a medium-sized Sanskrit word can easily reach twenty letters, the general reader may have great difficulty recognizing elements that can easily be learned, so either spacing or hyphenation is quite useful. Mahâśiva or Śivadeva are only eight-letter words but they are instantly recognizable as Mahâ-śiva or Śiva-deva. The use of Mahâ (great) before a name—Mahâ-Lakshmî or Mahâlakshmî, Mahâ-Devî or Mahâdevî, Mahâvishnu or Mahâ-Vishnu—demonstrates variant forms of names. I will use these variants interchangeably to both teach the reader to recognize elements that can be learned easily and to aid in the use of reference words and databases that employ alternate systems of spelling, spacing, capitalization, and hyphenation.

Capitalization is arbitrary when transliterating Sanskrit, as the written language made no distinction between upper and lowercases. I will use an upper case for the proper name of an individual god or goddess while lowercasing names that apply to groups, such as *devas, asuras, daityas, indras,* and so on—all classes of gods or demons.

I suspect that most of my colleagues will approve of these decisions about Sanskrit orthography. I also suspect that even a student in the first year of Sanskrit studies will be able to move from these popular spellings to their *Devanâgarî* (Sanskrit alphabet) equivalents. If so, the *Handbook* should meet the needs of the widest variety of readers.

There is a trend not to italicize well-known religious literature such as the Christian Bible, but then one finds oneself looking to *Webster's Dictionary* to see if the *Vedas* should be italicized or not. For consistency's sake, all Hindu scripture, well-known or not, will be italicized.

Certain names have become so well-known in English works and databases—such as Krishna (Kṛṣṇa) and Vishnu (Viṣṇu)—that hopefully the general reader and those more familiar with Sanskrit and Hindu terminology will feel equally comfortable.

Footnotes have been integrated into the text in all but a few cases. Likewise, references to the precise scriptural text—for example, *Mahâbhârata, Adi Parva,* chapter 167, verses 190–220, documenting Draupadî being cited as one of the five ideal women of Hindu mythology—have been omitted as too technical for current purposes. Select entries have additional readings to help the general reader gain familiarity with the richness of bibliographic resources that are ever increasing.

Finally, certain concepts that are so common as to need no explanation in academic circles—such as sanskritization or brâhmanization (drawing an element of the low tradition into the high tradition and giving it a Sanskrit name or term) or orthoprax/heteroprax (opposing *praxis* or practice rather than belief of the orthodox and the heterodox)—will be discussed in chapter 1. Besides these common notions (and even they will be explained briefly), each article will attempt to be self-contained or need only the connected articles for fuller understanding.

Special thanks is due to ABC-CLIO and its fine editorial staff: to Todd Hallman for his early leadership of the project, to Bob Neville, and to Anna Kaltenbach. I am especially grateful for the careful reading of the manuscript given by Silvine Farnell. Lastly, I would be remiss if I did not thank my Sanskrit professors who, decades ago, introduced me to this wondrous language and its literature, and to a host of dedicated scholars like Wendy Doniger O'Flaherty, who have influenced this work in one way or another.

George M. Williams
April 2003
Semester at Sea, somewhere in the Indian Ocean

1

INTRODUCTION

Most Hindus do not separate myths from ordinary experience the way Hindu philosophers and theologians do. Hindu intellectuals make sophisticated distinctions between existential truths (what you experience with your own senses and know from your own experience) and what others teach. The Buddha taught his followers to test everything in life and only believe what they had verified through their own life experiences. Most Hindu intellectuals are very comfortable with the Buddha's counsel as a beginning point for their explorations. Yet, even in the thinking of most intellectuals, and as for other Hindus, there has always been some room for the imaginal—for myth.

Many historians of religions insist that what distinguishes a myth from a legend is myth's dealings with gods and demons—legends deal with humans, especially heroes and heroines. However, this distinction does not hold well in India. In Hindu narratives gods and demons are brought into even the most ordinary legend, seemingly as a device of the storyteller that warrants it being heard. There is such a familiarity with the sacred that the supernatural adorns almost everything. From another perspective, Lee Siegel has connected this attitude with India's fondness for magic and the belief that magical powers are both a sign of the divine and an attribute of those gifted by the divine. Siegel has shown, in *The Net of Magic*, that India utilizes magic so freely that one cannot easily gain attention without it. Thus India's mythology seems filled to a higher degree with magical or miraculous elements than other mythologies are. The extent of this infilling with the miraculous will be explored in these pages.

This text will follow the academic custom of not capitalizing the words *god* and *demon*. This can be justified from most Hindu perspectives as well, since the Absolute, the Supreme Being, is not being referred to as a whole. When the Absolute, or the entirety of the Godhead, is indicated, then God will be capitalized. There is no theological truth claim intended.

THE LIVING POWER OF HINDU MYTHOLOGY

A Hindu does not have to "believe in" the details of the myths. These details are open to variation. In fact, there are often many versions of the same story, and one version may contradict the details of another. A Hindu can participate in the mythic meaning of a tradition simply by identifying with the myth's ability to help one locate oneself within the community's worldview. Insiders will find themselves at home within the worldview of their tradition's myths; outsiders will hear or read these myths and find them strange and even "untrue." That is the nature of being an outsider. For the insider, the myths will be validated simply in the experience of belonging to a community. For the outsider, the same myths will be objects outside of one's experience. However, even the outsider can see universal themes—mythology's timeless contributions to human reflection.

Any study of myth that does not recognize myth's potential to be alive and existentially powerful, even in modern life, has missed something. Myths are not true in any scientific sense—nor are they true philosophically, theologically, metaphysically, or ontologically (that should about cover all the perspectives that study absolute truth). Myth's power arises from its ability to articulate the existential need for identity. Myth answers questions about origin or creation (where we came from), purpose and meaning (why we are here, what we should do with our lives), morality (what is right or wrong), and destiny (above all what happens at and after death). Myths are not children's stories. They are often violent and filled with sexuality. There are many reversals; sometimes the people who are supposed to be good (such as teachers or priests) turn out to be bad examples in a particular version of a myth. That is why the hearer has to be alert—or have a good teacher. The many versions treat a theme or topic from many different angles and teach more than a single "true answer." The cast of characters, the themes, and even the core meanings of the entire mythology become second nature to the insider. One comes to know what one's culture believes about itself and what it expects.

MYTHIC IDENTITIES

Cultural and religious identity in Hinduism is amazingly broad. In Hindu mythology there are as many as 330 million different role models (gods, or *devas*) that can validate an individual identity. One's identity is not stereotyped by being a Hindu; there is not just one way to approach life. One's appropriation of this vast treasury of wisdom is one's own responsibility (that is what the notion of *karma* is about—personal responsibility for each and every action—

and *svadharma*—one's own appropriation of truth and one's responsibility to live what one's own *karma* has necessitated).

Thus, a living mythology is quite different from a dead one. One does not study Hindu mythology in the same way one studies Greek mythology. Or if one does study Hindu mythology as dead, or monolithic, one will never grasp its current power. There are still hundreds of millions of Hindus who appropriate Hindu mythology into their own lives in a variety of ways. We will study Hindu mythology's general patterns and articulations, constituting its macro, or larger, view. However, there are microscopic versions of Hindu mythology: hundreds of millions of Hindus have their own understandings and live their own appropriations. One must never say, "I know all about Hindu mythology," even with a mastery of the macro level. A living mythology is full of surprises, since every Hindu potentially may appropriate Hindu mythology in her own way. One must be humble and realize that every Hindu is the authority about her own appropriation of Hindu mythology and what each believes is just that—what is true for her (and that is the micro level of mythology).

ALIVE WITHIN HINDU MYTHS

Roy Amore and Larry Shinn, in *Lustful Maidens and Ascetic Kings*, described what it is like to grow up with Hindu myths and stories:

> To grow up in India is to mature in a world alive with demons and water nymphs, goblins and irate goddesses. Wisdom is often measured not by degrees or formal education, but by the ability to tell the right story or recite a passage of scripture appropriate to a particular situation. Mothers and fathers teach their children religious and family responsibilities through stories. Householders scold their servants with reference to the fate of a character in a particular tale. In classical times, the student priest had to commit to memory vast quantities of scriptures, which varied in subject matter from the techniques of sacrifice to the proper conduct of the king in peacetime and at war. The moral tales and fables as well as myths relating the feats of the gods were common fare for any person who sought to be educated.[1]

HINDU WORLDVIEWS

Before any attempt to describe a mythology that has remained alive for four millennia, a brief summary of the most basic Hindu beliefs, of the Hindu worldview, is needed. A summary from the prevalent "Hindu Renaissance" point of

Pûjâ is worship, devotion, service to the divine, and a means to acquiring merit. (TRIP)

view, given by Prof. D. S. Sharma, should be adequate for our needs.[2] Sharma stated that Hindus share a unity within diversity, a unity that has five commonalities: (1) a common scripture (the *Vedas*); (2) common deities (one supreme spirit, *Brahman,* with many manifestations); (3) a common set of beliefs in the evolution of the world, the organization of society *(varna dharma),* the progress of the individual, the fourfold ends of human life *(aśrama dharma),* and the law of *karma* and *samsâra* (rebirth); (4) common ideals; and (5) a common group of practices *(varna-aśrama-dharma),* leading toward deification through worship *(pûjâ, japa, bhakti),* yoga, knowledge *(jñâna),* and meditation *(dhyâna, samâdhi).* Sharma admitted that there is great latitude in the ways Hindus understood each of these five elements. It is that very latitude that myth often explores best. These basic concepts will be developed more at the end of this chapter.

This statement of commonalities represents an attempt to characterize the majority of Hindus in the present. Yet, even though a living mythological tradition currently shares common beliefs, there has also been a "situated tradition"—with particularities that require attention to more aspects of the tradition. The entire tradition must be studied within historical periods or contcxts; within myth cycles, perspectives, and communities; within cognitive ways of understanding; and within broad cultural themes. To these we now proceed.

HISTORICAL CONTEXTS OF HINDU MYTHS

Myths are situated within historical periods. The same myth told in the medieval period of India as it was articulated in the *Purânas* (a body of scriptures of later Hinduism) may differ from earlier contexts and meanings. For example, Śiva has not always been the same supreme deity that he became in some of the *Purânas*. There was no Lord Śiva in the earliest extant stories of the *Âryas* (anglicized as Aryans), a people who were the Sanskrit-speaking arrivals to the Indian subcontinent approximately four millennia ago (though since the "arrival hypothesis" and the non-Aryan origin of Śiva are controversial, both will be discussed later). The origins of myths about Śiva appear to be among the native, tribal, or indigenous peoples who did not speak Sanskrit. So even the name of this god would have been in a tongue that was not part of the central community that was evolving into what would later be called Hindu.

Pre-Aryan Period (c. 2500–1700 B.C.E., Indus Valley or Dravidian civilization)

Indian culture has many roots. Two of the most important for modern Hinduism are the Indus Valley culture (c. 2500–1700 B.C.E.) and the Aryan culture (appearing in the Indus region around 1500 B.C.E.). The indigenous culture of the Indus is shrouded in mystery, as its script has defied translation. However, its archeological remains are extensive and seem to suggest some correspondences to later Hindu mythology. Indologists maintain a Web site to track activity and claims on the subject: http://www.indology.org. The tiny "sealings" that may have been used to label grain bags depict mythical beings of great imagination—beasts that are often a composite of real and imaginary creatures. Some have multiple heads, others a single horn. Taken together with the archeological sites, these sealings have allowed scholars to construct a picture of the mythology of the Indus Valley culture (or Harappan culture, as it has been named after one of its principal cities): (a) male gods worshiped by the ruling elite; (b) yogic practice and a lord of *yoga,* called the proto-Śiva; (c) mother goddesses worshiped by the masses; (d) public baths for ritual bathing; (e) tree spirits; (f) worship of snakes (later known in Sanskrit as *nâgas*) and theriomorphic (animal-shaped) beings, images of which were often tied to ritual objects to indicate their imminent sac-

The oral Sanskrit prayers became the holy Vedas. (TRIP)

rifice. (For a slightly dated but elegantly written summary of this culture, see Joseph Campbell, *The Masks of God: Oriental Mythology* [New York: Viking Press, 1962], pp. 155–171.)

The Vedic or Samhitâ Period (c. 1500–900 B.C.E. Aryan Civilization)

The *Vedas,* the sacred scriptures of the *Âryas,* define both a period of time and a culture. Almost all who consider themselves Hindu believe that the *Vedas* are eternal, that they exist eternally at the most subtle level. However, they must have become manifested in the form that scholars study them at some point in time. Therefore, it should not be offensive to even the most ardent Hindu fundamentalist that scholars have found that point of time to be less than four millennia ago, or more precisely, circa 1500 B.C.E.

The Aryan culture appeared full-blown on Indian soil in the *Rigveda,* a collection *(samhitâ)* of more than a thousand hymns *(rik-s),* which later became the first of three *(triya)* and then four Vedas. The three *Vedas* were the *Rigveda, Sâmaveda,* and *Yajurveda.* These, plus the *Atharvaveda* (a collection full of shamanic magic), became the *Samhitâs* and the first limb of a later conception of the fourfold *Veda* that then included the *Samhitâs* (collections that included the Rigveda), *Brâhmanas* (commentaries), *Âranyakas* (forest texts), and *Upanishads* (a treasury of mystical and devotional texts). But the fourfold *Vedas* evolved slowly in several stages.

The Vedic language was Sanskrit, with mythic and ritual elements memorized by priests, and unwritten for almost a millennium. Whether the Aryans were indigenous or arrived as warrior nomads from the steppes of Russia is a matter of contentious debate, reflecting agendas of colonialism and independence, postmodernism and Hindu fundamentalism. However interpreted, this culture contributed much to Hindu myths from its vast solar pantheon (Sûrya, Indra, Ushas) and its fire rituals and sacrifices (*agni yâgas*, literally "fire sacrifices"). By approximately 1200 B.C.E. Rigvedic mythology had reached its greatest expanse, and its influence over later Indian history was enormous. In fact, each succeeding age has related back to some remembered or imagined Vedic (i.e., Rigvedic) past, to which they have usually claimed to be the heirs. The exception would be those who consistently used the *catur-yuga* (four ages) theory of declining righteousness and thought that the *Vedas* were no longer suited for an evil age—only later scriptures like the *Purânas*.

The Brâhmanical and Aranyâka Period (c. 900–c. 600 B.C.E.)

The mythological point of view changed between the period of the *Samhitâs* (collections) and that of the *Brâhmanas* (commentaries). The *Brâhmanas* were more concerned with ritual and its effectiveness and less concerned with the older Rigvedic gods (*devas*). The role of Agni, the god of fire, had increased, and the symbolism of the fire sacrifice was more explicit. In the later *Brâhmanas* there were thirty-three *devas*, enumerated as eight *vasus*, eleven *rudras*, and twelve *âdityas*—with two gods unnamed. The period of the *Brâhmanas* and *Âranyakas* (forest texts) reached its fruition approximately 900 B.C.E. This period witnessed the ascendancy of the *brâhmanas* (priests), referred to in English as *brâhmans* and *brâhmins*, to the top of a social hierarchy, the caste system. The foundation had already been laid for the priestly assertion that their role was more essential than that of the Vedic gods, since they knew and controlled the sacrificial rituals. A tension between Brâhmanical (sacrificial) religion and later forms of Hinduism that tended to subordinate Vedic sacrifice became a constant in both the liturgy and the mythology from this point onward.

The Upanishadic Period (c. 900–c. 600 B.C.E.)

This period, the time of the major *Upanishads* (though minor Upanishads were produced for many more centuries), saw at first a reaction to and revolt against the caste system led by priests and against the blood sacrifices to the Vedic gods. Later, however, these texts were coopted by the priestly (orthoprax) tradition and made the fourth *Veda*—and for a majority of Hindus this most important and last section of the *Vedas* has been referred to in English as *Vedânta* (*anta*, or "end," of the *Vedas*).

About half of the *Upanishads* were mystical and unitive, speaking of experiencing the divine as the one *(ekam)*, while the other half promoted devotion to one or more deities. New gods and goddesses were celebrated, and devotional practices began to be introduced.

About this time (c. 600 B.C.E.) non-Hindu elements (Buddhist, Ajivika, Jain, and later elements from invaders such as the Yanavas, Shakas, and Pahlavas) made their "heteroprax" contributions ("other" or "alien practice") to Hindu mythology—such as temples, indoor shrines, and rituals modeled after service to a divine king. One can find ascetics (*munis*, yogis, *samnyâsîs*, *tapasvins*, and *taposdhanas*) on the periphery and among indigenous people (Dravidians, tribals). Renunciate traditions contributed elements that questioned blood sacrifice and the killing of animals, and promoted asceticism (even the gods should constrain themselves), vegetarianism, and much more. But within a few centuries, these too would be integrated into orthoprax, Brahmânical religion. All of these elements were picked up by Hindu mythology and modified in the following periods.

The Epic Period (c. 400 B.C.E.–c. 400 C.E.)

The period of India's great epics, the *Mahâbhârata* and *Râmâyana*, continued the expansion of mythology, emphasizing divine action on earth in incarnations and manifestations. Gods and demons multiplied as did their stories. Epic mythology foreshadowed the rich polytheism of the next two periods. The *Mahâbhârata* contained two appendices that were extremely important sources for later mythological development, the *Bhagavad Gîtâ* and the *Harivamśa*.

The Purânic Period (c. 300–800 C.E.)

The mythology of the *Purânas* can be broken into three periods (300–500; 500–1000; 1000–1800), or the whole period may simply be referred to as the Hindu middle ages or medieval period. During the previous periods, everything had been prepared for the banquet of Hindu mythology. Its table was now a

Vishnu is centered in this slightly sectarian image, with Brahmâ and Śiva smaller and above with Krishna and Râma, his avatâras or incarnations, below. (TRIP)

smorgasbord of mythic delights. Everything from the past could be found on the table, but most elements were characterized by new mixtures, with Hindu sectarianism on one hand (with each sect centered around one of the principle gods and goddesses—Vishnu, Śiva, or Devî) or Hindu universalism on the other (all paths are the same; all paths lead to the Absolute). The three sub-divisions within this period help locate in time historical developments within the sectarian communities, the rise and decline of Tântrism and its influence on mainstream mythology, the tendencies in Purânic mythologizing of subordinating Vedic gods and past heroes to ever-increasing moral weaknesses, and the like. This is a period of exuberant polytheism.

The Tântric Period (c. 900–c. 1600)

Imbedded within the Purânic period was a shorter one of *Tantra* and *Śâkta,* so called from the *śaktî,* or cosmic energy, associated with the Divine Mother (Devî). This period appeared full-blown by 900. Some say that it finally became visible again, having disappeared from historical sight at the time of the Aryan dominance of indigenous, Indus Valley culture. Some say that it never died and that it continues secretly today. Others point to a revival encouraged by the New Age movement in the West. And indeed, it is true in some way about every period of mythology in India. The old myths and beliefs do not really die but are reborn, though usually in a metamorphosis, to continue into the present. During the Tântric period, the mythology of Tântra and Śâkta revived and enriched blood sacrifice and the pursuit of pleasure as central themes. Tântra's stories differed radically in meaning from those of epic mythology, which favored devotion, asceticism, and duty.

The Modern Period

The modern period is said to begin with Râja Rammohan Roy (1772–1833), who was a century ahead of his civilization, if not of world civilization. Roy demythologized Hindu mythology a century before Rudolf Bultmann demythologized Christianity. Roy particularly opposed the *Purânas* and their polytheism, championing a rational and sometimes mystical interpretation of the *Upanishads.* The analysis of "core mythologies" begun by Rammohan Roy is not within the scope of this study; briefly, it promises a way for a culture's mythology to be studied in order to see its influence even when that influence is unknown or denied.

The modern period also contributed two quite different approaches—the revivalism of such figures as Svâmî Vivekânanda (1863–1902) or Svâmî Dayânanda Sarasvati (1824–1883) and of Hindu fundamentalism (ranging from the Hari Krishnas to the Rashtriya Svayamsevak Sangh, simply known as the RSS). One of the novel uses of mythology by Hindu fundamentalists has been in the conversion or reconversion of Indian tribals and nonscheduled classes (modern India's name for former outcastes). Myths were found or invented to make tribals or former "outcastes" Hindu and bring them within the cultural whole of a reconstructed Hindu mythological community.

SOURCES: ORAL TRADITION, TEXTS, SCRIPTURES—AND MODERNITY

Besides the scriptural tradition that names each of the periods of Indian history, there are oral traditions. Among the oral sources are storytellers (including astrologers, palm-readers, priests, and teachers), plays (India's great dramatic tradition, received by the masses in live performances), and even movies and television (some say half of India's movies and television shows are productions of the myths or retellings in some modern form). Allusions and references to the myths are made constantly in everyday conversation and enrich life by giving it points of comparison with India's long and complex mythology.

However, the sources that are easiest to study in English are the written resources—and many have been translated from Sanskrit and Hindi, as well as from India's regional languages, half of which are not related to Sanskrit. Some collections, like the *Panchatantra,* are literary documents, not scripture. However, most of the resources for the study of myths are considered sacred—they constitute Hindu scripture. Because of the Indian notion that most Hindu scripture is timeless, there is some potential offense in handling it historically. Nevertheless, by using internal and external evidence (references within the text, words that are datable by looking in all extant Indian literature and finding the very first occurrence of that word, historical and archeological findings), scholars (both Indian and non-Indian) are able to date Hindu scriptures to the period in which they were composed, give or take one or two centuries.

MYTH CYCLES, PERSPECTIVES, AND COMMUNITIES

Hindu myths are most often nested within much larger myth cycles. For example, the rebirth of Vishnu as a dwarf to rescue the gods *(devas)* from the rule of the demon king Bali is nested within the Vishnu cycle of myths. One could view Vishnu from many perspectives. (For example, pan-Hindu, sectarian, and nondualistic, or *advaitan.* But whatever the perspective and its influence on inter-pretation, all knew the stories of Vishnu's coming down to earth in at least ten different incarnations *(avatâras),* including the dwarf *avatâra.* Minor characters in each of the myths would be known both individually and in relation to the larger stories.

Given this complexity, several approaches must be taken to study Hindu mythology. No single approach helps the student learn the entire story, discover the elements both above and below this story (a process of nesting one story within another), and keep track of all the characters and special terms found in a single myth.

There are many versions of a story, both oral and written, and the stories are retold not only in Hindu versions but also in Buddhist and Jain versions. For scholarly exploration one usually must pursue these variations in primary tex-tual sources, dissertations, or journals that work with original languages and sources. However, these variations are not unusual when the stories are told in daily life in India. In fact, myth tellers themselves often refer to another myth or indicate a specific version of a myth. These cross references demonstrate just how familiar Indian audiences are with multiple versions of the myths, so that a myth maker or teller can "play the myths" much like a musician who chooses the right chords to syncopate a rhythm or modify a melody, creating ever differ-ing or familiar renditions at will.

UNDERSTANDING MYTHICALLY

How do Hindus understand their myths? In a living tradition mythology func-tions dynamically within the culture—ranging from narrowly Hindu to broadly pan-Indian. At the same time, there will be numerous ways that Hindus under-stand their myths. One might be tempted to say, as some scholars have, that there are as many ways as there are Hindus. But there are several general pat-terns that deserve specific mention.

Literalistic

The literal understanding of the core mythology of one's community is the beginning point. All children take stories literally until they are initiated into a myth's special kind of deception. (Some American children can believe in Santa Claus literally until five or six, but seldom longer than seven, and all experience "the wounding of consciousness," or "loss of naïveté," perhaps at the hands of a knowledgeable peer.) However, religious myths may be lived and believed literalistically for a lifetime. Reform Hindus have appealed to psychology (specifically theories of cognitive development, personality development, and child psychology) and even neurophysiology (specifically theories of brain development) to argue against holding a majority of people at this stage of cognitive development.

Nevertheless, there is something special about medieval and modern Hindu culture that permits a literalistic understanding of Hindu mythology for a lifetime without damage. Gods and demons are not outgrown. Priests, who might not be literalistic in their own faith, often justify the literalizing of Hindu myths for their "childlike" followers.

Hindu fundamentalists in modern times have added a new dimension—taking a narrow view of a literalistic Hinduism that does not tolerate other views. Slogans seldom translated into English include "India for Hindus" and "Drive Muslims and Christians out of India." Literalized myths about the incarnation of Vishnu as King Râma and about his birthplace, Ayodhya, figure prominently in their militant fundamentalism. Their power rests upon a noncritical, nonhistorical approach to living myths.

Sectarian

Biology is informing us about our human behavior of taking our group or community to be the only one that is true. In religion this is called sectarianism—that only one sect or religion is true; all others are not. There is an overlap between sectarian religion and sectarian mythology.

During the middle ages of India many examples of sectarianism in Hindu mythology emerged. This happened chiefly in Hindu devotionalism, where Vishnu, Śiva, and Devî (the Mother Goddess) competed as supreme deities. Logically there can only be one supreme deity of the universe. Followers championed one or the other of these three and literalized all of Hindu mythology into myth cycles that proved their god or goddess to be Supreme. (Followers of these three respective deities are called Vaishnavas, Śaivas, and Śâktas.)

Pan-Indian

This is a cultural approach. The myths are known as stories (as Americans know the story of George Washington and the cherry tree). The myths inform cultural expectations about truth telling, about relationships, about society. The myths are felt. They inform one's identity. They can be questioned and can even be doubted, but one identifies with a Hindu view of life and does not reject it. Thus, Hindu mythology still helps one to be Indian.

Reformed

The reformed and pan-Indian way of understanding often overlap. Rammohan Roy, the great Hindu reformer, believed that the mythic frame of reference had to be outgrown for Indians to "progress" from "superstition" to scientific and rational thinking and living. He foreshadowed modern movements in philosophy and theology to "demythologize" religion. He used the principles in the *Vedas,* especially in the *Upanishads,* to critique Hindu mythology and pointed out that myth was not literally true but only pointed to something higher than itself. Myth was never more than a symbol of truth. Thus, the myths and the gods were metaphors of truths, and if believed literally myths became idols. He did not mean idol in the Purânic sense of *mûrti*—physical forms that help the worshipper to conceive of the formless divine. Rammohan Roy meant that mythic thought and idols led to "idolatry"—worshipping something that was both false and dehumanizing. He thought it led to deceiving oneself and others.

Living at the beginning of the nineteenth century, Roy did not have the benefit of modern psychological research on human cognitive development to reconstruct what he had deconstructed. Roy did not see a value in mythology, even for children, but he might have modified his total rejection of mythology had he lived today. Indeed, the basis for using mythology developmentally was part of his interpretation of myth—that myths served as pointers to the truth, to the Absolute, no more. Just how deceptive they are and whether or not a "deceptive" notion might be developmentally necessary for easier comprehension is the issue he might have addressed if he had been born in the twentieth or twenty-first century. This has not been adequately addressed in modern Hinduism (for example, from Svâmî Vivekânanda to Sarvepalli Radhakrishnan) and will have to remain beyond the scope of this study.

HINDU MYTHOLOGY'S CONTRIBUTION TO WORLD MYTHOLOGY

Besides its adaptation from period to period within India, Hindu mythology has been assimilated into other mythologies or worldviews. Early explorers of India brought back stories about *yoga* and the wonders of the *faqirs* (Persian for illusionists or magicians). Translations of the *Upanishads* by Rammohan Roy were read by Emerson and Thoreau and influenced American Transcendentalism and its notion of the oversoul.[3] However, it was Hindu mythology's influence on Theosophy and Christian Science that bore more direct fruit. The New Age movement is a second or third generation of succession from this earlier influence. Hindu mythic themes and attitudes thrive in this new soil. Even as Ken Wilber[4] was outgrowing and rejecting the New Age movement of which he had been the greatest theorist, Hindu philosophy's influence on him cannot be denied. It has become a fixture in American—and more broadly Western—culture, creating new mythologies.[5]

Finally, let us turn to Hindu mythic themes—those that are nearly universal in the mythologies of the world and those that are more specific to Hindu mythology.

HINDU MYTHIC THEMES: UNIVERSAL

All mythologies probe the great themes of life: good and evil, the purpose of living, death and what lies beyond, struggle and suffering, challenge and determination, hope and perseverance. Some themes address a time before human life began—cosmic time at the beginning, or what was before the beginning of time. Other themes probe an ambiguity in existence that stretches concepts of good and evil, making them relative to an absolute perspective—ethics viewed from a divine or cosmic viewpoint.

As already noted, Hindu myths presuppose entire core systems, of which there are many. Amazing contradictions populate Hindu mythology, and yet these have not been a problem, as each hearer has been located in one of the many Hindu identities and its corresponding mythological core system. This applies both within a given period (as in the Vedic period or in the present) and within the membership of a particular community (as a Vaishnava—a worshipper of Lord Vishnu—or as a Tântra—a member of a sect with its distinctive core mythology and so on).

Myths speak of various ways that life has come to be as it is. There are a number of explanations as to why life is so miserable (if it is). Later Hindu myths with a single deity who is responsible for everything—creation, fate, destiny—speak of divine play *(lîlâ)* as one reason behind human suffering. However, earlier conceptions involved ritual and its effectiveness: that human beings were unhappy because the gods of the Vedic fire sacrifices had not been properly appeased. Some myths taught that one's fate was ruled by the cosmic justice of *karma*—that one always reaped exactly what one sowed, whether in this lifetime

Scholarly Terms in the Study of Mythology

Anthropogony	origin of humanity; how humans came to be the way they are
Anthropology	study of humanity and its evolution
Cosmogony	origin of the cosmos; how the cosmos came to be the way it is
Cosmology	concerning [study of] the origin of the cosmos and its evolution
Eschatology	concerning [study of] the end times
Theogony	origin of the gods; how the gods came to be the way they are
Theology	concerning [study of] the gods
Theomachy	a battle with or among the gods (and demons)
Soteriology	concerning [study of] salvation or release from suffering and chaos

or another. This would be "hard karma." However, there could also be "soft karma," *karma* softened by grace and devotion—myths that told of a god or the Supreme forgiving all one's past deeds and awarding heaven, even when it was not deserved by the "karmic facts."

Thus, the myths accounted for evil or suffering in a variety of ways. Perhaps the most remarkable notion was the news that there is no evil at all. Apparent evil is but an illusion *(mâyâ)* from a cosmic or divine perspective. So, finally, there is always hope. Hinduism is hardly pessimistic—as so many Westerners of the nineteenth and twentieth centuries have charged. Each Hindu mythology, comprised of ever expanding circles of mythic elements and themes, had at its disposal all the Hindu myths of all previous ages. And these included cosmologies and cosmogonies, theogonies and theologies, theomachies, anthropogeneses and anthropologies, eschatologies and soteriologies. (See the table above.)

However, to speak of these constructions—cosmologies and so on—was to bring them to analytical consciousness as rational and narrative systems. That is what a philosopher, a teacher, or a priest may do. The ordinary hearer only needs to draw from the psychological, spiritual, and social resources of myth. By the time there is analytical consciousness, there is already distance, doubt, and danger of evolution and change. Mythology works best in the early stages of human and civilizational development. However, the larger questions about life and death have changed little.

The mythic way of addressing them was distinct to each culture at that stage of development. So Hindu myths minister to persons struggling with life's existential crises and offer hope, suggest ways of cheating fate, and provide examples of those who have not been fortunate.

Cosmogony, Theogony, and Anthropogony

How did the cosmos, the gods, and humans come into being? Which came first? Some Hindu myths say that humans created the gods, so the order has been debated.

Hindu mythology accounts for the origin of the cosmos (cosmogony) with four of the five general cosmogonic solutions human beings have advanced, leaving out only the notion of creation from nothing. Many myths recall a cosmic battle, such as the one between Indra and Vritra. This kind of cosmogony is common in mythology, where creation comes from a victory over chaos. In the earliest Rigvedic hymns Vritra was a water demon (chaos), and Indra gained a victory that brought order (and thus creation). An even older cosmogonic myth had being come into existence as a cosmic egg, *hiranyagarbha* (a golden egg). It appeared or was created—depending on the version. Creation by divine dismemberment was another cosmogonic solution—the dismembering of the cosmic man *(purusha)* or of Agni the fire god, who resided or hid in the depths of the ocean; the latter joined two kinds of cosmogonic solutions (the separation of creative fire from chaotic water and the creation by the ritual sacrifice of a god). The "earth diver" as a cosmogonic solution can also be found in Hindu mythology, in the story of when Vishnu in his incarnation as Varâha plunged into the ocean and brought forth the earth (Bhûmî or Prithivî) from chaos. There were three more solutions in Hindu mythology to the cosmogonic mystery: creation from mind, creation from sound *(vâc),* and creation from parents (coition). The later was the most common form of creation and re-creation in the later mythology of the *Purânas* and had many versions.

Prajâpati was the first creator or father of all, but he was soon replaced with Brahmâ. There was always something available for the production of life, the most common source being the creator's seed. Perhaps the most interesting cosmogony was the "emission" *(prasarga)* of Brahmâ's sons from his own mind (making them *mânasâ-putras,* mind-born sons).

Some of these myths spoke of the creator becoming androgynous and producing offspring—a self-embrace transcending the opposition of male and female. A few accounts had Prajapati or Brahmâ create a woman (a mind-daughter) with whom he begot all beings. These births could either be by ordinary sexual relations or by magical means *(tapas).*

The creations *(srishthis)* had to be repeated again and again. Each age *(kalpa)* was followed by its destruction *(pralaya),* and there would eventually be fourteen great creations. We are now in the seventh age. Each age was ruled over by its first human being, its Manu. And each age received the Vedas and was required to live the *dharma,* but eventually would go into a decline that precipitated another destruction and another creation. (For more on time and the creations, see chapter 2.) So, which came first: time, the cosmos, or a god who created one or both? Hindu mythology is rich in answers.

Cosmology

What is the nature of the cosmos? What are the various realms or regions of the cosmos? Are there separate realms for the gods and demons?

In Indo-European mythologies there was usually a center of the earth directly under heaven, supported or separated from heaven by a sacred mountain or tree. In India that sacred mountain was Mount Meru, wider at the top than the bottom. Meru was situated at the center of an island continent, surrounded by an ocean. Around that island continent were six more concentric oceans and six donut-shaped continents. Above were the heavens, below many underworlds and hells. The sacred banyan tree was much like Meru in shape. A magical plant, *soma* (the plant of immortality and of healing), grew on the mountains of heaven but was brought to earth by Indra. Once the monkey god Hanuman had a difficult time finding *soma*, so he simply brought a mountain with its magical herbs to Râma, an incarnation of Vishnu.

In a late myth about the struggle between the gods *(devas)* and demons *(asuras)*, the snake Vâsuki was used as a rope to churn *soma* from the Great Milky Ocean. The gods and demons had to work together to accomplish this, but then they fought over the spoils. Finally, *soma* was replaced with rituals, austerities, and then devotion as means of sustaining or empowering the gods.

The sacred stories connected the landscape of India and Nepal to the gods. Wherever the *devas* touched the earth, there was a potential site for a temple or shrine—and a place for pilgrimage *(tîrthas)*, a central element in Hindu devotional life. Each temple or group of temples tended to develop their own mythologies, stories that proclaimed their importance and made clear why they must be visited. "The most sacred place in India" varied over the centuries and according to sectarian affiliations, but all lists would include most of the following: Badrinath, Hardwar, Varanasi (Benares or Kâsî), Pushkara, and Prabhâsa (Somnath). There were also *asura tîrthas* (pilgrimage sites of demonic activities where demons had played a role), such as Gâyâ, where Vishnu vanquished the demon Gâyâ, perhaps as allusion to the Buddha.

Once again myth has slipped over into what is thought of as the territory of religion: rituals, pilgrimage, temple worship, and religious merit. However, in India Hindu mythology is still living and plays a central role in religion, pilgrimage, art, literature, drama, and the subjects of modern film and video.

Theogony and Theology

Where did the gods come from? What is their nature? Who are they? Are they like us in form and character? What is our relationship to them? What do they want from us?

The origin of the gods varied most in Vedic mythology. In the earliest hymns some were simply there—Dyaus, the sky father, and Prithivî, the earth mother. However, their time of honor was already over, and their myths were not even retold. Then there were the central triad of gods—Sûrya, Indra, and Agni. However, in the *Vedas* the title of creator is bestowed on Prajâpati, lord of the beings or creatures. Yet there was no cosmogonic myth about him either. In the *Brâhmanas* and *Upanishads* a cosmic force or process known as *Brahman* would be either the totality of all that existed or the only Real, while all else was merely apparent. However, *Brahman* was not an object of human narration and thus not a proper subject of Hindu myth. In late theistic mythologies a supreme deity (Vishnu, Śiva, or Devî) was described as bringing everything into being—even time and causality (see chapter 2).

Theogony is composed of two Greek words—*theos,* or god, and *gonia,* related to our *genesis,* or beginning. Thus, a theogony concerns the beginning of the gods, where they came from, and their genealogy. Hindu polytheisms entail, like all polytheisms, stories about the life of the gods, their families, and their struggles for order (theomachies). They have a life! So a portion of Hindu mythologies simply tells stories about the gods, answering basic questions about their origin and activity. These stories are not pointless—they address social concerns and personal salvation (soteriology).

If we begin with the latest developments of Hindu mythologies in the *Purâ-nas,* we find myths centered on a single god as the supreme deity of the universe. There were three who competed for this honor: Vishnu, Śiva, and Devî. Since each of these deities was supreme for their devotees, there could be no myths of origin for them. They each must be the cause and agency of everything that exists. In other religious traditions, we would find any study of a supreme deity leaving mythology and entering a more rationalized theology. However, in Purânic "Hinduisms" myths were still constructed about the supreme deity, even though Supreme Being would be beyond having a life that was imaginable in human terms or amenable to story.

The Śiva of Purânic mythology was either supreme or subordinate to Vishnu or Devî. Śiva's core mythology included his marriage to Pârvatî or Umâ or both. He had two sons, Ganeśa and Skanda (or Kârttikeya). His vehicle was Nandi, the bull. Kailâsa was his abode. Although all Hindus would probably know the entire myth cycle and its elements, the themes of supremacy or inferiority

Śiva and key visual elements of his core mythology (TRIP)

┼-│0-│ tally alter the meaning (and even the details) of any episode depending
~r Śiva is seen as supreme or inferior to the Supreme Being. Both
Devî had their own myth cycles demonstrating that each could also
~~ supremacy and be seen as the sole origin of the universe.

In most later Hindu mythologies, Brahmâ was considered the creator god or
at least given that title. He might be presented as having "mind-children" or as
being the divine parent directly. In the latter kind of story, Brahmâ created a
female with whom he then had children. Later Hindu thinkers charged Brahmâ
with incest, because this was seen as marrying his own daughter, who was called
Vâc (speech). Brahmâ's role was further compromised by the sectarian mythologies that made Śiva, Vishnu, or Devî the author and creator of the universe—the
only self-existent *(svayambhû)* one. Eventually, Brahmâ was depicted as only
sitting on a lotus flower growing out of the navel of Vishnu, his function to create each new age, only to fall asleep or to be destroyed in the cyclic doomsday
(mahâpralaya), to be reborn anew from the thought of the real creator, Vishnu
(or one of the other supreme deities). Later mythology changed the Vedic myth
of the spontaneous appearance of the golden egg *(hiranyagarbha),* from which
the universe emerged, to its origin upon the release of Brahmâ's seed into the primordial ocean. Both Brahmâ and the cosmic egg had become subordinate parts
of other myths.

The gods were also bothered by marital problems. The great ascetic Śiva, ·
lord of *yoga,* was troubled as much as any human with love and family life. Some
myths resorted to magic to overcome Śiva's asceticism (portraying the god as
being shot by one of Kâma's magical love arrows), some to feminine wiles, some
to common sense—surely Śiva would be attracted to his beautiful wife. Other
myths had him chasing his wives from one lifetime to the next, even in the form
of animals. Their lovemaking in these myths even threatened the universe with
an early destruction. From a mythological point of view these stories can be seen
as an extension of the cosmogonic battle to create, now projected into the chaos
of male-female relationships.

The gods must be followed through their mythic relationships. Vishnu has
a wife or consort who goes by two names, Śrî and Lakshmî—although sometimes the names belong to separate individuals. In later myths she was known
as Mahâlakshmî and Bhadrakâlî. Vishnu's second wife is Bhû Devî (the earth
goddess). His vehicle was Garuda, the sun bird. During his sleep at the end of an
age, Vishnu reclined on his serpent—either Śesha (the remainder) or Ananta (the
endless one, eternity). But to complete the myth of Vishnu one must know the
stories of each of his ten avatâras—fish, tortoise, boar, man-lion, dwarf, Râma
the Ax Wielder, Râma of the *Râmâyana,* Krishna, the Buddha, and Kalki.

Śiva was first associated with Rudra and then became a being in his own right. He was married to Pârvatî, by whom there were two children, Ganeśa and Skanda (or Kârttikeya). Durgâ is also his wife in some myths. His vehicle is Nandi (or Nandin), the bull. He is lord of *yoga*, lord of the animals *(pasupati)*, and lord of the dance *(natarâja)*. He is the only god who left a part of himself to be worshiped by his devotees, the *linga*. His manifestations have the same purpose as Vishnu's incarnations of ending evil or granting grace, but his sovereignty over the universe was preserved in another way. In one of his manifestations he is united with his feminine power (his *śaktî*, in other stories enjoying a separate existence as Śaktî, his wife) so that he becomes androgynous. As a *śarabha* (a fierce mythical animal), he is able to conquer the boar *avatâra* of Vishnu—yet another manifestation of his supremacy.

Devî is encountered in many feminine manifestations; the first is Durgâ (who was at first associated with Vâc). Some of these manifestations are terrifying (Durgâ, Mahishamardinî, Candikâ, Kâlî, Vindhyavasinî, Câmundâ, and many more), others quite benevolent (Satî, Umâ, Pârvatî, Śivâ, and Gaurî). Any of these goddesses might be portrayed as a wife or consort of a god, or they can be a manifestation or the emphasis may be on her power as a manifestation of Devî—and therefore beyond any subordination to a mere husband. Devî also appeared as Yoganidrâ (cosmic sleep), Vishnumâyâ (world illusion), Ambikâ (the mother), and Śaktî (divine energy).

Theomachy

What kept creation from being perfect? Against whom do the gods fight? Who are the demons or the demonic forces? Where did they come from? Why do they seek to destabilize the divine order that the gods created? How do they get their power? Will there ever be a final victory over evil and disorder?

Vritra, opponent of Indra in the *Rigveda*, had no genealogy (theogony). Vritra was a personification of chaos. Later demons *(asuras)* were born from the very same Prajâpati (progenitor or grandfather) as the gods, Kaśyâpa. However, in many of the myths the *asuras* were the older brothers of the gods (or, much later, cousins) and therefore were the rightful rulers of heaven and earth. How they lost their right to rule was a recurring theme of the myths. During the ritualistic periods of the *Vedas* and *Brâhmanas*, it was the sacrifices that sustained the power of the gods, so they fought over their share. However, this situation taught nothing but brute force, cunning, or deception. Later, as faith in the sacrifices waned, the myths found a way around this problem. Ascetic practice *(tapas)* could be engaged in by gods, demons, and humans with equal results: one gave up pleasure to acquire power *(siddhi* or *śaktî)*. This approach allowed an

Devî manifests as Durgâ to destroy Mahesha, the buffalo demon. (TRIP)

ascetic morality by which there was a real struggle between forces of (relative) good and (relative) evil. During the later mythology even devotional practices were thought to be as effective as purely ascetic ones. It was by these practices that magical powers *(siddhis)* could be acquired—invisibility, invincibility, or an immortality that was always limited to an apportioned lifetime according to one's species. (The myths allowed six individuals *(ciranjivis)* to attain true immortality, so that they would never die.) Hindu theomachy never completely solved the problems involved in personifying the *devas* and the *asuras* and gave mixed messages about the sources of evil and the purposes for good.

The gods *(devas)* typically fought the demons *(asuras)*, and humans struggled with flesh-eating monsters *(râkshasas)*. There were also other beings that might just appear or be sent by the gods to steal ascetic power *(śaktî)*, such as the Aśvins, *gandharvas,* or *apsaras* (the divine twins, celestial musicians, and celestial damsels—see entries in chapter 3).

There would be many stories told of the gods in combat with demons (theomachies). Establishing and maintaining order was a recurring problem. Indra had to defeat the serpent-dragon Vritra, and various gods reestablished order again and again. Vishnu fought demons in each age, but only as an incarnation, or *avatâra,* such as the fish, the boar, Krishna, or Râma, never in his own form as the Supreme. There were always contests for supremacy—if not with another god or a demon, then with a sage like Nârada. Ascetic practice, or *tapas* (giving up pleasure in order to gain power), was the currency that made one a rival of the gods. Indra's throne heated up when god, demon, or sage gained too much power by their *tapas.* He was thus forewarned, so he could act to protect his office as king *(indra)* of heaven.

In the *Purânas* it was not always clear who was supreme. Of course, it was clear in the mind of a devotee of one of the three contenders for supremacy—Śiva, Vishnu, and Devî (and that point of view is called sectarian). However, stories abounded about the contests between them. The devotees of one particular god wove a version of the myth to show how their god was lord of the universe. For example, Devî took her *śaktî* (power—a feminine word ending in "*î*") away from Lord Śiva. This was proved linguistically by a clever argument based on Sanskrit's syllabic spelling. With the *i* subtracted from the first syllable, *śiva* (the auspicious one) becomes *śava* (the corpse). In another example of sectarianism, the story goes that Vishnu took the form of his boar *avatâra,* Varâha, and plunged into the cosmic ocean, where he claimed that he had found the base of the cosmic *linga* (the divine phallic form of Śiva). Then he took the shape of the divine eagle (Garuda), and after his flight he claimed that he had flown to the top of the universe and seen its top, though the linga was known to be infinite by Śiva's followers. Nandi, Śiva's bull vehicle, could not stand by and allow such lies, so he kicked Vishnu in the forehead, knocking him silly (his devotees thought that he was meditating). This blow left a hoofprint on the god's fore-head, which Vishnu's devotees copied, making on their own foreheads a distinc-tive mark *(tîlaka)* of three horizontal lines. These stories were endless.

Anthropogony

Where did we come from? Were humans always like this? How are we supposed to live? What are the correct traditions? What are the laws we should live by?

Besides all of the creation or evolution stories, there were stories about the four castes—*brâhmins, kshatriyas, vaiśyas,* and *śûdras*. When human origin was traced to the dismemberment of the cosmic man *(purusha),* the castes were described as originating from different parts of his body. Humans were a part of the same sacred web of being as animals, demons, and gods. Myths of declining goodness (the *yugas,* the four ages) explained that humans were once great heroes and teachers *(gurus, rishis),* but now there was an ever-lessening attention to righteous living *(dharma).* The incarnations *(avatâras)* were necessitated by a loss of the correct traditions found in the *Vedas* from which knowledge *(jñâna)* of the eternal truths came. The divine rule of King Râma, himself an *avatâra,* had clearly established the correct laws that should govern all of human life. Hindu myths would have examples who are arch villains and true heroes and heroines, both illustrating how life ought to be lived no matter what one's station or cir-cumstance. There are the five great women *(pañcakanayâs):* Ahalyâ, Draupadî, Mandodarî, Sîtâ, and Târâ. The five Pandava brothers have all the attributes of greatness, and Arjuna certainly joins the select few as a great friend and devotee of Krishna. Sages such as Vyâsa and Nârada abound with awesome powers. Kings, maidens, prostitutes, rouges—from all castes and in all stages Hindu mythology provides good and bad examples of our possibilities and our frailties.

MYTHIC THEMES: SPECIFIC

Dharma (life's duty) and *karma* (ultimate responsibility), sin and error, knowl-edge and ignorance, mercy and grace, pollution and purification, mortality and immortality, birth and fertility, asceticism and enjoyment, piety and ritualism, demons and gods—these weave their way throughout Hindu mythology.

Dharma

What is righteousness? How can we know and do good? What is our duty?

Dharma is one of the most pregnant notions in Hindu philosophy, religion, and mythology. It can be translated in English as religion, virtue, truth, or duty.

For our purposes it is the duty that one is born into (*varna-dharma,* caste) and the responsibilities one must shoulder according to one's stage of life (*aśrama-dharma*). In the *Bhagavad Gîtâ* Krishna told Arjuna that it is better for him to do his own duty *(svadharma)* than to try to do someone else's. Arjuna was trying to avoid the duty of a warrior and renounce war.

This varying standard according to caste and stage of life is constantly illustrated in the myths. In the Epic and Purânic periods *dharma* became the standard by which good and bad *karma* could be judged, as it meant that one had performed one's duty in that particular circumstance. But there will be a noticeable tension between *dharma* and *tapas,* duty and austerities, especially the more magical austerities of the later myths. Unrighteous *asuras* (demons) are able to practice severe *tapas* and gain their desires, usually for power over the *devas* (gods). But there are humans who also use the fruits of their *tapas* to get revenge, with some sages going so far as to curse others from the power of their *tapas* with death or deformity. The ethical connections between *dharma* and *tapas,* duty and austerities, truth and religious practice, will be given great latitude in some of the Purânic stories.

Karma

How does *karma* work? Does *karma* carry over from one lifetime to the next?

Karma is one of the causative principles of Hindu philosophy and mythology. It is the accumulated results of actions done as causative instruments for future blessing or punishments. In this wide-ranging mythology *karma* has both its hard and soft versions—as will be discussed further in chapter 2 in "Nimitta (Causality)": one quite mechanistic in its strict sense of justice and punishment, the other allowing for interventions such as divine grace. Hindu mythology never defines its usages of *karma* but appeals to its eternal law in every narrative.

There is probably no single myth that illustrates *karma* better than the story of Kamsa, the uncle of Krishna. This myth has a series of nested stories that go forward and backward in time to examine the changing relationships of the principle characters and their *karma.* Kamsa's karmic chain began at the beginning of a new cosmic creation, at the beginning of this *kalpa.*

Kamsa was, in his first birth of this aeon, Kâlanemi, a son of Virocana, an *asura* (demon) and the brother of Bali. The brothers were famous demons, which would suggest that there had been a lot of bad *karma* in the previous kalpa. Kâlanemi had six sons, whose bad *karma* from a previous lifetime was explicitly stated in another myth. They had been the six sons of Marîci, a semidivine figure clouded in some mystery. Marîci was associated with Indra and was apparently a *marut,* with powers of storm and battle. Marîci's sons were so powerful that they rivaled the creator, Brahmâ. They openly mocked him and accused Brahmâ of marrying his daughter, Sarasvatî. Weakened by their own actions, they were victims of Brahmâ's curse—that they would be reborn as *asuras*. Thus, they were born the sons of Kâlanemi, the future Kamsa.

The story goes back and forth to show good and bad actions of Kâlanemi and his six sons. Kâlanemi was later born as Kamsa, and his six sons were reborn twice before being born as Kamsa's nephews. At that point they were born to Devakî (mother of Krishna), and the Krishna nativity story tells how Kamsa killed each of them. (For a concise retelling of this karmic puzzle, see the entry on Kamsa in chapter 3.)

After many lifetimes of opposing Vishnu's incarnations, Kamsa, or Kâlanemi, was finally redeemed, as his *karma* burned out in the presence of the Lord's grace. The final fate of the six sons also demonstrated this dissolution of *karma* by grace.

Samsâra or Transmigration

Cosmogonic questions take on a specifically Hindu character when the answers involve transmigration. How does chaos become order? How does the undifferentiated one become many? What is the interrelation of all living things in the cosmic web of being? How does rebirth work?

Samsâra (flow) points to a conception of the universe in constant change, a universe following nature laws *(dharma)* and rhythms *(yugas)*, the declining ages of each cosmic cycle. Humans fit into a chain of life that Hindu mythology explicates with stories about births and rebirths of the soul *(jîva)* on its path to find the divine.

While transmigration seems to be the common territory of all Hindu religions and philosophies, Hindu myths come at this concept from many differing points of view and even conflicting solutions, sometimes offering alternatives that are in direct conflict with prevailing religious and philosophical views. One solution would involve the notion of the *gotra* (an order of being), positing long chains of past lives in the various rebirth orders (*gotras*), and progression and regression within the orders of being during many rebirths.

The problem of mythic and historical overlap can again be seen in the term *gotra*. Although *gotra* currently means the ancestry or lineage of a *brâhmin* (something like a Brâhmanical clan), the term was historically used before the caste system came into existence and indicated a Vedic clan. Later in Hindu mythology the notion of *gotras* was used as part of the solution to the problem of how all orders of living things could come from the same parents (one *prajâ-*

pati and his wife). According to the *Mahâbhârata* (an Epic), four *prajâpatis* participated in the moment of creation of the current *kalpa,* thus placing all living beings into four orders, four *gotras.* But this notion of some separation in creation did not prevail, as it blurred the generally accepted idea of the interconnectedness of all beings.

Instead, a deep interconnection between the animal, human, demon, and divine orders was seen to exist. Myths connected all living beings to the same father or grandfather *(prajâpati).*

Kâla

What is time *(kâla)*? Was there a beginning and will there be an end to time? What happens at the end of time? Is there something more in life than what is apparent? What is our ultimate fate?

The various answers given by Hindu mythologies to these questions form the material of the next chapter. In the earlier periods of Hindu mythology knowledge of time, space, and causality *(kâla-deśa-nimitta)* seems to be the requisite in ordering the rituals that control the *devas* that grant life's blessings and even arrange matters concerning life and death. In some of the Hindu mythologies time *(kâla)* falls within the power and control of a supreme. In these instances it is the Supreme that rules time and usually everything else; in such a case *kâla* as time and *kâla* as death are totally in the hands of God, as will be seen in chapter 2.

Cosmogonic Return to the One

The paradigmatic Hindu myth of the return to the one is that of the destruction of the cosmos by Śiva in one version or by Vishnu's sovereign agency in another. Everything goes back into the cosmic ground of being and will once again be recreated into all the multiplicities of life. Yet there is a paradox: Despite being dissolved in the divine fire of cosmic destruction, one's *karma* survives (at least the minor dissolutions, according to many myths) and one's karmic chain continues until divine grace intervenes.

Each re-creation demonstrates the interconnectedness of life, as the myths connect the order of being—gods and demons, animals and birds, and humans, every possible form of life—on the same web of being. In the mythic past, all were able to talk together, compete with each other, and even mate with each other. No other modern mythology survives into its modern religious traditions to the same extent that Hindu mythology extends into modern Hindu traditions. Stories of gods mating with animals or shape-shifting into animal form to have animal progeny are still taken literally by many, which causes some adverse reaction in outsiders—and Hindu reformers. In primordial or mythic time there was shape-shifting from one species to another (changing orders of being). *Rishis* mated with *apsarâs* (celestial damsels); gods like Indra were attracted to *rishis'* wives and on occasion raped them (also the behavior of demons).

All this was not taken as confusion but related to the problem of primordial unity (or chaos) before creation and differentiation into the separateness of creation. Gods like Indra feared a return to the primordial unity where all orders of being are truly undifferentiated, but gods like Indra did not necessarily represent the highest wisdom. A return to oneness was seen as a desirable goal by the truly wise. The paradigmatic situation was symbolized by a sage practicing austerities in order to change the cosmic order—back to its original oneness.

A belief in an original undifferentiated oneness seems to be reflected in the myth of Vishnu-Varâha and Bhûmî-devî, when it tells of their continuous love play *(lîlâ)*, lasting for three hundred years (some versions say a thousand). This love play seems to be a re-creation of the cosmogonic moment of nondifferentiation beforc the separation of being and nonbeing and of male and female. There are no offspring, only an embrace. This lovemaking is without the desire for a climax or for offspring. It is without passion. This divine play became a model for later Tântric practices in which the participants embraced as the divine androgyne. And even as a divine couple became one, so also most myths would agree that the entire differentiated cosmos ought to seek oneness in the Absolute.

Renunciation, Sacrifice, and Magic

Renunciation, sacrifice, and magic are themes that are hardly unique to Hindu mythology. However, the part they play in the myths is distinctive. Renunciation *(tapasya)*, when it first appeared, was in marked contrast to the various kinds of life affirmation found in many early Hindu myths. Since it is so commonly accepted that Hinduism in general and Hindu mythology specifically are life-negating, one needs to be reminded that in the Vedic and Brâhmanical periods in particular, long life and good health were worthy and constantly sought goals. There were originally three stages of life *(aśramas)*—student, householder, and retiree. One's social and religious duties overlapped in a series of sacraments *(samskâras)* that celebrated life and its activities. An artifact of that life affirmation was the desire for the boon of immortality *(ciranjîva)*. One sought to become immortal because there was nothing to escape. This existence was the place of joy and blessing. Perhaps even reincarnation or transmigration *(samsâra)* began as an affirmation of the goodness of life.

However, from the time of the Buddha (c.600 B.C.E.) Hindu mythology developed a new logic and emphasis. The pleasures and attractions of this life could be renounced through ascetic practices *(tapas)*, and by so doing one could acquire supernatural or transhuman powers *(siddhis)* or creative energy *(mâyâ, śaktî)*. This new desire for divine powers led to a search for knowledge *(jñâna)* about these powers and to practices *(tapas, yoga, tântra)* that helped in their acquisition.

Ascetic practices were developed extensively outside of Vedic religion—among the Ajivikas, Buddhists, Jains, and independent sages. But ascetic practice became part of Hindu tradition in *yoga* and its supportive philosophies and theologies. It was a new form or conception of sacrifice. One would not perform a blood sacrifice of an animal, involving its "murder" (as the Buddhist and Jains charged in their call for *ahimsa*, which literally means non-murder and later became non injury). Asceticism embraced a change in consciousness that included an individual (not a clan or group) who controlled his or her own actions and desires. This mastery of the "self" seemed god-like, and the myths taught that this is exactly how the gods and demons acquired their phenomenal powers—through austerities, not conquests or fire sacrifices as earlier in the Vedic age. So not only was a new individual consciousness produced, but also austerity *(tapas)* and powers *(siddhis)* were connected in a new way. Now the hearer of these new myths would learn of ascetic powers, those produced by *yoga*, fasting, vows, pilgrimages, donations of wealth, and other tangible and intangible sacrifices. All of these led to an experience of non-attachment or non-addiction to the ordinary things of life and the resulting power to operate in the world with new strength—and even miraculous abilities *(siddhis)*.

Myths often told of who practiced and what they achieved. Again, in primordial time animals, humans, demons, and gods all practiced austerities, acquired powers, used them against each other, and admired great accomplishment *(tapasya)*, even when it might be used for unworthy ends—as was almost always the case with the demons *(asuras)*.

Austerities *(tapas)* that generated powers *(siddhis)* were thus not always ascetic. Most myths not only linked austerities *(tapas)* with powers *(siddhis)* but also linked the use of those powers with nonascetic and often immoral goals (killings, cursings, and the like). One practiced *tapas* in order to gain *siddhis*. The demons *(asuras)* usually would quit their practices (fasting, yoga, meditation, worship) as soon as they acquired the *siddhi* they sought (immortality, invincibility, and the like). But some did not and made defeat impossible except for intervention of the Supreme (in sectarian myths). Brahmâ, and sometimes

Indra or other *devas,* granted the boon *(vara)* of a particular *siddhi* simply because these austerities pleased the gods. At least so the mythmakers often said; nevertheless, it seemed that Indra and the other gods were actually operating under some kind of compulsion—if austerities were done, a boon had to be granted. Something very much like the law of *karma* seemed to be at work. Seen in this way, austerity *(tapas)* was analogous to Vedic sacrifice, which could be seen as providing the *devas* with something they wanted so that they would give human beings what they wanted, but which actually operated rather differently. In fact the inner logic of *tapas* was quite close to the "science" of controlling the gods with Vedic rituals, except that the rituals had been replaced by austerities. The rewards for austerities could include heaven *(svarga),* but even in late mythology the powers were often used for more ordinary human desires. Myths about the way the *asuras* would first practice *tapas* to obtain a boon from Brahmâ suggested that repeating a chant *(mantra)* of praise a thousand times either pleased Brahmâ or obligated him to grant the desired boon. When *tapas* was equated with purification rituals, austerity was linked to the notion of penance. However, when one's motive for becoming purified by austerities was to obtain a *siddhi* of invincibility or immortality in order to be victorious in war, that only emphasized the connection to magic *(mâyâ).*

Many myths mention the use of magic directly. The myth of Bala, an *asura* (demon), mentioned that he knew and taught ninety-six kinds of magic to trouble the *devas* (divinities). Hanuman was said to practice the eight superhuman powers *(ashta siddhis).* The *asuras* had a life-restoring magic *(mritansañjîvanî)* that they had been using in their battles against the *devas.* It was this magic that necessitated giving *amrita,* a potion that bestowed immortality, which was churned up from the Milky Ocean, to the *devas.* Sîlavatî was a wife who, by practice of austerities *(tapas),* was able to cast a spell that prevented the sun from rising.

The practical understanding of power as *mâyâ* (magical power) and *śaktî* (creative energy) rested on a "science" of observation and experimentation that proved the effectiveness of both ritual and ascetic practices. *Brâhmins* had concluded that rituals worked when done precisely, as did incantations of *mantras* as prayers of praise or formulas of magical control. Further, this understanding of *mâyâ* as control of the mysteries of life concluded that austerities (*tapas*) led to powers that controlled nature, including the gods, or to the acquisition of any object of desire, including heaven (*svarga*) or immortality. The mythological view was the practical one: that there were practices (rituals, austerities, devotion, or a combination of these) that gave mortals some control over the results of their action (connecting with *karma*) and hope for the future. Many, many myths mention the use of magic directly, and many terms are used in the myths for the practitioners of this art, as well as for the art itself: for example, *mâyâvî* (one with power) or *tapasvinî* (magician) and *indrajala* (magic or illusionism).

In Hindu mythology renunciation, sacrifice, and magic did not always follow the clear logic of the philosophical systems *(darśanas)*, but the myths do intend to be logical: Theirs is a logic of magic with earlier understandings of renunciation and ritual sacrifice. This might not be the true renunciation of the ascetic, but it constitutes one of the main supports of a mythic worldview.

Mâyâ as Illusion

During the Upanishadic period a new meaning for the concept of *mâyâ* began to be illustrated in Hindu mythology. That theme was the illusory nature of the seemingly real. This theological and philosophical notion could have totally undercut the assurances of Hindu mythology that attention to correct actions *(karma)* would have positive results in this life and the next. But it did not. Paradoxically, *mâyâ* could be used as a new storytelling device as the succeeding periods became more and more like Indian music. There was no actual musical score, but only an essence that needed to be maintained. There was no single account in which all the details had to be consistent, coherent, and logical, since the myths pointed to a reality beyond, behind, above the illusion *(mâyâ)*.

Metaphysically and epistemologically, *mâyâ* pointed to the process of mental creation and its correspondence to material creation. Like the mind-creations of Brahmâ, this creation as projection by the Absolute *(Brahman)* seemed to involve a dreamlike state of the Absolute in which the world was dreamed into being. Later mythology picked up this notion explicitly, when Brahmâ or, more properly, one of the supreme deities (Vishnu, Śiva, Devî) was the dreamer and creation was the dream. This critical usage of *mâyâ* as illusion or dream allowed for a contradiction or rejection of the practical usages of *mâyâ*—performance of ritual or austerities to acquire magical powers. Meditations to become one with the One (the cosmogonic embrace) or devotions to the supreme deity (to receive grace and love) allowed the cosmogonic problem of multiplicity and improper order after creation to be finally corrected in oneness with the Supreme or with the Absolute.

With the broad outlines of Hindu mythology's approach to the cosmogonic and cosmological mysteries of life sketched in, it is time to explore further a central problem in mythology: mythic time, space, and causality. That will be the subject of chapter 2.

NOTES

1. Roy Amore and Larry Shinn, *Lustful Maidens and Ascetic Kings* (New York: Oxford University Press, 1981), p. 5.

2. D. S. Sharma, "The Nature and History of Hinduism," in *The Religion of the Hindus*, edited by Kenneth Morgan (New York: Ronald Press, 1953), pp. 3–47.

3. J. P. Rao Rayapati, *Early American Interest in Vedanta* (New York: Asia Publishing House, 1973).

4. Ken Wilber, *The Spectrum of Consciousness* (Wheaton, IL: Theosophical Publishing House, 1977) and *The Atman Project* (Wheaton, IL: Theosophical Publishing House, 1980).

5. There is a New Age genre of literature arising from this influence that is one reason that Ken Wilber has disassociated himself from the term. Examples would be the books by Elizabeth Clare Prophet, *The Lost Years of Jesus: On the Discoveries of Notovitch, Abhedananda, Roerich, and Caspari* (Summit University Press, 1984) and Holger Kersten, *Jesus Lived in India: His Unknown Life before and after the Crucifixion* (Dorset, UK: Element Books, 1986; 2d edition, 1991). This genre has the same kind of scholarly weight as a depiction of Krishna as a warrior with superpowers who arrived in India on a UFO.

2

MYTHIC TIME, SPACE, AND CAUSALITY

When Svâmî Vivekânanda (1863–1902) spoke of time *(kâla)*, he connected it with the concepts of space *(deśa)* and causality *(nimitta)*, in much the same way as centuries of Indian philosophers had done. While the gods and goddesses were seen as being held within the operational power of *kâla-deśa-nimitta*, the Absolute would certainly not be. That would be true for both the impersonal Absolute, *Brahman*, as well as the theistic supreme deities, such as Śiva, Vishnu, or Devî. Svâmî Vivekânanda's handling of time as relative to the Absolute and time limiting all creatures (those who are created) is sufficiently representative of the interconnectedness of time, space, and causality in most Hindu mythological periods to remind us that any division between these three concepts is purely for purposes of convenience.

MYTHIC TIME

Mythic time provides a temporal plane that shapes all the cosmogonic elements of Hindu mythology (associated with the origin of every thing and every being, purpose, duties, stages of life, meaning, and so on) and turns mere stories into a cosmic drama of necessity and urgency. One's very actions *(karma)* are related, even though they may be infinitesimal, to the greater stories of the transmigration (both evolution and involution) of the cosmos.

Mythic time (cosmic, divine) and existential time (the time of ordinary human experience) tend to interpenetrate each other in the living mythologies of India. Human measurements of time—from the experience of divisions of time in a day to those of a yearly (human) calendar—blend into the ritual cycle commemorating divine birthdays and other festival events. However, a ritual calendar pales when placed alongside a chart of mythic time. (See chart on p. 38.)

Birth and death are the normal markers for human or existential time. However, mythic time intrudes, and birth must be viewed as rebirth. For in mythic time, this birth or lifetime was preceded by the prior "causes" in the karmic chain that shape this birth—always answering why one was born in this caste *(varna)*, into this marriage group *(jati)*, with these disabilities, and so on. Since one is now human, there would have been many, many lifetimes and rebirths as animals and, prior to that, possibly as plants. There may even have been regressive rebirths, as was made clear in the myth of Kamsa and the six sons (referred to in chapter 1 in the section on "Karma"; see also the entry on Kamsa in chapter 3). The mythic view of rebirth is cyclic—there is no moment that one can declare as the absolute beginning of one's own life cycle.

Quite telling is the fact that *kâla* is the word for both time and death. Kâla was personified as the god *(deva)* of time, but he was also referred to as Yama, the god of death. (See entries in Chapter 3.) Kâla worked within a fixed universe: he would come only at the appointed time of death, which was governed not by him but by a causality regulated by *karma* and the time believed to be allotted for each species, from plants and animals to humans and gods. Even Brahmâ, the creator, had a fixed allotment of one hundred divine years (see chart below).

In the *Mahâbhârata* (Anusasana Parva, chap. 91, verse 36) the sage Ganita was given credit for calculating the course and duration of the *yugas*, the vast cycles of time. The *yugas* were of extraordinary duration, but they were only parts of even larger cycles—*kalpas* and *mahâkalpas* (defined below).

There is a way in which time could be said to have a beginning, for in most later Hindu worldviews there was something outside of time that could begin and end it. But, technically, these are re-beginnings. In the devotional *(bhakti)*, or theistic, systems a supreme deity ruled time, bringing it into being along with Brahmâ, as in the myth cycle of Vishnu, where Brahmâ is born at the beginning of each *mahâkalpa*. Also in the least mythological worldview, that of Advaita Vedânta and its foremost philosopher-theologian Śankara (c. eighth century C.E.), the Absolute *(Brâhman)* was both beyond and unaffected by *kâla-deśa-nimitta*. These cosmic principles subordinated both humans and gods to the rule of time, putting them on essentially the same level in the myths.

Each beginning of time was a creation *(srishthi)*—or, as already observed, a re-creation. Even the notion of revealed knowledge *(veda)* did not fully reconcile the many revealed versions of creation found in the many Hindu scriptures (both *shruti* and *smritî*, different orders of scriptures in their authority and origination).

There would be found in scripture creations from the mind *(manas)*, and creations by division, sacrifice, dismemberment, coition, and so on. The logical contradictions were noted by early thinkers, but later resolved by the simple device of stating that there were many creations, and these accounted for all of the differences. There were minor creations (re-creations) after each set of the four *yugas* (ages) and major creations after the *mahâkalpas*. (See chart on p. 38.) A further notion removed one last discrepancy seen by some Hindu thinkers—

the various Prajâpatis (creative "grandfathers") had proliferated in the later mythology so that even the notion of multiple creations did not remove all of the logical problems. So the notion of *gotras* (families of created beings) placed all of the creatures of each creation within four *gothas*, each "grandfathered" by its own *prajâpati*. (But what seemed to fix the problems in the conception seemed to disturb the fundamental insight concerning the interconnectedness of all being as emanating from the One, as a projection from the One, and ultimately becoming one with the One.)

Mythic time had placed a judgment on this present moment in human or existential time. In the present, human history is occurring at the worst of all times, the mythic time of the *kali-yuga* (defined below), a time of lessened spiritual possibilities because of loss of the full *Vedas*, and the inability to live the Hindu way of life (the complete *varna-asrama-dharma*, the ethical system involving the interrelationship of the individual and group's obligations in every aspect and stage of life). It further implied a current need for yet another restoration of the *dharma*, but with the likelihood that there would only be partial incarnations of God *(amsa-avatâras)* before the final dissolution *(pralaya)* of this *kalpa* and the coming of the tenth incarnation, Kalki (Kalkin), the last *avatâra* of this yugic cycle.

Mythic time is complicated by a cross-referencing with periods of time referring to Hindu scriptures. There is a notion that there was a time at the beginning of this yugic cycle (in the *krita-yuga*, also called the *satya-yuga*, "age of truth") that was Vedic. That is, those who lived in the *krita-yuga* were able to live the truths of the *Vedas*. However, by the *kali-yuga* human beings were in need of simpler scriptures, representational aids to worship the divine (idols and temples), and rules for living that were adjusted to a dark (benighted) age—thus, the time governed by the devotional practices of the *Purânas* and consequently called Purânic time.

The *Mahâbhârata* (Bhisma parva, 4–12 and Santi parva 12.224) and the *Manu Smritî* (1.64–86) were among the first scriptures to record what later became the prevailing view of mythic time. As mentioned before, the sage Ganita was credited with making the first calculations that defined mythic or divine time in terms of human time. Thus, the *yugas, catur-yugas* (the fourfold yuga cycle), *kalpas, mahâkalpas*, days and nights of Brahmâ, and lifetime of Brahmâ could be calculated in human years. (See chart on p. 38.) Yet there were always variations in these calculations. The following chart is based on the *Vishnu Purâna*, which saw time (*kâla*) as the body of Vishnu, the supreme creator of all, including the time-space-causality continuum (*kâla-deśa-nimittâ*).

Creation (*srishthi*) is followed by an active phase of evolution (*sthiti*) and then of dissolution or involution (*laya*). At the end of one *ardha-kalpa* there is a

Time: Human, Mythic, Cosmic

Sanskrit Term	Comparative	Explanation
kashtha	15 twinklings of the eye	
kala	30 *kashthas*	
muhurtta	30 *kalas*	
ahorâtra (and *vâra* or *tithi*)	30 muhurttas; 405,000 *kasthas*	a human day and night
mâsa	a lunar month	30 human days
paksha	half of a lunar month	15 days waxing and 15 days waning
ayana	6 human months	180 days
	2 *ayanas*	human lunar year of 360 days
southern *ayana*	night of a *deva* (god)	human lunar half year of 180 days
northern *ayana*	a day of the gods	human lunar half year of 180 days
—*sandhya*	period that precedes each *yuga*	it lasts for 400, 300, 200, and 100 divine years, depending on the *yuga*
krita-yuga	4,000 divine years	1,728,000 human years (144,000+1,440,000+144,000)
—*sandhyansa*	period that follows each yuga	it lasts for 400, 300, 200, and 100 divine years, depending on the *yuga*
treta-yuga	3,000 divine years	1,296,000 human years
dvapara-yuga	2,000 divine years	864,000 human years
kali-yuga	1,000 divine years	432,000 human years
catur-yuga (four *yugas*), or *mahâyuga*	12,000 divine years	4.32 million human years
manvantara, or *mahâyuga*	4 *yugas*; the reign of a Manu	4.32 million human years
ardha-kalpa	a half *kalpa*, the night or day of Brahmâ, 1,000 *mahâyugas*	4.32 trillion human years
kalpa	2 *ardha-kalpas*; a day and night of Brahmâ	8.64 trillion human years
a day or night of Brahmâ	1,000 *ardha-kalpas*	4.32 quadrillion human years
a day and night of Brahmâ	2000 *kalpas*; reign of 14 Manus	8.64 quadrillion human years
a year of Brahmâ	360 Brahmâ days and nights	3.1104^{15} human years
mahâkalpa	100 Brahmâ years; a Brahmâ lifetime	3.1104^{17} human years
laya	the destruction at the end of a *manvantara* or *mahâyuga*	
pralaya	after each day of Brahma, a dissolution of the universe	
mahâpralaya	the great dissolution after the lifetime of a Brahmâ	
srishthi	creation (literally, "discharge")	
prasrishthi	creation before each *kalpa*	
mahâprasrishti	great creation before each Brahmâ	
mahâprasthiti	the entire period of evolution in the lifetime of one Brahmâ	

greater destruction of the cosmos *(pralaya)* followed by a great preservation *(prasrishthi)* and its subquent destruction *(pralaya)*. The period before and after each *yuga (sandhya* and *sandhyansa,* respectively) are periods of awakening and dissolution proportional to the time of the particular *yuga.* There are even notions of time in terms of the lifetime of one Brahmâ—the great creation *(mahâprasrishti),* the great evolution *(mahâprasthiti),* and the great destruction *(mahâpralaya).* There is no ending, as this cycle starts over again. Also, according to the *Vishnu Purâna* there is no purpose to cyclic time either, as it is just for the play *(lîlâ)* of Vishnu.

The list of words for mythical time is not exhaustive. Some of the myths were quite creative and invented more units of time. For example, in the story about Mahâvishnu incarnating as Varâha, Vishnu and Bhûmî-Devî made love for a *devavarsha*—300 human years, less than one divine day.

Additional Systems and Units of Time

Astrological time (used to calculate horoscopes), calendar time (involving naming the days after reigning planets, or *graha,* the solar months for the twelve solar mansions, and the lunar months for the twenty-seven or twenty-eight lunar mansions, or *nakshatras*), and musical and dance time all contributed to the total culture's conceptions and terminology about time. Of course, any myth might introduce these notions of time into a story set in mythic time without fear of inconsistency or contradiction.

DEŚA (SPACE)

In the Hindu continuum of *kâla-deśa-nimitta,* space is the second component of the cosmogonic mystery. *Deśa* too must be created or brought into being and order at each beginning, or re-beginning. What is the shape or dimensions of space? What is above and what is below? Where is the center? Where do the gods live? What are the names of the regions? Where does space go at the destruction? The myths know and occasionally even ask these questions but never quite answer them.

There were many conceptions of space during the various periods of Hindu mythology. In the Vedic period there was a decidedly Indo-European three-tiered universe with three hierarchical regions, as well as the notion of the cosmic egg *(Hiranyagarbha).* The latter concept involves imagining space from "above" as an egg enclosing existence, with the human beings within the egg looking up at its roof, the heavens, and being supported below, so that the enclosure was a golden womb. This notion could be affirmed even as an hierarchical notion of ascending regions or worlds *(lokas)* became the dominant conception.

The Vedic notion of space was limited to three regions: earth, midair, and the heavens. A member of the principle divine triad of the Vedic period ruled over each region—Agni over earth *(bhû)*, Indra over midair *(bhuvas)*, and Sûrya over heaven *(svar* or *svarga)*. Over time, these regions *(lokas)* were elaborated until, in the *Purânas,* they had multiplied, with a *loka* for each of the major gods, arranged hierarchically. Mount Meru (Mahâmeru, the cosmic mountain) began with its base at the center of an earth island known as Jambudvîpa (rose-apple tree island). Meru, or Mahâmeru, was shaped like a banyan tree, smaller at its base and larger above. In the upper regions of Mount Meru were the regions for the gods and their respective palaces *(lokas)*. All had names—Brahmâloka, Indraloka or Svarga, Vaikuntha (this name was also given to the watery realm where Vishnu rested on the serpent Ananta, or Śesha), Kailâsa (for Śiva), Mahodaya (for Kubera), Śraddhâvatî (for Varuna), and so on.

Jambudvîpa was either the island at the center of a series of concentric islands or the first of seven donut-shaped islands with Meru at the center; in either case, Meru was at its center. Each island had an ocean filled with a different liquid surrounding it (salt, sugar-cane juice, wine, ghee, buttermilk, milk, and sweet water). Some sages and kings were said to have wandered until they reached the Himâlayas and then finally Mount Meru. Others needed divine transport to reach it. Not only could the occasional human reach Meru, but also many other beings: animals (some divine like Hanuman and others who were just companions or vehicles of the gods), semidivine beings *(apsaras* and *gandharvas)*, and demons—even armies of them could invade Meru.

Jambudvîpa was divided into many lands, with Bhârata (India) subdivided into nine regions, each ruled over by descendants of the solar and lunar races of kings. Bhârata was known for its sacred geography. Where gods and goddesses had touched the soil of India in their births, play, or rule, it had been made sacred. When there had been dismemberment of a god or goddess and divine body parts had fallen to earth, those spots too were holy. (See the story of the dismemberment of Satî after Daksha's sacrifice in the entry on Satî in chapter 3.) At such spots, mythic space and mundane geography overlapped at least at the pilgrimage sites *(tîrthas)*. All these places became sites for pilgrimage *(tîrthas)* and for temples and temple-cities.

Sometimes what had been in divine or mythic space came down to earth. The Gangâ was a celestial river, from which, according to some versions, Śiva only brought down one drop to make the mighty earthly Gangâ. A piece of Mount Meru was broken off and made Lanka. Conversely, what was sacred space on earth, such as a river, a tree, or a mountain, could have been a goddess in her previous lifetime in heaven. Almost every river in India was mythically connected with a goddess who had been reborn as a river—sometimes a blessing, sometimes a curse. Occasionally, a mortal was blessed to be reborn as a river (and thus a goddess).

Below the earth were the nether regions or underworlds. The *nâgas* (snakes) inhabited great rivers, the sea, and the primordial ocean, ruling over the treasures of the internal, or inner region, known as *pâtâla*. However, the *nâgas* were also to be found in Śiva's heavenly realm, Kailâsa, and in other places like graveyards in association with Śiva.

The underworlds changed radically from period to period. As the kingdom of Yama, lord of the dead, the underworld was named Yamapurî (city of death). Yama and Kâla were the same god, and so space and time are one in death. The Upanishadic lad Naciketas could report that the accommodations were fine and the occupants well cared for in Yamapurî. However, subsequent rulers, all kings of the *asuras,* turned the place into a living hell. Probably influenced by Buddhist and Jain conceptions of hell, medieval Hindu mythology treated the seven *narakas* (and some incorrectly added the Vedic netherworlds or *pâtâlas*) as places of torment and punishment for evil deeds.

An alternate way of seeing the universe conceptualized space *(deśa)* as consisting of eight spheres (sphere translating *vasu,* "that which surrounds"). These spheres included the earthly sphere *(prithivî),* the spatial sphere *(antariksha),* the heavenly sphere *(dyaus),* and the stellar sphere *(nakshatra).* In older mythology divinities *(devas)* both inhabited the various spheres and ruled them. Agni ruled the earthly sphere, Vâyu (the wind) ruled the sphere of space, and Sûrya (the sun) ruled the heavenly sphere. The constellations ruled the stellar sphere (leading to their designations in the lunar and solar calendars). This notion of *deśa* contained within it faint memories of a mythological hierarchy that differed from those mentioned in chapter 1, memories of a time when Vâyu was the second member of the divine triad instead of Indra.

NIMITTA (CAUSALITY)

The last component of the cosmogonic puzzle in Hindu mythology was effective causality. Most Hindus had held that the effective cause *(nimitta)* of the universe would have to reside inside of the *time-space-causality* continuum. Thus, time *(kâla)* and *karma* as the result of ritual or ethical actions could be controlled by the direct actions of the ritualist or by heroic effort as in *yoga* or asceticism *(tapasya).*

If the gods *(devas)* were governed by *karma*, then they would be subordinate to the forces of existence (or reality, consciousness, creation, or whatever one might call it). Therefore, the law or laws of causality would be prior to the gods, and a creator would only be like Brahmâ, a re-creator—existing within and governed by time-space-causality.

The way causality was conceived of as governing within the universe, the way the laws of *karma* operated, did not remain the same over the centuries. Causality was not always seen as tight; it could be hard or soft. When causality was seen as tight, that meant that the universe was seen as following rules of causality that could not be changed under any circumstances. There would be no miracles. One could only reap what one had sowed. There could be no gain or loss. There could be no favoritism, no cheating, no deceit. *Karma* had to be tight, or hard, to be fair, just, equal.

A preponderance of evidence suggests that Brâhmanical ritualism (also known as Brâhmanism) was based on a belief in a tight causality. If the priest had the correct knowledge *(jñâna)* of the proper rituals and sacrifices *(yâyus, yâgas, yâjñas)* and knew the correct formulas of address and praise for each god *(deva)*, and knew the sections of scripture *(karma kanda)* about Vedic ritualism that dealt with this "science," the laws that governed this tight causality, only then could the priest *(brâhmin)* expect perfect success in obtaining from the *devas* exactly what had been asked. In the next-to-last section of chapter 1, "Renunciation, Sacrifice, and Magic," the connection is made between the control exercised over the gods in the sacrificial ritual and the control exercised by the practice of austerities. Hindu myths on asceticism also implicitly used a concept of tight causality to explain how demons (always the test case) could acquire power over the gods, bring disorder once again to all of creation, and drive righteousness *(dharma)* from the world. Ascetic myths that used this tight causality believed so strongly in the superpowers *(siddhis)* to be gained by ascetic practices that a Śankara had to come along and dismiss their ritual and ascetic "sciences" as *mâyâ*—changing the way this term was used forever. Moreover, after Śankara, no one would think that *mâyâ* referred to a tight causality. Śankara had turned their magical science *(mâyâ)* on its head and, through the "paradigm shift" that he achieved, *mâyâ* would subsequently mean "illusion" or "projection" *(vivarta)*.

Hindu mythology could not work with Śankara's concept of relative or illusory causality. Hindu myths about ascetic practice and ritual performance needed a tight causality to provide the certainty needed for communal identity and karmic hope, so Purânic mythology countered with a concept of theistic causality. The world was not an illusion; there was a supreme deity in whom all causality resided. What ritualists sought with their sacrifices and ascetics sought with their renunciations, theistic Hindus could now achieve with devotional practice. A supreme deity, who both ruled *kâla-deśa-nimitta* and transcended it, could provide unmerited grace (something their good *karma* had not fully bought or earned) and liberation *(moksha).* The Supreme—be it Vishnu, Śiva, or Devî—could thus provide a soft *karma,* granting refuge in a community of those who followed the eternal truths *(sanâtana dharma)* of the scriptures and who lived according to the expectations of the stages of life *(aśramas)* and the obligations of the organic society *(varna).*

Hindu mythology, like Indian music, did not require a fully explained or precise cosmology. It knew the essence of the musical piece and had learned to enjoy great latitude in performance and theory. In fact, lack of variation would be boring to Indian taste and sensibility. Nothing was discarded, and mythmakers could and can draw on it all, without worrying about consistency or incoherence in their worldview.

3

CHARACTERS, THEMES, AND CONCEPTS

ÂDI

An asura (demon)

The demon Âdi was the son of Andhak, who had been killed by Śiva. To gain revenge, Âdi did austerities *(tapas)* with the sole purpose of receiving a boon *(vara)* from Brahmâ, the creator. In due course Brahmâ granted him the *vara*, so Âdi asked for invincibility in battle. But boons, especially to demons, are provisional, and may be invalidated by a flaw in the wording of the request. The literal wording of Âdi's request won for him invincibility only while in his *asura* form.

Not knowing this limitation and quite certain of his invincibility, Âdi went to Kailâsa, Śiva's heavenly abode, to avenge this death of his father. Âdi first changed into the form of a serpent. Since snakes are natural friends of Śiva, who is lord of all creatures, Âdi was allowed into Śiva's presence. But once inside Śiva's palace, Âdi again changed his form to appear like Śiva's wife, Pârvatî. Śiva recognized the deceit and killed Âdi, who had lost the boon of immortality by being in another form than his own.

See also Andhak; Pârvatî; Paśupati; Śiva

ÂDI-KÛRMA

An avatâra of Vishnu

The original *(âdi)* turtle, or tortoise (Kûrma), was involved in a creation, or re-creation, myth, the Churning of the Milky Ocean. For the main entry see Kûrma.

See also Avatâra; *Kshîrâbdhi-Mathanam*; Kûrma; Vishnu

ADITI

A devî (goddess), mother of the gods

There are few interesting myths to tell about Aditi, but her status and roles change so remarkably that she illustrates the fluidity of Hindu myths. Her name literally means eternity (free, boundless, infinity), so philosophically she is a personification of time. Aditi slowly evolved as the prototype of the Great Mother, Devî, or Śaktî.

In the early *Rigveda* she was described as the mother of seven (and later twelve) *âdityas* (children of Aditi), and was prayed to for protection. There are prayers to her in this period asking her to give the Aryans children and cattle, protection and forgiveness.

In the epics (the *Mahâbhârata* and the *Râmâyana*), Aditi is the wife of Kaśyapa, a progenitor or grandfather of creation. She is explicitly the mother of Vishnu, the twelfth âditya. But Aditi's earlier praise as *Deva-mâtri* (mother of the gods) led to her highest role, in the early *Purânas*. The âdityas came to include all the *devas*, so she became mother of the 330 million gods and goddesses who made up all the various classes of medieval polytheism. Her opposite, in both name and role, was Ditî (bound, finite). Ditî's children were the *daityas* (born of Ditî), who were also known as the *asuras*.

In the sectarian *Vishnu Purâna*, where Vishnu was the supreme god, Aditi was only the mother of Vishnu's dwarf incarnation (Vâmana). In the *Matsya Purâna* she was given a small part: she received a pair of earrings from Indra at the churning of the ocean.

In the *Vedas* Aditi was the wife of Daksha, grandfather of all creatures. But in the *Vishnu Purâna* Aditi had become the daughter of Daksha and wife of Kaśyapa. Her role as the parent of the gods was continued into her rebirth as the mother of an incarnation of Vishnu. According to the *Devî Bhâgavata*, Aditi was reincarnated as Devakî, the mother of Krishna.

All the variations did not go unnoticed. The great medieval commentator Yâska explained that all these variations could be true because the gods were born of each other. Another explanation accounted for differences in parentage or marriage by saying that these were the results of rebirths, not just in this age but in the many ages *(yugas)*, with varying roles in each.

> *See also* Âdityas; *Kshîrâbdhi-mathanam*; Daksha; *Deva*; Devakî; Kaśyapa; Krishna; Vâmana

ÂDITYAS

Devas (gods)

The sons born to Kaśyapa-prajâpati (a grandfather or procreator) and Aditi (mother of the gods) are called the *âdityas*. In the hymns of the *Rigveda*, Aditi only had seven or eight children. But by the time of the *Brâhmanas* there are twelve âdityas: Dhâtâ, Mitra, Aryaman, Rudra, Varuna, Sûrya, Bhaga, Vivasvân, Pusha, Savita, Tvashta, and Vishnu. They are among the most important of the earliest

Vedic gods. This grouping could represent the twelve months, as they are celestial deities. In another context *âditya* (singular not plural) referred to the sun (Sûrya).

But as the centuries passed Aditi's role as mother expanded to all of the *devas*. First, she became mother of Indra, who was called the king of the gods in later mythology. The next addition to the myths spoke of twenty-one children (besides the twelve) who were also called âdityas. And finally, as a prototype of the Great Mother, Aditi became the mother of the entire world of *devas*, who have become 330 million, all born from the 33 children of Aditi.

In the earliest stage of their conception, the âdityas seem to have been personifications of light and of the phenomena of the heavens. The seven âdityas were the sun, moon, and five planets. They were rulers of the celestial realm and symbols of kingship and sovereignty, especially Varuna, Mitra, and Aryaman. But their importance must have been developed in myths prior to the Aryans' arrival in India (or for those who find the Aryans a transformation of local tribes, before the composition of the hymns of India's earliest literature, the *Rigveda*). Their myths are not retold in the *Rigveda*, and their supreme importance receded rapidly. Three more brother gods—Bhaga (the dispenser), Amsa (the share), and Daksha (the capability, "ritual skill")—were celestial models for the social and ritual relationships of the earliest Aryans. But their myths were also not to be found in the *Rigveda*, as the âdityas were in the process of being replaced by the Vedic fire ritual (the Agni cult) and the Rigvedic triad of Agni, Indra, and Sûrya.

The myths of the seven âdityas can be found in Old Persia (Iran) in the form of their equivalents among the Persian gods (Amesha Spentas) of the *Avesta*.

See also Aditi; Agni; *Deva*; Indra; Kaśypa; Mitra; Sûrya; Varuna

AGASTYA, AGASTI

A rishi (sage) who conquered the Vindhya mountains

Agasti was mentioned in a hymn in the *Rigveda* dedicated to Mitra, a solar deity. That hymn said that two of the *âdityas*, Mitra (comradeship) and Varuna (binder, "all-seeing"), placed their semen in a pot and set it before Urvaśî, an unusually beautiful *apsara* (celestial maiden). Because she had aroused their desires, Mitra and Varuna cursed Urvaśî to live on earth as the wife of the *rishi* Purûravas. Agasti (or Agastya) and Vasishtha were the sons born to her. Later versions expanded and elaborated on the details.

Agastya was the form of his name used in later myths. It was said that his name came from his command that the Vindhya mountains bow down and worship him. He received another name of Ocean Drinker (*Samudra-Culuka*) when he drank up the ocean to reveal the demons hiding there and aid the gods in a victory over them.

According to the *Purânas* Agastya happened upon his ancestors' spirits *(pitris)* hanging upside down on a limb. They told him that they were in this condition because the proper death rituals were not being performed and that he must bear a son to carry out his duties to his ancestors. So he created a baby girl from all the beautiful parts of the beings of the forest and placed her in the king's palace. And when she was of marriageable age, he asked the king to give her to him in marriage. So he married Lopâmudrâ. He lived with her in a hermitage south of the Vindhya mountains. The myths about him include stories of how he ate the *râkshasa* (demon) Vâtâpi, how he stamped down the Vindhya mountains, how he cursed the god Kubera, how he set the *asuras* on fire, how he made Indra send rain, and many more. The râkshasas of South India were said to be in fear of this great sage. Râma visited his hermitage, and Agastya became his friend, advisor, and ally. He gave Râma the bow of Vishnu. And when Râma returned to Ayodhyâ, Agastya joined him there as one of his priestly advisors.

In the epics and *Purânas* Agastya was also celebrated as one of the greatest writers of sacred literature. Agastya was said to have been an author of everything from Vedic hymns to texts on medicine, but it was as the father of Tamil literature and science that he was most important in the south. There are temples in modern Tamil Nadu in which Agastya worship is still practiced.

See also Haritâsva; Râkshasa; Urvaśî

AGNI
A deva (god), god of fire

At his earliest appearance in the Rigveda, Agni was a complex deity. He was the fire of the sacred sacrifices that were the heart of Vedic religion as well as the central rituals of a seminomadic warrior culture. Agni was addressed as the *deva* who ruled earth, a third of the entire cosmos. Two other gods with the characteristic of fire formed a triad with Agni. The solar fire (deified by many names, especially that of Sûrya) was ruler of heaven; and the fire of the middle air, lightning, was deified as Indra, god of storm and god of war. A few Rigvedic hymns addressed Agni as one of the supreme triad (India's first set of three), with Sûrya and Indra. Agni was also the purifier of the offering to a Vedic pantheon and was next to Indra in the number of hymns dedicated to him. (Later this function as purifier of offerings was the only important role left for him.) Phrases from these hymns suggest an Agni myth cycle and a separate cult. He was fathered by Dyaus (sky) and the waters, or born of Indra between two clouds, had a triple existence (in heaven, middle air, and earth), and was lord of the house, friend of man, enemy of *râkshasas* (whom he crushes in his teeth), beloved of the *hôtris*

The Great Mother as Kali (TRIP)

(priests who make the Vedic sacrifices), and the one who knows when to make the offerings that gain boons from the other gods.

S. M. Bhardwaj, in his study *Hindu Places of Pilgrimage in India,* uncovered a connection between the Agni cult and the Aryanization of the regions eastward along the Gangetic plain, north toward the Himalayas, and slowly south along the coast but barely into the interior. Recorded in the *Mahâbhârata,* the world's largest myth about an ancient war, were the places sanctified by Agni that provided great merit for those who visited and worshipped at these sacred sites *(tîrthas).* They had become places to perform a fire ritual (i.e., they had been Aryanized). Thus Agni seems to have been central in spreading Aryan (literally, "noble") culture from its beginnings in northeast India throughout the subcontinent.

In the *Atharvaveda,* Agni takes the soul of the deceased from the funeral pyre to one of the worlds *(lokas)* of heaven *(svarga),* Indraloka or Brahmaloka, or to hell *(naraka).* Fortunately for Agni, later accounts give this function to Yama, god of death.

There are many forces at work in Agni's reduction over the centuries to a minor deity. There was the attack from outside the Vedic tradition by Buddhists and Jains on the Vedic triad and its sacrificial system. The Agni cult included the killing and eating of animals. One of the responses inside the Vedic tradition was to begin to internalize sacrifice, and another was to adopt the principle of *ahimsa* (noninjury, or literally "no murder"). In addition, later devotional Hindu traditions that championed minor Vedic gods like Vishnu or non-Vedic gods and goddesses like Śiva and Devî had a more subtle effect on Agni's role. As these divinities rose to supreme importance, Agni became a messenger to the gods and one of the eight guardians of the universe *(ashtha-dikpâlakas).*

Finally, in the *Purânas,* Agni becomes the name of a class of gods; his sons and grandsons were also Agnis. In the medieval period Agni had a scripture named after him, the *Agni Purâna,* as he became merely the recipient of a revelation from the rest of the *deva*s. This scripture is a vast collection dealing with the incarnations of Vishnu, injunctions relating to the worship of gods, and a variety of subjects such as astrology, architecture, sculpture, and drama. In the scripture, Agni himself was completely overshadowed by Vishnu, who is presented as the supreme lord of the universe.

The Holi Festival (a two-day holiday at the end of winter in February or March) is connected to Agni. According to one version of the myth that explains the connection, he had been cursed by a sage (and great sages and yogis could become more powerful than the gods by practicing austerities, *tapas).* This *brâhmin* was named Bhrigu. He worshipped Agni every day, feeding him with ghee (clarified butter). While Bhrigu took his morning bath, he would leave his beautiful wife Puloma under Agni's care and protection. But the *asuras* (demons) came one morning while Bhrigu was away and fed Agni so much ghee that he fell asleep. And they promptly stole Puloma. Bhrigu became so angry that he cursed Agni so that he began to die. Vishnu was able to get the old sage to modify his curse, but once a sage's curse had been made it could not be taken back. So now, only on the day before Holi are worthless offerings thrown into the fire. On Holi Agni again receives his due—and is saved by divine grace. Another version has Ganeśa, the elephant-headed son of Śiva, taking pity on Agni and fanning his flames back to life with his ears.

In the Kathikai Festival in Andra Pradesh and Tamil Nadu, Śiva is worshipped in the form of the five elements, including Agni (fire). Another Shaivite festival worshipping Śiva as lord of the elements (i.e., the universe) is the Batesar Mela at the ancient pilgrimage site of Bhuteshwar. It is quite likely that this was originally a pilgrimage site (*tîrtha*) of the ancient Agni cult.

Agni was given a role in many Purânic myths: in the birth of Śiva's son Skanda, in numerous battles with the *asuras,* as a dart emanating from Śiva, and in the chorus of gods pleading their many cases with Brahmâ, Vishnu, or Śiva. But none of these roles indicated any memory of Agni in his glory in Vedic India.

Early verbal descriptions gave Agni two heads, four horns, three feet, and seven arms. Centuries later Agni was sculpted in stone or carved in wood with one or two heads, two or three eyes, and two or four hands. He was given a chariot drawn by four parrots or was shown riding his animal vehicle, the ram. These images included a wife, Svâhâ.

See also Indra; Skanda; Sûrya; Tapas

AHALYÂ
The first woman; one of the five perfect women

The story of Ahalyâ has as many dimensions as it has versions. She appeared in the epic *Râmâyana* but was also projected back to the beginning of the creation of this age *(yuga).* One account stated that Brahmâ created her as the first and most beautiful woman on earth. Then he gave her to the *rishi* (sage) Gautama. In most tellings, the rest of her story illustrated how a perfect woman should behave under the worst of circumstances. The villain was Indra, the Vedic god, reduced in the *Râmâyana* to a minor but despicable role. In one version Indra changed his shape to appear to be Ahalyâ's husband and deceived her. In another he first changed into a rooster, crowed to make Gautama go outside for his morning devotions, and then took his place in bed. Another version attempted to mar her image, stating that Ahalyâ recognized Indra and was flattered by his advances. When the rishi discovered Indra's crime, he cursed him, at the same time putting a curse on his wife that took away her beauty and expelled her into the forest. After many years of austerities and purification she was found by Lord Râma, rewarded for her devotion, and restored as chaste to her husband.

Ahalyâ was esteemed as one of the *pañca-kanyâ,* the five ideal women of Hinduism, along with Draupadî, Mandodarî, Sîtâ, and Târâ.

See also Indra; Râma; Râmâyana; Rishis

AIRÂVATA

An elephant; the vehicle of Indra

Airâvata was the celestial elephant-king and the vehicle of Indra. Airâvata was popularly known as the white elephant with wings. He was a descendant of the lineage of the sage Kaśyapa. Airâvata came from a maternal line (Kaśyapa's wife Krodhâvasâ, their daughter Bhadramatâ, her daughter Irâvatî, and then Airâvata). Such parentage would certainly explain how it was possible for Airâvata to be born as king of the elephants. In mythic time gods might simply change into an animal species with their spouses and have children of that species, or they might spend a rebirth in an animal species. So the storyteller does not have to say just how the descendant of a sage became an elephant.

Another version of the birth of Airâvata stated that he was born or appeared out of the Churning of the Milky Ocean (*Vishnu Purâna,* chap. 22). But in this account he had four tusks. Another Purâna, upon noticing the discrepancy, added a new dimension—the story of an Airâvata with four tusks was about the sixth cycle of creations *(manvantaras),* but this was the seventh. Each cycle had its own Indra, with his elephant who was again named Airâvata.

Airâvata was used in another context as one of the eight elephants who guarded the eight zones of the universe *(ashtha-dikpâlakas).* Airâvata protected the eastern zone.

See also Indra; Kaśyapa; *Kshîrâbdhi-mathanam;* Manvantara

AMBARÎSHA

A king of the Ikshvaku dynasty

Ambarîsha, king of Ayodhyâ (birthplace of Râma), was one of the sixteen great kings who ruled Bhârata (Marutta, Suhotra, Paurava, Sibi, Râma, Bhagîratha, Dilipa, Mândhâta, Yayâti, Ambarîsha, Sasabindu, Gâyâ, Rantideva, Bharata, Prithu, and Parasu-Râma).

In the *Vâlmîki Râmâyana* there was a story about the theft of one of Ambarîsha's sacrificial cows by Indra. (In the *Bhâgavata Purâna* the theft was from King Hariscandra.) Ambarîsha was forced to find a proper sacrifice to complete his rituals. So he bought the second of three sons, named Śunahśepha, of a greedy *brâhmin* named Ricîka (also know as Ajîgartha). King Ambarîsha traded 100,000 ordinary cows for the sacrificial substitute—the young *brâhmin* Śunahśepha. But Śunahśepha prayed to Indra, and Indra not only blessed him with long life but also bestowed upon King Ambarîsha the rewards of the sacrifice *(yâjña)* as if it had been properly completed.

See also Ayodhyâ; Bharata; Hariscandra; Indra; Parasu-Râma; Râma

AMRITA

Immortal; immortality; a drink or food

In the *Vedas*, *amrita* was a characteristic or quality of a suitable offering in the fire sacrifices to the gods. Soma (the divine plant) had more amrita than other offerings. Later amrita (or amritam) was a substance produced by the Churning of the Milky Ocean *(kshîrâbdhi-mathanam)*. There were different versions of this myth in the *Mahâbhârata*, the *Râmâyana*, and the *Purânas*. According to one version the demons *(asuras)* had triumphed over the gods *(devas)*, so the *devas* sought Lord Vishnu's help. He told them about amrita and how it would bestow immortality on those who drank it. Because the *devas* were able to take all of the amrita with Vishnu's help, they were able to prevail over the *asuras.*

In the *Purânas* there were many stories about the stealing of this ambrosia of immortality. But amrita was no longer the sole source of immortality. Immortality was given by Brahmâ as the result of great austerities *(tapas)*, but this was only a provisional immortality—a guarantee of living as long as one's allotted time. In many of the later myths it was the *asuras* who did the difficult austerities and gained immortality, which was only a kind of limited invincibility, in order to torment the gods.

Later mythology conflates amrita and *soma* as the drink of immortality.

See also Kshîrâbdhi-mathanam; Môhinî; Soma; Vishnu

ANANTA

A celestial snake

Ananta literally means "without end," "infinite." It was a descriptive term used of Vishnu and other gods. It was also used as a name of Vishnu's serpent.

Ananta was the giant serpent that floated upon the Milky Ocean and formed the bed for Vishnu as he slept during the involution of the universe *(pralaya)*. Ananta (also known as Śesha) was the son of Kaśyâpa, the grandfather of all beings, by his wife Kadrû. Other serpents, such as Vâsuki, Takshâka, and Karkkotaka, were his brothers. Bala-Râma was a partial incarnation of Ananta.

See also Bala-Râma; Kaśyapa; Pralaya; Takshâka; Vâsuki; Vishnu

ANASÛYÂ

A heroine and role model for women

Anasûyâ was the wife of the sage Atri. As with all major figures in later mythology, her lineage was completely spelled out: granddaughter of Svayambhuva-Manu (Manu of his Yuga) and his wife Śatarupâ; daughter of Kardama-prajâpati (progenitor of his age) and Devahutî.

Anasûyâ (charity) was famous for the power of her austerities *(tapas)*. Once Anasûyâ used her powers to bring rain when there had been a continuous drought; even the Gangâ had dried up. Another time Anasûyâ changed ten days into night to help the gods. And when Sîtâ was drawn by her austerities to the forest hermitage of Anasûyâ and Atri, Anasûyâ was able to give Sîtâ an ointment (created by austerities) that gave Sîtâ eternal beauty.

Anasûyâ played an important role in the story of Shîlâvatî's curse, which prevented the sun from rising. (See entry under Aruna.) The gods asked Anasûyâ to help, so she convinced Shîlâvatî to remove her curse and allow the sun to rise. Anasûyâ was given a boon, which she used to have sons born of the Trimûrti (Brahmâ, Vishnu, and Śiva). Anasûyâ thus became the mother of Dattâtreya, Durvâsa (famed for both his psychic powers and his bad temper), and Candra. Her sons were partial incarnations of Brahmâ, Vishnu, and Śiva.

See also Atri; Dattâtreya; Durvâsa; Prajâpati; Tapas

ANDHAK, ANDHAKA

An asura (demon)

In one version of his birth Andhaka was a *daitya* (demon), born of Ditî and Kaśyapa. He had a thousand arms, a thousand heads, and thus two thousand eyes, hands, and feet (in another version, two thousand arms, two thousand legs). And even though he could see, it was said that he walked like a blind man. Andhaka means "blind" or "blind one."

In another version Andhaka was born from the love play (lîlâ) of Pârvatî with her husband, Lord Śiva. Pârvatî placed her hands over Śiva's eyes in jest, only to throw the universe into total darkness. But her touch heated Śiva so that a drop of sweat fell from his brow and became an angry, deformed, dark, hairy demon, Andhaka. Pârvatî and her attendants were told by Śiva to protect "her son" and care for him.

On earth the demon Hiranyanetra (the golden eye) was practicing severe austerities *(tapas)* to win a boon from Śiva. And eventually the lord of yoga (Śiva) was pleased and granted Hiranyanetra's wish for a heroic son. Śiva gave his own son, Andhaka, to the demon yogi.

In the *Kûrma Purâna,* Andhaka desired the beautiful goddess, Pârvatî, and

went to Mount Mandara to abduct her. Śiva had gone to the Pine Forest to manifest himself there to its sages. He had left the gods, Vishnu and the rest, to
attend to and protect Pârvatî. The attendant gods became women in order to
serve the empress of the universe. But when Andhaka (who in this myth may not
be seen as being already Pârvatî's son) attempted to molest her, Śiva appeared
and impaled him on his trident and began to dance. But by the mere touch of
Śiva, Andhaka's sins were burned away. Śiva transformed this grotesque demon
into a handsome young man. And when Andhaka prostrated before Pârvatî and
Śiva, he was accepted as their son.

See also Pârvatî; Śiva; Tapas

ANGÂRAPARNA

See Citraratha

ANGIRAS

A Sage

Angiras appeared in many roles, some contradictory. The *Rigveda* called him the
first of the fire-gods. As such he was a mediator between gods and men. At times
he appeared as a *mahârishi,* a composer of many Rigvedic hymns to the gods. He
was also a *prajâpati,* or progenitor of humankind. As such his origin or lineage
was important, at least for later mythology. He was said to be born from the mind
of Brahmâ, as were five other sages: Marîci, Atri, Pulastya, Pulaha, and Kratu.

There was a quite different version of his birth. Once Brahmâ went to see a
sacrifice performed by Rudra. He was attracted by the celestial damsels present
there and had a seminal release. He offered the semen to the sacrificial fire, and
from that fire were born three sages: Angiras, Marîci, and Bhrigu. The meaning
of Angiras is "one born from the fire."

When Angiras was considered one of the sixteen grandfathers (prajâpatis), it
was by the appointment of Brahmâ. Angiras had two wives, Smritî and Khyati,
and fifteen children, in one account, and four wives in another: Smritî (memory),
Śraddhâ (faith), Svadhâ (oblation), and Satî (truth). The famous sage Brihaspati
was his son.

Late myths tell of the great austerities *(tapas)* of Angiras that so frightened
Indra. Indra's throne became overheated by these tapas, increasing his anxiety.
Indra had to act to stop these austerities, which could result in Angiras usurping
his rule of heaven. One version had Indra being reborn on earth as the son of
Angiras, by the name of Savyâ, to frustrate Angiras's austerities.

See also Brahmâ; Brihaspati; Prajâpati; Tapas

ANI-MÂNDAVYA

A sage

Mândavya was a sage who was doing penance at his hermitage *(ashram)* when several thieves ran past being chased by the king's men. The thieves left the stolen property near Mândavya and ran away. The king's men found Mândavya with the stolen property and took him before the king. Since he did not answer the questions put to him, Mândavya was condemned to death—along with the thieves, who were finally caught. They were all pierced through with a trident. The thieves died, but Mândavya stayed alive. After some time Śiva appeared before him and granted him long life. The king learned that Mândavya was still alive, made further inquiries, and realized that Mândavya was innocent. He asked Mândavya to forgive him. Mândavya did so, even though it was not possible to take the trident completely out of his body. The tip *(ani)* of the trident was left. And thenceforth Mândavya came to be known as Ani-Mândavya (Mândavya with the tip).

Ani-Mândavya asked the gods why he had to undergo this punishment, even though he had committed no sin. The god Dharma (Dharma-deva) answered that Mândavya in his childhood used to pierce butterflies on broomsticks. Being pierced with the trident was punishment for that sin. Ani-Mândavya argued that, according to the scriptures, sins done before the age of twelve would not be punished. So Ani-Mândavya laid a curse on Dharma-deva to be reborn as the son of a lower-caste, *śûdra* woman. And so it was; Dharma-deva was born as Vidura, the son of the palace maid and the sage Vyâsa. There is another version of this myth in which both cursed each other to be born of śûdra mothers in their next rebirth.

As in the Jewish story of Job, Ani-Mândavya, who had been a just man and fulfilled his *dharma* (duty, righteousness), was betrayed by the divine, personified as Dharma-deva. The story of Ani-Mândavya in the *Purânas* is but one example of a strong protest against institutionalized duty.

See also Dharma; Śiva

ANJANÂ

A monkey; mother of Hanuman

Once Śiva and Pârvatî were playing in the woods in the form of monkeys. Pârvatî became pregnant. The fetus was given to Vâyu, the wind god. Vâyu gave it in turn to Anjanâ who was doing austerities *(tapas)* at that time in order to obtain a son. Thus, Kuñjara, the monkey chieftain, and Añjanâ gave birth to Hanuman.

In her previous birth Anjanâ was a goddess named Puñjikastalâ (also known as Mânagarvâ). She was born as a she-monkey, Anjanâ, as a result of a curse. She was redeemed from the curse and regained her original nature after the birth of Hanuman.

See also Hanuman; Pârvatî; Śiva

APÂLÂ

A daughter of the sage Atri

A story in the *Rigveda* says that Apâlâ was abandoned by her husband when she came down with leprosy. She began living in the *ashram* of her father Atri and did austerities *(tapas)* to please Indra. One day when she was coming back from her daily rituals beside the river, she happened to taste *soma (amrita)* that was to be offered to Indra. Perhaps she could be healed by this magical ambrosia of the gods, or she could even gain immortality. But when Indra appeared, she immediately gave the soma offering to him. Indra was so pleased by Apâlâ's action that he cured her of leprosy.

See also Amrita; Indra; Soma; Tapas

APSARA

A celestial being

An *apsara* was a celestial damsel or nymph *(devastrî)* found in Indra's heaven, Devaloka. Apsaras were born at the Churning of the Milky Ocean. Another version, in the *Manu Shastra,* stated that these damsels were created along with the seven Manus. They were called wives of the gods and daughters of pleasure.

The thirteen apsaras were also said to have come from the union of Kaśyâpa and Arishtâ. The apsaras were known as heavenly charmers (as was Urvaśî) of heroes and temptresses (as were Menakâ and Rambhâ) of sages. Their numbers swelled from 13 to 34 to 1,000 and finally to 35 million. Their roles changed from celestials in Indra's court to wives of the *gandharvas* (celestial musicians) to the reward for warrior-heroes in Indra's heaven.

See also Gandharvas; Manu; Urvaśî

ARÂ

Daughter of the sage Śukra

Her story was a warning to kings who abused their power, who did not live by the rules of civility, or who harmed the family of a *brâhmin.*

A haughty young king named Danda ruled a large kingdom that extended to the Himâlayas. One day on a hunting expedition King Danda saw Arâ, daughter of the great sage, Mahârishi Śukra. In his lust he raped the young *brâhmin* girl.

Arâ told her father, and he advised her to practice austerities *(tapas)*. This must have been for purification, for it was the *rishi* (sage) who gained the boon from Indra to rain fire upon the kingdom of Danda. The entire region was turned into an impenetrable wasteland where neither animals nor birds lived. The place became known as Danda-kâranya. (This story was nested within the Râma myth cycle, serving to explain the place and its name.)

See also Râma; Tapas

ARAYANNA

The heavenly swans (hamsa)

The *arayanna* were described as having a heavenly abode on Mânasasaras, one of the Himâlayas. *Ara* denoted royalty. The swans did not like rain, so they came to earth when it rained in their heavenly abode and returned as soon as rain began on earth. Their parentage was traced to Kaśyâpa by his wife Tâmrâ through her daughter Dhritarâshthrî. Vâlmîki's *Râmâyana* stated that this lineage alone gave the swan its divinity *(devatva)*.

Swans were at first black and white, according to a myth in the *Uttara Râmâyana*, but pure white was given as a blessing from the god Varuna, who took their form to hide from the great demon Râvana. (The gods had assembled for a sacrificial meal and had to change into the shape of various birds when Ravâna came to attack them.) The swan was blessed by Varuna to be as white as milk.

There are many stories about the arayanna. A swan was once stuck in a water tank, and Prince Nala found and captured it, but then took pity on the trembling bird and released it. The arayanna was so happy that it flew to the next kingdom and helped in gaining Princess Damayantî as Nala's wife.

The swan could be used in a more obvious moral lesson. A story was told to Bhîshma: why this sage is so unreliable. An old arayanna lived by the sea and preached righteous actions to the birds of that region. Then because of a famine the birds needed to look farther away for their prey, so they entrusted their eggs to the swan, and he grew fat eating the very eggs he had promised to watch. Finally one of the birds noticed the declining number of eggs and told the others, and they killed the deceitful arayanna. This theme of reversal in the myths—of a king or priest or even a god failing to be righteous—illustrated the importance of following *dharma* (ethical duty) just as clearly as if the story had given a positive example.

Swans (*hamsa* or *arayanna*) were considered to be celestial birds having the capability of separating water and milk. They were often used in Vedantic literature metaphysically as a metaphor for one who had the ability to distinguish between the material and the spiritual. Even Krishna would be called a *hamsa*, as was Shrî Râmakrishna in the modern period.

See also Brahmâ; Kaśyapa

ARISHTÂ
Wife of Sage Kasyapa

Arishtâ is one of the mothers of all beings. She gave birth to the four gandharvas (the celestial singers: Haha, Hûhû, Atibahu, and Tumburu) and the thirteen apsaras (celestial maidens).

See also Apsara; Gandharva; Kaśyapa

ARISHTHA, ARISHTHAKA
A demon

Arishtha was the servant of Kamsa and was sent to Gokula in the form of an ox to kill Śrî Krishna. The ox terrified the cowherds *(gopis)* as it tore up the hills and mountains around Vrindarvin. The youth Krishna faced and killed the ox, throwing it an incredible distance. As he died, Arishtha appeared in his *asura* form.

See also Asura; Kamsa; Krishna

ARJUNA
A hero and warrior

Arjuna's story was one of the best known in Hindu mythology, yet it is fully intelligible only if one is familiar with the many other stories related to it. It is nested in or overlaps with the story of the great Bharata war, the story of Krishna, the story of Krishna's mother, Kuntî, and with the other larger stories, many of which are told in the *Bhagavad Gîtâ* and the *Mahâbhârata*.

Kuntî received a *mantra* (magical formula) from the sage Durvâsa as a five-fold boon so that she could become the mother of a son from any *deva* she thought about as she chanted the mantra. Before marriage she tried one of its five uses and gave birth to Karna by the sun god Sûrya. But Kuntî abandoned Karna, and he was raised by a low-caste family without knowledge of his miraculous birth. After marriage, with the permission of her sick husband Pandu, Kuntî used the boon three times and gave birth to three more sons: Dharmaputra (or Yud-hishthira) from Yama (god of death), Bhîma from Vâyu (wind god), and Arjuna from Indra (king of the gods and god of war). She gave the fifth use of the mantra to Mâdrî, the other wife of her husband. Mâdrî thought upon the Aśvins as she

Arjuna is driven into battle by Lord Krishna. (TRIP)

chanted and gave birth to twins, Nakula and Sahadeva. These five sons became know as the five sons of Pandu (the Pandavas). In the *Devî Bhâgavata* Arjuna is said to be the reincarnation of the rishi called Nara. But this twist in the story is not part of the narrative in the *Mahâbhârata*.

Arjuna, his brothers, and their one hundred cousins, who were known collectively as the Kauravas, received training in archery from the great master *(acarya)* Drona. Arjuna surpassed everyone except the dark-skinned and low-caste Karna, Arjuna's unknown half-brother. Karna later became allied with and the champion of the Kauravas, who had become the enemies of the Pandavas.

Three episodes about Arjuna stand out of the hundreds nested in the *Mahâbhârata*: Arjuna's marriage to Draupadî, the loss of the kingdom to the Kauravas, and the single episode told in the *Bhagavad Gîtâ*.

Arjuna won the hand of the princess Draupadî in an archery tournament, and when he announced to his mother that he had won a great prize, she declared that the prize must be shared equally with his brothers as always. Obediently, Draupadî married all five brothers, but Arjuna was her favorite. The brothers agreed that none could intrude upon the brother who was alone with Draupadî on pain of a one-year exile of celibacy. By mistake Arjuna broke the agreement and went into exile. But he did not remain celibate and married three more times. The most interesting of these was the marriage to his cousin Krishna's sister, Subhadrâ. She bore him a son whom they named Abhimanyu, who died on the plains of Kurukshetra in the great war. This exile was the beginning of the epic relationship between Arjuna and his cousin Krishna. Together they destroyed the Khândava Forest to appease the god of fire (Agni), riding on two chariots as "the two Krishnas." A nested story told how they were the seers Nara and Nârâyana in a previous life. Nara has his own myth as the cosmic man, or the original soul *(purusha)*. Nârâyana would metaphysically connect Krishna with the cosmic form of Vishnu. This warrior pair joined again for the greatest of all battles on the fields of Kurukshetra, with Krishna as Arjuna's charioteer, the two Krishnas in one chariot.

The great war had so many causes that the storytellers nested one myth inside another to create the world's longest epic, the *Mahâbhârata*. At the same time the theme was simple and understandable. The Pandavas had been cheated out of their kingdom by the evil of their cousins, the Kauravas. The eldest Pandava, Yudhishthira, lost everything including Draupadî in Indian literature's most notorious dice game. Draupadî would have been stripped naked in the great hall had not divine intervention provided an infinite amount of material to her sari. This humiliation of their joint wife would be avenged. Now all the Pandavas were exiled from their kingdom.

Arjuna used the time of this exile to further prepare as a warrior. He performed severe austerities *(tapas)* to Śiva and was granted use of the doomsday weapon (a divine bow and missiles that destroyed his enemies). He was even transported to heaven and taught by his father, Indra, god of war. Arjuna became a celibate dance instructor—an episode that associated him with Śiva, who was lord of the dance. Later in the great war Arjuna danced on his chariot and saw Śiva as the real agent of the destruction before him.

Arjuna's most famous moment, one of the most loved in Hindu mythology, was a single episode in the great war, the episode described in the *Bhagavad Gîtâ.* Arjuna had lost heart as a warrior and questioned whether he should fulfill his duty *(dharma)* as a warrior. He refused to continue a fight that would mean killing of family and friends and incurring sin. Krishna argued with little success until he appeared in his true nature as the supreme lord of the universe— as Vishnu. Arjuna was taught that he must do his duty, he must act without attachment to results, and he must offer all the fruits of his actions to the divine in loving devotion. Thus even in killing he would be free of sin.

Arjuna's belated recognition of the charioteer Krishna as Vishnu, the supreme lord of the universe, earned for him a place in Vaishnava mythology as the role model for all true devotees *(bhaktas).* But Arjuna transcended any narrow sectarianism. He became a pan-Indian example of one who does their caste duty *(varna-dharma).* He fought for a just and righteous society based on the rules of the Hindu tradition. He was an ideal husband, whose *karma* (in the sense of previous actions) earned a marriage with the Goddess in her incarnated form as Draupadî. He was the ideal human, connected to the divine as son of Indra, as pupil of Śiva, and as the friend of Krishna, the incarnation *(avatâra)* of Vishnu.

> *See also Bhagavad Gîtâ;* Dhritarâshthra; Draupadî; Durvâsa; Indra; Krishna; *Mahâbhârata;* Nara; Nârâyana; Pandu; Pandavas; Sûrya; Vâyu; Vishnu; Yama

ARUNA
Charioteer of Sûrya

Aruna's story must begin with an account of how he became the charioteer of the sun god, Sûrya. Aruna's father was the famous Kaśyâpa-prajâpati (grandfather of all creatures). Two of Kaśyâpa's wives, Vinatâ and Kadrû, pleased him so much that he granted each a boon. Kadrû asked for a thousand *nâga* (snake) sons, and Vinatâ wanted only two sons, more powerful than those of Kadrû. So Kaśyâpa granted their wishes and went to the forest to practice austerities *(tapas).* After some time Kadrû gave birth to a thousand eggs and placed them in pots to incubate. Vinatâ gave birth to two eggs and placed each in a pot. After five hundred years Kadrû's pots broke open with her thousand *nâga* sons. So

Vinatâ opened one of her pots, but that son was only half developed. This deformed child was named Aruna. He became the charioteer of Sûrya (the sun). His brother finally developed and was named Garuda, the great sun eagle, and was eventually chosen as the vehicle of Vishnu. (There are some accounts that say that Garuda's mother was Kardu.)

In the *Ramâyana,* Aruna appeared in an episode with Râma and his brother Lakshmana. Jatâyu, a bird hero, was wounded by the demon king Ravâna as he escaped with Sîtâ. Ravâna gained victory by cutting off Jatâyu's wings. When Râma and Lakshmana found him wounded in the forest, Jatâyu explained that he had been Aruna in his previous birth. In another version Jatâyu was only the son of Aruna.

Aruna was used in a Purânic myth to account for the birth of Bâli (a demon)—a tale of sex changes and deception. This episode was nested in the story of Shîlâvatî, who had performed *tapas* to prevent the sun (Sûrya) from rising, in order to save her husband. And while the sun slept, the sun's charioteer Aruna used his time off to change into a female and go to Indra's heaven, Devaloka. He had learned that the women were dancing naked in their reserved area. But as he sported with them, Aruna, in his female form as Ârunîdevî, excited Indra—an Indra who had become the example of desire and excess in the Purânic myths. Indra enjoyed the night with Ârunîdevî, and they had a child, who was immediately given to Ahalyâdevî, wife of the sage Gautama. Of course this introduced the need for another story to be told about what happened to this child and how it became Bâli. But Aruna's story continued. He had to return to his job as charioteer of the sun. Shîlâvatî had stopped her *tapas,* Sûrya had awakened and was ready to be driven across the heavens in his chariot, but Aruna was late getting back. Sûrya made him explain the reason for this dereliction of duty, and Aruna told how he had changed himself into a woman and deceived the women in Indra's heaven and been caught by Indra—and with what result. Now the sun—whose purity was never questioned in the Vedas but who had also become in later myth an example of how not to behave—reacted. Sûrya made Aruna show his female form, and of course Sûrya too had a child by Aruna; this child was also turned over to Ahalyâdevî, wife of the sage Gautama. This child was named Sugrîva. And this story continued when Indra gave both Bâli and Sugrîva to the monkey king, Riksha-râja.

See also Ahalyâ; Bâli; Garuda; Kaśyapa; Sûrya; Vishnu

ASCETICISM

See TAPAS. See also discussions in chapter 1 of "The Upanishadic Period," "Theomachy," and "Renunciation, Sacrifice, and Magic."

ASHTHÂVAKRA

A sage

Sage Uddalaka's daughter Sujatâ married his disciple Khagodara, and to them was born Ashthâvakra. The word *ashtha-avakra* means "one with eight bends," referring to his deformed body.

There are two versions of how he acquired the eight bends. According to one version, once Khagodara was reciting holy *mantras*. Sujatâ sat beside him, but the baby inside her womb heard his father's chants and said loudly that Khagodara was chanting the mantras in the wrong way. Khagodara became very angry and cursed him to be born with a crooked body.

Another Purânic version stated that Devala was Ashthâvakra's original name, and that he was the son of the sage Asita. In this version Devala was cursed by Rambhâ, one of the celestial nymphs *(apsaras)*. She had fallen in love with Devala, but when Devala did not yield to her wishes, she cursed him with a crooked body. He thereafter was called Ashthâvakra. He later regained his original form by doing *tapas* (austerities).

The *Agni Purâna* added that once Ashthâvakra laid a curse on the celestial nymphs *(apsaras)* when they teased him about his crooked body, dooming them to be reborn on earth as humans, and thus the celestial nymphs were reborn as the many wives of Shrî Krishna.

See also Apsara; Devala; Krishna

ASIKNÎ

Wife of a prajâpati and mother of many beings

Asiknî must be ranked among the most fertile of all wives in Hindu myth. The myths only gave her this one dimension. Daksha, an alternative creator to Kasyâpa, found that he could not create all of the species from his own mind. So he married Asiknî and immediately begat five thousand Haryashvas, creatures who were to populate the earth naturally. But the old sage Nârada, the *deva-rishi* (divine sage) with the golden words, shamed the Haryashvas with their ignorance. He told them that they must first know the extent of the world before they peopled it. So they left to explore the world and never returned. Finally Daksha concluded his Haryashva sons were lost, so he fathered a thousand Sabalâsva sons by Asiknî. But dear old Nârada tricked them with the same quest, and they followed their brothers to the ends of the world, not to come back. This time Daksha begat sixty girls by Asiknâ, and he gave them to lesser *prajâpatis* (grandfathers of the various species). And this worked.

See also Daksha; Kasyâpa; Nârada; Prajâpati

ÂSTIKA

A sage; son of the sage Jaratkâru and his wife, the goddess Manasâ-devî

This Purânic myth illustrates how many steps might be involved in a divine plan. Long ago snakes were overrunning the earth, so everyone pleaded with Kaśyâpa-prajâpati, the great progenitor, for protection. Kaśyâpa created a goddess from his mind, and she was appropriately named Manasâ (mind). While she was practicing *tapas* (austerities) in the forest to gain a boon from Śiva, a sage named Jaratkâru discovered a reason why he must give up his celibate life and marry. He discovered the spirits of his ancestors in a very sad state, hanging upside down on a single blade of grass over a precipice. When asked, they told him that it was because he had no children for the annual rites *(samskâras)*, and without living descendants they would perish and never reach heaven. So the sage decided he must marry and fulfill his duty *(dharma)* toward his ancestors. Jaratkâru had only one condition: that the woman should have the same name as his own.

This condition could be met, because Manasâ incarnated as the sister of Vâsuki, the great serpent, in order to save the serpents, who were threatened with total extinction by a soon-to-be-undertaken snake sacrifice, foreknown by her *tapas*.

Vâsuki, the great serpent, appeared to tell the sage Jaratkâru that he had such a sister (or half-sister as it turned out to be). So Jaratkâru and Jaratkâru were married. And all was bliss until the sage Jaratkâru overslept in the lap of his wife, who was supposed to wake him up to do his rituals. He cursed her for not awaking him. But she thought of the gods, and so great was the power from her austerities that they appeared immediately. They were finally able to convince the *brâhmin* that he should not exile his wife before she had a son. So he touched her with his hand, and she became pregnant with Âstika. In many accounts, he then retired to the forest.

So Manasâ-devî (in her incarnation as Jaratkâru) traveled to Kailâsa and was instructed by Śiva and Pârvatî. Her unborn child, Âstika, heard all the teachings. He grew up being taught by gods and sages. Finally Âstika and his mother Manasâ-devî went to visit Kaśyapa, who was overjoyed to see his grandson and daughter. Kaśyapa passed the merit of feeding a million *brâhmin*s to his grandson. Now the stage was set for Âstika's role in the divine plan.

A king named Parîkshit had insulted a *brâhmin* during his meditation by throwing a dead snake on him. The sage's son, Śamîka, was offended by the joke and put a death curse on King Parîkshit—that he had only seven days to live. But the king had his engineers build a new palace on a pillar in the middle on the ocean with psychics and *yogis* protecting him. The giant serpent Takshâka made a final attempt on the seventh day. Disguised as an old priest, Takshâka met

Dhanvantari, the physician of the gods, on his way to protect the king. After they became friends, Dhanvantari returned home. Takshâka changed his shape and entered an apple being taken to King Parîkshit. When the king picked up the apple, Takshâka changed into his true shape and size and killed Parîkshit instantly. But the king's son, Janamejaya, sought revenge. After all the proper rituals were carried out, the new king Janamejaya enlisted many *brâhmin*s, who began a snake sacrifice. So many snakes were called into the fire by their powerful chants (mantras) that Takshâka fled to Indra and curled himself around Indra's bed. But the *brâhmin*s increased their chanting and used even more powerful mantras and were about to bring Takshâka, the cot, and Indra into the fire. So the gods rushed to Manasâ-devî and asked her protection of the surviving snakes and Indra. Manasâ-devî sent her son Âstika. Âstika knew that a king must grant a *brâhmin* a reasonable request. So Âstika asked King Janamejaya to give him the lives of Takshâka and Indra as a gift. His advisors saw no way out of this request, so the king gave Âstika his wish, and the snake sacrifice was ended. All the requests for divine help, all the way back to the people of the world praying to Kaśyapa to protect them from the snakes, were fulfilled. But the snakes were also protected from annihilation.

See also Dhanvantari; Janamejaya; Kailâsa; Kaśyapa; Nâga; Takshâka; Vâsuki

ASURA

Demons

The term *asura* is so ancient that it has a separate mythology among the Aryans' cousins in ancient Persia. In the *Avesta*, the word *ahura* (*asura*, Sanskrit) was a positive term that meant the gods. But the *ahura* were mainly gods of agrarian values, and the greatest *ahura* was Varuna, the god of the justice in the sense of cosmic order *(rita)* that a farmer could depend upon to reap what he had sowed. The original meaning of the word *asura* was "spiritual, divine."

Even in the *Rigveda* there was an admission that the *asuras* were the older brothers of the *devas*, the gods of the Vedic, or Aryan, peoples. Varuna was the only *asura* who was honored as a god in the *Vedas*. For the Aryans the *asuras*—except for Varuna—had become demons. It was not that they were really evil; they just opposed the *devas*.

In the later mythology everyone had to have a genealogy; so the *asuras* belonged to the dynasty of demons, sons of Kasyapa-prajâpati born to two of his wives, Danu and Ditî. The sons born to Danu were called *danavas*, and those born to Ditî were called *daityas*. The danavas and daityas together constituted the class of demons, or *asuras*.

The *râkshasas* are another class of demons not included with *asuras,* as they descended from Pulastya, not Kaśyapa.

See also Deva; Kaśyapa; Râkshasa; Varuna

AŚVA-MEDHA

The horse (aśva) sacrifice (medha)
A wild stallion was released by a warrior king to roam freely. The king or his general would follow the horse with an army and defeat in a battle any kingdom that the horse crossed that would not pay tribute and recognize the king's sovereignty. There was a chance for great honor, but only a "world conqueror" *(cakravartin)* could complete such random warfare. At the end of the year the horse would be brought back to the king's capital, where priests would sacrifice it in one of the most elaborate and expensive of Vedic rituals. The cost of the *aśva-medha* alone required much booty from the year of conquests. The ritual had a number of features involving fertility and renewal.

Performing a hundred such sacrifices *(yâgas)* was the definition of an Indra. Thus, later mythology taught the descent of royalty from the gods and their upward rise back to divinity, even the status of king of the gods, an Indra.

AŚVATTHÂMA, AŚVATTHÂMÂ

A Kaurava general and a brâhmin
Aśvatthâma became the commander-in-chief of the Kauravas when their great army had been reduced to three—plus the dying Duryodhana. Those three entered the camp of the Pandavas and slaughtered many heroes and their children. Five young sons of the Pandavas were beheaded and taken back to Duryodhana. Draupadî, wife of the Pandava brothers, wanted revenge, but she allowed her husbands a way out of slaying a *brâhmin.* They only had to bring back the jewel Aśvatthâma wore. Bhîma, Arjuna, and Krishna pursued Aśvatthâma and brought back his jewel to Draupadî. Aśvatthâma went into the forest with the sage Vyâsa where they both are said to continue to live as *ciranjivis* (ones who do not die).

See also Ciranjivis

AŚVINS, AŚVINI-DEVAS

The celestial Twins
Satya and Dasra were popularly called the Aśvins (possessors of horses) and were the physicians of the *devas* (gods). Their father was the sun, Sûrya. They were

proud warriors who drove their chariot across the sky, paired as driver and fighter. They were associated with the goddess of the dawn, Ushas. It was their exploits against the demons Namuci and horse-headed Dadhyañc that proved them to be physicians of the gods.

Twinning would pair them by association with all other twins in Hindu mythology: twin wives, the twin children of Tvashthri, the twins Yamî and Yama.

See also Sûrya; Ushas

ATIBALA

A samnyâsin (world renouncer)

Yama took the form of a *samnyâsin* and was the indirect cause for the death of Râma and Lakshmana.

After Râma had killed Râvana in the Lanka war, the main reason for the incarnation of Vishnu as Râma was fulfilled. There needed to be a cause for Vishnu to return to Vaikuntha (his heavenly abode). Brahmâ asked Yama to go to see Râma. Yama went to see Râma in the guise of a samnyâsin called Atibala and said that he had a secret to tell Râma. During their meeting with him nobody was to enter. Lakshmana was asked to guard the entrance, and if anybody entered Lakshmana would forfeit his life.

At that time sage Durvâsa approached Râma's tent, after doing austerities *(tapas)* for a thousand years. He was hungry and wanted to ask Râma for food. When Lakshmana asked him to wait for a while, Durvâsa threatened to turn everybody into ashes if he was not allowed to go inside. With no other alternative Lakshmana had to go inside and inform Râma about the situation. Durvâsa was given sumptuous food. But in order to keep the promise with Atibala, Lakshmana had to die. He went to the river Sarayu and drowned himself. Beset by despair, Râma entrusted the affairs of his kingdom to others and went to the river Sarayu. There he renounced his earthly body and also drowned himself—returning to Vaikuntha in his original form of Lord Vishnu. (Another Purânic version is given in the entry on Lakshmana.)

See also Durvâsa; Lakshmana; Râma; Râvana; Vaikuntha; Vishnu

ATRI

Son of Brahmâ

Brahmâ had six *mânasâ-putras*—sons created from his mind. Atri was one of them. The other five sons of Brahmâ are Marîci, Angiras, Pulastya, Pulaha, and Kratu. Another version of the *mânasâ-putras* increased the number to seven, or the seven sages *(sapta-rishis)*.

Atri married Anasûyâ, and they had three sons, Soma (or Candra), Durvâsa, and Dattâtreya. Atri was also known as the author of a part of the *Rigveda*. His story is told at more length in the entry on Anasûyâ.

See also Anasûyâ; Brahmâ; Dattâtreya; Durvâsa; Mânasâ-putra; Sapta-rishis; Soma

AUM
See Om

AURVA
A fierce sage

The Aurva myth was told only in the *Mahâbhârata* and portrayed a time of mutual killings between the *kśatriyas* and *brâhmin*s. It took some of the motifs of the Agni myth cycle, such as the submarine fire, and reshaped them, portraying the fiery priest Aurva, whose horse-headed descendants would consume the world at the end of the age. The Aurva myth may have been a model for that of the later Paraśu-Râma incarnation in the *Purânas*.

A generous king named Kritavîrya made the priestly descendants of the sage Bhrigu very rich. But with his death the kingdom and its ruling family fell on hard times. They asked the Bhrigus for help but were refused and felt humiliated. When they learned that some of the priests had hidden their wealth in the ground, the impoverished *kśatriyas* vowed to kill them all. So a slaughter of the Bhrigus (also called Bhargavas) began. Even women and children were killed. One woman hid her unborn child in her thigh, but the *kśatriyas* learned of it. As she fled from their pursuit, she fell, and her thigh split open. A boy too bright to be looked at fell from her thigh *(ûru)*, and thus he was called Aurva (of the thigh). As he grew, his austerities *(tapas)* frightened both gods and men. After years of wrath against the *kśatriyas*, only his ancestor spirits *(pitris)* were able to get him to release his anger. When he threw it into the sea, it became a fiery being with the face of a horse that was called Hayashiras (another name in the *Vedas* for the sacrifice itself, *yâjña*).

Aurva retreated to the forest and while there stopped the *satî* (widow-burning) of the pregnant wife of King Bâhu. She finally delivered, after carrying the baby for seven years. Aurva became the child's protector and named him Sagara (ocean). Aurva gave him the fiery weapon of Agni, the Âgneyâstra, which later helped Sagara conquer barbarian invaders. One account stated that Aurva had a son named Ricîka. Another version stated that he begat progeny who began destroying the world. Brahmâ had to intervene and gave an abode to them in the "mouth of the ocean" so that together they could consume the world with fire at the end of each age. *Asura* was clearly linked in this version with the submarine fire.

See also Bhrigu; Manu; Parasu-Râma; Sagara; Tapas

AVATÂRA

A concept meaning incarnation, or "coming down of god"

The term *avatâra* is usually associated with divine incarnations, especially the ten incarnations of Vishnu. But there were lists with as many as twenty-six incarnations. The ten avatâras, *dashâvatâra* (*dasha*, "ten," and *avatâra*, "incarnations"), were Matsya the fish, Kûrma the turtle, Varâha the boar, Narasimha the lion-man, Vâmana the *brâhmacâri* (second stage of life) dwarf, Parasu-Râma (or Râma with the ax), Shrî Râma, Balabhadra-Râma, Krishna, and the future avatâra, Kalki. The incarnation of Vishnu as Kalki is expected at the end of the Kali Yuga when this evil age ends in fire. One account stated that there are an innumerable number of the incarnations of Vishnu, both partial *(amsâvatara)* and full. In some lists the Buddha was considered an incarnation of Vishnu, taking upon himself the form of a false teacher in order to lead those who were evil away from the *Vedas*. Traditionally, each avatâra appeared in order to perform a specific cosmic duty that was necessary to maintain or restore cosmic order. Having performed that task, the avatâra then disappeared, or merged back into Vishnu.

The myths of each of the avatâras will be told under its own heading, but those of Râma and Krishna need further attention. These deities became so popular that they transcended their regional origins. As early as medieval Hinduism, each began to be seen as a deity in his own right, and indeed as the supreme lord of the universe, not just an incarnation of Vishnu. This change also involved a reversal. Since either Râma or Krishna was the Supreme, then Vishnu, and all other gods for that matter, were but manifestations of Râma or Krishna.

The myths about the Divine Mother, Devî (Durgâ), and Śiva also involved the notion of divine descents (avatâra). But there were subtle differences in the philosophical and theological concepts of Śâktism (worship of the Divine Mother) and Shaivism (worship of Śiva). Both maintained philosophically that the Absolute did not come down into the limitations of time, space, and causality. The Absolute remained beyond these limitations, while only a manifestation, not technically an avatâra, appeared to reveal the truth or to correct what only God could.

Krishna's promise in the *Bhagavad Gîtâ* expressed the concept well:

In order to protect the good and punish the wicked,
In order to make a firm foundation for righteousness,

I come into being age after age.
(*Bhagavad Gîtâ* 4.7–8)

See also Bala-Râma; Buddha; Kalki; Krishna; Kûrma; Matsya; Narasimha; Parasu-
Râma; Râma; Vâmana; Varâha; Vishnu

AYODHYÂ
A city
Ayodhyâ was the capital city of the kings of Ikshvaku. But it then became one
of the seven most sacred cities in India because it was the birthplace of King
Râma. Ayodhyâ was also where Râma ruled as king after he defeated Râvana.
Râmanavami is the festival that is still celebrated there, one of the five great
fasts (*maha-vratas*) of Vaishnavism.

Ayodhyâ has become a flash point for communal struggles in modern India
since a four-century-old mosque was destroyed by radical Hindus there. They
believed that it had been built over the very birthplace of Râma.

See also Râma

BALA
A demon (asura)
Bala lived in Atala (one of the seven hells), teaching ninety-six kinds of magic to
trouble the *devas* (divinities). Out of one of his own yawns, he created three
women with the power to entice whomever they wanted. These three women had
an aphrodisiac called *hataka*. They gave *hataka* to men and enjoyed them as long
as they liked—and then would abandon these poor mortals, drained of their energy.

In a battle with Indra, king of the *devas*, Bala defeated him. Indra "took
refuge in Bala" and glorified him with the highest praise. Bala fell into Indra's trap
by asking Indra what were his wishes. Indra said that he wished for Bala's body.
Bala then gave his body to Indra, because he had given a boon and would keep his
word. Bala's body was cut into pieces and thrown about. Wherever these pieces
fell, they turned into gold mines (some accounts say diamond mines). This was
the result of Bala's merit for honoring his promise to grant Indra's request.

After the death of Bala his wife Prabhavatî went to the teacher of the *asuras*,
the *âcârya* Śukra, in an attempt to bring her husband back to life. Śukracharya said
that he was unable to do so but was able to bring back Bala's voice. And it asked
Prabhavatî to leave her body and join him. Prabhavatî immediately abandoned her
body and joined Bala. She thus became the river Prabhavatî, for posterity.

See also Asura

Bala-Râma plays with his younger, dark-skinned brother Krishna. They are both avatâras *of Vishnu. (TRIP)*

BALA-RÂMA, BALARÂMA, BALABHADRA-RÂMA
Elder brother of Krishna and an avatâra of Vishnu

This myth is nested within the great myth cycles of Lord Vishnu and Shrî Krishna. Bala-Râma was involved in many episodes as an adoring, supportive older brother of Krishna. It was a role deserving of a divine lineage, demonstrating the kind of person who deserved to be near so great an incarnation as Krishna, and how important it is to live one's own *dharma* (duty). Bala-Râma's birth was particularly miraculous.

On the day of the marriage of the Yâdava king Vasudeva to Devakî, a voice was heard from the sky that the eighth child of this couple would kill Kamsa, the wicked brother of Devakî. Kamsa immediately jailed both Devakî and Vasudeva. He killed the first six children born to them. The seventh child was the incarnation of Ananta, Vishnu's serpent. Vishnu, in order to protect him, ordered Mâyâdevî to take the child from the womb of Devakî and to place it in the womb of Rohinî, another wife of King Vasudeva in the city of Madhurâ. Rohinî gave birth to Balabhadra-Râma. The eighth child was Krishna.

Bala-Râma was the constant companion in all the boyhood adventures of

Krishna in Madhurâ, killing demons and demonesses and even his uncle Kamsa at a Câpa-pûjâ (worship of the bow).

According to the *Bhâgavata Purâna*, Bala-Râma was the partial incarnation of Vishnu, and Shrî Krishna is a full incarnation. Other *Purânas* identified Bala-Râma as the incarnation of Ananta, the serpent on which Vishnu reclined upon when floating on the milky ocean. In versions where Bala-Râma was considered a partial incarnation, another figure was inserted in the list of the ten incarnations of Vishnu, such as Buddha. When Bala-Râma died of disappointment with the Yâdava clan and all of their failures at kingship, his spirit left his body through his mouth as a white serpent and was welcomed into the netherworld by the Nâga kingdom.

In art and iconography Bala-Râma is exactly the same in appearance as Krishna except he is white and Krishna is black or dark purple.

See also Devakî; Kamsa

BALI

A king of the asuras

Bali was present at so many times and places that the mythmakers had to employ one of their greatest discoveries, the various periods of the Manus *(manvantaras)*, a repeating of the cosmic ages each with its own "first man" (Manu). Thus the stories of Bali and his *deva* (god) opponents were never in conflict.

Mahâbali (or "great" Bali) was present at the Churning of the Ocean in the Câkshusa-manvantara, the period ruled by the Manu Câkshusa. He fought Indra and the gods, constantly defeating them with the magic of *mritansañjîvanî* (life restoration) taught by their great guru Śukra. So complete were his victories over the gods, that his priest Śukra performed the sacrifice of *viśvajita* (conqueror of the world), and Bali completed one hundred *aśva-medhas* (horse sacrifices). (For a description of an *aśva-medha* see under "Yudhishthira.") Bali was anointed as king of heaven—he had become an Indra.

The *asuras* possessed *amrita* (the magical no-death nectar) and its container. Once when Bali was killed in a battle with the gods, the demons carried his dead body to their teacher Śukra, and Bali was brought back to life. He completely drove the gods from the heavens, but in his victory he denied both *devas* and *brâhmins* (priests) their due. So with the help of the priests, the gods were finally able to appease Lord Vishnu, who had been upset with their pretenses. They realized that Bali's devotion to Vishnu was the reason for his triumph over the gods and that it had been the ultimate reason for Bali's invincibility. Only Vishnu could contrive a plan that would both restore the *devas'* rule over heaven, their *dharma*, and reward his devotee Bali with a greater destiny.

So Bali's story folded into the more significant story of the incarnation of Vishnu as Vâmana, the dwarf. In that incarnation, Vishnu defeated Bali by his very devotion to Vishnu and confined Bali to Pâtâla (the netherworld, hell).

Some accounts gave the Bali myth a perfect *bhakti* (devotional) ending. Vishnu incarnated as a small, some say dwarf, *brâhmin* who came to Bali and was honored by him. Even when his own priest and advisor recognized Vishnu and warned Bali, the king granted the young *brâhmin* a wish. And the wish—for all that could be covered by his three steps—ended in Bali losing everything. Some versions have Garuda, the sun eagle, binding Bali and taking him to Pâtâla. Other versions had Vishnu rewarding Bali with a direct entrance into heaven. There was one account that said that Bali became a *ciranjivi* (one who lived forever), just like Hanuman, the faithful servant of Râma.

Bali played a role in Vâlmîki's *Râmâyana* in an encounter with the demon Râvana. Râvana went to Pâtâla to free Bali but could not even obtain the earrings of Bali's great-grandfather, Hiranyakaśipu. Râvana returned to Lanka in shame. In a myth featuring the goddess Lakshmî, Bali's loss of his kingship of heaven came from his neglect of service to the *brâhmins*.

See also Aśva-medha; Ciranjivi; Vâmana

BÂLI

A great monkey king

Bâli's myth is nested within a number of interlocking myths. His part in the story of Râma and Sîtâ is mostly negative, as Râma has to kill him. But this is because he has turned from the very practices that made him a great king. He had a divine birth, one of miracle and magic. And that birth was set in motion by a woman sage of great power whose pronouncement stopped the sun from rising.

Bâli was the son of Indra by Aruna, but Aruna was a male—the charioteer of Sûrya. This was a late myth that highlighted the lust of Indra and devotion to Râma as an incarnation of Vishnu. But before we can get to the gender-shifting birth of Bâli and his brother, Sugrîva, there is another story of the events that set this one in motion.

Sîlavatî was a devoted wife and had acquired great power through her austerities. One night according to the wish of her leprous husband, Ugratapas, Sîlavatî carried him on her back to a harlot. On their way the sage Animandavya saw them and cursed Ugratapas for his lust: he would die before sunrise. Sîlavatî heard this and cast a spell so that the sun would not rise the following day. And the next day the sun did not rise at the right time, and the night was prolonged.

Because of the magic of Sîlavatî, the sun continued to sleep. Aruna, the charioteer of the sun, seeing that the sun was not rising at his appointed time, thought of spending this free time watching the dance of the apsaras in the court of Indra. He went to Indra's court disguised as a beautiful woman. But Indra noticed and was attracted by this new woman. He took her to a remote place, and out of their union was born Bâli. Aruna was late getting back to Sûrya, so the sun was angrily waiting for him and demanded an explanation. When Aruna told the whole story, Sûrya became interested in seeing this female form. Aruna again became a woman for the sun and out of their union was born Sugrîva.

The brothers, Bâli and Sugrîva, were given to one of the most pious of women, Ahalyâ, wife of the sage Gautama, and brought up in their hermitage. Later the monkey king, Riksha-râja, prayed to Indra for sons, and Indra brought him the divine brothers. Thus, Bâli, the elder, became the king of the monkey tribe when Riksha-râja became too old to rule.

After some time Bâli learned that a monkey was born of Śiva and Pârvatî, and he feared for his kingdom. He tried to kill that monkey, Hanuman, before he was born by pouring five molten metals into the womb of his foster mother, Anjanâ. But since Hanuman was conceived of the sperm of Śiva, he could not be injured by heat or metal. And Hanuman's presence protected his monkey mother as well.

Bâli had been given a boon from the *devas* that he would receive half the strength of his opponent in battle, thus enabling him to defeat anyone he wanted. So his kingdom grew in every direction. The demon king of Lanka, Râvana, was envious and devised a plan to kill Bâli. One morning as Bâli did his rituals on the eastern seashore, Râvana quietly sat down behind him, planning to attack from the rear and outwit the boon from the gods. Bâli pretended that he did not notice Râvana but tied him up like a bunch of sticks with his long tail. He jumped about India as usual on his way back to his kingdom. When everyone saw the demon tied up by Bâli's tail, he was laughed at and humiliated. Râvana returned to Lanka in defeat.

There is an interesting story, an excursion into magic and deceit, to explain how the two divine monkey brothers turned into blood enemies. The son of Maya, a carpenter of the demons, sought to use his abilities in magic and wrestling to defeat Bâli. But when he challenged Bâli in the middle of the night, Bâli and his brother Sugrîva chased the magician into a cave. Bâli left Sugrîva at the mouth of the cave with the command to seal it if red blood indicated he was killed. And if the milk of a sorcerer appeared, it would mean that Bâli had succeeded. But after a year blood appeared, and Sugrîva sealed the cave, returned to the monkey kingdom, and was crowned king. But the sorcerer's magic had worked in spite of his death as his blood appeared red instead of white. Thus Bâli believed that his brother had tried to kill him for the kingdom. Bâli would have killed his brother, but Sugrîva took refuge on a mountain that Bâli could not go to because of a sage's curse that he would meet death there. So Bâli practiced rituals and austerities *(tapas)* on the seashores, jumping back to his kingdom in a single bound after each attack. On his way, he would kick his brother on the forbidden mountain in mid-flight. Hanuman was Sugrîva's minister, and this torture of his king troubled him. One day he leaped into the sky as Bâli jumped from the sea toward the kingdom, kicking Sugrîva in passing. If Hanuman could have pulled Bâli into the mountain, the touch of the mountain would have ended his life and the torment of Sugrîva. But Hanuman and Bâli were equal in strength and finally had to make a truce.

Finally, the stage has been set for Bâli to be a worthy opponent of Râma on his march to Lanka to free Sîtâ. Râma met Sugrîva, and they became allies. Sugrîva and his prime minister, Hanuman, were to help Râma attack Râvana, and Râma was to help Sugrîva take back his own kidnapped wife from Bâli. But Bâli, the son of Indra, had such great powers that none had been able to defeat him. Sugrîva had two duels with him, losing half of his energy to Bâli each time, and was near death. Finally Râma killed Bâli from his hiding place, robbing Râvana of a powerful ally. As he died, Bâli questioned Râma's honor as a warrior, saying that it was not right for the king of Ayodhyâ to kill from ambush. In each version of the story, Râma's answer was revised. Since he was the perfect king and husband, and an incarnation of the supreme god, his answer needed to be satisfactory. But each version had attempted to solve a perceived weakness in his character and his divinity. Râma had done what was needed: Bâli could not be defeated in direct combat and needed to be punished for violating his *dharma* by stealing Sugrîva's wife. So Râma had killed him by the only method that was available to him. But such a utilitarian justification of his actions was not an ideal solution, which sought glorifications of dharma and honor.

After Bâli was killed by Shrî Râma, the kingdom was given to Sugrîva, and Râma proceeded to Lanka to attack Râvana.

See also Ahalyâ; Apsara; Aruna; Gautama; Indra; Râma; *Râmâyana*; Sûrya

BHADRAKA

A sinful brâhmin

Bhadraka had lead such an immoral life that some accounts say that he was outcasted. But one day he took a ritual bath for three days at Prayâga, during the month of Mâgha (a month in the Hindu calendar that falls in February or March). It had been said that those who took a bath at Prayâga in the month of Mâgha would be absolved of all their sins. So Bhadraka was awarded rebirth in heaven after his death because of this single act.

This type of myth advertised the powers of a particular pilgrimage place. So great were Bhadraka's sins that everyone could believe that they had sinned less and would surely get to heaven by taking a pilgrimage to Prayâga and bathing there.

BHADRAKÂLÎ

An incarnation of Pârvatî

When Śiva learned of his wife Satî's self-immolation in the sacrificial fire of her father Daksha, he loosened his matted hair in full anger. Out of this angry energy were born two attendants: Vîrabhadra and Bhadrakâlî. Bhadrakâlî was the angry energy of Pârvatî in a feminine form. Śiva sent them to kill Daksha.

This part of the Śiva myth cycle involves the killing of a *brâhmin*. Even Śiva could not do that directly. Devotees of Lord Vishnu used this myth to argue that Śiva was not invited to Daksha's Vedic sacrifice because of his impurity and that his killing of a *brâhmin*, even indirectly, by sending his creations, made him guilty of the greatest sin against *dharma* (duty, righteousness).

In a later myth Bhadrakâlî made a dramatic appearance in the Krishna birth story. In order for Krishna to escape death at his birth at the hands of his evil uncle Kamsa, a baby girl was substituted. As Kamsa tried to kill her, Bhadrakâlî appeared in full glory and power.

She also played a role in the Râma-Râvana war. Pârvatî complained to Śiva that she had not been given a role in Vishnu's Râma incarnation. So Śiva caused her to lose consciousness of her true nature and be reborn as Lankâ-Lakshmî, a doorkeeper or guardian in Lanka for Râvana. She fought with Hanuman, who knocked her unconscious with a blow from his left hand. When she regained consciousness, she remembered that she was Bhadrakâlî. She thanked Hanuman and returned to Kailâsa and Śiva.

See also Daksha; Dharma; Hanuman; Krishna; Pârvatî; Râma; Satî

BHAGA

A deva

Bhaga (inherited share) was a Vedic deity of wealth, power, and happiness. He was also, according to the *Rigveda,* one of the seven *âdityas*. The other six are Mitra (friendship, comradeship), Aryaman (honor, or chivalry), Varuna (binder to tribal rules; "all-seeing"), Daksha (ritual skill, or rules of ritual), and Amsa (gods' share).

Later, in the *Mahâbhârata* and the *Purânas,* there are twelve âdityas, born to grandfather Kaśyâpa-prajâpati and his wife Aditi. Bhaga was given a wife, Siddhi (psychic power). He made brief appearances: in Indra's assembly, at Arjuna's birthday celebration, at the burning of the Khândava forest, at Daksha's sacrifice, and at the sacrifice in which the *devas* forgot to give Rudra a share. In each of the last two stories, Bhaga's eyes were plucked out. At Daksha's sacrifice Bhaga was one of the presiding priests. After Śiva's anger over Satî's suicide in her father's sacrificial fire was manifested as Vîrabhadra and Bhadra-kâlî, Vîrabhadra plucked out Bhaga's eyes. Another version had Śiva doing it himself. This blindness was later seen as appropriate to Bhaga's way of bestowing wealth—without regard to purity, devotion, or honor. Bhaga bestowed wealth blindly.

In one account that did not become universal, Bhaga was associated with Rudra (a fierce god appropriated by the Śiva myth cycle) and gave his name to eleven Rudras. This association with Rudra came from a role Bhaga played in the myth that told of the dividing up of the sacrifice among the *devas* at the end of the *deva yuga*. Rudra was left out and in a rage attacked the gods, causing great injury. Bhaga was blinded. Another version had Rudra giving back Bhaga's eyes as well as the body parts taken from other gods. Some accounts would have Śiva returning these items.

But the point about wealth being given blindly was lost in the episode of dividing up the sacrifice, while it remained intact in the myth about Vîrabhadra's blinding Bhaga at Diksha's sacrifice.

See also Aditi; Âdityas; Daksha; Kaśyapa; Rudra; Śiva

BHAGAVAD GÎTÂ, BHAGAVADGÎTÂ

A scripture

The *Bhagavad Gîtâ* (Song of the Lord) is one of the most loved scriptures of India. It is pan-Indian, even though its central character, Arjuna, discovered that the driver of his war chariot, Krishna, was the supreme lord of the universe, Lord Vishnu. If this claim were taken literally and exclusively, the *Bhagavad Gîtâ* would be limited to devotees of Vishnu (Vaishnavites, or Vaishnavas). But many interpreted Krishna's revelation of the Godhead metaphysically: he was, according to them, speaking of the vastness of the divine and Vishnu as only one of its manifestations. Because of the sheer beauty of this poem the *Bhagavad Gîtâ* has become the song (the *Gîtâ*) of all songs.

The *Gîtâ* was been added as an appendix to the great epic, the *Mahâbhârata*. The presence of the *Gîtâ* in the epic meant that the myth cycles of both Krishna and Vishnu included a recognition that Krishna was a full incarnation of Vishnu.

The story of the *Gîtâ* occupied but a moment in the great Kurukshetra battle between the Kauravas and the Pandavas, nested within both the larger story of the battle and a story about a sage telepathically seeing and hearing what was happening many miles away and telling it to the blind king. Krishna was attempting to convince Arjuna to continue fighting as a warrior in order to uphold *dharma*, the sacred order of life. Arjuna could only see the sin of killing his kinsmen in a war that seemed selfish and cruel. He even questioned the activity of war itself.

Except for the revelation of his true nature as Vishnu, Krishna's story was that of a charioteer in the *Mahâbhârata*. But the *Gîtâ* provided support for the central claim of the Krishna cult—that Krishna was the Supreme. Krishna's divine birth and childhood are not found in the *Gîtâ* but in the *Purânas*, especially the *Bhâgavata Purâna*. Krishna's myth cycle was nested within Vishnu's, since he was the eighth *avatâra* (incarnation) of Vishnu.

The *Bhagavad Gîtâ* received so much praise from around the world after its early-eighteenth-century translations into English and German that Indians discovered its pan-Indian character. Svâmî Vivekânanda's (1863–1902) praise of the *Gîtâ* as the "gospel of Hinduism" raised it to a rank almost equal to the *Vedas* in holiness and example.

> *See also* Arjuna; Dharma; Dhritarâshthra; Krishna; Kurukshetra; *Mahâbhârata*; Vishnu
>
> *For further reading:*
>
> There are many excellent translations in English since the first, in 1885. One that represents devotional interests is Swami Prabhupâda's *Bhagavad-Gîtâ As It Is* (New York: Bhaktivedanta Book Trust, 1968). A fine scholarly translation is by Kees Bolle, *The Bhagavadgîtâ* (Berkeley: University of California Press, 1979). Almost every major thinker in India has written a commentary on the Gîtâ, many of which have been translated into English.

BHÂGAVATA PURÂNA

A scripture

The *Bhâgavata Purâna* is a highly devotional scripture that articulated the views of tenth-century South India and of those worshippers of Krishna known as the Bhagavatas. It is quite large, even by Indian standards, containing 18,000 verses *(slokas)*, in twelve books *(skandhas)* of 332 chapters. All the incarnations of Vishnu are described, but the tenth skandha is a masterpiece on the divine Krishna. The *Bhâgavata Purâna* should be given as a gift on the full moon day of Proshthapada (September), along with an image of a golden-colored lion.

> *See also* Krishna; Vishnu

BHAGAVATÎ

The goddess

Bhagavatî (feminine form of "lord") is another name for Devî, or Shaktî; when it elevated the goddess to the role of the Supreme, it became a term used by her sect, the Śāktas. In the *Devî Bhâgavata Purâna* the mother of the universe, Devî, taught Vishnu about the eternal reality of time, space, and the universe *(brahmânda)*. The name Bhagavatî could be interchangeable with Prakriti (nature), indicating the eternal and all-powerful. The Śāktas taught that everything is grounded in the energy (śaktî) of the mother and by her all things exist. Such an understanding would be considered sectarian, but Bhagavatî may also be used as a nonsectarian name for Devî.

See also Brahmânda; Devî; Prakritî; Śaktî

BHAGÎRATHA

An ascetic king

Bhagîratha's story is part of the myth of the coming to earth of the Gangâ (Ganges). These interlocking stories gave Bhagîratha a great royal lineage, with prior events in that lineage requiring him to do a thousand years of austerities *(tapas)* in order to ask Śiva for a boon. And all this explained the coming down to earth of the Gangâ.

Bhagîratha's great-grandfather, Sagara, had two wives and sons from each. All 60,000 sons of one wife were killed by the sage Kapila as they disturbed his rituals. Indra had stolen the sacrificial horse that King Sagara had been using in the battle before the *aśva-medha* (royal horse sacrifice) and hid it near Kapila's place for rituals. The warriors' noise, upon their discovery of its hiding place, ended their lives. But a proper burial was not possible for lack of water, so neither Bhagîratha's grandfather or father could complete their duty. In order to obtain enough water Bhagîratha worshipped the celestial river goddess Gangâ. She appeared and told him that her descent to earth would destroy it in a worldwide flood. Gangâ told Bhagîratha to ask Lord Śiva's help. So to get Śiva's attention, Bhagîratha did austerities *(tapas)* for a thousand years, and Śiva allowed the river to fall on his head and go through his matted hair. After another thousand years none had reached the earth. So Bhagîratha worshipped Śiva fervently, and Śiva shook a single drop of the celestial Gangâ from his own matted hair. That became the mighty earthly Gangâ with sufficient water for Bhagîratha to complete the burial rites of his ancestors.

See also Aśva-medha; Gangâ; Śiva; Tapas

BHAIRAVA

An attendant of Śiva

Bhairava (the terrible) is a popular Tântric deity—of the type scholars like Wendy Doniger classify as hot, or nonorthodox. Once, overcome by pride, Brahmâ the creator insulted Śiva. Out of the fire of Śiva's anger Bhairava was born. Instantly Bhairava rushed at Brahmâ and pinched off the fifth, or crowning, head of Brahmâ. Śiva turned Bhairava into the *damanaka*, or *tâtirî* tree. But Śiva was technically guilty of taking the life of a *brâhmin (brahmahatyâ)* by cutting off one of Brahmâ's heads. So in expiation of that sin, he—some say Śiva, others say Bhairava—had to become a begging ascetic carrying a skull (Brahmâ's fifth head). Some accounts gave Bhairava a self-created female assistant for his journeys, named Brahma-hatyâ. (These versions point to left-handed Tântric practices that require a female assistant.)

At last Bhairava—some accounts say on the suggestion of Śiva—went to Vârânasî (modern Benares) and took a bath in the Gangâ. This washed away his sin. He left the fifth head of Brahmâ there, and that place became a famous pilgrimage place named *Kapâla-mochana-tîrtha* (skull-liberating ford). The Kapâlikas copied Śiva's austerities as naked ascetics devoted to Bhairava, carrying a skull as their begging bowl. Bhairava's sacred tree (the damanaka, or tâtirî) is still worshipped because of its association with Śiva as Bhairava.

Iconographically, Bhairava is horrific, adorned with snakes and symbols of Śiva, such as a crescent moon and matted hair. His weapons are the sword, arrow, bow, dagger, trident, and rope. He can have five faces and is often clothed, if at all, in an elephant skin.

See also Brahmâ; Śiva; Tantra; Tîrtha-Yatra

BHAIRAVÎ

A manifestation of Devî

The Bhairavî is "the horrific one," a "hot," as scholars say, or nonorthodox, form of Devî and a counterpart of Bhairava.

She was also one of a very ancient group of eight Ambâs, or Mâtrikas (mothers), who were non-Vedic and identified with the feminine energies of great gods (Brahmânî from Brahmâ, Maheśvarâ from Śiva, and so on). The seven other Ambâs were Rudrârcikâ, Rudracandî, Nateshvarî, Mahâlakshmî, Siddhacâmundikâ, Siddhayoeshvarî, and Rûpavidyâ. The count increased until the Ambâs, or Mâtrikas, were beyond number. They can also be shown as worshipping Śiva and attending his son Kârttikeya.

See also Bhairava; Devî; Kârttikeya; Śiva

BHAKTI

A religious practice of worship

Most Hindu mythologies are built upon a logic of devotion *(bhakti)*, connecting worship *(puja)*, purity (*shuddhi; śauca*), morality (dharma), responsibility *(karma)*, and austerities *(tapas)*. Bhakti can be more than just "being religious," since it can lead to liberation *(moksha)* from life's addictions and even from the cycle of rebirth *(samsâra)*. This sense of liberation is often connected to an afterlife with a personal supreme god, such as Śiva, Vishnu, or Devî. It has always involved a loving relationship with the divine. Some myths are told from the perspective of bhakti.

Indian philosophers and theologians began at least by the time of the *Bhagavad Gîtâ* to classify religious or spiritual experience according to three or four types, which are called ways *(margas)* or disciplines *(yogas)*. Bhakti appears in both lists. Devotionalism is the way (marga) or practice (yoga) known as bhakti marga or bhakti yoga.

Bhakti encompassed worship, prayers, and both elaborate and simple devotional rituals. But myths were not always linked to religious practice. Sometimes, devotion was a strategy of praise that was performed in order to gain power, a blessing, or a boon. What was gained by this kind of praise would then be used by the "hero" to complete his or her "quest," or "pilgrimage." This use of bhakti in these myths would be more a part of a world of magic or shamanism than of devotional spiritual practices.

See also Tapas; Yoga
For further reading:
On the interconnection between Hindu mythology and magic, read Lee Siegel, *Net of Magic: Wonders and Deceptions in India* (Chicago: University of Chicago, 1991).

BHARADVÂJA

A sage

Bharadvâja was the son of Mahârishi Atri. He lived thousands of years, years that he used for the study of the *Vedas*. He was a disciple of the great Vâlmîki. Many Vedic hymns are credited to Bharadvâja's authorship.

When Râma was beginning his exile, he went to Bharadvâja's *aśrama* and was blessed by him. Later when the great king Bharata visited with a huge retinue, Bharadvâja used his powers as a magician and called the architect of the gods, Viśvakarman, to arrange a banquet, with dishes of food floating down from heaven and entertainment by some of the most famous celestials—*devas, gandharvas, apsaras,* and *ashthadikpâlas.*

During the time when Vishnu was incarnate as Krishna, Bharadvâja had a momentary liaison with the great temptress, Ghritâcî. This famous apsara gave Bharadvâja a *brâhmin*-warrior son, Drona. Drona was the great archery master of the Bhârata war, training both Pandavas and Kauravas.

See also Drona; Ghritâcî; Vâlmîki

BHARATA
A brother of Râma

There were five Bharatas in Hindu mythology: (1) the brother of Râma, (2) a partial incarnation of Vishnu who ruled for 27,000 years and whose land was called Bhârata, (3) a king of Hima who reigned for 100,000 years and, according to one tale in the *Bhâgavata Purâna*, was the king from whom India received its name, (4) a sage and writer of the *Nâtyasâstra* (art of theater), and (5) a late collective term for the sons of Agni, god of fire.

Bharata, son of Dasaratha and brother of Râma, was interesting from a number of points of view. There were so many twists and turns in this myth that a skillful teller could find something for almost any occasion—from positive examples of loyalty and duty to negative ones of deceit and jealousy.

King Dasaratha of Ayodhyâ had no children, so he performed the *putra-kameshti* (the ritual to beget children) on the advice of the sage Rishyasringa. From the sacrificial fire emerged a pot of pudding (some accounts say the very ambrosia of the gods, *amrita*). The pudding was equally divided between his three wives: Kausalyâ, Kaikeyî, and Sumithrâ. Srî Râma was born to Kausalyâ, Bharata to Kaikeyî, and Lakshmana and Satrughna to Sumithrâ. The four sons married well, and arrangements proceeded for Râma to succeed his father. But Dasaratha's second wife, Kaikeyî, had two boons from the old king that she had not used. So she used these to force him to exile Râma to the forest for fourteen years and crown her son, Bharata, king. Râma, his wife Sîtâ, and his brother Lakshmana went without complaint to the forest. But even before Bharata returned from a visit to be crowned, the old king died of remorse at what he had been forced to do by his evil wife Kaikeyî. Bharata was so furious with his mother that he would have killed her had his half-brother Satrughna not prevented it. Bharata and Shatrughna then set out to find Râma and get him to come back to the kingdom. A huge procession from Ayodhyâ followed them to the banks of the Gangâ. At Râma's forest *asrama* the brothers completed funeral rites for their father but were unable to get Râma to return as king. Râma believed that it was his duty *(dharma)* to fulfill his promise to his father. So Bharata took Râma's sandals back to Ayodhyâ to symbolize that he was ruling for his brother until Râma returned after the fourteen-year exile. Bharata left the palace vacant and ruled from a village near the capital. After fourteen years Râma returned and was crowned king of Ayodhyâ.

Bharata was sent by King Râma on a mission to kill *gandharvas* who were molesting people in Kekaya, a nearby region. When he had freed these regions of demons, his two sons were made their rulers. Bharata's final act of loyalty and devotion to his divine brother was to give up his life when Râma drowned himself in the Sarayû River. Śatrughna committed suicide as well. When Râma became Vishnu again, Bharata and Śatrughna became Vishnu's conch and wheel.

See also Daśaratha; Kaikeyî; Lakshmana; Râma

BHARATA

Son of King Dushyanta and Śakuntalâ (another of several kings named Bharata)
See Dushyanta.

BHÎMA

One of the Pandava brothers, a hero of the Mahâbhârata War

Bhîma (the terrible) was the product of his mother's union with Vâyu, the wind god. (For more details see Kuntî.) Bhîma had a terrible temper but was courageous and a great warrior. He was the Pandava brother with the most strength and appetite. He would eat half of the family's food. During the first exile from the Pandavas' lost kingdom, Bhîma saved the family from a burning house and subdued *asuras* (demons) to stop them from molesting humankind. After defeating the demon Hidimbha, Bhîma married the demon's sister Hidimbî as his second wife. Bhîma enjoyed a memorable honeymoon of a year, aided by Hidimbî's magical ability to fly to the mountain tops. So by day Bhîma honeymooned with Hidimbî, and each night he returned to be with the Pandava brother's joint wife Draupadî.

Bhîma had vowed to avenge the humiliation of Draupadî caused by Duryodhana. He finally kept that vow on the battlefield of Kurukshetra. However, Bhîma had to resort to an unfair blow from his war club, which crushed his cousin's thigh, and then he kicked his despised foe brutally as he lay wounded. His brothers had to pull him away. That blow earned him the title of an unfair fighter, a blot on his honor as a warrior.

Despite one episode that tarnished his record, more than a hundred stories made Bhîma an example of raw courage and strength, fighting to follow the way of a righteous warrior.

After the end of the Mahâbhârata war, he followed his elder brother Yudhishthira on the final journey to Kailâsa (heaven). Nevertheless, he died on the way and was waiting for Yudhishthira when he finally got there.

See also Draupadî; Duryodhana; *Mahâbhârata;* Pandavas; Vâyu

BHRIGU

A sage, son of Brahmâ

There are many versions of Bhrigu's birth. Depending on the account, Bhrigu was born as one of the *mahârishis* or as a demon *(asura).* One account said that he was the son of Brahmâ, born of Agni at a sacrifice *(Brahma-yâjña)* presided over by Varuna as the chief priest *(hotri).* In yet another Bhrigu was born from Brahmâ's skin. And still another account said that he was born of Manu and then sired the greatest of sages and *rishis,* the class of Bhârgavas, called the Bhrigu-vamśa (Bhrigu's family). Nevertheless, he was one of the grandfathers *(Prajâ-patis)* of a minor class of gods, the Bhrigus, with a family from each of his births, and he started at least two different family lines, one from Brahmâ and a second from Varuna.

Bhrigu was the officiating priest *(hotri)* at Daksha's sacrificial feast, to which Śiva was not invited. Sîtâ cast herself into the sacrificial fire because of the humiliation she felt that her husband was not invited, which implied that he was not worthy to attend. In anger Śiva produced two demons who avenged the loss of his wife—either pulling out the beard of Bhrigu or, according to another account, killing all the officiating priests, including Bhrigu.

Bhrigu was used often in the *Purânas* in myths about psychic powers and the curses that sages would put upon evil kings and demons. Bhrigu's most famous action was his curse of Śiva, whom Bhrigu condemned to be worshipped as a *linga* (a phallus). Śiva had killed Bhrigu's wife Puloma to end her ascetic practices *(tapas)* in support of the demons. In Bhrigu's mouth was put an anti-Shaivite proclamation: that no one who was pious or respectable would ever worship Śiva—only Śiva's *linga.*

See also Daksha; Linga; Śiva; Varuna

BHÛMÎ

The goddess of earth

Bhûmî (the earth) was a Purânic addition to the Hindu pantheon. There are a number of versions of her birth, and her children had so many different gods and demons as fathers that another myth had to provide a curse from Pârvatî to explain this flaw in her character.

Some of the versions of Bhûmî's birth in the *Purânas* involved a physical earth that then became a goddess. But in others she is the daughter of Brahmâ. In one version of the first kind, during the period of floods, the earth was in a liquid state. Śiva cut his thigh and let a drop of blood fall into the waters. It coagulated as an egg *(anda)*, which Śiva split open. Man *(purusha,* the cosmic man) emerged, and from him was made nature *(prakriti).* One half of the eggshell became the sky and the other the earth. In another such version, in the beginning Mahâvishnu lay on the surface of the waters. A lotus sprang from his navel, and on its blossom sat Brahmâ. From Vishnu's earwax was born two demons who tried to harm Brahmâ, so Vishnu killed them. The demons' fat hardened into the earth.

Another myth began in the *Varâha Kalpa* (the age of Vishnu's incarnation as a boar), with the demon Hiranyâksha abducting Bhûmî and taking her under the waters. However Vishnu took the form of a boar and brought Bhûmî to the surface on his tusks. Bhûmî stood up on a lotus leaf on the surface of the waters in her most charming shape. Vishnu was so overcome by her beauty that he made love with her for one *Deva-varsha* (a god's moment of three hundred human years). Mangala was born from this contact. From that time Bhûmî-devî became Vishnu's wife.

Nevertheless, it was assumed by many of the myths that, if the demon Hiranyâksha abducted her, she would have become his "wife." These accounts stated that the mere touch of his tusk made Bhûmî the mother of the sage Naraka and, therefore, the mother of the *asuras* (rather than Ditî). Therefore, she was referred to as the wife of Hiranyâksha. Her marriages to Vishnu and to Hiranyâksha with children from each was explained by a curse from Pârvatî. It was said in the *Vâlmîki Râmâyana* that Pârvatî and Śiva's love play rocked the foundations of the heavens and the earth, so both the gods and Bhûmî complained to Śiva. He stopped, but Pârvatî became angry. She cursed Bhûmî-devî that she would become many forms and the wife of many. Pârvatî also stated that, since she had been prevented from having a son, Bhûmî-devî would have no more children.

In various *Purânas* Bhûmî received a number of minor roles. Bhûmî-devî was turned into a cow and milked dry by the magic of the sage Prithu. She appeared in the Narasimha myth to catch Prahlâda, the demon devotee of Vishnu, when Prahlâda was thrown from a high building by his father Hiranyakaśipu. And Bhûmî got Paraśu-Râma to stop killing *kṣatriyas* before all were eliminated from the earth during that incarnation of Vishnu. Finally, in Vishnu's incarnation as Râma, Sîtâ was Bhûmî's daughter. It was to her that Sîtâ returned when life with Râma became unbearable.

See also Devî; Hiranyâksha; Narasimha; Sîtâ

BRAHMÂ

A deva (god)

Brahmâ rose to importance in the late Vedic period of the *Âranyakas* and *Upanishads*, after the first Hindu triad declined—that of Sûrya, Indra, and Agni. Brahmâ's temple at Pushkara was the beginning point for pilgrimages from the time of the two great epics. However, it turned out to be the only temple dedicated to Brahmâ as the primary deity that has survived the centuries. His cult may have once been important enough to command the respect of pilgrims, but he was badly used in most of the later myths. Even though Brahmâ has had roles in more myths than any other god or goddess, his parts have left him flat and one-dimensional.

In the *Brâhmanas* he was associated with Prajâpati and later replaced him as the creator. His creations, however, came to be seen as re-creations. It was Śiva, Vishnu, or Devî who was said to be the ultimate origin of the universe. Brahmâ was only its current creator (or re-creator).

In his many myths Brahmâ rewarded austerities *(tapas)* of men and demons by granting them their most frequent wish, the wish for immortality. Although that boon was limited and did not bestow complete immortality, it always caused a great deal of trouble for the gods. So Brahmâ was usually in trouble with the other gods. In these instances, Vishnu or Śiva, depending on the viewpoint of the myth, would save the gods from the demons. The supreme god, Vishnu or Śiva, would find the limitation of Brahmâ's boon of immortality in order to defeat the demon who had gained the boon and return the world to its proper order.

In the *Purânas*, Brahmâ the creator was joined in a divine triad with Vishnu and Maheśvara (Śiva), who were the preserver and destroyer, respectively. The universe was created by Brahmâ, preserved by Vishnu, and destroyed for the next creation by Śiva. However, the birth of Brahmâ was attributed to Vishnu in some myths. Brahmâ was often depicted as sitting on a throne arising from the navel of Vishnu, who was resting on the cosmic serpent, Ananta (also Śesha). In the very beginning Vishnu alone was there. When Vishnu thought about creation, Brahmâ was created from a lotus that came from his navel.

There was a Śaiva myth that told of Śiva's appearance to Vishnu and Brahmâ as a cosmic *linga*. Vishnu attempted to go to the top and bottom of this giant pillar. He was only able to go to the top of the universe and the bottom of the sea, but he did not find the end of the linga. Brahmâ lied that he had reached its end, thus claiming to be superior to Śiva. So Śiva cursed him, so that Brahmâ would never again have temples dedicated to his worship, and except for the temple to him at Pushkara, the myth seemed to fit the facts of history so that the curse seems to have been fulfilled.

The four-headed Brahmâ is the creator in the Trimûrti or Hindu Triad, which also includes Śiva and Vishnu. (TRIP)

His final roles in the later *Purânas* were reminders of how mighty Brahmâ was debased. One myth claimed that Brahmâ committed incest with his daughter, goddess of speech (Vâc). But this myth had already been told about Prajâpati, lord of creatures.

Iconographically, Brahmâ's image had four heads. (A fifth had been cut off by the fingernail of a horrific aspect of Śiva.) He carried a water jar, offering ladle, meditation beads, a lotus, and a bow or scepter. His vehicle was the swan *(hamsa)* or goose.

> *See also* Prajâpati; Śiva; Vishnu
> *For further reading:*
> B. K. Chaturvedi, *Brahmâ* (Delhi: Books for All, 1996), vol. 2 in a series on the
> *Gods and Goddesses of India.* Although uncritical, this book covers most of
> the myths concerning Brahmâ.

BRAHMACÂRI, BRAHMACÂRYA

The stage of life (âsrama) of student

This is the first of the four *âsramas,* or stages of life. The other three are householder *(grihastha),* forest dweller *(vânaprastha),* and renunciate *(samnyâsa).*

A brahmacâri was one who stayed in the household of the teacher (*guru,* or *âcarya*) and learned scriptures, rituals, and ascetic practices. It was a period of chastity, ended by dying a symbolic death involving a bath in a river and being reborn to marry and enter the duties of a householder.

> *See also* Catur-Varna; Samnyâsa. The *varna-aśrama-dharma* system is addressed in
> chapter 1 in the sections on "Hindu Worldviews" and "Dharma."

BRAHMAN

An early term; the Absolute

The word *brahman* is more context-sensitive than most Sanskrit terms. It is neuter in gender and evolved into one of the most important concepts in Hindu theology and philosophy. For one school of Hinduism *Brahman* came to mean the Absolute as impersonal and formless—and should be capitalized in English. It could not be described in terms of anything lesser—even the most well-meaning personifications and projections that worshippers might attribute to the divine.

In the earliest sections of the *Vedas,* however, *brahman* was used to mean the magic power behind the efficacy of the Vedic sacrifices or the performative power in the prayers or chants of the priests. As such it was associated with *vâc* (speech, personified as a goddess) and *prâna* (breath; later, energy). *Brahman* was all the enigmas of the universe. It is not surprising that throughout the centuries *brâhmins* were associated with *Brahman*, because the prayers *(brâhmanas)* were performed by the *brâhmins.* Any confusion among these three terms was advantageous to the priests. Some scriptures and myths taught that the priests were gods on earth. However, such personifications were misrepresentations of a term that denies every comparison. (*Neti. Neti.* Not this. Not this. The Absolute was not to be described at all, declared the *Upanishads.*)

But in later mythology *Brahman* was neither the hidden power behind the verbal contest in the *brahmodya* (contests in sacred knowledge) at the horse sacrifice *(aśva-medha)* nor the only reality that exists of itself. *Brahman* became another superlative for whatever supreme god was being worshipped. The great modern teacher, Shrî Râmakrishna, used to say that *Brahman* and the Great Mother Kâlî were the same. That kind of identification was also made in Hindu mythology—that the infinite and the finite were the same.

See also Cosmology in chapter 1

BRÂHMANAS

A division of the Vedas; a collection of scriptures

The *Vedas* came to be divided into the *Rigveda* (hymns), *Brâhmanas* (commentaries), *Âranyakas* (forest texts), and *Upanishads* (a treasury of mystical and devotional texts). The *Satapatha-brâhmana* was considered to be the oldest *Brâhmana.* It was a great source of *mantras,* or incantations.

The mythological point of view changed between the period of the *Rigveda* and that of the *Brâhmanas.* The *Brâhmanas* were concerned with ritual and its effectiveness. There was a triad of gods who were most important: Agni, Indra, and Sûrya. Agni's role had increased, and the symbolism of the fire sacrifice was more explicit. In the later *Brâhmanas* there were thirty-three *devas* (gods), enumerated as eight Vasus, eleven Rudras, and twelve âdityas—with two gods unnamed.

See also Âdityas; Rudras; Vedas

BRAHMÂNDA

A cosmogonic principle in the Rigveda

Brahmânda, or the egg of Brahmâ (immensity), may have been the subject of an entire book describing a creation myth, the *Brahmânda Purâna.* But it is no longer extant, existing only in fragments of other works. The description of the origin of the universe as a golden egg appeared in both Vedic and Purânic literature.

In the beginning there was nothing but the golden egg in space alone. From it was born the Cosmic Person *(virât purusha)*, whose different body parts became the different planets and the four castes *(varnas)*.

See also Purusha; Varna

BRÂHMIN (ALSO BRÂHMANA AND BRÂHMAN)

One of the four castes

The Rigveda described the origin of the four castes from parts of the cosmic person, *Virat Purusha.* The *Manu-smriti* (the law code of Manu) said that the four castes where born from different parts of the body of Brahmâ. *Brâhmanas (brâhmins)* were born from the face, *kśatriyas* from the arms, *vaiśyas* from the thighs, and *śûdras* from the feet of Brahmâ. The place one found in this hierarchy of privilege ordained by birth was founded on the actions one had done in previous lifetimes, that is, on one's karma.

The duties of a *brâhmin* include performing sacrifices and learning and teaching the scriptures. A *brâhmin* was also called a *dvija*, which means twice born; members of the upper castes were seen as being born a second time when they were invested with the sacred thread at the *upanayana* (the sacrament concerning one's spiritual birth).

See also Purusha; Varna

BRIHASPATI

A sage

Brihaspati was the teacher of the *devas* (gods). He was born of Angiras and Vasudhâ (or Śraddhâ). Angiras was the son of Brahmâ, the creator, who had lost his seed in the sacrificial fire at the sight of a celestial maiden. Sage Brihaspati was also identified with a celestial star or planet, Jupiter. In the *Rigveda* there was a god of this name (also known as Brahmanaspati).

The sage Brihaspati was married to Târâ, who was unusually beautiful. Consequently Târâ was abducted by Soma (or Candra, the moon), and that resulted in a war known as Târaka-maya. Rudra and the demons were on one side with Soma, and Brihaspati and the gods led by Indra were on the other. Brahmâ finally restored Târâ to her husband. However, she was with child. Both Soma and Brihaspati claimed the child, who was named Budha (planet Mercury). Finally, Târâ said that the child was fathered by Soma.

There are many other late tales of Brihaspati where he appeared as a *rishi* (sage). One sectarian episode in the *Padma Purâna* has him turning *asuras* (demons) into Jains and Buddhists. His character was totally reversed in the story that told of his rape of his brother's wife, Mamatâ, and his cursing of the unborn child in her womb (Dirghatamas) with blindness.

See also Angiras; Brahmâ; Dirghatamas; Soma

BUDDHA

A negative incarnation (avatâra) of Vishnu

In some accounts one of the ten incarnations of Vishnu was as the Buddha. Vishnu came to earth in order to delude those who already deserved punishment for their bad deeds *(karma).* Deceived by the Buddha's false teachings, these individuals renounced the *Vedas* and ceased to do their duty *(dharma).* They were then punished in hell or by inferior births.

In a number of later texts, this Buddha *avatâra* was given a positive purpose. Vishnu was said to have chosen the incarnation as the Buddha in order to teach nonviolence and compassion to humanity.

See also Avatâra; Vishnu

CAÑCALÂKSHMÎ

(1) A famous prostitute

Once while the prostitute Cañcalâkshmî ("one with moving eyes") was waiting in the night for her lover, she was attacked and killed by a leopard (or in another version, a tiger). Following her death both the attendants of Vishnu and Yama came to take her soul. They began to argue. Yama's servants pointed out the fact that she had sinned throughout her life. Vishnu's emissaries argued that she had on one occasion in her life gone into a temple to Vishnu and spilled some lime juice on the wall. That act was seen by the all-gracious Vishnu as the service of cleaning the walls of a temple. For that Vishnu had chosen to give her life with him in Vaikuntha, his heaven. So she gained paradise almost by accident.

If one worshipped Vishnu with mindful intent, how much more would one be rewarded, was the message of this myth.

See also Vishnu; Yama

(2) A Vidhyadhara girl

Cañcalâkshmî, the celestial, was raped by the demon Râvana, while her mind was fixed in prayer. She was praying to the goddess Mahâlakshmî. Cañcalâkshmî cursed Râvana, stating he would be killed by Lâkshmi. In the course of time Lâkshmi was incarnated as Sîtâ. Râvana abducted Sîtâ, and Râvana was killed by Lord Râma. Thus the curse was fulfilled. Râvana's act was avenged by Lâkshmi, born as Sîtâ, at the hands of her husband Râma.

See also Lakshmî; Râvana; Sîtâ

CANDA AND MUNDA

Two asura (demon) brothers

Canda and his young *asura* brother Munda allied with the great demons, Śumbha and Niśumbha. The latter two *asura* brothers had just returned from heaven after receiving a boon from Brahmâ that they could only be killed at the hands of a woman. After receiving this boon Śumbha and Niśumbha and their *asura* armies conquered the three worlds of heaven, earth, and Pâtâla (the netherworld). On the advice of the sage Brihaspati the frightened *devas* (gods) went to Pârvatî, the wife of Śiva. After hearing their pitiful plea, Pârvatî-devî went into a deep state of meditation, and out of her body emerged Kâlî (or Kausikî). Kâlî disguised as a beautiful woman sat alone in the forest, where she was seen by Canda and Munda. They reported their great discovery to Śumbha and Niśumbha. Canda and Munda (some accounts say another demon named Dhûmrâksha, a cohort of Râvana) were sent along with sixty thousand soldiers to bring the beautiful woman to their court. By the sound *hum* Kâlî reduced all of them to ashes and then killed Śumbha and Niśumbha for good measure.

See also Asura; Kâlî

CANDAKA

A hunter and an ardent devotee of Śiva

While hunting in the forest one day Candaka saw a Śiva temple in ruins. He reported the dilapidated condition of this temple to Simhaketu, the king of Pânchala. After consulting the scriptures, Simhaketu allowed Candaka to install a Śiva *linga*, the phallic symbol of Śiva, and said Candaka could start worshipping it on one condition: that he smear himself with the ashes from the nearby cremation ground. Candaka and his wife Pulindî worshipped the *linga* for a long time. Then one day Candaka did not have any ash and hence could not worship. At this point Pulindî suggested that she should become the ash that Candaka would wear so that he would not have to interrupt his worship *(bhakti, pûjâ)*. Candaka agreed with great reluctance. Pulindî burned into ash, and Candaka performed his worship of Lord Śiva. When he finished, to his utter surprise Pulindî regained her life and stood before him. A celestial chariot came from Śivaloka (Śiva's realm) and took both of them to heaven.

See also Bhakti; Śiva

CANDIKÂ

A ferocious form of Pârvatî (or Durgâ)

Candikâ was the furious aspect of the Goddess, having ten, eighteen, or twenty hands, each holding a weapon. Her vehicle was a lion, and she stood with her left foot on the corpse of the demon called Mahisha-asura and held his severed head aloft. From the bloody neck of the felled demon emerged a red-headed, red-eyed man with weapon drawn but already noosed by Candikâ's rope.

In the *Devî Mâhâtmya* Candikâ has become the *śaktî* of the Goddess herself so that Durgâ (or Devî) possesses a feminine manifestation of her divine activity rather than needing a masculine actor; in the final evolution of this myth cycle the feminine is complete in itself.

See also Durgâ; Mahishâsura; Pârvatî

CANDRA

The moon, a deva

In the Vedic period Candra, the moon, and Soma, the entheogenic plant, were connected by associations *(bandhus)* in the early hymns. However, Candra was not one of the *âdityas* with Sûrya (the sun), but was one of the eight Vasus with Vâyu (the wind). By the Purânic period Candra's very essence had changed to that of just another Vedic deity to use as a bad example in the self-elevation or pride of medieval priests.

Candra's highest birth in the myths was as an emergence from the Churning of the Milky Ocean *(kshîrâbdhi-mathanam)*. He was also described as the son of the sage Atri and Anasûyâ. Other accounts said his father was Dharma. The *Brihadâranyaka* said that he was not a *brâhmin* at all but a *kṣatriya*. These inconsistencies were usually explained away by using the notion of different births in different *yugas* (world ages) or *manvantaras* (world cycles). But his essence had become something that did not need a worthy lineage—he had been transformed from a companion of Soma, at the very center of Vedic religious experience, to a marginalized seducer of the wife of a great *brâhmin* sage. (The story of Târâ illustrates the Purânic mentality of defaming its heroes and heroines, since some accounts make her a willing participant in adultery and others exonerate her and present her as one of the *pañcakanayâ*, five perfect women.) This episode had a strange ending: the usual seducer of *brâhmins'* wives, Indra, acted as the defender of moral duty *(dharma)* and fought great battles with Candra. Candra was finally given the son of his misdeed—the beautiful star-child born to Târâ was Budha (the planet Mercury).

The *Devî Bhâgavata* contained a fragment of what could be an older myth of the moon. Candra was said to have married the twenty-seven daughters of Daksha, a progenitor. His twenty-seven wives were the twenty-seven brightest stars of the Vedic sky. However, the *Purânas* used his plural marriage to make Candra an example of a bad husband. When twenty-six of Candra's wives complained to their father Daksha that Candra loved Rohinî more than the rest and did not give them enough recognition, Daksha asked Candra to love his wives equally. Candra did not obey, so Daksha cursed Candra: he would suffer various diseases and would lose part of his body for fourteen days every month. That curse accounted for the waxing and waning of the moon.

See also Kshîrâbdhi-mathanam; Magic, Blessings, Cursings; Mâyâ; Pañcakanayâ; Soma; Târâ

For further reading:

R. Gordon Wasson, *Soma: Divine Mushroom of Immortality* (New York: Harcourt Brace Jovanovich, 1968).

CANDRÂNGADA

A prince

Candrângada's story has another myth nested within it of a curious gender transformation. The Purânic mythmakers did not portray a supreme god or goddess remedying the situation in this case, as they so often did. In fact, neither sages nor the divine mother (Pârvatî) seemed able to reverse this permanent gender change, which had resulted from cross-dressing.

Prince Candrângada has married to Sîmantini, a *brâhmin* (daughter of Yajnavalkya and Maitrcyi). Later when Candrângada was riding in a boat with his friends in the river Kailindi, a storm broke out, and the boat capsized. All his friends were drowned. As Candrângada sank to the bottom of the river, the serpent *(nâga)* king Takshâka took him to the underwater world of the serpents *(pâtâla)*. While Candrângada lived there for a long time, his funeral rites were performed. Sîmantini began living as a widow, and his father's kingdom was conquered by their enemies. After Candrângada had enjoyed a time of sporting with the *nâga* damsels, Takshâka proposed that Candrângada should marry them. This helped him remember that he had been married to Sîmantini and had to go back home.

Candrângada was sent back to the earth with many presents from Takshâka. There was a joyous reunion with Sîmantini, and they began living again as husband and wife. The enemy kings even released Candrângada's father and gave back his kingdom.

Both Candrângada and Sîmantini were great devotees of Pârvatî and observed a specific ritualistic fasting on Mondays called the *soma-varavrata* ("Monday boon-seeking fast"). Pârvatî appeared and blessed them. Observing this piety, three impoverished *brâhmin* brothers, Sumedha, Sârasvata, and Sâmavan, thought they would be able to obtain enough money from Candrângada and Sîmantini to gain brides for themselves. After listening to their story, Candrângada and Sîmantini took Sârasvata and Sâmavan in a procession around the palace—with Sâmavan dressed as a woman. But Sâmavan's womanhood manifested itself and could not be changed back into manhood. Even the attempts by sages and fervent appeals to Pârvatî to change him back to a man failed. Pârvatî suggested the solution, according to the *Śiva Purâna*. Sâmavan was renamed Sâmavatî. So Sârasvata and Sâmavatî lived as husband and wife. There was no report that the former brothers were married by priestly rites.

See also Pârvatî

CANDRASHARMAN

A sinner who had killed his teacher

Candrasharman's story was told along with that of three other sinners in the *Padma Purâna*. These four had committed that period's four most terrible sins: killing a cow *(go-hatyâ)*, killing one's teacher *(guru-hatyâ)*, killing a *brâhmin (brâhma-hatyâ)*, and sleeping with the wife of one's *guru (agamyâgamana)*. The outcaste Vidura, a Pâncâla deśa [Pâncama jana—an outcaste], had killed a *brâhmin* and had visited all the pilgrimage sites *(tîrthas)* to no avail. Before committing the greatest of all sins, he had been a *kṣatriya*. Candrasharman, a *brâhmin*, had killed his teacher (who might have been a *brâhmin*, but in any case Candrasharman's sin was considered less, perhaps because he was himself a *brâhmin*). Vedasharman, another *brâhmin*, slept with his teacher's wife. The final sinner was a vaiśya (merchant caste) named Vañjula who had killed a cow. Although they gathered in the same place to share their stories, the myth made it clear that they did not add a further sin: that of breaking caste law. They did not have food together, sit on the same seat, or lie on the same bed sheet. And the three who had not become outcastes did not touch the outcaste. Then an evolved soul, a *siddha*, instructed them to wash in the Gangâ. When they did, all were absolved of their sins.

See also Varna

CATUR-MUKHA-LINGA

Four-faced emblem of Brahmâ

After creation of the world, the five-headed Brahmâ was resting and thinking about the next creation when a beautiful woman appeared before him. Even though she was born of him, Brahmâ became attracted to her and let his passion go. For this sin one of his heads broke off. He went to Sthânu *tîrtha*, one of the famous pilgrimage sites on the Sarasvatî River. Undoubtedly punning, the myth made Brahmâ construct a *linga* with his own four faces (thus the *catur-mukha-linga*) from the fifth head that had broken off. Worship of the linga absolved

Brahmâ of his sin, just as it would for pilgrims coming to Sthânu *tîrtha* to worship that shrines' linga.

See also Linga; Śiva; Tîrtha-yatra

CATUR-VARNA (CATURVARNYAM)

The four *(catur)* castes *(varna)*

The *brâhmin, kśatriya, vaiśya,* and *śûdra* castes originated from the body of Brahmâ, according to the *Rigveda.* The later *purusha* (cosmic man) myth posited their origin from the self-sacrifice of the "first man," god creating by self-division. By the late Vedic period four castes, instead of three, and a definite hierarchy with the *brâhmins* at the top had been firmly established. The first three castes were twice born, leaving the śûdras without a second or ritual birth. Therefore, śûdras could be not eligible to study Sanskrit or learn the *Vedas* and the accompanying rituals.

Caste is an unhappy translation of *varna,* as *varna* is the ancient ideal social system of Vedic religion whereas "caste" refers to actual *jati* (birth) system of today. The myths mix praise of *varna dharma* (the ideals of an ordered and righteous society) with criticism of a mixing of races and groups that reflects a decline of society into the moment that another destruction will be inevitable.

The *varna-aśrama-dharma* system is addressed in chapter 1 in the sections on "Hindu Worldviews" and "Dharma."

See also Candrasharman; Dharma; *Purusha*
For further reading:
Morton Klass, "Varna and Jati," *Encyclopedia of Religion,* vol. 15 and *Caste: The Emergence of the South Asian Social System* (Philadelphia: ISHI, 1980); Louis Dumont, *Homo Hierarchicus: An Essay on the Caste System,* translated by Mark Sainsbury (Chicago: University of Chicago Press, 1970).

CATUR-YUGA

See Chapter 2, "Mythic Time, Space, and Causality."

CHÂYÂ

A goddess (a replica of a goddess; literally, "shade," or "shadow")

The goddess Samjñâ created her replica, Châyâ, in order to fool her husband, the sun (Sûrya). After having three children by Sûrya (Manu, Yama, and Yamî), Samjñâ could no longer stand the heat of his affections. So she created Châyâ to take her place. Things went well for a while, and Châyâ gave birth to Sani (the planet Saturn), a Manu (first human of a cosmic age) known as Savarni, and a river goddess, Tapatî. Châyâ treated her own children so well that Yama, who had been fooled as completely as his father Sûrya, tried to kick the woman he believed was his mother out of jealousy. Châyâ cursed him so that the foot that he raised against her would forevermore be afflicted with sores and worms. That was certainly fitting for the future god of death. Sûrya suddenly realized that she could not be the real mother of Yama, so he searched for his real wife. He found Samjñâ and brought her home.

Another version makes Châyâ the daughter of Viśvakarma and therefore the sister of Samjñâ.

See also Samjñâ; Sûrya; Viśvakarma; Yama

CHURNING OF THE MILKY OCEAN
See Kshîrâbdhi-mathanam

CIRANJÎVI, CIRANJÎVIS
Immortals
These were the seven beings who did not have to experience death. Hanuman was one among the *ciranjîvis.* The other six chiranjîvis were Aśvatthâma, Mahâbali (Bali), Vyâsa, Vibhishana, Kripa, and Parasu-Râma. Accordingly, they are all still alive in this creation and perhaps will be in all others.

See also Aśvatthâma; Bali; Hanuman; Parasu-Râma; Vyâsa

CITRAKETU
A king who longed for a son
This nested myth within a myth begins with a king and queen being granted a child; they then gain the blessing of becoming *gandharvas* (celestial musicians), but the story ends with the king cursed to become a demon.

According to the *Bhâgavata Purâna* King Citraketu and his queen had been childless for many years before they received a blessing from the sage Angiras. From that blessing came a son. However, not long after the infant died. With great sorrow Citraketu took the body of his son to Angiras. Angiras was being attended by Brahmâ and the sage Nârada. Angiras used his great powers and gave life back to the infant. Upon regaining his life, this child could not recognize his parents and asked Angiras to choose for him his parents from his many previous births. Brahmâ and Nârada became confused with the complex questions on birth and rebirth, but before leaving they gave their spiritual wisdom to King Citraketu.

Citraketu concentrated this mind for eight days on the divine, and both he and his wife were turned into gandharvas. One day while they were enjoying their powers of flight, they flew over Mount Kailâsa and saw Pârvatî sitting on the thighs of Śiva. Citraketu laughed. Pârvatî, enraged by this rude act of Citraketu, cursed him to become a demon. Citraketu was then born as Vritra-asura.

See also Angiras; Gandharvas; Magic, Blessings, Cursings; Mâyâ; Nârada; Vritra

CITRALEKHÂ

Daughter of the demon Bana

This little story has great popular appeal. One even finds it alluded to or even added as a scene within modern Indian films or video serials.

According to the *Bhâgavata Purâna* Chitralekhâ had an unusual ability to draw portraits. She drew one from an account of a dream that Ushâ, a princess, gave. The portrait actually was the picture of someone whom Ushâ was yet to meet. Ushâ fell in love with the portrait and then discovered that it was Aniruddha, grandson of Krishna. Later, when Aniruddha was brought to Ushâ's room and saw his own picture, he too fell in love with her, and they were married.

See also Ushâ

CITRÂNGADÂ

(1) The third wife of Arjuna

This myth is nested within several other myths within the *Mahâbhârata*. There was a devout worshipper of Śiva who has been promised a son but could not produce one himself. His daughter, Princess Citrângadâ, succeeded in bearing a son by the hero Arjuna, who is given this reason for leaving his joint wife Draupadî (taking another wife in order to fulfil a boon granted by Śiva).

Previously, Prince Arjuna was forced to leave home because he broke an agreement that the five brothers (the Pandavas) made in order to have privacy with their common wife Draupadî (also called Pâncâlî, princess of Pañcâli). Any brother interrupting another would go into exile or on a pilgrimage for a year. So it happened that Arjuna made the mistake of intruding and honorably set forth. But before he could get to the right kingdom and be the agent of Śiva's grace for King Citravâhana, Citrângadâ's father, Arjuna had another adventure in a *nâga* (serpent) kingdom. He married the nâga princess Ulûpî, who later became the nurse of his son with Citrângadâ. One *Purâna* added the detail that Arjuna had a son by princess Ulûpî before leaving the land of the serpents.

With this background, enough of the elements of Citrângadâ's story were in place for the story itself to be told. Of course there were always more connections and versions that could be added for a really good audience.

Citrângadâ, daughter of King Citravâhana of Manalûr, instantly fell in love with Arjuna, and he with her, and she proposed to him. The king was overjoyed to acquire such an important prince and warrior as his son-in-law and sanctioned the marriage. A son was born to them named Babhruvâhana before Arjuna needed to return home from exile. The *nâga* princess Ulûpî became Babhruvâhana's nurse.

Much later, after the horse sacrifice *(asva-medha)* following the great battle of the plains of Kurukshetra, Arjuna had the honor of following the wild stallion in battle. Where the stallion wandered, Arjuna and his army followed, conquering each kingdom in turn. But when he reached Manalûr, a young warrior, Babhruvâhana, met Arjuna in battle and slew him. Then both Chitrângadâ and Ulûpî came to the battlefield and saw their dead husband. Ulûpî used the magic diamond, Mrita-sañjîvanî ("making alive the dead"), to bring Arjuna back to life. Then Arjuna took his two wives and his son back home to the Pandava capital of Hastinâpura.

See also Arjuna; Asva-Medha; Draupadî; Kurukshetra

(2) The daughter of Visvakarma, the celestial architect

One day while she and her friends were taking a bath in a forest pond, Citrângadâ saw Prince Suratha, son of Sudeva, walking by. She recognized that Suratha was in love and that she would give herself to him. Her friends tried to restrain her impulse but could not. Learning of this, her father, Visvakarma, cursed her that she would never marry. Citrângadâ fainted, but her friends believed that she was dead and took her to the cremation ground beside the Sarasvatî River. They left her there while they looked for firewood for her pyre. She awoke and, believing that all had abandoned her, attempted to drown herself in the river. The Sarasvatî pushed her into the Gomatî River, and it in turn washed her ashore far from home. She awakened this time and saw a sage called Ritadhvaja. She told him her sad story. Ritadhvaja blessed her with a boon that reversed the curse and cursed her father Visvakarma to be reborn a monkey for his cruel deed. Citrângadâ then married Prince Suratha.

See also Magic, Blessings, Cursings; Mâyâ; Visvakarmâ

CITRARATHA

A gandharva (celestial musician)

In the *Mahâbhârata* while the Pandavas were walking in the forest after killing the demons Hidimbha and Baka, they heard a sound in the river nearby of somebody taking a bath. Arjuna went to see who was taking a bath at night. He saw the *gandharva* king Citraratha and his wife Kumbhinasî bathing together. It was the only moment that it was possible for a human to see a gandharva—at twilight when it was between night and day. Citraratha was furious at having a human spy on his privacy and began a battle with Arjuna. Arjuna defeated the gandharva, and Citraratha taught Arjuna the magic science of *cakshushi-vidya,* the ability to see anything in the three worlds. He also gave Arjuna many other gifts, such as chariots and horses. Arjuna in return taught Citraratha about his magic weapon called the Agniśira.

See also Arjuna; Magic, Blessings, Cursings; Mâyâ

CITRASENA

A gandharva (celestial musician)

Citrasena had many roles in the Purânic and Epic literature.

While flying overhead in his celestial chariot, Citrasena accidentally spat on the sage Gâlava, who complained to Krishna, who in turn vowed to kill Citrasena before sunset. The good old sage Nârada telepathically learned of all this and told Citrasena. So Citrasena's two wives, Sandhyâvalî and Ratnâvalî, made a firepit before the abode of Subhadrâ, wife of Arjuna and sister of Krishna. They planned either to win her help or to die with their husband on his funeral pyre. Subhadrâ granted them the boon that they could live with their husband before knowing the full story. So Arjuna had to come to the aid of Citrasena and to stop all of the arrows that Krishna aimed at Citrasena. He did this so well that it became a fight between Arjuna and Krishna. Subhadrâ was finally able to stop their fight, and Krishna allowed Citrasena to apologize to the sage Gâlava.

On an occasion in the *Mahâbhârata,* at a time when mortals could see *gandharvas,* Duryodhana and his army came into the Dvaitavana forest to kill the Pandavas. They stumbled upon Citrasena and his troop bathing in a forest pond. Haughtily they ordered the gandharvas out so that their king could bathe alone. A fight ensued, with Citrasena routing the Kaurava army and binding the captured Duryodhana. A helpless Kaurava went to Arjuna and begged his help to free Duryodhana from this terrible foe. Of course Arjuna went to his enemy's aid and fought a foe that he did not recognize. Finally after much combat, Citrasena took the form that Arjuna recognized. So Arjuna was able to ask Citrasena to release Duryodhana. After a short time Duryodhana and the Kauravas expressed their gratitude by renewing their evil ways. (It still delights the hearers of all ages that they know the nature of Duryodhana better than Arjuna.)

Next Citrasena taught Arjuna dance and music in the court of Indra. While there the much-celebrated *apsara* Urvaśî became attracted to Arjuna. However Arjuna declined her advances. The frustrated Urvaśî cursed Arjuna to become a eunuch. This curse was a blessing to Arjuna and enabled him to stay incognito as a dance teacher in the palace of King Virata during a year when he needed to go unrecognized. It was through Citrasena that Indra sent a message to Urvaśî to remove her curse.

See also Arjuna; Magic, Blessings, Cursings; Mâyâ; Urvaśî

CÛDÂLA

A queen and great scholar

Queen Cûdâla's accomplishment was placed long ago in the first *Dvâpara yuga* of the seventh *manvantara* (world cycle). Perhaps that placement in an age of greater spiritual potential was why *kṣatriyas* were able to achieve great powers *(siddhis)* without mention of a *brâhmin* teacher and a woman could learn faster than her husband. It seemed also to be a time when humans did not wish to yield to the temptation of calling for help from a god. An alternative interpretation is that we are dealing with an anti-priestly myth with a revolutionary notion that spiritual practice rather than high-caste birth was the more important factor.

Acccording to the *Jñânavâsishtham* King Śikhidhvaja and Queen Cûdâla of Mâlava practiced *jñâna-yoga* (the discipline of knowledge) together. (This myth and its scriptural source are proof of a time when jñâna-yoga was more than just mystical practice.) Cûdâla began to gain powers *(siddhis),* including levitation and travel through the air. The king decided that he would not be able to achieve such powers living in the palace, even though his wife had. So he retired into the forest and performed austerities *(tapas)* there. Cûdâla finally went to him in disguise and stood before him without touching the ground. Śikhidhvaja naturally assumed that a being whose feet did not touch the ground must be a *deva,* so he began to reverence this being. Cûdâla assumed her true form and convinced Śikhidhvaja to return to the palace and practice jñâna-yoga there. However, before they left the forest, Cûdâla used her great power to create a seductress named Urvaśî as well as gods like Indra to test her husband's resolve. Then she took him back to the palace, where they both advanced in jñâna-yoga.

See also Siddhi; Tapas; Urvaśî

CYAVANA

An asura (demon) sage

Cyavana was a son of the great teacher and priest of the demons, Bhrigu. Cyavana had become a great magician like his father, but he had grown old and blind. The Aśvins, the Divine Twins, cured Cyavana of both his old age and blindness. After getting back his youth, Cyavana was extremely happy with the

Aśvins, who had won their fame as physicians to the gods. Now Indra had banned the Aśvins from partaking of *soma*, the celestial drink. Cyavana promised that he would help them get soma, even if it meant opposing Indra, king of the gods. Cyavana organized a soma sacrifice *(soma-yâga)* and invited all the *devas*, including the Aśvins. Indra was furious to see the Aśvins at the *yâga* and ordered them to leave. Consequently, Cyavana started a fight with Indra using all his magical powers. He made a demon called Mada out of the sacrificial fire and sent it to kill Indra. Indra attempted to use his *vajrâyudha*, his war disc, to retaliate, but found all his limbs frozen. Indra prayed to his *guru* Brihaspati. And Brihaspati advised him to give up and apologize to Cyavana. Cyavana accepted Indra's apology, but then Indra used that moment of truce to tear the demon sage into four pieces. These four pieces became the game of dice, hunting, wine, and women. And all still have magical power over men.

See also Aśvins; Bhrigu; Magic, Blessings, Cursings; Mâyâ

DADHÎCI OR DADHÎCA

A sage

Dadhîci had been made from the essence of the world by his father, the great ascetic Bhrigu. He too became an ascetic and engaged in severe *tapas* (austerities). Indra became afraid that his position of Indrahood (as king of the gods) was threatened by a *yogi* with such power *(siddhi)*. So Indra sent Alambushâ, one of his *apsaras* (celestial damsels), to deter Dadhîci from his austerities. Watching the dance of Alambushâ at his hermitage, Dadhîci had a seminal discharge, which fell into the river Sarasvatî. Sarasvatî gave birth to a son named Sârasvata. The sage blessed him with the divine power to cause the rain that would end a twelve-year drought. Sarasvatî took their child to her abode and raised him.

Dadhîci was also known for his readiness to sacrifice even his own life for a noble cause. Unable to defeat a demon named Vritra, Indra went to Brahmâ for his advice. (Vritra had been a serpent monster that prevented the rains in Vedic mythology.) In this myth from the epic period, Brahmâ advised Indra that he would be able to kill Vritrâsura with a weapon made of the bone of Dadhîci. With much hesitation Indra went to the sage and told him about Brahmâ's advice. Without a moment's reflection Dadhîci abandoned his body for this noble cause. Indra killed the demon and his army with the weapon made of Dadhîci's bone. It became Indra's powerful *vajra* (diamond) weapon.

See also Apsara; Magic, Blessings, Cursings; Mâyâ; Siddhi; Tapas; Vritra

Kâlî, wearing a kapâla-mâlin (garland of skulls) and leaving all evil as a corpse, is the destroyer of fear. (TRIP)

DÂKINÎS

Class of women who are proficient in magic

Women magicians were not given much of a role in nonsectarian Hindu mythology. The magicians known for their country and mentioned in the *Mahâbhârata* as the Kshudrakas were one exception. They came to the aid of Duryodhana and the Kauravas. Bhîshma even had the Kshudrakas attack Arjuna. In another incarnation myth most of the Kshudrakas were exterminated, along with the *kśatriyas,* by the *brâhmin*-warrior Paraśu-Râma (Râma-with-the-ax, an avatâra).

Later in Śâkta myths the dâkinîs were transformed into the blood drinkers *(ashrapas)* of Kâlî and were her fiendish helpers, who feed on human flesh. The dâkinîs would acquire an even more important role in the mythology and iconography of Tântric Buddhism, especially as it developed in Tibet (see Detlef Lauf's *Secret Doctrines of the Tibetan Books of the Dead.* Boston: Shambala, 1989).

See also Kâlî; Magic, Blessings, Cursings; Mâyâ; Paraśu-Râma; Śâktism; Tantra

DAKSHA

A prajâpati (creator or progenitor)

In the *Rigveda* (2:27:1) Daksha (ritual skill) was one of the six âdityas, deities related so closely to Vedic sacrificial ritual that they may be called personifications of its logic and method. During the Vedic period the six expanded to twelve, with Daksha always among the most important. Ritual skill in sacrificial magic-science was then central to Vedic and Brâhmanical religion and mythology.

In the great Hindu epics, references to Daksha abound, as numerous versions of his myth were recorded without much regard for consistency. Daksha was born from the right thumb of Brahmâ, or had his origin with the six or seven *mahârishis* or with the eight *prajâpatis,* or was even one of the mind-born of Brahmâ. His fluid nature ranged from being father of energies like Garuda (the sun bird) to being father of some minor demons. The idea of Daksha's sacrifice began in the epics. Daksha, whose very name must be associated with sacrificial ritual, presided over a sacrifice in which Śiva misbehaved by kicking out the teeth of the god Pûshan (the nourisher and protector of cattle), put out the eyes of the god Bhaga (inheritance), and broke the arms of the solar god Sâvitrî (vivifier).

In the *Purânas* the myths reached a point where there were either two separate Dakshas or Daksha's life must be interpreted in two cycles—one as a prajâpati and another as a rebirth as the Daksha who would not invite Śiva to his sacrifice. In his role as Prajâpati, following the account in the *Vishnu Purâna,* Daksha was ordered by Brahmâ to create all the subjects *(prajas).* So Daksha created *devas,* sages, *gandharvas, asuras, nagas,* and so on. Turning these out one at a time was not efficient. So he invented coition and produced with his wife Aśiknî five thousand sons, the Haryashvas. However, Nârada—a sage whose Purânic role was to make trouble or to tell secrets—sent the Haryashvas to learn the wonders of the world, and they never came back. Again Daksha and Aśiknî went back to work and created a new race—a thousand Śabalâśvas. And once again Nârada sent them to the ends of the earth, and they too were lost. Daksha angrily cursed Nârada to be a homeless wanderer (and all know this curse as the reason why Nârada was always available for a grand entrance into any myth). Then wise Daksha created by coition sixty daughters, giving them as wives to the gods and lesser *prajâpatis:* ten to Dharma, thirteen to Kaśyâpa, twenty-seven to Soma (or Candra, the moon), four to Arishthanemi, two to Angiras, and two to Krishâshva. Daksha had twenty-four more daughters by Prasûtî, one of whom, Sîtâ, he gave to Śiva and another to Bhrigu, his father in the *Epics* but now his son-in-law. At this point the Purânic mythmakers chose to end the myth of the venerable and wise Prajâpati Daksha or to re-introduce him in another lifetime in a Śaiva myth cycle.

In the *Śiva Purâna* Daksha became a very negative figure who tried to humiliate the Absolute, which in this Purâna was Śiva. Daksha objected to his daughter Satî's relationship with Śiva. Even though it was assumed that Satî was already Śiva's wife, there was a noteworthy omission of a proper wedding. Such a wedding would have legitimated Śiva ritually and would have made Daksha's objection to Śiva's presence at an orthodox sacrifice to the gods without meaning. This myth addressed something that has had currency even in the modern period: that Śiva and his cult were not Vedic and his presence would pollute Daksha's ritual. Most accounts present Śiva as being unconcerned about not receiving an invitation, but everything changed because of what happened when Satî went alone—against Śiva's advice. Daksha's later Purânic persona behaved badly, humiliating Satî so totally that she threw herself into the sacrificial fire, turning it into a funeral pyre, and becoming an example of a woman's ultimate sacrifice *(sati)*, the self-immolation of a wife, who thereby becomes a model of purity). Satî became a *satî* ("a pure one" feminine) by committing *sati.*

Śiva became outraged. From his anger two demonic figures were created, Vîrabhadra and Bhadra-Kâlî, and they killed Daksha and destroyed his sacrifice. But what Śiva won in this myth by brute force, he also lost: he was the causal agent in the killing of the *brâhmin* Daksha. And non-Shaiva myths added this sin to other reasons Śiva and his cult were less Vedic and less orthodox.

This myth was important devotionally, however, as it taught that devotion to Śiva was more important than sacrifices or rituals performed without devotion.

See also Bhadrakâlî; Prajâpati; Śiva; Satî

DÂLBHYA

A sage

This is an example of a myth about a priestly curse that explains the bad fortune of a king and a kingdom. Such a myth served as an advertisement of the powers *(siddhis)* of *brâhmins* and their ability to bless or curse. This late story in the *Vâmana Purâna* referred back to the setting of the great war told in the *Mahâbhârata* and why King Dhritarâshthra's kingdom was destroyed. The listeners would appreciate an addition to the many other reasons that they already knew from the episodes of the *Mahâbhârata.*

A group of *brâhmins*, including the sage Dâlbhya, asked King Dhritarâshthra for alms in the holy Naimisha forest. But he refused them and they vowed revenge. Dâlbhya officiated at a sacrifice intended to cause the kingdom of Dhritarâshthra to decline. Realizing his mistake, Dhritarâshthra went to Dâlbhya and gave him money and presents. So Dâlbhya stopped the curse and blessed Dhritarâsthra. But *karma* is cumulative—and the listener knew what the final result would be, despite Dhritarâshthra attempt to buy his way out of bad karma.

See also Dhritarâshthra; Magic, Blessings, Cursings; Mâyâ; Siddhi

DAMAYANTÎ

Daughter of King Bhîma of Vidarbha and wife of Prince Nala

Damayantî was born from the blessing of her childless parents by the sage Dama. She grew into a beauty whose fame reached the attention of Prince Nala. Damayantî also knew of this handsome prince from those divine messengers, the swans. The two fell in love without even meeting.

King Bhîma announced a *svayamvara* (a *kśatriya* custom in which the princess could select her own husband). Nala set out for the kingdom of Vidarbha with the hope of being chosen by Damayantî but was met by four gods—Indra, Agni, Varuna, and Yama. He did what was proper and promised to do their will. They gave him the power *(siddhi)* of invisibility to allow him to get past the other suitors and the palace guards so that Nala could tell Damayantî to choose one of them. However, Damayantî did not agree to chose one of the gods. When the contest began, the gods took the shape of Nala so that there were five Nalas in the line of suitors. But love aided Damayantî's choice. The gods were pleased with the respect they had been given and with the fine characters of the couple. So they blessed them. Nala was given a special blessing from each god: divine presence from Agni, righteous action from Yama, the ability to obtain water with a thought from Varuna, and liberation *(moksha)* after completing a sacrifice to the gods from Indra.

Their story was nested in a story told by the sage Brihadasva to Dharmaputra (another name for Yudhishthira, the oldest Pandava brother), while he was lamenting Arjuna's absence during their stay in the forest. Arjuna had gone to Kailâsa to do austerities and to win a boon from Śiva—the divine weapon called Pasupata.

This myth about young love is one of the most popular love stories in Indian literature. It continues with many episodes, including a gambling episode in which Nala lost everything, modeled on another famous gambling story of the Pandavas.

See also Agni; Indra; Magic, Blessings, Cursings; Mâyâ; Nala; Siddhi; Varuna; Yama

DAŚARATHA

A king, father of Śrî Râma

To be so great a figure as to have a god born as one's son, one must have a distinguished lineage, excellent *karma* (based on what one had done in past lives), and a record of devotion and service to the gods. All of these elements were provided in the various episodes about King Daśaratha. Various compositions and retellings of the *Râmâyana* nest one myth within another, to the great delight of Indian audiences throughout the centuries. There were enough blessings and cursings, magical powers, and divine visitations reaching into the future and turning back into the past to fully satisfy. Several episodes must suffice to illustrate these rich myths: a curse from the king's youth, great deeds and a boon to one of his wives, temple worship and austerities for a son, and death by a predicted curse.

Once while he was hunting, Daśaratha heard a sound from the river that was similar to the sound of an elephant drinking water. Daśaratha, without thinking, shot his arrow, only to discover that he had mortally wounded a *brâhmin* boy collecting water for his aged parents. Śravana, the young boy, asked Daśaratha to take water to his parents at their hermitage, since they did not have anybody else to help them. Daśaratha took the water to the hermitage and told the aged parents about the accidental death of their son. They asked Daśaratha to take them to their dead son. They made a funeral pyre for Śravana. Then the aged parents cursed Daśaratha to die from the loss of his own children. Then both parents jumped into the funeral pyre of their son and died.

Years passed. The *devas* (gods) asked for Daśaratha's help in their battles with the *asuras* (demons). During this service to the gods one of his three wives, Kaikeyî, twice saved his life on the battlefield and gained two boons, which she was to use much later. Years and episodes rolled by. Daśaratha and his wives remained childless. He entrusted his kingdom to his ministers and began to practice devotion by building a temple and worshipping an image of Lord Vishnu. He also gained the help of an ascetic named Rishyaśringa, who performed the magic incantation for children *(putrakâmeshthi)*. From the sacrificial fire and the chanting *(mantrayâna)* a luminous figure arose with a pot of pudding and placed it before Rishyaśringa. He gave it to the king with more *mantras*. According to Rishyaśringa's instructions King Daśaratha gave a portion to each of his wives: half to Kaushalyâ, who conceived Râma, a half incarnation of Vishnu, a fourth to Kaikeyî, who conceived Bharata, a one-fourth incarnation of Vishnu, and a fourth to Sumitrâ, who conceived two sons, Lakshmana and Śatrughna, each a one-eighth incarnation of Vishnu.

Years passed. The sons married, and Daśaratha was prepared to pass his kingdom to the son of his first wife, Kaushalyâ's son Râma. Now the boon to Kaikeyî had its karmic unfolding. She demanded that her son, Bharata, be crowned king and that Râma be exiled for fourteen years to the forest. Thus, all this was nested in the Râma myth cycle, which in turn nested within the Vishnu myth cycle.

However, Daśaratha's story must be brought to an end. It was because of the curse of the *brâhmin* boy's parents that Daśaratha died of intense sorrow after exiling Śrî Râma to the forest. Śrî Râma and Lakshmana along with Sîtâ would have to spend fourteen years in exile because of Daśaratha's deeds (karma).

See also Magic, Blessings, Cursings; Mâyâ; Siddhi

DATTÂTREYA
A sage

Dattâtreya had wonderful parents: the sage Atri and his wife Anasûyâ. Dattâtreya was an incarnation of Vishnu according to some *Purânas.*

Why did Lord Vishnu incarnate as Dattâtreya? The *Brahmânda Purâna* traced the story back to a hermit named Ani-Mândavya who meditated under a vow of silence. In pursuit of robbers who dropped their loot beside Ani-Mândavya, the king's guards bound the *yogi* and dragged him off to prison. The king ordered his execution on a trident, and Ani-Mândavya suffered but did not die.

Adding another element of the divine plan, Sîlavatî, a devoted wife, was carrying her leprous husband Ugratapas on her shoulders to the house of a harlot, as was his wish. They passed by Ani-Mândavya, who was still alive even though he was skewered on the trident. Mândavya saw them and cursed Ugratapas to die before sunrise. (See "Ani-Mândavya" for the ending of that episode.)

Sîlavatî used her acquired *siddhis* (ascetic powers) to cause the sun not to rise. And when it did not rise, the gods went to the Trimûrtis (Brahmâ, Vishnu, and Śiva) and prayed that the problem be solved. The Trimûrtis went to Anasûyâ and asked for her help with Sîlavatî. Anasûyâ and the gods succeeded in getting

Sîlavatî to allow the sun to rise by granting that her husband Ugratapas would not die. Then the Trimûrtis gave Anasûyâ a boon. She stated that she did not want any boon, except that the Trimûrtis take birth as her sons. The boon was granted. Vishnu was born as Dattâtreya, Śiva as Durvâsa, and Brahmâ as Candra.

Dattâtreya grew up as a hermit with wonderful siddhis. Arjuna under the patronymic (a name formed from that of a father or ancestor) of Kârtavîrya (also Kârtavîryârjuna) came to Dattâtreya and worshipped him. This pleased Dattâtreya, and he gave King Kârtavîrya a boon of a thousand arms. The *Brahma Purâna* stated that further worship brought gifts of a golden chariot, power to rule justly, a boon to conquer the earth and to rule it righteously, and invincibility—death only at the hands of a warrior whose fame had spread over the entire world. King Kârtavîrya (Arjuna) then ruled for 85,000 years of peace and prosperity. The bringing about of such a rule of *dharma* would be a worthy reason for the incarnation of Vishnu as Dattâtreya. However, though the longing for such a rule to supplant that of Muslims in late medieval India may have influenced the myth, the expectation failed. And Dattâtreya failed with it. He became a victim of Râvana's conquests, confined like a wild beast in the corner of his city. Another ending of his life made him a thief, robbing the wife of Jamadagni of the calf of the divine milk cow. He was punished by another *avatâra* of Vishnu, Paraśu-Râma (Râma with the ax), with some versions stating that Paraśu-Râma came into human form just to kill Dattâtreya (one incarnation of Vishnu killing another).

See also Ani-Mândavya; Candra; Durvâsa; Siddhi

DEVA, DEVAS; DEVÎ, DEVÎS

A god, deity; one of a class of celestial gods

In Hinduism the divine may be viewed as having form *(murti)* and attributes *(gunas)* or being without any form or qualities at all *(nirguna)*. The former perspective was for those with little understanding and in need of every hint possible. Myths about *deva*s added shape and form to the divine mystery.

The word *deva* is derived from the word for light, since a *deva* is one who shines forth. It was said in some sacred texts that it was related to the word for play as well. The word is older than its use in the *Rigveda* with a parallel in ancient Persian. In Sanskrit *deva* referred to the gods, those beings of light that might even be seen at the sacrifice when *soma* (a possible hallucinogen) was drunk by the worshippers. Opposing the *deva*s were the *asura*s (demons). In ancient Persian *(Avestan)* the terms meant the opposite: *ahura* referred to the "lord or lords," and *daivas* to the loud, aggressive beings who did not follow truth *(asha)*. Persian *ahura*s to be taken as gods *(deva*s) in India were Varuna, lord of truth (in Sanskrit, *rita*) and ruler of night, and Mitra, lord of the day.

Although *deva* is masculine, there are also a few *devîs*, the feminine form, in the Vedic period: Aditi, mother of universe; Ushas, dawn; Nirritî, destruction; and Vâc, speech. But most were *devas*, who competed among themselves, as well as with the *asuras*, who seem to have been thought of first as their older brothers and then later as their cousins. Both competed for territory, for female companions (drawn from all kinds of beings), for shares from the sacrifices, and for praise and reverence from worshippers (humans, animals, gods, and demons).

The *devas* and *devîs* occupied and, at least in the Vedic period, ruled the three worlds: heaven *(svar)*, mid-air *(bhuvas)*, and earth *(bhûr)*. The principal *devas* of heaven were Dyaus, the sky god; Varuna, lord of *rita*; Mitra, lord of the day; Pûshan, nourisher; and Vishnu, the pervader, or three-strider. The main *devas* of the mid-air were Indra, lord of storm and war; Vâyu, lord of wind; the Maruts, warrior lords; and Rudras, howlers and lords of killing fire. The greatest of the earthly *devas* were Soma, lord of the plant soma, and Agni, lord of the sacrificial fire.

The evolution of the *devas* was already apparent in the *Rigveda*. Dyaus had no real authority or role, only a faint memory of his past glory. The first triad took shape in the middle period of the *Vedas*, with the heightened importance of Sûrya, Indra, and Agni as rulers of the three domains. As the soma experience of seeing and hearing the *devas* began to be referred to in ancient hymns, the magical formulas of the prayers *(mantras)* and the science of control of the universe through the Vedic sacrifices placed the priests *(brâhmins)* at the center of the Vedic worldview. The *devas* and *devîs* multiplied, and the classifications of divine beings expanded to include more and more classes. The gods were even given a teacher, Brihaspati, the name of an ancient *deva* who was also known as Brahmanaspati (lord of the prayers, or lord of ritual magic).

Creation myths appeared in the middle Vedic period, as did creators and progenitors, with mind-creation, creation by division, creation by coition, and so forth. Some *devas* were given these roles: Paśupati (lord of the creatures; earlier one of the Rudras), *Purusha* (the first being or man), Brahmânda (the cosmic egg), Virât (the cosmic essence)

The sacrificial, or ritual, religion of the Brâhmanical, Epic, and Purânic periods achieved order and control of the divine worlds by classification. A devotional revolution took place alongside this ritualism. Since its notion of the divine involved something higher than the *devas* and *devîs*, a supreme lord of the universe, these competing notions of divinity were able to be harmonized in their literal expression. Both ritualism and devotionalism *(bhakti)* could accept the myths, classifications, and iconography of the *devas* and *devîs*—only devotionalism maintained that all these divine beings were only manifestations of the one supreme lord of the universe (whether seen as Sûrya, Śiva, Vishnu, Devî, Krishna, Râma, or others).

As the *devas* and *devîs* grew from 33 to 330,000,000 the threefold classification changed many times. The 33 presiding *devas* were the 12 *(dvâdasha)* âdityas, the 11 *(ekadasha)* Rudras, the 8 *(ashtha)* Vasus, and the 2 Aśvins. Indra was their chief. These 33 ruled over the 330,000,000 *devas.* One classification divided the gods and goddesses into Âdityas, Viśvadevatas, Vasus, Tushitas, Âbhâsvaras, Anilas, Mahârâjikas, Sâdhyas, Rudras, Vidhyâdharas, and Pitri-devas.

Further divisions added Apsaras, Virûpâkshas, Bhadras, Kinnaras, Gandharvas, Kumbhândas, Râkshasas, Nâgas, Ashvinîs, Kimpurushas, Piśâcas, Guhyakas, Siddhas, Câranas, Matris, Kûshmândas, Bhûtas, and Vetâlas. Later Purânic classifications even included Lokapâlas, Lipikas, Rishis, and Prajâpatis as *devas* and *devîs.*

The *devas* could be classified with reference to Bhûtaganas like Prithvî or different types of *devatâs* such as the Bhûdevatâs, Agnidevatâs, Vâyudevatâs, and so on. Kubera was the presiding spirit of the Bhûdevatâs, Varuna of the Jaladevatâs, Vâyubhagavân of the Agnidevatâs, and Indra of the Âkâshadevatâs.

Hindu polytheism gave control to the ritualist; focus and loyalty to the devotionalist; a desire for unity to the philosopher or mystic; a sense of divinity in everything to naturalist, farmer, and artist—a myriad of responses to a multi-leveled manifestation of divinity that no one could claim to totally comprehend.

See also Âdityas; Prajâpati
For further reading:
Alain Daniélou, *The Myths and Gods of India* (Rochester, VT: Inner Traditions International, 1991), originally published as *Hindu Polytheism* (New York: Bollingen, 1964).

DEVAKÎ

Daughter of a Yadu leader and mother of Śrî Krishna

Devakî was said to be the rebirth of Aditi, the mother of the *devas* and wife of Kaśyapa-prajâpati. She was more famous as the mother of Śrî Krishna. (Vishnu pulled two hairs from his head, one white, another black, and implanted them in the wombs of Rohinî and Devakî. Each divine fertilization became a full incarnation of Vishnu.)

One account stated that Devakî held a *svayamvara* (the self-selection of her husband by a *kśatriya* princess) in which she chose Vasudeva. At their marriage a voice from heaven announced that her eighth child would kill Kamsa, her brother. Kamsa drew his sword and would have killed her, had not her husband Vasudeva pledged to give him each of the sons when they were born. So began intermittent imprisonments of the couple and the killing of their first six sons, who were being reborn to work out *karma* going all the way back to their sin of mocking the creator.

Kamsa personally bashed the brains out of each baby boy. Kamsa's rule of Mathurâ became more and more evil. Some versions of the myth tell of the seventh child as an incarnation of Mâyâdevî. Even though the seventh birth was not a boy, Kamsa tried to smash her head against the ground. But she rose into the air and announced that Kamsa's death was near.

Another version made Bala-Râma the seventh child. Devakî's womb became a divine way-station for Bala-Râma on his way to Rohinî to carry him until his birth as the seventh *avatâra* of Vishnu. This makes these incarnations complicated theologically, since there were two full incarnations of Vishnu on earth at one time.

Finally, Krishna was born as her eighth child, and in due course fulfilled the prophecy that he would kill Kamsa.

Devakî's rebirth as Prishnî, wife of Sutapas (a *prajâpati*, or progenitor), seems to have been an example of inattention by the mythmaker. They placed her back in time without any explanation of the karmic necessity for such a story. Devakî had other such roles without development of character or purpose except for the use of her name.

See also Aditi; Bala-Râma; Bhadrakâlî; Kâlanemi; Kamsa; Krishna

DEVAKULYÂ
Granddaughter of Sage Marîci

Devakulyâ washed the feet of Vishnu, and she was reborn as the river goddess Gangâ. This myth had to be reconciled with another origin myth about the Gangâ: that the earthly Gangâ came by the grace of Śiva. The version featuring Devakulyâ in the *Bhâgavata Purâna* emphasized her merit for worshipping Vishnu and how she was rewarded with a rebirth as the river goddess Gangâ. Devakulyâ's rebirth as Gangâ exalted Vishnu and was noted in sectarian interpretations. But from universalist viewpoints both Vishnu and Śiva were a part of the One, and worship given to either honored both, and the Absolute as well.

See also Gangâ; Śiva; Vishnu

DEVALA
See Ashthâvakra

DEVASENÂ
Woman of great beauty and purity

As a daughter of Daksha, a Prajâpati, Devasenâ could be considered a minor goddess. In heavenly fields one day Devasenâ and her sister Daityasenâ were enjoying nature when they caught the lustful eye of the demon Keshi. The demon talked Daityasenâ into marrying him but could not persuade Devasenâ to do the same. She prayed to Indra, who drove Keshi away with his diamond weapon *(vajrâyudha)*, but the demon escaped with the submissive sister. Devasenâ asked for a husband who could defeat the *devas* (gods), *dânavas* (her half-brothers, sons of Danu, all demons), and *yakshas* (tree spirits). However, both Indra and Brahmâ could not find such a warrior in the three worlds. All the gods combined were able to create Subrahmanya for her. Later with Devasenâ's and Subrahmanya's help the gods defeated the demons.

This myth was nested in the Śiva myth cycle when Subrahmanya came to be seen as a son of Śiva and would need a worthy wife.

See also Daksha; Subrahmanya

DEVAYÂNÎ
Daughter of Śukra, teacher of the asuras

Devayânî's father, Śukra, was the greatest master of magic of his age, but he served the *asuras* (demons). The *devas* (gods) sent Kaca to learn how Śukra made the *asuras* invincible, and Kaca discovered that whenever the gods killed demons, Śukra restored them to life.

Kaca caused Devayânî to fall in love with him, and through her learned the magical power of *mritasañjîvinî* (giving life to the dead) from her father, Śukra. But after Kaca mastered the training, he left without marrying Devayânî. So she cursed him, so that what he learned would not be of use to him. Kaca cursed her back that no *deva* would marry her.

After a very long time, King Yayâti, a mortal, married Devayânî, and she had two sons by him named Yadu and Turvasu. Devayânî's divine ancestry made her a worthy wife for an eminent king of the lunar dynasty *(candra-vamśa)*, thus legitimating this ruling line and giving it semi-divine status.

See also Kaca; Magic, Blessings, Cursings; Mâyâ; Siddhi; Śukra

DEVÎ
A goddess; the Great Mother

Devî is a general term for all goddesses through all the periods of Hindu scripture and mythology. As such, it can be added to the name of particular mothers, sisters, wives, or lovers of male gods *(devas)*. In India it is such a common practice to be named after a god or goddess that the addition of *deva* or *devî* is help-

Devî manifests in many ways; here she kills yet more personifications of evil. (TRIP)

ful for clarification.

As one individual goddess, Devî may be seen as subordinated to Śiva as one of his wives. Or, as Mahâdevî (the "great mother goddess"), she is Śiva's equal, or she may even be held to be the supreme deity of the universe and the ultimate source of everything that has life, consciousness, power, or activity. While Mahâdevî's ontological nature was addressed by India's greatest philosopher-theologians, Devî's complex and ambiguous mythology held much of India under her spell. For specific information about each manifestation of Mahâdevî, see details in particular entries for names mentioned in what follows.

Mahâdevî's mythological cycle can gather all myths about *devîs* (goddesses) within its wide embrace. From the most humble stone of a tribal image representing a *matrikâ* (mother) to virgin goddesses *(kumâris)* to a myriad manifestations of power *(Śhaktî),* her presence was perceived and worshipped as the Great Mother. When subordinated as a wife and mother, her "cool" (orthodox) nature manifested in beautiful, obedient wives such as Pârvatî for Śiva, Lakshmî or Śrî for Vishnu, and Sarasvatî for Brahmâ. But even myths about these fully Brâh-manical *devîs*—goddesses who have respectable places in orthoprax temples, festivals, and rituals—may have reversals of gender roles and episodes that hint at her possession of more power than her consort, at an alternate world order, and even at another and more dangerous nature. For those who understand that Mahâdevî's *sakti* was the source of all energy and the very life and activity of the universe, the Mother was present even in the most sanitized myths of proper, subservient, and inferior female goddess roles.

Any doubt about Mahâdevî's status disappeared when her power was needed to correct gods and men and turn them from their errant ways. Her five most important manifestations *(pañcadevîs)* as Durgâ, Lakshmi, Sarasvatî, Sâvitrî, and Râdhâ included three cool goddesses and two "hot," or nonorthodox, ones. Durgâ was dangerous as a slayer of evil, personified as a buffalo demon, Mahisha. She drank wine before battle and decapitated her victims. Though beautiful and seemingly ready to be married and to be brought under the control of a husband, Durgâ reversed ordinary notions about the feminine. And Râdhâ, the earthly consort of Śrî Krishna, was only an earthly manifestation of Radhikâdevî, who was the formless, eternal beauty more powerful than all the gods. As Râdhâ she disregarded normal conventions and hinted that pleasure and power, not renunciation, were the divine reward of those who knew her play *(lîlâ)*.

The hottest of all the manifestation of Mahâdevî is Kâlî. She was the anger of Umâ, or Pârvatî, Śiva's wife. She has traditionally demanded offerings of wine, meat, and blood. Animal sacrifices are still given to her at her temple in Calcutta, or in Nepal, or in the villages in non-orthoprax rituals. At the village level any of the hot goddesses could be seen as Kâlî—Câmundâ, who drinks up the blood of the demon Raktabîja (bloody seed), whose blood was the seed of more demons, the Sapta-Mâtrikas (seven mothers), and even lesser goddesses of smallpox and disease like Śîtalâ and Mâriyamman.

Pan-Indian festivals like Durgâ Pûjâ celebrate Durgâ's great victories over demons like Mahisha, and in local celebrations Mahâdevî might take possession of male or female mediums, who speak with village wisdom and remind all of her ever present and powerful nature. Everywhere that there is a river, especially ones famous enough to have their own pan-Indian or even local myth, the goddess is there too, as Gangâ, Sarasvatî, Tapatî, or Gomatî.

See also Durgâ; Kâlî; Lakshmî; Râdha; Śakti; Tantra

DHANVANTARI

A sage or deva (god)

After a thousand years of Churning of the Milky Ocean Dhanvantari arose with a water-pot *(kamandalu)* in one hand and a staff *(danda)* in the other. He rose above the water and worshipped Vishnu. He delivered the *amrita*, the drink of immortality, which was supposed to be shared equally by *deva*s and *asuras* (demons). Vishnu promised him a wonderful rebirth.

So Dhanvantari was reborn to introduce the science of *Âyurveda* (the indigenous medicine of India), after his earthly father-to-be, Dhanvâ, worshipped his son-to-be as Abja-deva, the name Vishnu had given Dhanvantari as his divine name. Dhanvantari taught his disciples the *Âyurveda*.

See also Kshîrâbhdi-mathanam

DHARMA

(1) A deva (god)

In the *Vedas*, Dharma was a metaphor, a personification of duty. In later periods, however, Dharma was presented as a minor *deva*. Dharma was said to be born from the right nipple of Brahmâ, the creator. In the *Mahâbhârata* Dharma was given three sons: Śama, Kâma (god of love), and Harsha. In the *Purânas* Dharma married thirteen daughters of Daksha-prajâpati: Śraddhâ, Lakshmî (later to be given to Vishnu), Dhritî, Tushtî, Medhâ, Pushtî, Kriyâ, Buddhî, Lajjâ, Vapus, Santî, Siddhi, and Kirtî. Famous sons of Dharma were Hari, Krishna, Nara, and Nârâyana. Hari and Krishna were great *yogis*, and Nara and Nârâyana were great ascetics.

Dharma partially incarnated as Yudhishthira, eldest of the Pandavas and son of Kuntî, when she received the boon of having children by different gods. In one account, Dharma was reborn a mixed-caste human as Vidura, with the *brâhmin* Vyâsa as his father and a *śûdra* slave girl as his mother.

See also Brahmâ; Kâma; Kuntî

(2) A concept

This concept plays a major role in both Hindu mythology and religion. The word itself came from the verbal root *dhri*, meaning "to sustain, support, uphold." The older concept used in the *Rigveda* is neuter in gender, *dharman*. But the form of the word used in the following periods of mythology was masculine, *dharma*.

There is no single word for religion in Sanskrit, perhaps because that realm was so pervasive. The term *dharma* encompassed truth, tradition, teaching, right action (ethics or morals), correctness (ought), duty, and obligation. It had cosmic and social dimensions.

Its oldest connections were with the Vedic concept *rita*, the sustaining order presided over by Varuna. That connected to truth *(satya)* and proper action. *Dharma* developed within the tensions of Varuna's *rita* and *satya*, Brâhmanical (priestly) ritualism, and *kśatriya* (warrior) codes of ethics (honor, courage, and loyalty). The myths demonstrate this tension in the struggles between gods and demons, gods and humans, and gods and priests. Justice (*rita*) and truth (*satya*) was universal but it was articulated indirectly in stories of misunderstandings, failures, and conflicts.

Perhaps the most important connection was between *dharma* and the social system, comprising two aspects, *aśramas* (stages) and *varnas* (castes). These three, as *aśrama-varna-dharma,* became inseparable for orthoprax Brâhmanical society. For a more general discussion see the entries in Chapter 1, "Hindu Worldviews" and "Dharma."

See also Brâhmacâri; Catur-Varna; Jada; Rita; Samnyâsin; Varna

DHRITARÂSHTHRA

Son of Ambika and the sage Vyâsa (credited with receiving the *Vedas*)

The lunar dynasty was in danger of dying out. Dhritarâshthra's life story is an illustration of just how weak *dharma* (truth, righteousness, religion) had become on earth. Dhritarâshthra was the king under whose rule the great Mahâbhârata war would be fought. Evil could not be reversed as the great royal lineage fought amongst itself.

Dhritarâshthra's conception compromised the great sage Vyâsa who was not married to his mother, his resulting blindness disqualified him from being chosen king until there was no other choice, and his own past *karma* placed him on the wrong side of the Mahâbhârata war. His story is nested in the actions of his grandfather, his conception in his dead father's name by a substituted mother (and thus creating a glaring problem in the logic of his geneology), and his own past actions. It is Hindu mythology at its best and most complicated—the use of stories nested within stories illuminating right action through bad examples.

Dhritarâshthra's grandfather, King Śantanu, had sons by two wives, Gangâ and Satyavâtî. Gangâ had been reborn on earth as part of a curse by Brahmâ for exposing herself in heaven on one occasion. Gangâ threw seven of her eight sons into the earthly river Gangâ and gave her eighth son, Bhîshma, to Satyavâtî to raise alongside Satyavâtî's own two sons, Citrângada and Vicitarvîrya. Bhîshma took the vow of chastity *(brahmavrata),* so his half-brother, Citrângada, was enthroned as the king. But he was killed on a hunting expedition by a *gandharva*.

At this point storytellers could provide their audience with an adult or a children's version. Vicitarvîrya was appointed king. Bhîshma abducted three princesses from a neighboring kingdom. He sent one sister back and gave the other two, Ambikâ and Ambalikâ, to Vicitarvîrya. Unfortunately Vicitarvîrya also died before any children were born. The queen mother, Satyavâtî, solved the crisis of an heirless throne by remembering that she had had a child by a *brâh-*

min named Parâshara before she married King Śantanu. This son was none other than Veda-Vyâsa. Satyavâtî brought Vyâsa into the palace and sent Ambikâ and Ambalikâ, one after the other to Vyâsa so that they could produce heirs to the throne. However, they were shocked by this rustic, according to polite accounts, because he wore bark for clothes and had matted hair. Ambikâ was only able to stay with Vyâsa by closing her eyes, so her son, Dhritarâshthra, was born blind. Ambalikâ lost all her color when she saw the *muni* (wild one), and her son was born a leper or, perhaps only an albino, named Pandu. Queen Satyavâtî's maid was very happy to be with Vyâsa and had a normal and highly intelligent child who later became the great sage Vidura. Having done his duty, Vyâsa returned to his hermitage *(aśrama)*. The lunar royal lineage had been temporarily saved.

Dhritarâshthra was passed over as king because of his infirmity—blindness. Uncle Bhîshma helped arrange his marriage to a princess named Gândhârî, who just happened to have a boon from Śiva to be mother of a hundred sons. Vyâsa was the instrument of Śiva's blessing. Gândhârî had remained pregnant for two years, so she crushed her womb and forced out a lump of flesh. Vyâsa cut it into a hundred pieces and kept them in butter (ghee) pots. Duryodhana was the eldest son of the one hundred.

Pandu had become the king, but he was cursed by a hermit and died in the forest. Yudhishthira, his eldest, became king but later lost the kingdom in a dice game with Duryodhana. The Pandava brothers and their joint wife, Draupadî, were forced into exile and, after the agreed upon thirteen years, returned to claim the kingdom. However, Duryodhana would not return anything. So the hundred Kaurava brothers led by Duryodhana and the five Pandava brothers and their armies fought the great Bhârata war at Kurukshetra.

Dhritarâshthra opposed the war and was blessed with a moment's sight by Śrî Krishna and was able to see his cosmic form *(Viśvarûpa)*. During the battle the sage Sañjaya telepathically reported the events of the *Bhagavad Gîtâ* to Dhritarâshthra, who was again blind. After the great slaughter Dhritarâshthra and his wife Gândhârî retreated to a hermitage near Kurukshetra. Great sages like Nârada and Vyâsa visited them. Then Dhritarâshthra and Gândhârî along with the mother of the Pandavas, Kuntî, went to Gangâdvâra and performed severe penance. They died in a wildfire and entered the realm of Kubera, god of wealth and happiness.

See also Duryodhana; Pandavas

DHRUVA
A great devotee to Vishnu
Dhruva was the son of the second wife of Manu, the first human. Manu's first wife and son treated Dhruva and his mother badly, yet they both accepted the

abuse with gentleness and humility. When he grew up, even though he was a *kṣatriya* (warrior), Dhruva joined a group of *rishis* (sages) and eventually became one himself. He excelled in austerities *(tapas)*, to the point that he worried Indra, whose throne became hot from Dhruva's efforts. Because of his devotion to Vishnu, Dhruva was immortalized as the North Star.

Dhruva has been listed among the great devotees in Hindu mythology, like Arjuna, Hanuman, and Prahalâda.

See also Arjuna; Hanuman; Tapas

DIRGHATAMAS

A blind sage

The myths about Dirghatamas's parentage varied widely; he was described as a son of Kâsi-râja (according to the *Mahâbhârata*), of Uchâthya (in the *Rigveda*), and of Utathya by Mamatâ (in the *Purânas*). But this *brâhmin* came to be seen as having fathered a line of kings, so he inherited much more interesting parental *karma* in another version in the *Mahâbhârata.*

One day Brihaspati, the ancient teacher of the *devas* (gods), was overcome by passion for Mamatâ, his brother Utathya's wife. Mamatâ was already pregnant with Utathya's child and tried to dissuade Brihaspati saying that she could not hold the power of two sets of seeds at the same time. Utathya's unborn child had already mastered the *Vedas*. Brihaspati forced himself upon Mamatâ. During intercourse, the child inside the womb told Brihaspati that what he was doing was wrong and kicked the semen out of the womb with his foot. Brihaspati became angry and cursed the unborn child to be born blind. So Utathya's child received the name Dirghatamas, which means "one who is in eternal darkness."

Though blind, Dirghatamas equaled Brihaspati in brilliance. He married Pradveshi and had many children by her. Then he became so contemptible in his behavior toward his family that his wife and the members of their hermitage put him into a raft to get rid of him. King Bali rescued the blind old sage *(rishi)* and decided to have the sage produce brilliant children from his infertile queen. However, she substituted a maid, with whom the old *brâhmin* produced eleven brilliant children. Then the king discovered his wife's deception and sent her back to the old sage. The queen gave birth to five sons, who founded kingdoms with the modern names of Bhâgalpura, Bengâl, Ândhra, Râjasâhi, and Tâmravika.

See also Bali; Brihaspati; Magic, Blessings, Cursings; Mâyâ

DRAUPADÎ

Wife of the five Pandava brothers

Draupadî was the princess of Pañcâla (thus her name Pâñcâlî) who held a contest to choose her own husband *(svayamvara)*. Arjuna competed in disguise because he and his brothers had been exiled from their kingdom of Ayodhyâ. Arjuna, son of Indra and Kuntî, won the contest and took her away with him. When he announced to his mother that he had won a great prize, she declared that the prize must be shared equally with his brothers as always. Thus, Draupadî became the joint wife of the five Pandava brothers, although Arjuna always remained her favorite.

Draupadî was treated as property in Yudhiṣṭhira's famous gambling match with Duryodhana and lost twice to him. The second time Dushshâsana, Duryodhana's son, dragged Queen Draupadî into the Kauravas' great assembly hall and tried to disrobe her in front of her defeated husbands and the other members of the palace. She was helped by Krishna and saved from humiliation as her sari became unending. Draupadî vowed not to comb her hair until this humiliation was avenged.

Back in the forest Draupadî did not complain as each of her husbands acquired more wives and kept strange schedules. Bhîma honeymooned with Hidimbî, his *râkshasa* bride, during the day and each night returned to be with Draupadî. Arjuna went off for a year as a punishment for bursting into her bedroom when it was not his turn, acquiring wives and sons from his adventures. During the exile she may have been raped by a kinsman, King Jayadratha. Then she was so abused by a general named Kîcaka that Bhîma killed him and then had to rescue Draupadî from being burned to death as punishment for that killing.

Bhîma had vowed to avenge the humiliation of the Pandavas' joint wife Draupadî caused by Duryodhana. He finally kept that vow by mortally wounding Duryodhana with a blow from his war club.

On the eighteenth day of the Mahâbhârata war Draupadî and her five sons visited the Pandava encampment, anticipating that the war was finally over. That night Asvathâman and two warriors slaughtered most of the Pandava army, including Draupadî's five sons—one from each of her husbands. Draupadî wanted revenge but allowed her husbands a way out of slaying a *brâhmin*. They only had to bring back the jewel Aśvatthâma wore. Bhîma, Arjuna, and Krishna pursued Aśvatthâma and brought back his jewel to Draupadî.

With the end of the war the Pandavas regained their kingdom, only to find that they had no heart to continue as the royal family. When Yudhishthira, oldest of the Pandava brothers, renounced his kingdom and began the journey to the Himâlayas, Draupadî and her other four husbands joined him. Draupadî died on the way, but she was waiting in heaven *(svarga)* when Yudhishthira finally arrived.

Draupadî has been honored as one of the *pañca-kanyâ*, the five ideal women of Hinduism, being seen as one who lived her *svadharma*—all of life's obligations that she was responsible for observing.

See also Arjuna; Aśvatthâma; Bhîma; Dharma; Kuntî; Pañcakanyâ

DRONA

Son of a sage, and a warrior

Drona had a miraculous birth. His father, the *brâhmin* sage Bharadvâja, saw the naked body of the beautiful *apsara*, Ghritâcî, who lost her clothes as she ran from the mortal. Bharadvâja had a seminal discharge that was saved in a bucket or trough, a *drona*, thus giving his son that name. Drona mastered archery and taught both the Pandavas and Kauravas this martial skill.

Drona fought on the side of the Kauravas in the great Bhârata war, becoming their commander-in-chief upon the death of Bhîshma. He was killed when he put down his weapons after being told the lie that his own son had been killed. Drona was beheaded by the son of a king whom he had killed—even though he was a *brâhmin*. It was written that he transported himself to heaven because he had always fulfilled his *dharma* (duty).

See also Ghritâcî; Pandavas

DURGÂ

A goddess who killed Mahisha-asura (the buffalo demon)

The myths about Durgâ (the impassable) are like litmus paper. The paper indicates complete opposites (acid or alkaloid) as well as degrees of either. There are several oppositions: Durgâ as beautiful, peaceful sister of Vishnu, wife of Śiva, or Durgâ as ferocious, powerful, avenging destroyer. Another opposition is Durgâ as approved and Brâhmanical or Durgâ as heteroprax, left-handed, bloody, fully sexualized. Durgâ, the litmus paper, is the same. Some of her followers, Śâktas, say that she is the Parâdevî (the goddess as the Supreme). Some say Durgâ has manifested in sixty-four different forms (each appearing in many episodes), including Ambikâ (mother), Dakshinâ (goddess of the ritual gift), Kâmâkshî (goddess of love), Kâmadhenu (wish cow), Kâlî (goddess of time), Mûkâmbikâ (a horrific form of Durgâ), Pârvatî (goddess of the mountain), Shivâ (goddess of sleep).

There are three living myths, more important than the rest, seen in her images in temples, worshipped daily, or celebrated in her great festival, Durgâ Pûjâ. All agree that she came as Mahâmâyâ (goddess of cosmic illusion, mystery,

Durgâ in one of her eight-armed forms rides a tiger. (TRIP)

magic) to slay the personifications of evil formed at creation from the very ear-wax of Lord Vishnu. As Vishnu slept these demons attacked the creative agent, Brahmâ, who was saved by Durgâ's decisive conquest of this outburst of evil. In the brâhmanized form of her myth, Durgâ was produced by Vishnu. However, this myth can also be read to indicate another reality. Durgâ, in *Śâkta* texts and their mythology, controlled Vishnu's sleep, his *yoganidrâ* (yogic sleep after each *kalpa*). She was the active energy (*śaktî*) of creation and the necessary power to thwart evil.

Durgâ's most important myth involved her combat with Mahisha-asura. This powerful demon could not be killed by a male—not even by one of the Trimûrti (Brahmâ, Vishnu, and Śiva). In fact, Mahisha drove them from heaven *(svarga),* ruling it for several centuries. Most accounts credited the gods with combining all their powers to create a single being of light, a *devî* of celestial beauty with eighteen arms. She rode her lion to the entrance way into heaven (Devaloka, "place of the *devas,*" thus *svarga*) and proclaimed that she would become the wife of anyone who could defeat her in armed combat. Mahisha fell in love and was determined to have her. He sent his seconds, then his army, and lastly himself. Finally he changed into his ferocious form as a buffalo demon, but Durgâ cut off his head with a discus *(Vishnu cakra).* Iconographically, Durgâ, with her lion and perhaps a decapitated Mahisha-asura nearby or underfoot, is known as Mahisha-asura-Mardanî and Katyayanî with only ten arms.

The third myth about Kâlî springing from Durgâ's forehead, personifying her anger, has been used in some versions of the myths about Durgâ saving creation and Durgâ killing Mahisha. The world again was threatened by evil—by the demons Śumbha and Niśumbha. Durgâ's avenging energy, Kâlî, destroyed them.

Durgâ appears in many modern contexts. Perhaps her most famous devotee was Shrî Râmakrishna, *guru* of Svâmî Vivekânanda. She is central to both Śaktism and Śakta Tantrism, where her heteroprax worship involves blood sacrifice, wine, and erotic rituals.

See also Devî; Kâlî; Mahisha; Tantra
For further reading:
For historical process of sanskritization or Brâhmanization of goddesses see
Thomas B. Coburn, *Devî-Mâhâtmya: The Crystallization of the Goddess Tradition* (Delhi: Motilal Banarsidass, 1984) and J. J. Tiwari, *Goddess Cults in Ancient India* (Delhi: Sundeep Prakashan, 1985). For art history see M. C. P. Srivastava, *Mother Goddess in Indian Art, Archaeology and Literature* (Delhi, 1979) and T. A. Gopinatha Rao, *Elements of Hindu Iconography*, vol. 1, part 2 (Delhi: Motilal Banarsidass, 1914, reprint 1985). For source materials see Wendy Doniger O'Flaherty, *Hindu Myths: A Sourcebook* (New York: Penguin, 1975).

DURVÂSA

A sage

Durvâsa (hard to dwell) was known for his bad temper and his imperious ways. He was also said to be a partial *(amsha)* incarnation of Śiva.

Durvâsa has three different birth myths, each accounting for his character. The first began in heaven. Śiva had behaved so badly, abusing the *devas* (gods) and his wife Pârvatî, that she decided to leave him. So Śiva discarded that portion of himself that was making life miserable for everyone—to be born as a sage. The rest of the story is told within the stories of Śîlavatî, the woman who stopped the sun from rising in order to reverse Durvâsa's curse, and Anasûyâ, the woman who gained a boon to have children from each of the Trimûrtis. In the first version of Durvâsa's birth Anasûyâ's third child was the son of Śiva—none other than Durvâsa.

The second account of Durvâsa's birth involved Brahmâ driving Śiva from heaven because of his sins. Śiva begged the help of the *rishi* (sage) Nârâyana. Śiva was told to pierce the sage with his trident *(shûla)*. Three streams of blood from Nârâyana's arm worked as a blood sacrifice: one stream went to heaven, another into the skull carried by Śiva, and the third became Durvâsa. Brahmâ was placated, and Śiva, now pure because of the blood sacrifice, returned to heaven. In the third account Śiva's rage in a battle with demons came back to him as the arrow that killed the demons and returned to his lap. That arrow was then born as Durvâsa.

Was it any wonder then that, in the later mythology, Durvâsa served as a fierce teacher, ready to chastise or curse any who crossed him. He made Krishna and Rukminî pull his chariot like horses, beating them all the way. Then he gave Krishna partial invincibility in battle, leaving only his foot unprotected. And that of course turned out to be where the arrow that killed Krishna found its mark. Durvâsa cursed kings and damsels, gave five magic *mantras* to Kuntî so that she could have children by the gods, and spent lots of time in Indra's heaven.

See also Kuntî; Magic, Blessings, Cursings; Mâyâ; Siddhi

DURYODHANA

The eldest of the Kaurava brothers and an arch villain

Duryodhana's birth was a miracle from Śiva, assisted by a blessing from Vyâsa. (See account under Dhritarâshthra.) Duryodhana was raised in the palace of King Pandu, who reigned because his blind brother Dhritarâshthra was disqualified by his infirmity. When Pandu died, his oldest son Yudhishthira became king. Duryodhana and his ninety-nine brothers had trained in the martial arts with their five cousins, the sons of Pandu, or Pandavas. However, jealousy grew into hatred, and Duryodhana turned into one of the arch villains of Indian literature and myth. The sheer length of the *Mahâbhârata*, the world's largest epic poem, provided dozens of lengthy episodes that illustrated his deceit, cruelty, and malice.

Duryodhana was also a clever opponent of the Pandavas. On one occasion, with the help of his uncle Śakuni, Duryodhana led Yudhishthira into a gambling match that ended with the loss of his kingdom and even of the wife he shared with his brothers, Draupadî. Dushshâsana, Duryodhana's son, dragged Queen Draupadî (also know as Pânchâlî after her birthplace) into the Kauravas' great assembly hall and tried to disrobe her in front of her defeated husbands and the other members of the palace. She was helped by Krishna and was saved from humiliation. It was the miracle of the unending sari.

The Pandava brothers and their joint wife Draupadî were forced into exile and after the agreed-upon thirteen years returned in the fourteenth to reclaim the kingdom, but Duryodhana refused to give it up. So the hundred Kaurava brothers, led by Duryodhana, and the five Pandava brothers assembled their armies. Duryodhana asked Krishna to join on his side, but Krishna gave him the choice: either Krishna or his army. Duryodhana took the army, and Krishna joined the Pandavas as Arjuna's chariot driver. The battle involved great slaughter, but it eventually went badly for the Kauravas. On the eighteenth day they were routed, and Duryodhana fled the field of battle and hid in a lake. He had the miraculous power of surviving under water. He was discovered and forced to fight in single combat with Bhîma, the giant Pandava. Duryodhana was winning, but Bhîma, remembering his vow to avenge Draupadî's humiliation, struck Duryodhana below the waist, a dishonorable act. Duryodhana was left to die, but three of his army found him—the very last survivors of his great army. That night the survivors went into the Pandava camp, murdering many and bringing back the heads of five Pandava grandchildren. Duryodhana mistook these for the heads of the five brothers whom he so hated. He asked for the head of Bhîma and when he found that he was able to crush it, he knew the deception. His dying words condemned the loss of life of innocents. He had died a "good fighter" (*suyodhana*).

One interesting reversal came at the end of the story of Yudhishthira's long quest to reach heaven. Yudhishthira found that Duryodhana, his enemy and cause of so much of his and others' suffering, had reached heaven years before. Duryodhana had done his duty (*dharma*) and for so doing had been granted his place with Brahmâ.

See also Dhritarâshthra; Pandavas

DUSHYANTA

A king of the mythical Puru dynasty

King Dushyanta was on a hunting expedition in the forest when he found a woman of extraordinary beauty named Śakuntalâ. She had been raised by an old sage named Kanva in his forest hermitage. However, Śakuntalâ had another sage as her father, the famous Viśvâmitra, who had begotten her after being seduced by an *apsara* (celestial damsel) named Menakâ. Viśvâmitra went in shame to the Himâlayas where he did penance for a thousand years, leaving Śakuntalâ to be raised by Kanva.

Dushyanta fell in love with Śakuntalâ and took her in *gândharva* marriage, as the kind of marriage formed without any Brâhmanical ritual was called. Śakuntalâ managed to get two promises from Dushyanta before he returned to his palace: that if she had a son that son would become the next king and that Dushyanta would send for her upon his return to the palace. When old Kanva returned to the aśrama, he knew psychically the whole story and blessed Śakuntalâ that her unborn son would in fact become king.

In the meantime, King Dushyanta had offended the irritable old sage Durvâsa, who cursed Dushyanta with loss of memory. After six years Śakuntalâ stopped waiting and took her son to the palace. However, Dushyanta did not recognize her or remember anything. They argued until a celestial voice told Dushyanta the truth. Then the king relented, and their son, Sarvadamana, was accepted and later ruled under the name of Bharata.

See also Bharata; Durvâsa

EKALAVYA

Disciple of Drona-acarya

This is a myth that sets unusual talent against *dharma* (the moral order), in this case the duty of accepting the restrictions of one's caste. The master *(acarya)* Drona was a *brâhmin* who refused to teach one who was not twice-born. Drona taught the Pandavas and the Kauravas to be great archers, but unknowingly he prepared them to fight each other in the great Bharata war.

Dronacharya had not accepted Ekalavya as his disciple because he belonged to a lower caste. Ekalavya made an idol of Drona, worshipped it, and started learning the lessons of the great sage without his knowledge. Arjuna learned that Ekalavya was as skillful as he in archery. He went to Drona and asked how could this have happened, when Drona had already announced that Arjuna was the best in archery. Ekalavya was questioned and confessed that he had learned the lessons without Drona's knowledge. Drona accepted Ekalavya as his disciple. Then Drona asked for *guru-dakshina*, the token payment given to the teacher. Drona asked for Ekalavya's right thumb, which he cut off and gave to the *guru*.

This is a cruel myth, illustrating that one must follow one's own *dharma* (*svadharma*) rather than someone else's. It taught a very rigid application of the Brâhmanism of the law books (the *Dharma Śâstras* and *Dharma Sutras*): one's life was already defined by birth and stage of life (*varna-aśrama-dharma*). As a student, Ekalavya had to obey his teacher. And without his right thumb, he no longer could strive to become a warrior (*kśatriya*).

See also Catur-Varna; Dharma; Drona

EKAVÎRA

A king born from horses

In the days when gods and goddesses changed into horses, and their offspring became human kings, Ekavîra was born and founded the Hehaya dynasty. The myth began in Vaikuntha (Vishnu's heaven). A friend of Indra, King Revanta, came to the abode of Vishnu and Lakshmî. Lakshmî was infatuated with the handsome Revanta. She flattered him by complimenting the beauty of his horse. Because her attention was on Revanta, she did not hear what Vishnu was saying. Vishnu became angry at Lakshmî's behavior and cursed her to be born as a mare. Lakshmî begged for some way to do penance. So Vishnu stated that she would be redeemed from the curse and would get back her original nature once she gave birth to a son that equaled the glory of Vishnu himself. The rest of the myth unraveled this puzzle: how a mare could possibly do that.

Once on earth, Lakshmî prayed to Śiva and Pârvatî for help, which, after a thousand years of her devotion, they promised to give. Śiva went to Vaikuntha and sent Vishnu to earth as a horse. Other versions take this superiority away from Śiva by simply having Vishnu miss Lakshmî and follow her to earth as a stallion. Either way, there was a time of *deva-lîlâ*, divine play. When a child was born, Vishnu and Lakshmî returned to Vaikuntha, leaving little Hehaya ("born of a horse"—the future Ekavîra) alone in the forest. Divine beings, Vidyâdharîs and Lakshmî-Nârâyanas, finally got him to the right parent, King Shatajit, who had been praying for a son. He named the infant Ekavîra, raised him, and eventually gave him his kingdom so that he and his queen could retire to the forest and gain heaven. After some years of penance *(tapas)*, they attained Vishnuloka (another name for Vishnu's heaven).

Ekavîra found his wife by retrieving her from hell *(pâtâla)*. He was wandering in the forest and came upon a weeping damsel. She told the story of a childless royal couple who had produced a beautiful daughter by performing a magic ritual *(putrakâmeshthi yâga)*. They named her Ekâvalî and planned to marry her to Ekavîra, king of Hehaya. However, a demon kidnapped her, and when she would not submit to his desires, the demon Kâlaketu imprisoned her in hell. Ekavîra went to Pâtâla, defeated Kâlaketu in mighty combat, and brought both Ekâvalî and the damsel who had told him her story, Yashovatî, who was really the princess's lady-in-waiting, back to her father's palace. The king of Raibhya was so pleased that he gave them both to King Ekavîra, who returned to his kingdom of Hehaya and founded a great dynasty there.

See also Magic, Blessings, Cursings; Mâyâ; Siddhi

EPICS
See Mahâbhârata and Râmâyana

GANAPATI
A title or concept

Most Hindus see Ganapati as an alternative name for Ganeśa, the elephant-headed son of Śiva. Ganapati, literally "father of the ganas (groups)," was a title or concept that first appeared in the Rigveda. During the Vedic period ganas were the metrical groups, each of which had three syllables. The eight ganas represented all the metrical combinations of long and short syllables. A father of these metrical groups, a ganapati, would be a master of the Vedas themselves.

By the time of the Aitareya Brâhmana, father of the ganas had become a title of Brahmâ, father of these Vedic meters. Brahmâ was also called Brahmanaspati, father of the commentaries, and Brihaspati, father of Brihat (the Vast), a title appropriated from Varuna. As father of the groups Brahmâ was not the leader of dwarfs or demons but the patron deity of the lists of the sacred words that were the vocabulary of Vedic schools. Brahmâ was the lord of wisdom who helped priests memorize the hymns and recite the prayers in the sacred meters. Two Vedic sages were also said to father ganas: Prâtishâkhyas and Yâska.

Sometimes mythology has layers of evidence, like archaeology. In the Ganeśa myth cycle there seems to be clear evidence that the title lord or father of the ganas was still linked to the metrical groups. Vyâsa dictated the entire Mahâbhârata with Ganeśa, lord of the ganas, as his scribe. Ganeśa used his single tusk as the stylus that marked green palm leaves with Vyâsa's verses. Ganeśa was lord of the sacred words of scripture.

The second meaning of gana as "association" would put Ganeśa in charge of a host of associates of his father, Śiva. He was entrusted to lead Śiva's army of Ganas, now a class of dwarfs. With this association with Śiva's friends of the cremation grounds, Ganapati, now firmly identified with Ganeśa, acquired the dual dimensions of benevolence and danger that has attracted such devotion to him in Hindu mythology and religion. Those who worship Ganeśa as Ganapati exclusively are known as Ganapatyas; they worship him sometimes as clan deity *(kuladevata)*, sometimes as personal lord *(ishtadevatâ)*.

See also Ganeśa; Śiva

GANDAKÎ

A river of Purânic fame

This myth was included in the *Skanda Purâna* as an elaboration on the myth of the Churning of the Milky Ocean, in which Vishnu appeared as Môhinî and tricked the *asuras* (demons) out of the nectar of immortality. The moral purpose of this myth is not clear. It does extend the notion that rivers are sacred.

Vishnu had taken the form of a beautiful woman called Môhinî that had appeared when the Milky Ocean was churned, which had been stolen by the demons. Śiva wanted to see this form of Vishnu and persuaded Vishnu to appear again as Môhinî. Upon seeing her great beauty Śiva made love to Môhinî. The sweat that was produced during their love play fell down and turned into a river called Gandakî.

See also Kshîrâbdhi-Mathanam; Môhinî

GÂNDHÂRÎ

Wife of King Dhritarâshthra

In the *Mahâbhârata*, Gândhârî had the quite traditional roles of daughter, wife, and mother. Even though her sons, the hundred Kauravas, proved to be on the wrong side of righteousness, she was an example of one who practiced *svadharma*, meeting the requirements of her caste and of the stages of life.

Gândhârî was the daughter of King Subala of Gândhâra, receiving a name referring to her birthplace. She was married to King Dhritarâshthra, even though he was blind—because of Dhritarâshthra's lineage and power. Gândhârî accepted her father's choice and literally wedded blindness. From the day they married, she wore a blindfold until her death. She did not wish to see the world that her husband could not see. She gave birth to a hundred sons, the eldest being Duryodhana, and a daughter, their youngest child, named Dussalâ. Their birth was made possible by divine powers *(siddhis)* associated with the sage Vyâsa. (For more on these births, see the entry on Duryodhana.)

Gândhârî's brother, Śakuni, was an evil influence on her sons. He trained the Kauravas in dark magic that gave them power to win by deceit. Duryodhana was his best pupil in cheating at dice. Gândhârî was not able to counter these male influences. When the Bharata war finally ended with the death of all her sons, Gândhârî wanted to curse the Pandavas. However, old Vyâsa reminded Gândhârî of her blessing at the beginning of the war: that victory should go to the side of righteousness. She realized that the deeds of Duryodhana, Śakuni, and others had been justly punished. She did, however, curse Krishna, whom she held responsible for everything: her curse was that all his heirs should be killed and that even he would die by deceit. This curse was said to be the cause of Krishna's death from a poisoned arrow of a hunter that hit him in the foot—the only place where he was not protected. (For more on Krishna's partial invulnerability, see the entry on Durvâsa.)

After the death of all her sons in the battle at Kurukshetra, Gândhârî retired into the forest and stayed in a hermitage (aśrama). Because of her austerities (tapas), Vyâsa came and granted her wish to see her sons and relatives again before she died. After she had bathed in the Gangâ, all her dead relatives appeared on the shore. Two days later she died in a forest fire, along with her husband, and their companion Kuntî, mother of the Pandavas.

See also Dharma; Dhritarâshthra; Durvâsa; Duryodhana; Krishna; Mahâbhârata; Siddhi; Vyâsa

GANDHARVAS
A class of devas (gods)
This class of gods appeared first in the Vedic period. They were sky beings, associated with the preparation of soma. The Atharvaveda said that there were 6,333 gandharvas. They liked mortal women and sported with them, using their powers to shape-shift and fool all but the most disciplined of wives. There were, however, a number of great heroines whose austerities (tapas) were a match for the magic powers (siddhis) of the gandharvas. In later mythology they were said to be children of the progenitor, or grandfather, named Kaśyapa-prajâpati, by his wife Arishthâ. An appendix to the Mahâbhârata, the Harivamsa, stated that they came from Brahmâ's nose. They were adept at music and were known as the heavenly musicians.

Gândharva marriage was one of the six forms of marriage. It could be a love marriage or a seduction, even a seduction by force—getting its name from the gandharvas' example. Even under the best of circumstances, gândharva marriage was not blessed by the sacrament (samskâras) of Brâhmanical ritual.

See also Siddhi; Soma; Tapas

GANDHAVATÎ
A heroine
See Satyavâtî

GÂNDÎVA
The bow of Arjuna
The distance between gods and heroes in Purânic mythology was not very great. Divine weapons, like the Gândîva, the great bow of Brahmâ, could be given to mere mortals, since the mortals were so often partial divine incarnations or from mixed marriages between gods and mortal women. Such was the case with Arjuna who did not have a human father, as he was born of Indra (god of war) and Kuntî.

The Gândîva was made by Brahmâ. He kept the Gândîva for 1,000 years and then passed it on to Prajâpati (a "grandfather") who kept it for another 1,000 years. From Prajâpati the Gândîva went to Indra who used it for 3,585 years. Indra gave it to Candra (the moon), who had kept it for another 500 years and then gave it to Varuna, who used it for 100 years. Varuna gave the Gândîva to Arjuna. Arjuna used it for 65 years.

The Gândîva was famous for having the power to punish evil and wicked people. It made its user capable of fighting against one *lakh* (100,000) of warriors at a time. The Gândîva was also an object of worship for *devas* (gods), *asuras* (demons), and humans.

When the Kurukshetra war ended, the Yâdava dynasty declined rapidly, and even Krishna was killed. The Pandavas lost interest in ruling their kingdom. Parîkshit, grandson of Arjuna, was appointed king. The Pandavas started their journey *(mahâprasthana)* of renunciation toward heaven. On the way, Arjuna gave back the Gândîva to Varuna by throwing it, along with the quiver of divine arrows, into the sea, Varuna's abode.

See also Arjuna; Siddhi

GANEŚA
Son of Śiva; a god
Ganeśa's mythology came to be nested within that of Śiva and Pârvatî. The theriomorphic past, where animals are gods, has been sufficiently sanskritized and brâhmanized for Ganeśa, with all his associations as Ganapati, leader of the dwarf demons of Śiva, to become pan-Indian, losing ancient tribal and regional origins. Ganeśa even transcended his association with Śiva, for all Indians are likely to have his image in their business or on a family shrine.

The most important features of his mythology involve his birth story, how he came to have an elephant's head, how he received the power to remove obstacles, and how he became the god of wealth.

An account in the *Linga Purâna* gave one version of his origin. The *asuras* and the *râkshasas* performed sacrifices and austerities and received a boon from Śiva by which they were able to defeat the *devas* (gods) in battle. Indra and the other gods complained to Śiva and prayed that he would create an obstacle for the *asuras* and *râkshasas*. Śiva created from himself a being, Vighneshvara, the lord of obstacles, who would place all sorts of objects in the way of the *asuras* and *râkshasas* and frustrate their attempts to gain merit from their sacrifices and austerities, thereby decreasing the effectiveness of their boon. Vighneshvara came from Śiva's *amshas,* a part of his power, that was placed in the womb of Pârvatî. As soon as Vighneshvara was born, he obstructed the wicked and aided the righteous.

The account of Vighneshvara's birth in the *Śiva Purâna* acknowledged other versions but utilized an interesting device to both affirm them and give a new version, saying that in different ages *(kalpas)* of creation there have been different origins of Vighneshvara. Then it continued to tell about the origin of Vighneshvara in the *Śveta-kalpa* (a long ago cosmic age). In that *kalpa* Pârvatî's companions, Jayâ and Vijayâ, tried to convince her that she needed her own servant. And when Śiva intruded into her bath, she decided to create a gate-keeper *(dvârapâlaka)* from a little dirt from her skin. In so doing, she created a formidable being, Vighneshvara. The next time that Śiva attempted to burst in upon his wife, Vighneshvara prevented him—even driving him away with a cane that left a few cuts on Śiva. Furious, Śiva sent his *Bhuta-ganas* (demons), who were also promptly defeated. The gods, including Vishnu, tried to gain Śiva's favor by defeating this upstart. Pârvatî saw the gods ganging up on her son and sent two fierce goddesses to help with magic. They protected Vighneshvara from injury by using *mâyâ* ("magic," "illusion") to misdirect the aim of the god's weapons. Then Vishnu, lord of mâyâ, confused the goddesses, and they returned to Pârvatî. At that moment Śiva attacked Vighneshvara and easily cut off his head. Of course, the meddling sage Nârada appeared to tell Pârvatî about the death of her son, and Pârvatî created a thousand fighting goddesses to punish the slayers. The gods were suffering pitifully, so Nârada and other sages raced to Pârvatî and begged that she end her revenge. This she did as soon as her son was brought back to life.

In all versions of this myth, Śiva sent attendants to find a head, and one of a dead elephant was brought back. That head had only one tusk *(eka-danta)* and would make Vighneshvara into the elephant-faced god *(gajânana),* Ganeśa. When Pârvatî saw her restored son, she took him before the assemblage of gods,

Ganeśa, son of Śiva, is worshipped for protection and as giver of wealth and remover of obstacles. (TRIP)

presided over by her husband Śiva, and presented her son. Śiva promptly apologized to all and gave Ganeśa command of his demon forces *(ganas),* acquiring a role that gained him the title Ganapati. Thus this version accounted for the origin of Vighneshvara, Gajânana, Ekadanta, and Ganapati, all different names of Ganeśa, without compromising Śiva as Lord of Yoga, asceticism. He was both father of Vighneshvara and still chaste.

Three *Purânas* offered another version (*Varâha, Matsya,* and *Skanda Purânas*). This version made Vighneshvara a material aid in the operation of *karma.* The gods, immortals, and sages noticed that both good and bad actions involved the same effort. So they went to Kailâsa and asked Lord Śiva to create some force that would make bad actions more difficult. While Śiva was contemplating their request, he looked at his wife Pârvatî, and that look produced a radiant youth with all of Śiva's *âkâshic* (psychic) qualities. But Pârvatî (referred to in these works by her other name, Umâ) was excited by Śiva's creation and cursed their son so that he would not become a temptation for all the female inhabitants of heaven. She cursed him with an elephant's head and a huge belly. Even so, Śiva gave him his names: Ganeśa Vinâyaka (the guide, the remover), Vighnarâja (king or lord of obstacles), Son of Śiva, Chief of the Vinâyakas (guides) and of the *ganas* (demons), Ganapati.

One of the alternate versions involved Parasu-Râma. Ganapati was guarding the entrance to Kailâsa while his father Śiva was sleeping. Meanwhile the sage Paraśu-Râma came there and tried to go inside. When he was continuously denied entrance by Ganapati, Parasu-Râma cut off one of Ganapati's tusks. Thereafter he had only half a tusk on his right side.

Ganapati has a prominent place among Hindu deities as the god who removes all obstacles. This is a natural extension of his strength as an elephant. He is worshipped as Vignesvara, the remover of all obstacles. A *puja* (ritual worship) is done to him by breaking a coconut at the *garba griha* (inner sanctuary) of the temple. Any activity should begin with a prayer to Vignesvara to remove all the obstacles in the way of accomplishing it. The form of Ganapati with his huge ears, trunk, and big belly is philosophically interpreted by Hindus as symbolizing openness of mind for acute receptivity and alertness.

In temple images, Ganapati (Ganeśa) is most often found in ensembles with Śiva and Parvatî. He has a large rat for his vehicle and, in many images, one broken tusk. His image is almost obligatory for businesses, since he has become the god of wealth.

See also Ganapati; Parvati; Śiva

GANGÂ

A river goddess

Gangâ is the holiest river of India. She is the Mother who washes away all sins and redeems one from the fetters of life. There are many folk songs about the Gangâ, which testify just how much the river has been personified, deified, and made an integral part of Hindu spiritual life.

The origin of river Gangâ is connected with the *avatâra* (incarnation) of Vishnu as Vâmana. When Vâmana measured the three worlds, the nail of his left foot caused a hole in the upper side of heaven's shell. From that hole, Gangâ originated and fell into heaven. The point of her origin is called Vishnupadî. For a long time Gangâ remained in the heavens. The spot where she originated on earth is called *Dhruva-mandala,* since the sage Dhruva did austerities *(tapas)* there for many years, resulting in the Gangâ's descent to earth.

The seven Rishis, who are the sages that begin each cosmic age, continually take their holy baths in the Gangâ. The holiness of the Gangâ is described in scripture (such as the *Mahâbhârata* and the *Agni Purâna*). Even today, in spite of its polluted water, a dip in the Gangâ is believed to remove all sins and bless one with heaven. The festival of Kumbhamela (celebrated every twelve years) is attended by many tens of thousands of people to offer their worship *(pujas)* to Mother Gangâ.

The heavenly Gangâ prepares to flow to earth through Śiva's matted locks. (TRIP)

The descent of the celestial Gangâ to earth is described in the *Bhâgavata Purâna*. Many of the names are mythical, referring to heavenly regions and sacred geography. Gangâ originated from Vishnupâda (the foot of Vishnu) and flowed to *devayâna* (literally, the way of the Gods). From *devayâna* it descended to Candramandala. From Candramandala, Gangâ divided into four tributaries called Sîtâ, Cakshusa, Alakanandâ, and Bhadrâ, and then fell into Brahmaloka (Brahma's land in heaven). It fell in various directions from Brahmaloka. Of the four tributaries, Sîtâ fell on the head of Mount Meru and then flowed down to earth around Gandhamâdana, went around Bhadrâsvavarsa, and emptied into the eastern sea. Cakshusa fell on Mount Mâlyavân, went around the land of Ketumâla, and emptied into the western sea. Alakanandâ fell on Mount Hema-kuta, flowed around the land of Bharatavarsa (India), and emptied into the southern sea. Bhadrâ fell on Mount Sringavân, flowed around the land of Uttarkuru, and emptied into the northern sea.

One myth connected the river goddess Sarasvatî with Gangâ. Vishnu was talking to his three wives: Lakshmî, Sarasvatî, and Gangâ. During the conversation Gangâ passed playful glances toward Vishnu behind the backs of Sarasvatî and Lakshmî. Sarasvatî saw this and became very annoyed. She got up and started beating Gangâ. A fight raged between them. Meanwhile Lakshmî tried to intervene. Disliking her intervention Sarasvatî cursed Lakshmî to be born on earth. Gangâ cursed Sarasvatî in return to be born as a river on earth. Sarasvatî immediately cursed Gangâ back to be born on earth as a river too. At this juncture Vishnu pacified all three wives but said that the curses had to have their effects and could not be taken back. Lakshmî was born as the Tulasi plant (Ocsimum Sanctum) in the *aśrama* of the sage Dharmadvaja and grew up as his daughter. An *asura* (demon) named Sankhachuda who was a partial incarnation of Vishnu married her. In due course she became a river called Padmavatî. As the Padmavatî River, Lakshmî left her earthly form and returned to Vaikuntha (Vishnu's heavenly abode). Gangâ was led to earth by the prayers of King Bhagî-ratha and became a mighty river. She married a king called Santanu and gave birth to the Ashtavasus (eight Vasus who were attendants to Indra). After their birth she returned to Kailâsa and became the spouse of Śiva. Sarasvatî became a river on earth, and, leaving her mortal form there, went to Brahmaloka and became the spouse of Brahma. This version was given in the *Bhâgavata Purâna*. Many other versions are told, including the one when the Gangâ flows to earth from Śiva's matted hair.

See also Bhagîratha; Kailâsa; Lakshmî; Sarasvati; Śiva; Vishnu
For further reading:
Diana L. Eck, "Ganga: The Goddess in Hindu Sacred Geography," in *The Divine Consort: Radha and the Goddesses of India*, edited by John Stratton Hawley

and Donna M. Wulff (Berkeley: University of California Press, 1982); Steven
G. Darian, *The Ganges in Myth and History* (Honolulu: University of Hawaii,
1978)

GARUDA
The king of birds and the celestial vehicle of Vishnu
Garuda, or Garutman, as he was known in the *Vedas*, was appropriated in the
devotional myths of the epic and Purânic periods as the servant vehicle of Lord
Vishnu. The name Garuda has as its verbal root *gri* (to speak). In the Vedas
Garuda is the metaphor for, or, for those who would literalize these concepts,
the personification of, the magical words *(mantra, rik)*. Thus it was on Garuda's
wings that one was transported to the realm of the gods (either the mantras or
"the self," which could be understood metaphorically as either the subtle realm
where the mantras had their origin or as the Self, the deepest level of consciousness and of all reality). Before Garuda was completely literalized, Vishnu rode as
his vehicle *(vâhana)* on rhythms *(rik)*, sounds *(sâman)*, and sacrifices *(yâjña)*,
the components of Vedic ritual. Garuda's role in another mythology, the cult of
Sûrya (sun) as the Supreme, has left few traces except its late reconstruction at
the great sun temple at Konâraka.

In Purânic mythology Garuda myths abound. The vehicle of Lord Vishnu
had a great birth, worthy deeds, and supreme powers. His birth stories all
attested to his importance, even though they were otherwise inconsistent. One
version had him born on the basis of the great austerities *(tapas)* of his mother,
Vinatâ. Both she and her rival, Kadrû, were given boons by their husband
Kaśyapa-Prajâpati. Kadrû chose to have a thousands sons, the *nâgas* (snakes), and
they hatched first. Vinatâ chose only to have two sons, but ones greater than
Kadrû's. In her impatience Vinatâ opened one of her two eggs and brought Aruna
(the red one) half-hatched into the world. Aruna cursed his mother with servi-
tude and left to become Sûrya's charioteer. (For more, see the entry on Aruna.
Note here another connection between Garuda and Sûrya. Garuda was born from
the second egg and then served the god who appropriated Sûrya's powers and
attributes as a solar deity, Vishnu.)

Kadrû (the vessel for *soma*) and Vinatâ (personification of bowing to knowledge) are literalized as rival wives. These personifications sanskritize the myth
and turn Vedic concepts into goddesses. Vinatâ became the humiliated servant
of Kadrû, helping tend her sons.

Other versions told of Garuda as the product of Kaśyapa's practices *(yâjñas)*
combined with the magical practices *(yâga-śaktî)* of the Bâlakhilyas, a class of
tiny divine sages, each the size of a thumb. They gave their accumulated merit

to Kaśyâpa to have a son who would defeat Indra. Garuda was the result: so brilliant that he hurt the gods' eyes and worshipped by them mistakenly as Agni. Garuda was a shape-changer, going wherever he pleased, stopping the rotation of the worlds with the wind from his wings, with eyes of fire, and an enemy of snakes.

At this point the mythic versions merged. Garuda had to free his mother from the tyranny of Kadrû and her *nâga* children. A bargain was made for an exchange of the pot of divine nectar *(amrita)* for his mother's freedom. Garuda flew to heaven, fought the *devas* (gods), blinding them with a sandstorm from his great wings and taking the pot of amrita. He so impressed Vishnu that Vishnu granted him a boon of immortality. Garuda pledged that he would serve Vishnu and become his vehicle. Indra and Garuda fought again, and a respect arose between the two heroes after their combat. Garuda told Indra why he had stolen the pot of amrita, not for himself but to save his mother. He told Indra to follow and steal it back from the nâgas. Then he flew to their kingdom, exchanged the pot for his mother, and flew away. Garuda had told them that they must be pure before drinking the nectar of immortality. So, while the nâgas took a bath, Indra stole the amrita and took it back to the *devas.* The nâgas licked the *darbha* grass where the pot had been placed, and the sharp grass split their tongues.

More Garuda myths abound, both about the great eagle alone and as Vishnu's servant vehicle. He made an interesting mythological appearance in the royal symbolism of Buddhist Thailand, where, as the sun eagle, he represented royal power and divine approval.

See also Amrita; Aruna; Vishnu

GAUTAMA
One of the seven sages (sapta-rishis)
There were references to Gautama's name in the *Rigveda*. In a hymn that was later literalized, Indra as a metaphor of the morning carried off night. Indra's character became that of a seducer of sages' wives, and Ahalyâ ("unplowed"), the wife of Gautama, became one of them.

The number of versions of the seduction of Ahalyâ showed how many ways it could be utilized in Purânic mythology. (For another version see the entry on Ahalyâ). In a version where Ahalyâ was innocent, Indra came to the *âshrâma*, was given fruit by Ahalyâ, and left without harming her. But the old *rishi* Gautama returned, assumed she was guilty, ordered his son to cut off her head, and went back into the forest. Cirakâri sat down and pondered *dharma* (in the form of his duty to obey his father) and *karma* (in the form of the offense of killing his

*Gautama Buddha becomes merely an **avatâra** of Lord Vishnu in order to lead sinners astray with false teachings. (TRIP)*

mother). Fortunately, Cirakâri was not quick of mind, and his father had time to return in a better frame of mind and bless him for his thoughtfulness.

Gautama was given so many roles of blessings and cursings in the *Purânas* (cursing Ahalyâ, cursing Indra, blessing King Kalmâshapâda, blessing Dyumat-sena, and so on) that one might not be wrong in concluding that he was a personification of the complex logic of the curse and the blessing.

See also Ahalyâ; Magic, Blessings, Cursings; Mâyâ; Râma; *Râmâyana*; Sapta-Rishis

GAVIJÂTA

Son of a sage, who cursed a king

In the *Devî Bhâgavata* the sage Nâgabhushana ("one having snakes as his ornament," a sage whose name was a pun, pointing to the object of the story, Śiva) was deep in meditation at his forest hermitage. King Parîkshit, grandson of Arjuna, came to him desiring water after a long hunt. But Nâgabhushana did not respond. Parîkshit put a dead snake on the sage's neck, but there was still no response. The king returned to the palace thirsty. Nâgabhushana's son, Gavijâta, was teased by companions that his father really was "one having dead snakes as his ornament." The son immediately cursed the one who had done this to be bitten by the king of snakes, Takshâka, and die within seven days. When Gavijâta learned what the king's provocation had been, he went to the king and warned him of the curse so that there might be countermeasures. But Parîkshit stated that he was ready to die when the time for death came.

See also Magic, Blessings, Cursings; Mâyâ; Parîkshit; Takshâka

GHANTA-KARNA, GHANTÂKANTA

Râkshasa (demonic) brothers

Ghanta and Karna were brothers in some sources, but the older *râkshasa* was called by both names, Ghantâkanta, as the myths were about him. Ghanta's myth was nested within several others and modified in sectarian versions competing over who was the supreme deity, Śiva or Vishnu.

Ghantâkarna came into being because Śiva had to create a terrible demon to correct a misuse of a boon that he had granted to Mandodarî, wife of a demon named Dâruka. The story goes like this: Dâruka had done austerities *(tapas)* in order to gain a boon from Brahmâ and then used it to make life miserable for the *devas* (gods). They in turn sought relief from Śiva, who created Bhadrakâlî from his third eye. Bhadrakâlî killed Dâruka and left his wife Mandodarî grieving. Mandodarî then did severe *tapas* and won a gift from Śiva, some drops of sweat from his body. Śiva told her that these drops would cause smallpox to anyone upon whom they were sprinkled. So of course the demoness Mandodarî, as goddess of smallpox, made her first victim Bhadrakâlî. As Bhadrakâlî suffered from a life-threatening case of smallpox, Śiva created the *rākshasa* Ghantâkarna to help her. Ghantâkarna had the power *(śakti)* to lick the smallpox from her body. However, Bhadrakâlî stopped him before he licked her face, pointing out that Ghantâkarna and she were brother and sister, since both were from Śiva, and it would be wrong for Ghantâkarna to lick the face of his sister.

Ghantâkarna at first took Vishnu to be his enemy. He put bells *(ghantâ)* in his ears *(karnas)* to prevent hearing any mention of Vishnu. However, Śiva instructed Ghantâkarna that Vishnu was greater than he (Śiva). So Ghantâkarna became a devotee of Vishnu and sought to obtain salvation from him. One day Shrî Krishna was meditating at a hermitage called Badarya-aśrama and heard the sounds of *Piśâcas,* hungry souls of the dead, and their hunting dogs. They were led by Ghantâkarna, who was reciting the name of Vishnu (a practice called *japa).* Krishna blessed him and appeared as Viśvarûpa, the all embracing form of the supreme lord of the universe. At once Ghantâkarna brought the best offering a râkshasa knew to give, a dead corpse of a *brâhmin.* Krishna looked past the gift into the heart of this demon and touched his body. Immediately the demon lost his form and entered Vaikuntha, Vishnu's paradise.

Ghantâkarna's image with eighteen hands is worshiped in Vaishnava temples as the god who cures diseases that result from one's own sins. Ghantâkarna was the *râkshasa* who became a *deva.*

See also Magic, Blessings, Cursings; Mâyâ; Śiva; Tapas; Vishnu

GHATOTKACA
Son of Bhîma by his râkshasa wife Hidumbhî

In the *Râmâyana* the tale is told that soon after the Pandava brothers began their forest exile, a *râkshasa* chief sent his sister, Hidumbhî, to capture them for his dinner. However, Hidumbhî fell in love with Bhîma, the strongest and most physical of the brothers. The *râkshasa* chief came to collect his dinner himself but was promptly killed. Hidumbhî begged Kuntî, mother of the Pandavas, to intercede for her with Bhîma. So the clan allowed their marriage with the condition, that it would only be valid in the forest and the mountains during the day. At night Bhîma would return for his turn as husband of Draupadî, the brothers' joint wife. Ghatotkaca was born to Bhîma and Hidumbhî and became a great help both in the forest and later on the Kurukshetra battlefield. During the great war Ghatotkaca proved to be one of the greatest warriors, killing Kaurava allies, including kings on their war elephants, and winning great duels against other heroes. Finally, he was killed by Karna (son of Kuntî and Sûrya), who had to use his magical weapon *(vaijayantî śaktî)* to kill Ghatotkaca instead of using it on Arjuna. Thus Ghatotkaca died a hero's death. He appeared on the banks of the Gangâ with the rest when the souls of the heroes were called from death by Vyâsa for the Kauravas' mother, Gândhârî. After death, he lived in the heaven of the *Yaksha-devas.*

See also Arjuna; Bhîma; Draupadî; Gândhârî; Kuntî; Pandavas; Râkshasa; *Râmâyana;* Siddhi

GHOSHÂ

A woman sage

Ghoshâ was mentioned in the *Rigveda* several times. She was born from a fine lineage of sages. Her grandfather was the *mahârishi* Drigata and her father was Kakshîvân. As a child she contracted leprosy, and consequently no one would marry her. Consequently, she studied and practiced great austerities and became a great magician *(tapasvinî).* However, her greatest accomplishment was a hymn in praise of the Aśvins, the twin physicians of the *devas.* Greatly flattered, the Aśvins cured her of leprosy. Then she married.

See also Aśvins; Siddhi; Tapas

GHRITÂCÎ

An apsara

Ghritâcî was an *apsara,* a heavenly nymph. Her beauty was so overwhelming that many great *brâhmins,* whether married *rishi* (sage) or ascetic, fell victim to her charms. Several, Bharadvâja and Vyâsa, saw her and after years of ascetic practice *(tapasya)* had seminal emissions, followed by miraculous births of sons. Later Bharadvâja saw her again and lost control a second time, only to have a noble daughter, Śrutâvatî. Others of her conquests included King Pramati, sage Ashthâvakra, and sage Viśvakarman. She danced at Arjuna's birthday celebration without any serious disruption. Her myths were a reminder of how easy it was to lose decades of merit from austerities *(tapas)* for a moment's pleasure.

See also Apsara; Arjuna; Bharadvâja; Tapas

GOTAMA

A sage mentioned in the Rigveda

This sage was probably a historical person of the Vedic period. Gotama, son of Rahûgana, was not the sage Gautama, husband of Ahalyâ. There were many references to Gotama in the *Rigveda.* He wrote hymns contained in the seventy-fourth *sûkta* of the thirteenth *anuvâka* of the first *mandala* of the *Rigveda.*

There are two versions of a story about a well. Once Gotama was very thirsty and asked the Maruts for some water. The Maruts took a whole well to him and poured the water into a pot at his hermitage *(aśrama)*. Another version said that it was not the Maruts but the Aśvinidevas who took the well to the aśrama of Gotama. Because references to myths in the *Rigveda* were usually incomplete and seemed to presuppose the hearers' knowledge of the story's context and meaning, we are left to puzzle over its point. Having the gods bring a well of water to a sage would seem to prove the greatness of this sage, but if that was the point, one would think Gotama would have received more mention in later mythology.

See also Aśvins; Maruts

GUNASHARMAN
A brâhmin magician and sage and king
In the *Purânas*, Gunasharman's story is nested within an episode about his father Âdityasharman. The father used his great spiritual powers *(tapas)* to create an *apsara* (heavenly damsel) for himself, whom he named Sulocanâ. When a son, Gunasharman, was born to them, Âdityasharman became a *deva* (god) and went to *Brahmaloka* (heaven). One day Indra came to visit Âdityasharman, who could not be aroused from his contemplation. Indra was insulted and cursed him to be born a mortal again on earth. Âdityasharman immediately became alert and tried to placate Indra's anger. Indra decided that it would be punishment enough for his son Gunasharman to suffer the curse of his father.

Gunasharman grew up as a mortal and developed in all the sciences and arts, just as his father had done. He became an intimate of King Mahâsena and Queen Aśokavatî of Ujjayinî. He even used his spiritual powers to rescue Mahâsena when he was captured in battle. One day the king asked Gunasharman to give a dance performance, which he did with such beauty and grace that the king had Gunasharman teach dance to his wife. Naturally, the queen fell in love with her wonderful teacher. However, he rejected her love. Queen Aśokavatî then told the king that Gunasharman had acted improperly toward her, so Gunasharman had to flee the palace, evading the king's guards only by his magical powers. He hid in the hermitage of Agnidatta and married Agnidatta's daughter, Sundarî. There Gunasharman practiced austerities *(tapas)* to acquire more powers, propitiating Subrahmanya (also called Kârttikeya, son of Śiva and commander-in-chief of Śiva's minions) and receiving martial powers from him. Then he returned to the kingdom of Ujjayinî, used these powers to conquer it, and became its king. King Mahâsena and Queen Aśokavatî were exiled.

Was *dharma* served? Perhaps Gunasharman completed the ritual to change caste from *brâhmin* to *kśatriya*, but the myths do not add that detail.

See also Apsara; Magic, Blessings, Cursings; Mâyâ; Siddhi; Subrahmanya; Tapas

HALÂHALA

A poison

Some accounts stated that *halâhala* had been churned up from the Milky Ocean and absorbed by the *nâgas* (serpents) and became their venom. Other accounts said that *halâhala* was the poison vomited up by Vâsuki, king of the nâgas, during the time of the churning of the Milky Ocean. In order to prevent it from falling to earth and destroying everything, Śiva drank it. Pârvatî had to act quickly and pressed his neck to prevent the poison from going inside Śiva's body. The poison was absorbed in Śiva's neck, which turned blue. Henceforth, he was known as *Nilakanta*, which means the blue-necked one.

See also Kshîrâbdhi-Mathanam

HAMSA, HANSA

(1) An incarnation of Vishnu in Krita Yuga (the second age)

According to the *Bhâgavata Purâna* Hamsa was a *prajâpati*, a progenitor or creator. Hamsa taught *yoga* to sages like Sanaka and taught the way to liberation for the *Sâdhyadevas*, a class of divine witnesses of battles and celebrations in late mythology. Hamsa, like Vishnu, was also called the sacrifice *(yâjña)*. The teachings of Hamsa were known as the *Hamsa Gîtâ*, a sacred book no longer extant. Hamsa did not become important enough to be included in lists of incarnations of Vishnu and became one of the many incarnations to be forgotten or reduced to a category of partial incarnations.

See also Avatâra; Vishnu

(2) A gandharva (celestial musician)

Hamsa was given a partial incarnation as Dhritarâshthra, whose role in the *Mahâbhârata* deserved an important prior existence. As a *gandharva*, he was the son of Kaśyapa-Prajâpati by his wife Arishtâ.

See also Dhritarâshthra; Gandharvas; Kaśyapa

HAMSA (also HANSA)

Swans

See Arayanna

HANUMAN

A monkey and a god

Hanuman expanded the notion of the divine, perhaps more than any other being in Hindu mythology. He appeared as an agent governed by *dharma* like any human, yet while in an animal form he was divine. The myths of his birth from the elements of the gods, usually of Śiva and Vâyu (the wind god), proved his divinity. There were four different myths of his divine birth, ranging from the union of Śiva and Vishnu to one about his mother, Anjanâ, eating a divine pudding that made her pregnant.

Hanuman's name has traditionally been associated with the legend of Śrî Râma. Nevertheless, he has gained an independent status as a god in recent folk myths that have spread from northern to southern India. His status is evidenced by the popularity of the forty rhymes of Tulsidas (the great medieval poet), *Hanuman Câlisa,* glorifying Hanuman as a deity, by his presence in popular films and poster art, and by the reverence shown to ordinary monkeys in modern India.

Myths about Hanuman told of his mighty power and his ability to perform superhuman tasks. Hanuman lifted up the whole mountain of Kailâsa and brought it to Râma in order for him to find a special medicinal herb. Hanuman built the bridge across the ocean *(setubandhana)* to reach Lanka, slew the demoness of Mount Mainâka, and led his army of monkeys in the battle against Râvana.

Hanuman was portrayed in the myths as, and is still believed to be, a great *yogi* as well as an unusually talented musician. He was described as possessing the *ashtha siddhis* (the eight superhuman powers), such as being able to be light as a feather or impossible to move, to become invisible, to fly, and to reduce or enlarge his form. He was one of the rare beings who were truly immortal; he would never see death. Apart from all this, Hanuman was an erudite grammarian and poet. But what distinguished him from other Hindu gods was the way he acquired divine status—simply by his deep-rooted devotion to Śrî Râma, who was an incarnation of Vishnu. He was, and is, the best example to Hindus of an ideal devotee and the most adorable and worshipped among the popular devotees in the Hindu pantheon. (Other examples are Dhruva, Prahalâda, and Arjuna.)

An early reference mentioned Hanuman as an incarnation of the eleventh Rudra (a *deva*). It is quite possible that Hanuman might have been a deity of a local tribe, later adopted as a Hindu divinity.

The origin of this god can be traced back to the myth of the churning of the Milky Ocean as told in the *Śiva Purâna,* which stated that he was the son of Śiva and the feminine form of Vishnu as Môhinî. The semen of Śiva was deposited in the womb of Anjanâ by the seven *rishis (saptarishis).* (A recent variation of the

Hanuman, the paradigm of loyal friend in his service to Râma, takes his divine form in order to bring a mountain with healing herbs. (TRIP)

Hanuman myth associates the union of Śiva and Môhinî with the origin of Swami Ayyappa, a very popular deity in South India, merging past and present, theriomorphic deity and sage.)

Other variations of the story of the origin of Hanuman stated that he was the son of Vâyu, the wind god, or the son of Kesari, the monkey chieftain. One account said that both Śiva and Vâyu assumed the form of Kesari and had intercourse with Anjanâ. As the son of Vâyu Hanuman would be connected with the myths about Bhîma, who in the *Mahâbhârata* is also a son of Vâyu.

Hanuman was one of the few gods who has been given episodes in every period of Hindu mythology. His life stretched between two incarnations of Vishnu in this *kalpa* and involved associations with them both: with Śrî Râma in *treta yuga* and with Śrî Krishna in *dvâpara yuga,* the age that followed. His devotees put these different embedded myths together to prove that Hanuman had a presence in all ages and thus had perfect immortality, a boon Hanuman was given by Śrî Râma. He was known as one of the *ciranjivis,* the seven beings who would never experience death.

Iconographically, Hanuman is easily recognizable as a monkey who is either the loyal servant of Râma or the great warrior of the *Râmâyana.* As a servant his two hands are held together in a mood of devotion *(añjali-hasta).* As a warrior he holds a thunderbolt *(vajra)* in one hand, and his feet seem to tear up the ground beneath him.

See also Añjana; Ciranjivis; Râma; *Râmâyana;* Râvana; Sîtâ
For further reading:
K. C. and Subhasini Aryan, *Hanuman in Art and Mythology* (Delhi: Rekha
    Prakashan, 1970.); Hari Prasad Sastri, trans., *The Ramayana of Valmiki,* 3
    vols. (London: Shanti Sadan Publications, 1962).

HARA

An epithet of Śiva

Hara (the remover) was an epithet first associated with Rudra and the Maruts, both gods of storm. It had the connotation of death, the destruction that removes all things. By the Epic period Hara referred to Śiva, the destroyer.

There was a manifestation of the godhead as Harihara, the right half as Hara, or Śiva, and the left half as Hari or Vishnu. Found in a number of temples, Harihara has the matted hair of Śiva and all of Śiva's ornaments and weapons on the right, and the crown of Vishnu and all of his ornament and weapons on the left.

See also Hari; Śiva; Vishnu

HARI

(1) An epithet of Vishnu

Coming from the same root as the epithet Hara for Śiva (*hri*, to remove), Hari also means "the remover." There are many minor figures with this name, as well as a number of groups (some of the demon king Râvana's attendants, a group of *devas*, and others). Eventually, however, it became an epithet synonymous with Vishnu, the remover of the sorrows of the world. Hari has been heard around the world in its vocative form, *Hare*, chanted by Hare Krishnas as the opening word of the great *Hare Krishna mantra* of salvation.

See also Hara; Śiva; Vishnu

(2) A son of Dharma-deva, the god Dharma

Hari (the remover) was a son of the god Dharma (righteousness). The other three sons were Krishna (the dark one), Nara (man), and Nârâyana (moving on the waters). All these figures had characteristics and myths associated with love and devotion *(bhakti)* directed to a personal god.

See also Dharma; Krishna; Nara; Nârâyana

HARIDHÂMA

A sage

Haridhâma was a great sage devoted to Krishna who wanted nothing more than to be reborn near his lord. Consequently, he was reborn as Rangavenî, a female cowherd (*gopikâ* or *gopî*) in Gokula, the cow-tending colony. Thus, Rangavenî was near Krishna, which was the reward for his chanting the Krishna *mantra* so many times. The myth taught a devotion *(bhakti)* so great that one would become like a woman, longing for Krishna's love.

See also Krishna

HARIMITRA

A righteous brâhmin

In the *Padma Purâna* Harimitra had an *aśrama* (hermitage) on the banks of the river Yamunâ. A sinner named Vikundala became associated with Harimitra and followed his practice of a ritual bath in the Yamunâ. It just happened that he took a bath twice in the Yamunâ during the Hindu month of Magha. Vikundala was liberated from all his sins with the first bath, and with the second he was eligible to go to heaven. Vikundala's good *karma* came from right association with a righteous *brâhmin* and from following rituals prescribed in the scriptures.

See also Yâjña

HARISCANDRA

A king of Ayodhyâ

King Hariscandra of Ayodhyâ was very famous for his commitment to truth and for keeping his promises. Victim of a great magician's magical powers, Hariscandra represents all righteous persons who have suffered wrongly. Hariscandra lost his kingdom, his wife, and his only son, for the sake of keeping his word. For further details about the magician's wrath, see the entry on Viśvâmitra. There was also another story about his father, Triśanku (three sins), who could not get into heaven but had a heaven made for himself between heaven and earth.

Finally, Hariscandra was blessed by the Trimûrtis (the divine triad), was granted prosperity, and got back everything that he had lost.

See also Apunya; Viśvâmitra

HARITÂŚVA

A king of the Sûrya-vamsa (solar dynasty)

In the Epics kings could be as great as gods. One such king was Haritâśva, king of Ayodhyâ. He was greatly accomplished in the arts. He surpassed the sage Nârada and the goddess Sarasvatî in music. He pleased Brahmâ with his music and put Vishnu to sleep. Once Śiva was competing with Haritâśva and played a particular *raga*, a musical piece, called *sankarâbharana,* dedicated to Lord Śiva. Haritâśva pointed out that instead of the *santa rasa,* the emotion of peace, it should be played in *raudra rasa,* the emotion of anger. Śiva became furious and opened his third eye at Haritâśva. Gods like Kâma had been burned to ashes by Śiva's third eye. Haritâśva, however, was not intimidated because he knew that he was right. Śiva was pleased with his excellence and courage and blessed Haritâśva with wealth and prosperity.

A greater test came later. The gods were being abused by a great demon, Andhaka-asura. He conquered heaven *(svarga)* against the combined efforts of the Trimûrti (Brahmâ, Vishnu, and Śiva). Brihaspati, priest of the gods, advised them to get help from King Haritâśva. Agastya, a great *rishi* of superhuman powers, told Haritâśva that the demon was protected with images of Śiva and Pârvatî in his belly. Consequently, Haritâśva fired his arrows at Andhaka-asura's belly, removing his protection, and killed him. That was how a king restored Deva-loka *(svarga)* to Indra (king of the *devas*) and the gods.

See also Andhak; Nârada; Sarasvatî

HARIVAMSA

An appendix to the *Mahâbhârata*

This appendix to the *Mahâbhârata* is said to be authored by Vyâsa, as indicated in the Adi Parva (2.83–84) of the *Mahâbhârata*. The *Harivamsa* consists of glorifications of Vishnu and has about ten thousand verses. It is a rich source for the myths about the childhood of Krishna, as well as for myths about the Vâmana (dwarf) and Narasimha (man-lion) incarnations of Vishnu.

See also Mahâbhârata

HARYASHVAS

See Aśiknî

HAVYAGHNA

A râkshasa

Havyaghna had a miraculous birth, being created from the smoke of a sacrificial ritual *(yâjña)* of the sage Bharadvâja. Havyaghna ("leavings of the sacrifice") began eating the leftovers *(havis)* of that yâjña. Bharadvâja asked the demon why he would do this. Havyaghna explained that he was the Krishna that Brahmâ had cursed and could be freed from that curse if Bharadvâja would sprinkle him with Gangâ water, ghee, and *soma*. When Bharadvâja did as asked, Havyaghna was redeemed from Brahmâ's curse.

See also Bharadvâja; Magic, Blessings, Cursings; Mâyâ

HAYAGRÎVA

(1) A deva (god)

In the *Pañcavimsa Brâhmana* the story is told that four *devas* began a sacrifice *(yâjña)* with the agreement that the offering *(havirbhâga)* would be shared equally. They were Agni, Indra, Vâyu, and Yâjña. But Yâjña stole the offering and drove the others away with a divine bow given by Devî. So the *devas* created termites *(cital)*, and they ate through the bowstring. It straightened with such force that it severed Yâjña's head from his body. The *devas* took pity on his plight and put a horse's head on Yâjña's body.

See also Agni; Devî; Indra; Vâyu; Yâjña

(2) A demon *(asura)* and an incarnation of Vishnu

This Purânic myth told of two Hayagrîvas—one a demon and the other Vishnu, or rather his incarnation. The first phase of the story set the scene for the lord's rescue of the world from the demon's evil.

Hayagrîva the *asura* was the son of Kaśyapa-prajâpati by his wife Danu. He practiced austerities *(tapas)* for a thousand years and got the attention of Devî. She appeared and offered him a boon. He asked to become both invincible and immortal. She knew that even Brahmâ would only give these qualities as provisional boons, so Hayagrîva had to settle for the boon of only being killed by another Hayagrîva (one with the neck of a horse). Since there were no others in the entire universe, he went on a rampage. He even fought Lord Vishnu until even Vishnu needed a rest. However, Vishnu slept as a warrior should, sitting up with one end of his bow in the ground and the other end under his chin.

Unfortunately, there had been a curse that would make this sleep result in Vishnu losing his head. Long ago, Vishnu had laughed in Lakshmî's presence, and she cursed him, thinking that he no longer thought her beautiful. She said that his head would be severed from his body. That was about to happen. Hayagrîva tormented the gods until they had to awaken Vishnu. So Brahmâ created termites *(cital)* and bribed them with a promise that they could have the leftovers *(havis)* of the sacrifices *(yâjñas)* if they gnawed through the bowstring so that its release would awaken Vishnu. They did, but the bow cut off his head. Some accounts stated that he found a new head for himself, others that the gods did—but the result was the same. The head was from a horse, and Vishnu became a Hayagrîva (one with the neck of a horse). As in other incarnations, Vishnu was able to end the evil that had come into the world and restore its harmony. There were many versions of this story, but they all gave Vishnu the neck of a horse and victory over Hayagrîva, the *asura*.

See also Devî; Kaśyapa; Magic, Blessings, Cursings; Mâyâ; Vishnu

(3) An asura

During the time of the Vaivashvata Manu (also known as the Satyavrata Manu), while Brahmâ was reciting the *Vedas*, Hayagrîva stole them. Matsya, an incarnation of Vishnu, recovered the *Vedas*, which had fallen into the ocean from the mouth of Brahmâ when he fell asleep at the beginning of one of his nights—the end of a Yuga and the beginning of a Pralaya (period of dissolution and cosmic flood).

See also Brahmâ; Matsya

HEMAKÂNTA

A prince

While Brâhmanical ideology taught that killing a *brâhmin (brahmahatyâ)* was the worst of sins and required loss of caste, Purânic mythology told of those who had killed a *brâhmin* and escaped becoming outcaste *(candâla)*. This alternative view shifted the focus to devotion *(bhakti)* and its outward signs in gifts of compassion *(dâna)* and grace *(prasâda)* from the Supreme. So the story in the *Skanda Purâna* about Hemakânta, a prince, had real importance. Hemakânta, the son of the King Kusaketu, committed *brahmahatyâ,* the sin of killing a *brâhmin,* on a victim named Śatârcas. He was absolved of that sin when he gave a *brâhmin* named Trita some water to drink.

See also Bhakti; Catur-Varna

HEMAMÂLI

A celestial gardener

In this late myth in the *Padma Purâna,* Kubera, god of wealth, is portrayed as a devotionalist *(bhakta).* He had a wonderful garden with beautiful flowers that he used in temple worship each day. One day his gardener, Hemamâli, came back from a visit to the lake of the gods, Mânasasaras, filled with love for his beautiful wife, Visâlâkshî. He forgot all about his duty to get flowers to Kubera for his worship. Kubera waited all day at the temple, but Hemamâli was sporting with his wife. Kubera became very angry and summoned Hemamâli to his palace. Hemamâli apologized and told the truth. Kubera placed a curse on Hemamâli: that he would become a leper. Then Kubera expelled Hemamâli from Alakapuri, Kubera's heaven.

Hemamâli met the sage Mârkandeya, to whom he told his sad story. The sage advised him to observe a specific kind of fasting with *mantras,* called *aśâda Krishna ekadâshi* (worship of Krishna to remove a punishment). Hemamâli observed the *ekadâshi* and was cured of leprosy. From his *tapas* (austerities) he again gained Devaloka (heaven).

See also Kubera; Magic, Blessings, Cursings; Mâyâ

HIRANYAGARBHA

The golden egg or womb

The word *hiranyagarbha* is found in the Vedic literature referring to the primeval origin of the world within a golden womb or shell. It remained an image that was not greatly developed. For further details, refer to chapter 1 on creation myths, "Cosmogony, Theogony, and Anthropogony."

HIRANYAHASTA

Son of a princess

Hiranyahasta's story came from a time when gods had sons with princesses. Hiranyahasta's mother was Princess Vadhrimatî, who was married to a eunuch. Despondent that she could not have a child, Vadhrimatî prayed to the Aśvins, the divine twins. The physicians of the *devas* happily fulfilled her desire. Hiranyahasta grew up a sage, possibly even a *brâhmin*, since he married the daughter of the sage Matarisvan. Another version said he married a princess, the daughter of King Madirâshva.

　　See also Asvins; Varna

HIRANYAKASIPU
An asura (demon)

Hiranyakasipu was a worthy opponent of Lord Vishnu, born repeatedly, which necessitated multiple incarnations of Vishnu to conquer this powerful *asura* and restore *dharma* (righteousness) to earth. A demon of this magnitude would have quite a lineage and an appropriate source of his tremendous powers. There was a time before the life when he had this name when he was the very doorkeeper *(dvârapâlâkas)* of Lord Vishnu at Vaikuntha. His name in that previous birth was Jâya. His elder twin brother was Vijâya, also a doorkeeper. One day a group of hermits led by Sanaka came to Vaikuntha to see Vishnu. They were stopped by Jâya and Vijâya. But the sages took offense and cursed the doorkeepers to be reborn three times as demons *(asuras)*. The frightened doorkeepers begged the angry *brâhmins* for forgiveness, but they only slightly lessened the punishment: after three births, they would be redeemed by the weapon of Lord Vishnu.

　　Accordingly, the twins were reborn on earth as twin demons, Hiranyakasipu and Hiranyâksha, who came from the womb first. Their first earthly parents were Kasyapa-Prajâpati and his wife Ditî. After Hiranyâksha was killed by Lord Vishnu in his Vâmana (boar) *avatâra* (incarnation), Hiranyakasipu did austerities *(tapas)* in order to increase his strength and get revenge. He was so good at ascetic disciplines that he earned boons from Brahmâ and immediately conquered the three worlds. He was crowned Triloka Cakravarti (emperor of the three *lokas* [worlds]). He prevented everyone from saying Vishnu's name or even thinking about him. He instituted his own worship with the *mantra Hiranyâya namah* (salutation to Hiranya). However, his son, Prahlâda became a devotee to Vishnu and chanted *Nârâyanâya namah* (salutation to Nârâyana, in other words, Lord Vishnu). Hiranyakasipu was killed by the Narasimha incarnation of Vishnu (as man-lion).

　　See also Jâya; Kumbhakarna; Narasimha; Prahlâda; Râvana; Sisupâla; Vijâya

HIRANYÂKSHA
An asura (demon) and brother of Hiranyakasipu

Hiranyâksha was the elder twin of Hiranyakasipu. Their stories are intertwined through four lifetimes: first as Jâya and Vijâya when they were Vishnu's doorkeepers, then their first rebirth as Hiranyâksha and Hiranyakaśipu, a second rebirth as Râvana and Kumbhakarna, and finally their third rebirth as Śiśupâla and Dantavaktra.

Hiranyâksha was the eldest twin and began his rampage first. He stalked the three worlds with his war club and sent the *devas* (gods) running away in terror. In the meantime, the earth became flooded and the Manu of that age, Svayamb-huva, asked Brahmâ to raise the earth out of the waters. Some versions said that it was Hiranyâksha who had abducted Bhîmî (the earth) and taken her beneath the waters. So Brahmâ meditated on Lord Vishnu and a tiny boar *(vâmana)* came from Brahmâ's nose. The boar rapidly grew and then plunged into the waters and rescued Bhîmî. Hiranyâksha immediately knew that this enormous boar was Vishnu, so they fought a duel to the finish. Hiranyâksha was killed, and the proper order was brought back to the earth.

See also Bhîma; Jâya; Vâmana; Vishnu

IDÂ

A goddess

In the *Rigveda, idâ* was a word for food or refreshment, especially milk. In the hymns *idâ* worked metaphorically as the refreshment given to the *devas* (gods) as praise. Thus, it connected with *vâc* (sound) and could be personified as Idâ, the goddess who instructed the first Manu concerning the rules for an efficacious sacrifice.

In the *Taittirîya Brâhmana* the role of the priest can be seen as expanding; Idâ is described as created by the first Manu out of his sacrifice. She was sent by him to see how the *devas* performed the consecration of fire *(agnyâdhâna)*, and she returned with the shocking information that their method was less effective than hers. So she constructed the three firepits *(trividhâgnis)* properly. The *devas* invited her publicly to instruct them. The *asuras* (demons) seemed to have some reservations about being taught by a priestess, so they only invited her to come to them in secret. Idâ accepted the invitation of the *devas,* and her instructions were witnessed by all creatures. The story concluded that this was why all creatures came to worship the *devas* instead of the *asuras.*

The Idâ myth has elements that are quite ancient. There was a shamaness-priestess-goddess who taught gods and priests. There was, simultaneously, metaphor and personification. The clear process of ritualization can be seen as Idâ's birth from fire is changed to her birth as the daughter of the first Manu. And there is the boast in this myth that the sacrificial ritual *(yâjña)* of the *brâhmins* was more effective in controlling the powers *(mâyâ)* of the universe than the power of the gods.

See also Manu; Yâjña

ILÂ

Daughter of Vaivasvata-Manu and Śraddhâ

The myth of Ilâ is about the plasticity of gender, with Ilâ moving back and forth between male and female in the same lifetime. Ilâ's father, Vaivasvata-Manu, was the son of Kaśyapa-prajâpati and Aditi, the first parents in this myth. Her sons were all celestials and divine (*âdityas*) yet she was a mortal—this is one of the inconsistencies of Purânic myths.

Ilâ's parents, Vaivasvata Manu and Śraddhâ (trust), did not have children for a long time, so they asked Sage Agastya to perform a *yâjña* (sacrifice) to Mitra and Varuna for a son. However, a mistake was made in the ritual, and they received a daughter instead. They named her Ilâ (some versions say Idâ). They propitiated Mitra and Varuna, and Ilâ's sex was changed. Consequently, they named their son Sudyumna. But Śiva became displeased and changed Sudyumna back into Ilâ. At this point Ilâ married Budha (the planet Mercury) and gave birth to a son named Purûravas. Then by pleasing Vishnu, Ilâ was again changed into Sudyumna, married, and became the father of three sons.

There is another version that reverses all this. Vaivasvata-Manu and Śraddhâ did the sacrifice and received a son whom they named Ila. However, young Ila angered Pârvatî by trespassing in her sacred grove, so she turned him into a girl—Ilâ. After many prayers of supplication Śiva and Pârvatî changed the punishment to one month as a female followed by a month as a male for the remainder of that lifetime.

See also Âdityas; Agasti; Manu; Pârvatî; Śiva; Vaivasvata Manu

INDRA

A deva (god)

Indra's mythology underwent more change than that of perhaps any other god in the Hindu pantheon. Indra appeared in the oldest hymns of the *Rigveda* as the god *par excellence* of the warriors (*kṣatriyas*). This stratum of hymns was so ancient that Indra and Varuna were referred to as *asuras*, the older word for the "shining" gods. He was older than the *âdityas* but was later added as the fourth âditya. He battled an ancient monster called Vritra, who later became a serpent whose body encircled the celestial waters and, once defeated, released the rains. He even fought with Dadhyañc, an Atharvan priest, and the Aśvins to preserve the secret of *soma*. He used the bones of Dadhyañc's horse head to slay demons that were overrunning the earth. He pursued the magical cow of Tvashthri to the moon and freed the cows penned up in a cave. The fragments that allude to these exploits in the Vedic hymns do not allow for a reconstruction of the full story. Clearly, though, Indra rose to replace Vâyu (wind) in the first triad and was even prayed to as the most important of the gods in a number of the hymns. He brought the soma plant from heaven, taking it from the *asuras* (demons). He killed enemies, both *asuras* and non-Aryans. He destroyed stone cities and took slaves. There was no hint in these hymns that he was anything less than the greatest ideal warrior-god.

In the *Brâhmanas* (commentaries) Indra's status began to slip. As the power and magic of the Brâhmanical ritual increased, fear of Indra did as well. He became the focus of awareness that the gods were being challenged by the ideology of ritualism and a "science" of austerities that produced results because of an esoteric knowledge of causality that controlled even the gods. Indra began to lose battles with demons and to need help from *brâhmins* and the renewing power of their rituals and austerities.

In the *Epics* and *Purânas* Indra was reduced to the mere leader of demigods who were still called *devas* but had little power or energy. Indra was pictured as always being afraid of losing his position as *Indra,* the office of king of the *devas* that he did in fact keep losing. He began to employ the celestial damsels *(apsaras)* to distract or seduce sages whose austerities *(tapas)* were able to control gods and demons. Indra needed help constantly from supreme deities like Śiva, Vishnu, or Devî. Worst of all, Indra's character had changed. He was no longer a proud and powerful warrior, but a seducer of sage's wives, using his shape-shifting abilities to deceive them. Drunk and disorderly, he had become a mere clown with the honorary title of king of the gods.

His degradation benefited Brâhmanical ritualism, devotionalism (especially in the form of worship of supreme deities), the "spiritual-austerity sciences" *(tapasya, yoga,* and the like), and the metaphysical philosophies *(darśanas* like *Advaita Vedânta).* There were further degradations in his decline: his castration in an episode with Ahalyâ and Gautama, being cursed with a thousand *yonis* later made into eyes, and the reduction of the most voluptuous of all the god's wives, his wife Indrânî, to a demon wife, Sacî. He was turned into a killer of a priest, castrated, beheaded, and cursed to have no temple to worship him. In no other mythology has an orthodox priesthood so treated one of their most sacred deities.

See also Âdityas; Ahalyâ; Gautama; Indrânî; Soma; Tvashthri; Vritra
For further reading:

Sukumari Bhattacharji, *The Indian Theogony* (Cambridge: Cambridge University Press, 1970); Wendy Doniger O'Flaherty, *Hindu Myths* (Harmondsworth, UK: Penguin Books Ltd., 1975), *The Origins of Evil in Hindu Mythology* (Berkeley: University of California Press, 1976), and *Siva: The Erotic Ascetic* (Oxford: Oxford University Press, 1981); Georges Dumézil, *The Destiny of the Warrior* (Chicago: University of Chicago Press, 1970) and *The Destiny of the King* (Chicago: University of Chicago Press, 1973).

INDRADYUMNA

Son of King Sumati

In the *Bhâgavata Purâna* Indradyumna was a saintly king who was engaged in deep meditation. One day he was visited by the sage Agastya. Indradyumna did not notice the arrival of Agastya, who took the king's neglect for an insult. Agastya was enraged and cursed Indradyumna to become a mighty tusker, the elephant Gajendra. The grief-stricken Indradyumna asked Agastya to liberate him from the curse. Agastya said that he would be redeemed from the curse by Vishnu's touch.

Indradyumna, now as Gajendra, lived as an elephant for many years. One day he went to drink water from a lake at Mount Trikuta. In that lake lived a former gandharva named Hûhû, who also had been cursed. He had disturbed the sage Devala's devotions when the sage saw Hûhû frolicking with celestial maidens *(apsaras)* in the lake near his hermitage. Devala's curse turned Hûhû into a crocodile.

When Indradyumna as Gajendra the elephant stepped into the lake to drink, Hûhû the crocodile caught hold of his hind leg and tried to drag him under. They fought for a thousand years. Gajendra in great pain prayed to Vishnu, offering lotus flowers with his trunk. The prayer made by Gajendra on this occasion became a famous hymn in praise of Vishnu called the *Gajendra Stuti*. Vishnu came and killed Hûhû and redeemed Indradyumna from the curse. Indradyumna immediately attained Vaikuntha, the abode of Vishnu.

See also Agastya; Magic, Blessings, Cursings; Mâyâ

INDRÂNI

Wife of Indra

There are a number of references in the *Rigveda* to Indrânî but her story was not told. She was chosen by Indra as his wife from among many other goddesses because she was said to be the most voluptuous. But in the *Purânas* Indrânî became Sacî, daughter of Puloma, a demon. She was also called by the patronymic Paulomî. As Indra was reduced, so too was his wife—from a goddess richly endowed to a demoness.

See also Indra

ÎSVARA

The general term for the most powerful god

There are three terms *(îsa, îsâna, îsvara)* that all come from the root, *îs* (to have power). All can be translated as "lord," or "the one who possesses power." These terms were applied to many of the *devas* in the Vedic period—Indra, Mitra, Varuna, Soma, and Sâvitrî. In late Vedic texts Rudra, linked to Śiva, was called *îsâna*, master, or "the ruling one." *Purusha* was also called the *îśvara* of immortality and the immortal and imperishable *îsa* (in the *Svetasvatâra Upanishad*).

In later periods these terms came to be used exclusively for a god seen as the Supreme Being (either Vishnu or Śiva). That is why the term *deva* is sometimes translated demigod when it is used for the gods who are not supreme, to distinguish them from the Supreme. The term *îśvarî* meant "princess," but could also be used to indicate the Supreme as the Great Mother.

See also Devî; Śiva; Vishnu

For further reading:

Jitendra Banerjea, *The Development of Hindu Iconography*, 2d ed. (Calcutta: University of Calcutta, 1956); T. A. Gopinatha Rao, *Elements of Hindu Iconography*, Vols. 1 and 2 (Delhi: Motilal Banarsidass, reprint 1997).

JADA

A brâhmin

This is a Purânic myth about *dharma*—a father who failed to keep his *dharma* and sons who kept theirs. Jada was a *brâhmin* who became an unscrupulous businessman. But he was robbed and killed and reborn a *piśâca*, a hunger ghost. His sons were quite moral and did their duty toward their father. They decided to go to Kâśi (Benares) to perform proper rituals for the spirit of their father. As they recited the third chapter of *Bhagavad Gîtâ*, their father's angry spirit was redeemed from its state, and Jada was able to be reborn as a human.

See also Dharma

JAHNU

A sage

Jahnu gave his kingdom to his son and retired to a quiet spot to do austerities *(tapas)*. However, cosmic events disturbed his meditations. King Bhagîratha had been successful in his austerities to get Śiva's help in bringing the sacred river Gangâ to earth. And when it came, it flooded Jahnu's hermitage *(aśrama)*. Jahnu used some of his powers *(siddhis)* and drank up the Gangâ. Bhagîratha had to come to Jahnu and persuade him to allow the Gangâ to flow again. So Jahnu pushed Gangâ-devî out of his ear.

See also Bhagîratha; Gangâ; Siddhi; Tapas

JÂJALI

A hermit mentioned in the Mahâbhârata

This myth presents two competing spiritual paths: one of austerities *(tapas)* and another of spirituality located in a householder's life.

Jâjali had developed into a great ascetic. One day as he was doing a standing meditation, a pair of birds built their nest in his matted hair. So began a period when the mother bird laid her eggs, these hatched, and the young birds were raised. Still Jâjali remained motionless. Finally they flew away and did not come back. Only then did Jâjali go to the sea and bathe. He proclaimed to the sea that surely there was no more virtuous man than himself. But a voice—some texts say from heaven, others say that of a sea demon—spoke back to him: that there was a merchant *(vaiśya)* in Kâshî (Benares) named Tulâdhâra who was more virtuous than he. So Jâjali went to the city, found the *vaiśya* Tulâdhâra, and discovered that what was said was true. He became Tulâdhâra's disciple and thereby gained heaven.

See also Tapas

JAMADAGNI

A brâhmin sage, father of divine incarnation Parasu-Râma

Jamadagni was born by a miraculous birth in which his caste was determined not be birth but by a magical portion of rice pudding. His father, the sage Ricîka, a wonderous and powerful magician *(siddha)* gave his two wives different portions to determine the qualities of his future sons. Satyavatî switched her portion with the second wife and her son, Jamadagni was born with the qualities of a warrior *(kśtriya)* but the caste of his *brâhmin* father.

Jamadagni studied hard and mastered all the *Vedas*. Then he went to King Prasenajit (also known as Renu) and demanded to be given his daughter in marriage. The king gave him the princess Renukâ without complaint. Thus, she went to Jamadagni's hermitage to a life of austerities and bore Jamadagni five sons, the youngest being Parasu-Râma. (See more about her temptation and punishment in the entry on Renukâ.)

One day Jamadagni became furious with his wife when she was late with his meal because she had been watching love play at the bathing *ghat*. So he ordered his sons to kill her. Only the youngest, Parasu-Râma, a lad of fourteen, obeyed and cut off his mother's head with an ax (some versions said with a cutting arrow). The other four sons were cursed to become imbeciles by the old *brâhmin*-warrior Jamadagni. He was so pleased with Parasu-Râma that he granted him a boon. Parasu-Râma asked that his mother be restored to life completely purified of all sins and that his brothers become normal again.

Later King Kârtavîryârjuna and his hunting party came to Jamadagni's hermitage and asked for hospitality. Jamadagni called his divine cow Sushîlâ, and she immediately provided a feast for the king and his huge retinue. Unfortunately, however, the king never forgot about this cow. There are a number of versions of what happened next. In one, the king tries to give a thousand cows for Sushîlâ but finally, tired of being rebuffed, he (or his minister) stole the divine cow and her calf, leaving Jamadagni for dead.

In another account, Renukâ gave King Kârtavîryârjuna food and drink at the hermitage. Kârtavîryârjuna then destroyed their grove of trees and stole the divine cow. But in each version, Paraśu-Râma went after the cow, met the king and his army in battle, and killed them all. In a longer version his wounded father, Jamadagni, sent Paraśu-râma to Mahendragiri to do penance for killing so many people. And while Paraśu-Râma was away, King Kârtavîryârjuna's youngest son came with an army and murdered the old *brâhmin* Jamadagni. His sons and disciples built a funeral pyre and began the proper rituals. At this point Renukâ jumped into the fire of her husband, committing *sati* (suttee) by dying in the flames.

See also Parasu-Râma; Satyavâti

JÂMBAVÂN, JÂMBAVÂT

A great monkey or bear king

There is a lot of confusion as to whether Jâmbhavân was a monkey *(kapi)* or a bear *(riksha)*. Vâlmîki's *Râmâyana* presented some stories of Jâmbhavân as a bear and other stories of him as a monkey.

In one version Brahmâ sent the celestial damsels *(apsaras)* to be reborn around Râma and help him defeat the demon king Râvana and one was born as Jâmbhavân. Other versions stated that Jâmbhavân was reborn at each of Vishnu's incarnations, not just during his incarnation as Râma. It was in the Krishna incarnation that, as a bear or a monkey, Jâmbhavân came into possession of the magical gem, Syamantaka. The jewel protected the virtuous and harmed those who were evil. Sûrya, the sun god, had given the jewel to King Satrâjit, whose evil brother Prasena wore it hunting and was killed by a lion, which was in turn killed by the bear (or monkey) Jâmbhavân. Krishna went into the forest (or a cave in the bear version) and after a twenty-one-day battle was given the jewel by Jâmbhavân. Jâmbhavân became an ally of Râma and led his army (of bears or monkeys) against Râvana. He also became the father-in-law of Krishna, giving his daughter Jâmbavatî to Krishna as one of his wives. One version said that the jewel was given to Krishna as dowry. In any case, Krishna returned the divine jewel to King Satrâjit.

See also Krishna; Râma

JAMBHA

An *asura* (demon)

Jambha was the leader of the *asuras* who snatched away the pot of *amrita* (nectar of immortality) from the sage Dhanvantari when he emerged carrying it during the churning of the Milky Ocean. Jambha, along with his demon cohorts, was tricked by the beautiful woman Môhinî, the form taken by Vishnu to recover the nectar of immortality.

> *See also* Amrita; Dhanvantari; *Kshîrâbdhi-mathanam;* Môhinî

JAMBU

A divine rose apple tree mentioned in the *Bhâgavata Purâna*

This tree bore fruit throughout the year, fruit the size of elephants. The branches of the Jambu tree reached to heaven. The juice of the fruit flowed as a river. According to the *Bhâgavata Purâna* the Jambu tree was watered by *devas* (gods) called Siddhacaranas. Near the tree lived the goddess of the tree, who was called Jambvâdinî or Arunâ. She blessed everybody, even people who merely thought about her, and cured them of all diseases. The juice of the fruit mixed with soil and water turned into gold that was much more refined than ordinary gold.

JAMBUKA, JAMBUMALIKA

A sage who was a Śûdra in the *Uttâra Râmâyana*

Jambuka's ascetic practices threatened the very foundations of Râma's perfect rule as king *(râmarâjya).* Jambuka was a Śûdra who had adopted spiritual exercises *(tapas)* that he was not entitled to practice.

Râma had returned from twelve years of exile, and his rule in Ayodhyâ seemed to fulfill *dharma* (righteousness) in every possible way. Then one day a *brâhmin* and his wife brought their dead child to the king's court. It did not seem possible that there could be a child-death during a *râmarâjya.* The know-it-all sage Nârada pointed to a breach of *varna-aśrama-dharma* (social duties): there was a Śûdra sage in the land practicing *tapas.* Nârada stated that such a thing was *adharmic* and that it had caused the child-death. King Râma left his brother to take care of funeral rites for the child and a trusted minister to act in his place against possible invasions. Râma personally searched for this sage until he finally found Jambuka. When questioned, Jambuka told the king that he was hanging upside down from the limb of a tree until he bodily went to heaven. Râma solved this threat to social order by immediately cutting off Jambuka's head with his sword. Then everything was solved. Jambuka achieved liberation *(moksha)* that very moment and went to heaven. The *brâhmin* child returned to life before he was cremated. And the dharmic order in Râma's kingdom was restored.

See also Dharma; Nârada; Râma

JANAKA

A king (also known as Sîradhvaja) in the Epics and Purânas

Janaka's father, Nimi, king of Mithilâ, was childless and asked the venerable *brâhmin* Vasishtha to preside over a ritual *(yâjña)* for a son. Vasishtha was pre-occupied with another ritual and asked the king to wait. King Nimi left without making any commitment and then found another priest named Gautama to perform the *yâjña*. When Vasishtha finished his other business, he went to King Nimi, who told the priest that the ritual had already been performed. Vasishtha became so angry that he pronounced a death curse on the king, dooming him to be without a body *(videha)*. Nimi died instantly. He had no heir, so the *rishis* (seers) immediately churned *(mathana)* a son from his corpse. The son was named Sîradhvaja, but because of the churning he acquired the name of Mithi ("churned") Janaka, and his dynasty would be named Videha.

Now Janaka, king of Mithilâ, was also childless. One day he found a child born from the furrows of a plowed field. A voice from heaven told him that this child was Sîtâ and that she was his daughter.

Janaka became a great scholar. He was tested on one occasion by Sulabhâ, a great shamaness who changed into a beautiful woman and then entered into his soul while they discussed philosophical subjects. She left ashamed of herself and convinced that Janaka was both wise and pure. Janaka once clarified the doubts of Vyâsa's son Śuka when even the great sage Vyâsa had not been able to help. One account said the Janaka was an incarnation of all good qualities. He became Râma's father-in-law when Râma married Sîtâ.

The *Padma Purâna* has two long chapters about Janaka leaving his body when he was ready to die through his own yogic powers. He was met by a divine chariot *(vimâna)* but had a brief stop in hell. After learning from Kâla (time, god of death) of the torments of hell's inmates, Janaka chanted "Râm, Râm" *(jâpâ)* for them and gained their release. Then he asked Kâla why he had stopped briefly in hell. Kâla told him that he was the most righteous man of his age, with the most merit *(punya)* but that he had once prevented a cow from eating grass. That sin was now atoned for, and Janaka resumed his journey to heaven.

See also Gautama; Râma; Sîtâ

JANAMEJAYA

A king, father of Parîkshit

According to the *Devî Bhâgavata* Janamejaya was but an infant when his father King Parîkshit died from the poisonous bite of Takshâka, king of the serpents. At an appropriate age Janamejaya was crowned king of Hastinâpura. When he learned exactly how his father had died, Janamejaya sought a way to rid the world of snakes. Many great priests came to his kingdom to help perform a ritual called Sarpasatra. Soon their *mantras* and oblations, given to the sacred fire pit, called snakes of all kinds into the fire where they were burned to death. However, Takshâka escaped by going to Brahmâ and taking refuge with him. The high priest, Uttanka, searched for the king of snakes psychically and saw Takshâka beside Brahmâ. The priest was furious and decided to bring Brahmâ and his throne along with Takshâka into the fire. The magic worked so well that that they were pulled down from heaven and were within moments of being consumed in the flames. Exactly at that instance the *brâhmin* Âstîka arrived and was paid full respect by King Janamejaya. That included offering to fulfill any wish that Âstîka might have. Âstîka asked for an immediate end to the Sarpasatra. Thus, Takshâka and those snakes that were still alive survived because of this sage. (The account of the myth forgot to mention that poor Brahmâ was saved as well.) Âstîka blessed the snakes that had already died so that they attained heaven.

Janamejaya received an unusual blessing from Vyâsa: that he could see his father. Vyâsa called not only Parîkshit down from heaven *(svarga)* but also Samîka, upon whom Parîkshit had thrown a dead snake and whose son Gavijâta had cursed the king. Later Vyâsa was the presiding priest when King Janamejaya performed the prestigious horse sacrifice *(asva-medha yâjña)*.

See also Âstika; Asva-Medha; Gavijâta; Parîkshit; Takshâka; Vyâsa

JARA, JARAS

A hunter who killed Krishna

According to one version in the *Bhâgavata Purâna* Jara was hunting and shot an arrow through a bush at the sound of an animal. But the blind shot hit Srî Krishna in the foot, that only area of his body not protected by the magical potion from the sage Durvâsa. (For more details of this version, see the entries for Durvâsa and Krishna.)

There is a completely different version. The hunter, Jara, was the demon Bâli, who had been killed by Râma and in this rebirth killed Krishna in revenge.

See also Bâli; Durvâsa; Krishna

JARÂSANDHA

An evil king

Jarâsandha, mighty king of Magadha, was born by double magic, first from a *brâhmin* and second from a giant demoness *(râkshasî)*. His parents had been childless. They enlisted the sage Kakshîvân (some texts say Candakaushika) to help. As the sage meditated, a mango fell in his lap. He gave the mango to the king, who in turn gave half to each of his wives. They became pregnant. But when they delivered, each gave birth to half a child. They threw these misshapen globs of flesh outside the palace, where the *râkshasî* Jarâ found them. In putting them together as one perfect boy, she gave her name to him—Jarâsandha, "the one joined together by Jarâ."

Jarâsandha became a very powerful but wicked king. His two daughters were married to Krishna's uncle, King Kamsa. When Krishna killed Kamsa, the daughters went to their father, Jarâsandha, and provoked him into attacking Krishna. Finally after more than eighteen battles detailed in the *Mahâbhârata* and the *Bhâgavata Purâna*, Bhîma killed Jarâsandha in a duel.

See also Bhîma; Kamsa; Krishna

JATÂYU

A bird

Jatâyu was one of two sons born to Aruna, chariot driver of Sûrya (the sun god), and Shyenî, a divine bird. In his youth Jatâyu was saved by his brother Sampâti as they raced toward the sun, Sampâti allowing his wings to be burned as he shielded Jatâyu from the sun. It was Jatâyu's role to inform Râma that Sîtâ had been abducted by Râvana. Jatâyu saw Râvana escaping with Sîtâ through the air in his celestial chariot. Jatâyu intercepted Râvana, and a great air battle ensued. Râvana eventually cut off Jatâyu's wings. Śrî Râma and Lakshmana discovered the dying Jatâyu and learned about Râvana—and Sîtâ's abduction. Jatâyu died chanting Râma's name. Śrî Râma and Lakshmana lit his funeral pyre. The celestial bird's soul gained liberation *(svarga)*.

See also Râma; Râvana; Sîtâ

JATILA

A pseudonym of Śiva

Jatila was the name assumed by Śiva when he was disguised as a *brâhmin*. Śiva sought to test Pârvatî because she was doing *tapas* (austerities) in order to obtain him as her husband.

See also Pârvatî; Śiva

JÂYA, JAYAS

One of the dvarapâlakas (doorkeepers) of Vishnu

One day a group of hermits led by Sanaka came to Vaikuntha to see Vishnu. They were stopped by Vishnu's doorkeepers, Jâya and Vijâya. But the sages took offense and cursed the doorkeepers to be reborn three times as demons *(asuras)*. The frightened doorkeepers begged the angry *brâhmins* for forgiveness, but they only slightly lessened the punishment: after their three rebirths they would be redeemed by the weapon of Mahâvishnu.

In the first birth they were born as Hiranyâksha and Hiranyakaśipu. In the second birth they were born as Râvana and Kumbhakarna, and in the third birth they were born as Śiśupâla and Dantavaktra. After their three births they returned to Vaikuntha to serve Lord Vishnu.

See also Hiranyakaśipu; Hiranyâksha; Kumbhakarna; Râvana; Śiśupâla

KA

A letter

Ka is the first consonant in the Sanskrit alphabet, although, since Sanskrit is a syllabic language, one should say that it is the first consonantal-syllabic. Ka is also the ordinary word for *who*. It was used in an agnostic hymn of the *Rigveda* that asked "who" created all this, and when it had become inconceivable that a Vedic hymn should be agnostic, it became a symbol of and word for the creator: Prajâpati according to the *Mahâbhârata* and Brahmâ according to *Agni Purâna*.

See also Brahmâ; Prajâpati
For further reading:
Roberto Calasso, *Ka: Stories of the Mind and Gods of India* (New York: Alfred A. Knopf, 1998).

KABANDHA

A demon

In the Râma myth cycle in his previous life Kabandha was a gandharva called Visvâvasu. He was born to a gandharva called Śrî Visvâvasu, who was also known by the name Danu. Visvâvasu performed a penance *(tapas)* and received the boon of immortality from Brahmâ. Arrogant about this boon, Visvâvasu then attacked Indra. In the great battle that followed Indra used his divine discus *(Vajrâyudha)*. The head and thighs of Visvâvasu were squeezed into his body, and his mouth was pushed down to his abdomen. Upon Visvâvasu's pleading, Indra gave him two long hands and said that he would regain his original form when Śrî Râma cut off these hands. Because he did not have a head, only two long hands and a mouth on his belly, he came to be known as Kabandha, "the headless." Often he was depicted as a tree.

The fateful day came when Kabandha encountered Śrî Râma and Lakshmana in the forest. They were searching for Sîtâ. Before them appeared the horrible form of Kabandha, large as a mountain. The demon grabbed Śrî Râma in his right hand and Lakshmana in his left. Each cut off one hand. Kabandha then told them his story and fell dead. Śrî Râma and Lakshmana burned his body on a funeral pyre, and as Kabandha ascended from its flames, he told Śrî Râma and Lakshmana to go to Sugrîva, the monkey king, from whom they could learn more about Sîtâ's abduction. Kabandha was again Viśvâvasu, a *gandharva* king.

See also Râma; Sîtâ

KACA
The son of the sage Brihaspati

The *asuras* (demons) had become invincible in war because their priest, the *brâhmin* Śukra, knew the art of bringing the dead back to life *(mritasañjîvinî)*. No sooner would the *devas* (gods) kill the *asuras* than Śukra would perform the *mritasañjîvinî* and they were alive again. The *devas* dispatched their chief priest's son, Kaca, to learn this magic. Kaca presented himself so humbly in asking to become his disciple that Śukra could not refuse. Even Śukra's daughter, Devayânî, fell in love with Kaca. They became an inseparable couple. However, the *asuras* were not happy that the son of Brihaspati was at Śukra's *aśrama* (hermitage). One day they had their chance and killed him when he was in the forest looking for stray cattle. The *asuras* fed his body to wolves. Devayânî pleaded with her father to perform the *mritasañjîvinî*. Kaca was called back to life, and everything returned to normal, until the *asuras* killed him again. Kaca was again called back to life. But the third time the *asuras* killed him, they burned his body, mixed his ashes in Śukra's wine, and got Śukra to drink it. Again Devayânî pleaded for her lover's life.

Śukra could think of only one way to save Kaca. He communicated with Kaca in meditation and taught him the magical formula, the *mritasañjîvinî*. When Śukra performed it, Kaca came forth from Śukra's belly, splitting him open. Then Kaca performed the *mritasañjîvinî* and restored his teacher to life. Now Kaca knew the magical art and was ready to return to the *devas*. Devayânî was in love with him and pleaded to become his wife. But Kaca rejected her, so she cursed him to not be able to use the *mritasañjîvinî*. Kaca cursed her back, saying that no *brâhmin* would marry her. Kaca was able to get around Devayânî's curse by teaching his disciples how to use the *mritasañjîvinî* and restore the *devas* to life. But Devayânî had to marry a *kśatriya* (warrior) because of Kaca's curse.

See also Brihaspati; Magic, Blessings, Cursings; Mâyâ

KAIKEYÎ

One of the wives of King Daśaratha of Ayodhyâ

Kaikeyî was one of the three (some versions say five) wives of King Daśaratha. She had been a princess of the kingdom of Kekaya, seven day's journey from Ayodhyâ. When Daśaratha was summoned to *svarga* (heaven) to help the *devas* (gods) in a war with the *asuras* (demons), Kaikeyî rode with him in his war chariot and helped him. The *asura* Śambara used sorcery (black magic) to attack Daśaratha and the *devas* from ten thousand directions at the same time. So Daśaratha had to fight in ten thousand directions at the same time. As he was doing that, a lynch pin on one wheel of his chariot fell off, and the wheel seemed about to be lost—along with the battle. But Kaikeyî inserted her thumb into the hole so that the wheel stayed on. When Daśaratha discovered his wife's bravery, he granted her two boons. Wisely, she saved them.

Years later, evil advice from a hunchback maid named Manthurâ darkened her heart. Daśaratha was preparing to anoint as heir-apparent his son, Râma, by his first wife Kausalyâ. Kaikeyî demanded her two boons: that Râma be exiled to the forest for fourteen years and that her son Bharata be anointed heir-apparent. It was done. But Daśaratha died almost immediately.

The story of the rest of the queen's life will be found interwoven in the stories of Bharata's fourteen-year reign in the name of his half-brother, Râma, Râma's exile adventures, Sîtâ's abduction, the war with Râvana, Hanuman's help, and Râma's eventual perfect rule in Ayodhyâ. As with many other heroines the mythmakers gave her both good and bad roles in which her character vacillated between praise and blame.

See also Bharata; Daśaratha; Râma

KAILÂSA

The celestial abode of Śiva and Pârvatî

The *Mahâbhârata* describes the location of Kailâsa. Kailâsa is situated on the southern side of Mahâmeru (Mahâ-Meru), the great mountain. It is said that there are two celestial abodes on Mount Kailâsa, one of Śiva and Pârvatî and the other of Kubera, god of wealth.

See also Mahâmeru; section on Deśa (Space) in chapter 2

KAITABHA

An asura (demon)

There are two versions of the origin of Kaitabha and his brother Madhu. The version in the *Purânas* said that Madhu and his brother Kaitabha were born from the earwax of Vishnu. Vishnu was ending his cosmic sleep reclined upon the serpent Śesha (also called Ananta) floating on the Milky Ocean. Brahmâ emerged from the lotus that grew from Vishnu's navel. Some earwax emerged from each of Vishnu's ears, which became the two demons known as Madhu and Kaitabha.

According to the *Mahâbhârata* version, the two demons were born from the two drops of water trapped in the lotus that came from Vishnu's navel. Madhu had the attribute *(guna)* of darkness *(tamas)*, while Kaitabha's attribute was activity *(rajas)*.

Kaitabha and Madhu were taught a *mantra* of praise to Devî (the Mother), which they used for a thousand years. Pleased, Devî appeared to them and gave them a boon. They asked to die only of their own choosing. They became bored with the world before creation, a world that was totally submerged, so they decided to cause trouble. They stole the entire *Vedas* and plunged into the dark waters and reached Pâtâla (the underworld). Brahmâ had to waken Lord Vishnu, so he did it with praise. Vishnu agreed to retrieve the Vedas. Vishnu fought the haughty demons but was not able to win. Then he understood that they were invincible because of Devî's boon. So Vishnu called a truce and told Kaitabha and Madhu that he was pleased with them and would grant them a boon. But they mocked Vishnu and said they did not need anything from him, as they were more powerful than he was. So Vishnu said that if that was so, then they should grant him a boon. Without any fear, they said that they would. Vishnu crafted his boon carefully, asking that they grant him the boon to kill them.

The honorable demons had to keep their promise, but they placed one stipulation on their boon: that Vishnu could not kill them in water, since everything was flooded. So Vishnu expanded himself, and the demons found themselves high and dry on Vishnu's thigh. They enlarged themselves to be able to get their feet back into the cosmic ocean. But this time Vishnu's expansion was so great that the demons were unable to touch the ocean. Vishnu cut off their heads with his discus. The fat that flowed from their bodies coagulated on the sea and became the earth. That was how the earth received its name as Medinî ("having fatness"). They were reborn as Khara and Atikâya for more roles in later mythology.

See also Vishnu

KAKSHASENA

A righteous king

King Kakshasena, praised as an examplar in the *Mahâbhârata*, was the son of King Parîkshit and grandson of King Avîkshit. Kakshasena achieved an honored place in Hindu mythology because of his generous support of the priesthood. The lists of such donors included great kings of the epic period: Shibi, Pratardana, Rantideva, Ambarîsha, Paraśu-Râma, Śrî Râma, and a few others. King Kakshasena was said to have attained heaven because of his generosity to the *brâhmin* Vasishtha.

See also Paraśu-Râma; Râma

KAKSHÎVÂN, KAKSHÎVÂT

A sage mentioned in the Rigveda

The story of Kakshîvân is quite fragmentary, with some pieces quite ancient mixed with pieces from later mythology.

Kakshîvân was born according to a custom by which a priest would be requested to give the king a child by his childless queen. King Kalinga was without an heir. He consulted the sage Dîrghatamas and requested that he give him a son by his queen. But the queen did not want to sleep with the old, and probably smelly, sage. So she sent her maid Ushî instead. Kakshîvân was born of their union. This version was told in the *Rigveda*.

There was another version of the birth of Kakshîvân in the *Mahâbhârata*. This time Kakshîvân was born to a sage named Gautama (but not the Gautama who was married to Ahalyâ) and a śudra woman who lived in the land of Usînara.

The Aśvin twins once gave Kakshîvân a hundred pots of liquor to test his strength, according to a verse in the *Rigveda*.

According to the *Mahâbhârata*, Kakshîvân was one of the seven Barhishads, who were created by Brahmâ to teach Indra. Kakshîvân had completed his part of the training and was returning home. When night came, he slept by the roadside. The next morning he was found by King Bhâvayavya who, upon questioning him, found him so worthy that he gave Kakshîvân his ten daughters in marriage and loaded him down with gold, horses, cattle, and chariots. Kakshîvân arrived back at his father's home and wrote many hymns of praise. Kakshîvân had two daughters, Kâkshîvatasutâ and Bhadrâ.

See also Dîrghatamas; Kâkshîvatasutâ

KÂKSHÎVATASUTÂ

A woman sage

Kâkshîvatasutâ was one of two daughters of the *brâhmin* Kakshîvân. Kâkshî-vatasutâ (also known as Ghoshâ) contracted leprosy. She had mastered hymn writing and composed a *mantra* that praised the physicians of the gods, the Aśvins. They responded to her praise and cured her. She then was able to marry.

Bhadrâ, Kâkshîvatasutâ's sister, married King Vyûshitâshva, who died before they had children. Her lamentations were so great that Vyûshitâshva was called from the dead, and she was able to have six sons because of her austerities *(tapas).*

See also Aśvins; Ghoshâ; Kakshîvân

KÂLA

The god (deva) of death; time

As time is a great imponderable, it is related to death. The two words, time and death, are the same in Sanskrit. Kâla is popularly known as Yama. Born from the union of Sûrya (the sun god) and Samjñâ, daughter of Kaśyapa-prajâpati, Yama (Kâla) was given the duty to retrieve the souls of those whose allotted time was at an end.

After death the spirit of the body was taken by the attendants of Kâla to his court, and there the spirit was judged according to the virtue *(dharma, punya)* and vice that had shown in action in that lifetime. Depending on the judgment, the spirit *(pitri)* was sent to Vaikuntha (heaven) or Naraka (also called Pitriloka, the land of the spirits).

Kâla was one of the Dikpâlakâs, a guardian of the four cardinal directions. He guarded the southern quarter. His city was called Samyaminî (and Yamapurî). In the *Katha Upanishad* there was a discussion between a lad named Naciketas and Kâla (Yama) about the nature of death and that which is deathless.

In late Purânic mythology like that found in the *Vishnu Purâna*, there were twenty-eight Narakas (hells), each more terrible than the one before, with ever-increasing punishment and torments.

Kâla (Yama) fared just as badly as some of the other *devas*, like Indra in later mythology. He was ruled by the laws of *karma*, could be defeated by the magic of sages or the austerities of demons like Râvana, and was fooled by the play *(lîlâ)* of supreme deities.

See also Dharma; discussion of time at beginning of chapter 2

KÂLANEMI

A demon

Kâlanemi was a *râkshasa* (night-wandering demon) who was dispatched by the *asura* (demon) king Râvana to prevent Hanuman, the monkey god and loyal servant of Râma, from reaching the magic Drona mountain. Hanuman needed healing herbs for the wounded Lakshmana during the Râma-Râvana war. Kâlanemi appeared as a *brâhmin* in order to fool Hanuman, but this shape-shifting demon got himself killed in the process.

He also had a lifetime during the Krishna incarnation as Kamsa, the evil uncle of Krishna.

See also Hanuman; Kamsa; Krishna; Râkshasa; Râvana

KALÂVATÎ

Daughter of the king of Kâśi

Kalâvatî worshipped the sage Durvâsa and was given the powerful five-syllable mantra *(pancâkshara mantra)* in praise of Śiva *(śivayah namah).* By its use Kalâvatî became a saint.

Kalâvatî married King Dâhârha of Mathurâ. When he approached her, he noticed that he became overheated. Kalâvatî told him that, because of the *mantra*, sinners would feel hot if they touched her. The king consented to go with Kalâvatî to the *brâhmin* Garga. The king bathed in the Kâlindî River, and his sins flew away as tiny birds. When they next embraced, Kalâvatî's body was cool, and they had a son.

See also Durvâsa

KALI

The son of Kaśyâpa and his wife Muni

Kali (strife) was the personification of evil *(adharma),* as well as the worst throw in a game of Indian dice. He could also be called the god of sin and of bad luck. Kali was born as the fifteenth of sixteen sons of Kaśyâpa and his wife Muni.

In an encounter with King Parîkshit, Kali was cursed to be confined to five places on earth: gambling, drinking, woman, murder, and gold. According to the *Bhâgavata Purâna* Kali is the ruling power in the Kali Yuga—the present age.

See also Parîkshit; chapter 2 on time

KÂLÎ

A goddess (devî); the anger of Umâ, or Pârvatî

In the Vedic period Kâlî (the black one) was one of the seven tongues of Agni, god of the sacrificial fire. She was the black fire, though the specific meaning has been lost. She was referred to as one of the seven mothers of Agni—who nurtured him. There were also seven mothers (Mâtrikâs) whose natures seem far from Vedic rituals. Yet as she developed Kâlî seemed to combine both orthoprax Brâhmanical religion and the heteroprax religion of the cremation grounds. She was the dark side of Devî, the Great Goddess (Mahâdevî), assimilating tribal and non-Aryan goddesses and their myths.

The "hottest" (least orthodox) of all the manifestations of Mahâdevî is Kâlî. She is the anger of Umâ, or Pârvatî, Śiva's wife. She demands offerings of wine, meat, and blood. Animal sacrifices are still performed to

Kâlî, Hindu goddess of destruction, in an Indian painting from the nineteenth century (The Art Archive / Victoria and Albert Museum London / Eileen Tweedy)

her at her temples in Calcutta, in Nepal, and in the villages in non-orthoprax rituals. At the village level any of the hot goddesses may be seen as Kâlî—Câmundâ who drank up the blood of the demon Raktabîja (bloody seed), whose blood was the seed of more demons; the Sapta-mâtrikâs (seven mothers); and even lesser goddess of smallpox and disease like Śîtalâ and Mâriyamman. For many Kâlî and Durgâ are synonymous. Both have a lion as their *vahana* (vehicle), both kill Mahisha, both are goddesses that dance on their husband, Śiva.

In some myths Kâlî appears as a voluptuous woman enticing both demons and wicked warriors—only to reveal herself as an opponent who beheads men almost as a whim. Only male offerings can be presented to her and beheaded in her blood sacrifices. It is no secret that she symbolically castrates her victims.

In Tantra Kâlî's worship embraced the five pollutants, known as the "five m's" *(pañcamakâra)—madya* (wine), *matsya* (fish), *mâmsa* (meat), *mudrâ* (parched grain), and *maithuna* (sexual union). These could be utilized symbolically in right-handed worship *(dakshinâcâra)* or trangressively in left-handed worship *(vâmâcâra)*. Worship of Kâlî was dangerous, as her many bloody myths warned, but the rewards could be great.

See also Devî; Pârvatî; Tantra; Úmâ
For further reading:
Jeffrey J. Kripal, *Kâlî's Child: The Mystical and the Erotic in the Life and Teachings of Ramakrishna* (Chicago: University of Chicago Press, 1995).

KÂLINDÎ

A river and a goddess (devî)
Kâlindî was the daughter of Sûrya, the sun god. She was blessed to become a sacred river, also known as the Yamunâ. It flowed from the Kalinda mountain and entered the Gangâ at Prayâga, a very sacred confluence.

At the birth of Krishna, his father Vasudeva had to switch the infants of his two wives. He had to cross a flooding Kâlindî River. The goddess of the river miraculously helped him cross back and forth with the babies.

There is a strange story in the *Bhâgavata* (Skandha Ten) about Balabhadra Râma, Krishna's brother and a divine incarnation in some lists, and the Kâlindî. Balabhadra Râma had had a little too much liquor to drink and was playing with the cowherd girls *(gopis)*. He wanted to swim with them so he had to pull the Kâlindî over to them with his plough.

The *Bhâgavata Purâna* stated that Krishna and Arjuna were walking together along the Kâlindî and saw a beautiful woman, who turned out to be Kâlindî herself, practicing austerities *(tapas)*. Arjuna learned that she was doing these in order to gain Krishna as her husband. When Arjuna told Krishna, Krishna took the goddess Kâlindî in his chariot to Dvârakâ and married her. Krishna and Kâlindî had ten sons.

There was a story in *Vâmana Purâna* saying that Kâma-deva (the god of love) shot some of his love arrows at Śiva, when Śiva was very depressed over the death of Satî. Śiva became so excited that he jumped into the river Kâlindî—and that is why its water is black. In *Agni Purâna* the goddess Kâlindî was depicted as black in color and riding on a tortoise, carrying a water pitcher in her hand.

According to *Padma Purâna* the river Kâlindî was so holy that to drink her water or bathe in her divine flow would purify anyone from their sins and give them the merit *(punya)* to gain heaven *(svarga).*

See also Kâliya

KALIPRIYÂ

A prostitute

The story of Kalipriyâ is brief but nonetheless important. It represents the point of view of the devotional groups and the abundant grace *(prasâda)* that they promised. Kalipriyâ was absolved of her sins and received the merit *(punya)* to offset all her bad *karma* simply by performing a month-long fast *(kârtika vrata).* The *Padma Purâna* did not say that she achieved liberation *(moksha)* but stated that she gained a rebirth in heaven *(svarga),* the hope of devotionalists *(bhaktas),* who longed to be with their supreme lord.

See also Karma

KÂLIYA

A serpent

In the Krishna myth cycle Kâliya was a great serpent, born of the progenitor Kaśyâpa by his wife Kadrû, mother of the serpent kingdom. Kâliya lived in the Kâlindî River (also called the Yamunâ) and was well known because of his association with Krishna. Kâliya had a thousand hoods (although some texts say only five). One late version added that Kâliya was reborn as the *asura* (demon) Kâlanemi. While other Nâgas (serpents) had made an arrangement not to be eaten by Garuda, the sun eagle, Kâliya and his clan were protected by a boon that they could not be eaten by Garuda as long as they were in the Kâlindî. So they gave no offerings or tribute to Garuda.

Kâliya's poison became so strong that the entire Kâlindî River became poisonous, and trees along its banks died. One day the cowherds, *gopîs* and *gopâlas,* drank from its water and died. (One version said it was the cows that died.) Śrî Krishna became furious and attacked Kâliya. Krishna jumped from a tree upon the head of the giant, multiheaded serpent and danced on his head (the *Kâliya-mardhana, dance*). Beaten into submission, Kâliya and all his wives and children took refuge in Lord Krishna. Krishna blessed them and sent them to an island kingdom in the sea with the boon that Garuda still could not eat them there. From that time on Kâliya and his clan lived on Ramanaka Island. And of course the dead *(gopîs* or cows) were brought back to life, not by magical formulas or Brâhmanical rituals but by the will of Lord Krishna.

See also Garuda; Kâlindî; Krishna

KALKI

The tenth avatâra of Vishnu

Kalki is the form that Vishnu will assume at the end of this cosmic age, the Kali Yuga. As Kalki, Vishnu will appear in a human form riding on a white horse. He will bring a fiery end to the world, reward the virtuous, and punish the wicked. With his advent, evil will disappear, and the Krita Yuga (also known as the Satya Yuga, the age of truth) will begin again.

See also Vishnu; Yuga in chapter 2

KALMÂSHAPÂDA

A king of the Ikshvaku dynasty

Kalmâshapâda (one with polluted feet) was the name given a great king who had been turned into a man-eating *râkshasa* (night-wandering demon). Before the curse, he was Mitrasaha, king of Ayodhyâ, who lived in happiness with his beautiful queen Madayantî. There are three versions of how he was cursed.

The first version began on a hunt when King Mitrasaha killed a tiger cub that was really a râkshasa. The demon's brother took revenge by taking the shape of a *brâhmin* named Vasishtha and going to Mitrasaha's palace to perform an *aśvamedha* (horse sacrifice). The râkshasa, in the form of the presiding priest Vasishtha, asked the king to fix him a meat meal and bring it to his tent. Unknowingly Mitrasaha took the meat meal to the real Vasishtha, and the sage cursed the king and transformed him into a râkshasa.

The second version began with a hunt and the accidental killing of a râkshasa. Again the brother râkshasa took the form of a *brâhmin* cook. Vasishtha arrived, and a meal was needed for the sage. This time the cook prepared human flesh, and the king served it to the sage Vasishtha. Mitrasaha was cursed to become a man-eating râkshasa for twelve years. In the third version Mitrasaha was on a hunt. He met Śaktî, the son of Vasishtha, on the trail. Both thought the other should step off the path. Finally, the king struck the *brâhmin* with his whip. In anger, Śaktî cursed him, and another sage, Viśvâmitra, put a devil into the king's body. The king immediately became a râkshasa.

In one account King Mitrasaha tried to get even with Vasishtha for cursing him. Mitrasaha took water and was going to throw it down with a curse. However, the queen stopped him with the warning that it was not right to curse a *brâhmin*. So he threw the "cursed water" on his own feet, thus acquiring the name Kalmâshapâda, "one with polluted feet."

As a man-eating râkshasa, Kalmâshapâda was quite successful. He ate all one hundred of Vasishtha's sons, including Śaktî. Kalmâshapâda lived as a râkshasa for twelve years and had many adventures. Finally, at the end of twelve years he was returned to his original form by the blessing of Vasishtha himself.

See also Dharma

KÂMA, KÂMADEVA

The god *(deva)* of love

There are two versions of Kâma's birth. According to the *Mahâbhârata,* Kâma is the son of Dharma, who was born from the right breast of Brahmâ. Dharma had three sons: Kâma, Śama, and Harsha. All were very handsome like their father.

According to *Kâlikâ Purâna,* Kâma was born from the mind of Brahmâ. Brahmâ created ten Prajâpatis (progenitors) first and then an exceptional woman called Sandhyâ. When Sandhyâ was born, Brahmâ and the ten Prajâpatis were very much attracted by her beauty. At that moment of excitement a handsome youth sprang from the mind of Brahmâ holding a bow of flowers and arrows of sugarcane. The youth asked: "Whom shall I make excited?" And Brahmâ answered that he should excite men with *kâma* (love, desire).

Kâma was blamed by many versions of the myth for Brahmâ's creation of and marriage to Sarasvatî. She was mind-born from the creator—from his meditation. But then Brahmâ fell in love and married his own daughter, Sarasvatî. For this, he blamed Kâma, who, Brahmâ said, had excited him with his magic arrows. So Brahmâ cursed Kâma to be turned into ashes by the fire of the third eye of Śiva. (For more see the entry on Pârvatî.)

Kâma's greatest moment was when he was sent by Indra to wake up Śiva so that he could deal with Târaka, the great *asura* (demon) troubling the world. Śiva was angry and burned Kâma to a crisp. Kâma's wife Ratî pleaded with Śiva to restore Kâma to life. But all that Śiva would do was to give Ratî a rebirth as mother of a reborn Kâma who was reborn as Pradyumna. (See more in the entry on Rukhmini, Ratî's name when she was reborn.)

See also Brahmâ; Pârvatî; Rukhmini; Śiva

KÂMADHENU

The celestial cow

Kâmadhenu was born of Kaśyâpa and his wife Krodhavasâ. Kâmadhenu (desire-fulfilling milk cow) gave milk to the *devas* (gods), at any time and in any quantity they wanted. She was also known as Surabhî (the fragrant) and Nandinî (delight). The family of cattle came from Kâmadhenu. (Another source stated that Surabhî was the calf of Kâmadhenu.)

In the *Mahâbhârata* Surabhî worshipped Brahmâ for a thousand years and was blessed with divinity: she became a goddess and received her own world, Goloka (the celestial heaven of cows). Some late myths put Kâmadhenu in the possession of the sage Vasishtha. In one such myth, Satyavrata stole and killed Kâmadhenu, eating part of her body and giving the rest to the starving family of Viśvâmitra. Vasishtha cursed Satyavrata as one who had committed the three worst sins (*Triśanku*—according to this account, killing a *brâhmin*, one's teacher, and a cow). Vasishtha then restored Kâmadhenu to life.

> See also information about Satyavrata in Hayagrîva (3) and Viśvâmitra; more about Vasishtha as mentioned in Mitra-Varuna; more about *Triśanku* in Viśvâmitra

KAMSA, KANSA
Uncle of Śrî Krishna

The myth of Kamsa is told in a series of nested myths that are an excellent study of *karma* as a process over many lifetimes. But its primary location is within the Krishna myth cycle, where Kamsa plays a role in Krishna's nativity and his first great battle with evil (though in previous lives Krishna had already fought battles with demons of all sorts before the one with Kamsa).

Kamsa's karmic chain began at the beginning of a new cosmic creation. Kamsa was a rebirth of Kâlanemi, a son of Virocana, an *asura* (demon) and the brother of Bali. After that rebirth as an evil human, his next rebirth was as Kâliya, a serpent king.

Kâlanemi had had six sons, who were reborn from a curse by Brahmâ. The six sons had a karmic chain that brought them into contact with Krishna. They had been reborn as sons of Kâlanemi because of what had happened in their previous lifetime. Brahmâ had created Marîci, whose life remains clouded in some mystery. His greatness cannot be doubted, but some say that he was one of the Maruts (gods associated with Indra, thus gods of storms and battle). Others say that he was a Prajâpati (progenitor, or grandfather), or even one of the seven *mahârishis*, who were also the seven cosmic principles. According to the *Bhâgavata Purâna* Marîci (light) and Ûrnâ married (in the *Brahmânda Purâna* his wife was Anasûyâ, "without spite") and had six sons so powerful that they rivaled the creator. One day when they saw Brahmâ, they mocked him, saying that he was a father who had married his own daughter (Sarasvatî). Brahmâ cursed them to be born as demons. And thus these six had rebirths in two important incarnations of Vishnu as sons of demons—first of Kâlanemi and then of Hiranyakaśipu—and in one as humans, as sons of Vasudeva and Devakî.

As sons of Hiranyakaśipu the six brothers were pious and even received a boon from Brahmâ, that no one could kill them. But Hiranyakaśipu cursed them to sleep in Pâtâla (the underworld). After much pleading by his sons, he changed the curse so that they would be reborn as the first six sons of Devakî, so that their father in their previous life, Kâlanemi, who was going to be reborn as Kamsa, would be their uncle in the next lifetime and could kill them. That would allow another rebirth, which was better than being stuck in Pâtâla.

So the karmic chain of events brought Kâlanemi and the six sons of Marîci into a human rebirth. Kamsa was born as the son of Ugrasena, the king of Mathurâ. The meddling sage Nârada told Kamsa that he was the result of a rape of his mother by a *gandharva* named Dramila, and that that was why his mother hated him and cursed him to be killed by a member of his own family. So Kamsa was not really surprised at the wedding of his sister Devakî when a voice from heaven said that his sister's eighth son would kill him. Kamsa drew his sword and would have killed her, had not her husband Vasudeva pledged to give him each of the sons when they were born. So began intermittent imprisonments of the couple and the killing of their first six sons, who were being reborn to work out karma going all the way back to their sin of mocking the creator.

Kamsa personally bashed the brains out of each baby boy. Kamsa's rule of Mathurâ became more and more evil. The seventh child was a girl and an incarnation of Mâyâdevî. Even though the seventh birth was not a boy, Kamsa tried to smash her head against the ground. But she rose into the air and announced that Kamsa's death was near.

Śrî Krishna was born as the eighth son of Devakî and Vasudeva. Kamsa tried many ways to kill Śrî Krishna—all of which failed. Finally, he was slain by Krishna when an attempted ambush backfired. For the details about how Balarâma and Krishna escaped death at the hands of Kamsa, see their entries as well as that of Devakî.

See also Balarâma; Brahmâ; Devakî; Hiranyakaśipu; Kâlanemi; Krishna; Mâyâ; Nârada

KANDU

A sage of Purânic fame

Kandu appeared in the *Vishnu Purâna* as the archetype of sages who lose their focus. He was called chief of the *devajñas* (ones who know the divine). His powerful austerities *(tapas)* caused Indra to worry that Kandu would become more powerful than himself, the king of the gods. So Indra sent one of heaven's temptresses, the *apsara* (celestial damsel) Pramlocâ, to distract Kandu from his practice *(sâdhana)*. He moved with her from the banks of the Gomatî River to the Mandara valley and lived with her for a century enjoying conjugal bliss. After that century, and the next and the next, Pramlocâ asked if she could take leave, but Kandu insisted that she stay and enjoyed her more each day. One evening he noticed that the sun was setting and he prepared to do his normal Brâhmanical duty *(sandhyâvandana)* with a prayer *(ariti)* to the setting sun. Pramlocâ asked why tonight, since he had never done it before while they were together. Kandu protested, saying that he never missed doing any of his practices—and, besides, they had only met that morning.

When Pramlocâ finally convinced him that they had been together for many years, Kandu was shocked to learn the exact amount of time—nine hundred years, six months, and three days. Kandu became very angry and shouted at his former lover. Then he sent her away forever, so that he could try to start acquiring merit *(punya)* and power *(siddhis)* anew. As she left, flying up through the trees, her perspiration was left on the leaves of the trees of the forest, and the wind (Vâyu) gathered the droplets together into a woman. Mârishâ, "nursed by the trees," was given the name Vârkshî and later married ten husbands (the Pracetases), according to a *Mahâbhârata* account. And in a Bhâgavata Purâna version Vârkshî became the mother of Daksha (ritual skill), father-in-law of Śiva.

Kandu must have lost all his powers. He got only minor roles in stories after that. Losing his sixteen-year-old son in a forest, Kandu cursed the forest to become a desert, a desert that was later found by Hanuman. And he was just one of the many sages invited by Râma to his court when Râma began his divine rule of Ayodhyâ.

See also Apsara; Siddhi; Tapas

KANVA
A sage of Purânic fame
In the *Rigveda* Kanva was part of Kaśyapa's family. His father was Medhâtithi. Kanva became a teacher with many disciples at his *aśrama* (hermitage) on the Mâlinî River in the Himâlayas. He was credited with writing as many as fifty chapters of the first section *(mandala)* and the entire tenth section of the *Rigveda*.

In the *Mahâbhârata* Kanva had an aśrama on the Parvenu River. One day Kanva discovered Śakuntalâ (one *raised* by the birds). This little girl had been abandoned by her parents, the great *brâhmin* sage Viśvâmitra and the celestial temptress Menakâ. Indra had sent Menakâ to spoil Viśvâmitra's austerities, and the fruit of their dalliance was abandoned but kept alive by the birds.

Many of the *Purânas* used another name for Kanva, that of Kaśyapa. This led to quite a few mistakes when events about Kaśyapa-Prajâpati—who would have lived about twenty generations prior to this Kaśyapa (Kanva)—are confused. One of those confusions occurred around which sage was bribed so that the giant serpent Takshâka would be successful in killing King Parîkshit. It should not have been Kanva. Besides his excellence as a hymnist, his major fame was his adopted daughter, Śakuntalâ, who became the subject of love stories in every Indian language.

See also Viśvâmitra

KAPILA

A powerful brâhmin, a philosopher, a magician

Kapila, the historical founder of the Samkhya school of philosophy *(darśana),* lived long enough before the *Epics* and *Purânas* only to have his name be coopted and given a set of myths. In the *Purânas* Kapila became a master *yogi* as well as a master magician. He was said to be a partial incarnation of Vishnu in one section of the *Mahâbhârata* and a worshipper of Śiva in another.

Born very close to the beginning of this age, Kapila engaged in such severe austerities *(tapas)* that he developed the power to incinerate things with a glance. Some versions stated that Vishnu had incarnated to kill the sixty thousand sons of King Asamañjasa. Others make the sons' own behavior in the presence of a great sage the cause of their death. Kapila had chosen Pâtâla (hell) to practice tapas. Meanwhile on earth, King Asamañjasa had lost his wild stallion in the middle of a horse sacrifice *(aśva-medha).* Indra had stolen it and hid it beside Kapila. The king sent his sixty thousand sons throughout the world and then into the netherworlds to find his horse. They found it near Kapila and disturbed his austerities. That seemed enough reason to incinerate all of them. Their ashes lay in the underworld through four generations until King Bhagîratha did two one-thousand-year penances in order to win the boon of bringing the Gangâ to earth (and to hell, according to this version) with sufficient water to complete the funeral rituals.

See also Bhagîratha; Gangâ; Magic, Blessings, Cursings; Mâyâ

KARMA (KARMAN)

A concept

Karma (or *karman*) is a concept that is central in Epic and Purânic mythology. The term itself comes from the verbal root, *kri,* meaning "to act, to do, to bring about." In the *Vedas, karma* had referred to action performed in ritual and was associated with the logic of Vedic fire sacrifices and Brâhmanical incantations *(mantras)*. But through succeeding periods *karma* came to mean any correct ethical activity and was connected to *dharma* (righteousness, duty). So many myths explicitly connected rebirth, or transmigration *(samsâra),* with *karma* and *dharma* that the three must be considered together. (See chapter 1 for more details.) If one's *karma,* in the sense of action, is in accord with *dharma,* one will have "good karma" that will lead to a good rebirth. If one's *karma* (action) is adharmic, against *dharma,* the "bad karma" that results may play out in lifetime after lifetime. A favorite saying used to explain *karma* to Westerners is "As ye sow, so shall ye reap."

Karma is discussed in chapter 1, "Mythic Themes: Specific" and in chapter 2. In fact, the entire second chapter is about the relationship of *karma* to *kâla-deśa-nimitta* (the Hindu time-space-causality continuum). It is not the purpose of this study to prove that *karma* functions differently over the centuries of Hindu mythology, religion, and philosophy in Vedic *rita* (justice), Brâhmanical ritualism (*yajñâs, yâgas*) with its ritual science (*mâyâ*), Upanishadic *jñâna* (knowledge), Epic and Purânic *tapas* and their derived *siddhis,* Yogic *sâdhanas,* and devotional *bhakti* and *prâsada.* It is the purpose of these chapters to alert the reader to Hindu mythology's use of a more mechanical or hard *karma* than is taught by most Hindu philosophers and theologians.

The story of Kamsa, recounted in the entry of that name, illustrates well how later mythology understood the workings of *karma.* The fruits of his actions take effect over many lifetimes, flowing from one lifetime to the next. Not only are his rebirths affected, but others are reborn over and over with him in changing roles and genders to work out complicated causal chains of events.

One distinction might be of value: that between "hard" *karma,* a mechanical working out of karmic cause and effect, and "soft" *karma,* which allows for grace or purification rituals to remove the effects of *karma* without full recompense by the individual. Not that the situation is that simple; rather there is a continuum between these two extremes, with many cases falling somewhere in the middle. Grace gained from devotion (*bhakti*) that softened *karma* was the subject of many myths.

See also Dharma; Kamsa; Samsâra
For further reading:
> Wendy Doniger O'Flaherty, ed., *Karma and Rebirth in Classical Indian Traditions* (Berkeley: University of California Press, 1980), and Robert Baird, ed., *Karma and Rebirth in Modern India* (The Hague: Mouton, 1985).

KARNA

Eldest son of Kuntî

In the *Mahâbhârata* war Karna had a divine birth. His mother, Kuntî, was the daughter of King Shûrasena. As a girl Kuntî was in charge of arrangement in the palace for religious rituals. During a period of four months when the sage Durvâsa performed rituals for the king, Kuntî served him so well that Durvâsa gave her a wondrous *mantra*. She could only use it five times, but it had the power to call forth a god and to allow her to bear a child by that god that would have his qualities. Her curiosity got the better of her, and she chanted the mantra focusing on the sun. Sûrya descended from the sun in human form, told her that she would not lose her virginity, and gave her a son. Kuntî was able to keep the child a secret with the help of her stepmother, putting the baby into a box and sending it down the river Aśvâ. The box floated into the Yamunâ and then into the Gangâ. It was pulled from the river by King Dhritarâshthra's charioteer, Adhiratha, and taken to his childless wife Râdhâ. Karna was brought up by these foster parents in the country of Anga. Later Karna went to Hastinâpura and studied archery with the great master *(âcârya)* Drona. Karna lied about his lineage in order to study under another great teacher, Paraśurâma. He became an ally of Duryodhana and fought on the side of the Kauravas. In the Kurukshetra battle he was a heroic fighter but was eventually killed by Arjuna. After he went to heaven, he merged with his father, Sûrya.

See also Durvâsa; Kuntî; Pandavas; Paraśu-Râma

KÂRTTIKEYA
Son of Śiva and Pârvatî, god of war; the planet Mars

Kârttikeya's name derived from his having been raised by the six Krittikâs, the name given to six of the seven wives of the seven *mahârishis*. He was also named Skanda and Subrahmanya.

Kârttikeya appeared in the epics, the *Mahâbhârata* and the *Râmâyana*, as a son fathered by Śiva without being born from the womb of a woman. Śiva's seed landed in the fire, and Agni transported it to the river goddess Gangâ. But the seed became too hot for Gangâ, so Kârttikeya was born on the shore in a thicket. From this birth two of his mythic names were derived: Agni-bhû (born of fire) and Gangâ-ja (descendant of Gangâ). Some versions assigned his birth to Pârvatî, as Śiva's principal wife.

He had six heads and was born with the purpose of destroying the terrible demon Târaka, son of Ditî. He rode on a peacock named Paravânî. His wife was Kaumârî, or Senâ. He was never as popular as Śiva's other son, Ganeśa. As a warrior he was called Mahâ-sena (great conquering army) and Senâ-pati (lord of a conquering army); he was also called Kumâra (boy—one who is always young), Guha (mysterious one), Śaktî-dhara (spear holder), Gangâ-putra (son of the Gangâ), Sara-bhû (born in the thicket), Târaka-jit (vanquisher of Târaka).

See also Krittikâs; Pârvatî; Śiva; Skanda; Subrahmanya

KAŚYAPA

A *prajâpati* (progenitor) who fathered all beings; a sage

Kaśyapa-Prajâpati has a major role in creation. However, there were variations concerning his birth and his status. In the *Mahâbhârata* Kaśyapa was only the son of Marîci, who was one of the six mind-born sons *(mânasâ-putras)* of Brahmâ. The *Vâlmîki Râmâyana* added Kaśyapa as the seventh and youngest sons of Brâhma and thus a brother of Marîci. Thus, Kaśyapa was either the son or grandson of Brahmâ.

As chief of the prajâpatis, Kaśyapa was the primary progenitor of this creation. Kaśyapa married twenty-one daughters of Daksha (See entry on Daksha to see how the mythmakers saw Daksha as an *âditya*, thus a son of Kaśyapa, or born from the thumb of Brahmâ.) Kaśyapa was the father of both the *devas* (gods) and the *asuras* (demons). His more important wives were Aditi, whose children were the âdityas (gods, *devas*), and Ditî, whose children were the daityas (demons, *asuras*). His main *daitya* children were Hiranyakaśipu, Hiranyâksha, and Simhikâ. Kaśyapa's wife Danu gave birth to the Dânavas: Kapila, Śankara, and Târaka were among those who gained fame. Surabhî gave him another order of children including Rudra (a storm god) and Tvashthri (the divine architect). Vinatâ gave birth to Garuda (king of the birds) and the bird kingdom, while Kadrû became mother of the Nâgas, the serpent kingdom.

There were an astonishing number of appearances and roles that Kaśyapa was given in late myths. These are distributed over three rebirths. In the *Câk-shusha Manvantara* he was the sage Sutapas and married to Prishnî. After twelve thousand years of austerities he won Lord Vishnu's promise that Vishnu would be born as his son. In the next *Manvantara* of Vaivasvata Manu, Sutapas and Prishnî were reborn as Kaśyapa and Aditi, and Lord Vishnu was their son as Vâmana-deva. Surasâ was one of Kaśyapa's wives in that lifetime and was reborn with him in his next rebirth. Then in the next lifetime these three—Kaśyapa, Aditi, and Surasâ—became Vasudeva and his two wives, Devakî and Rohinî.

See also Brahmâ; Devakî; Mânasâ-putra; Prajâpati

KAUTHUMI

Son of a brâhmin

A young *brâhmin* named Kauthumi, son of Hiranyanâbha, challenged the royal priests of King Janaka in debate. But he lost his temper and killed one of them, thus committing *brahmahatyâ* (murder of a *brâhmin*). He was cursed and became a leper that very day. After much suffering he followed the advice of his father and used a magical incantation to Sûrya, the sun god (an incantation known as the *shrâvya-smajñaka-sûkta*). He was healed of his leprosy and redeemed from his sin.

This story warrants notice, as it recommended neither Brâhmanical rituals *(pûjâ)* nor devotion *(bhakti)* but the magical power of secret *mantras*. Such a myth would appear to be recommending the special role of the teacher *(guru)* and esoteric knowledge.

See also Sûrya

KETU
An inauspicious celestial

Ketu had two levels of appearance in Hindu mythology. Astronomically Ketu was a comet, as well as the descending node (waning) of the moon. Ketu's mythological persona expanded from these associations. Ketu was one of the thirty-three children of Kaśyapa and Danu, so that he was technically a *dânava* and really an *asura* (demon). But his descending nature marked his character, as did his association with Râhu, the lunar eclipse (who tried to steal *soma* from the gods and had his head cut off). Ketu became the demon who created meteors and comets. He was visualized holding a sword and a lamp—a monster with a dragon's head.

See also Kaśyapa; Râhu

KRISHNA
Ninth incarnation of Vishnu; the Absolute itself

The Krishna myth cycle has been integrated in such a way that most Hindus do not know its real complexity. Some of its elements are very ancient, showing that many myths have come together to form modern versions. First, there was the Krishna myth of a divine king, possibly with tribal or even Dravidian roots. This Krishna, whose name literally means "dark" or "black one," may have elements of a historical figure from the first millennium before the common era. The Krishna of the *Mahâbhârata*, a warrior in most sections, but the incarnation of Vishnu in two of the epic's appendices (the *Bhagavad Gîtâ* and the *Hari-vamsa*), could be merged with the tribal Krishna into what scholars call the Vâsudeva Krishna, son of Vasudeva, being both royal and divine. But without doubt, the most complex Krishna was found in the *Purânas*—especially the *Bhâgavata Purâna*. Here we find Krishna as the divine baby and child, the amorous cowherd, the slayer of demons, and the victor over all forms of evil. This Krishna Gopâla must be the most popular deity in India. And certainly for many, the mythic streams from the *Epics* and the *Purâna* are harmonious. Finally, one must

Śrî Krishna manifests in pure love, playing his magical flute in a call to devotion.
(TRIP)

return to the *Mahâbhârata* for the aged Krishna, once again all too human, with stories of weakness and finally death. The stories selected from this wealth of materials could fit into all the mythic traditions of India, universalist or sectarian. The account given here will summarize the most widely accepted versions.

Krishna was born as the eighth son of Vasudeva and Devakî. Vasudeva and Devakî in their previous births were Kaśyâpa and his wife Aditi. Another wife of Kaśyâpa, Surâsa, was reborn as Rohinî, to fulfill the task of being the foster mother of Balarâma, Krishna's brother.

His parents' complex stories are nested in Krishna's birth narrative and employ one of the arch-villains of Hindu mythology, Kamsa, Krishna's uncle, who tries repeatedly to kill him.

Krishna was born with four hands holding the signs of Vishnu (conch, discus, club, and lotus). After instructing his father Vasudeva concerning past lives, Krishna revealed what needed to happen in this one. He then changed to a baby with more human characteristics. Vasudeva took Krishna and traded him with the baby who had been born to Nandagopa and Yashodâ in the village of Ambâdi. Vasudeva had to cross the Yamunâ River, but it changed its course to aid in his mission. Once Vasudeva returned with the substitute baby, he reported the birth to Kamsa. The evil uncle raced to the prison cell and attempted to kill the incarnation of Mâyâdevî as a baby girl, but she rose into the sky and spoke a chilling message: that the one who would kill Kamsa had already been born. Kamsa began a massacre of boy babies, so Nandagopa took Yashodâ and Krishna as well as Rohinî and Balarâma and moved to Gokula.

Krishna spent his childhood in Ambâdi (Gokula) amongst the Gopâlas ("cow keepers") and the Gopîs ("female cowherds"), whose main profession was looking after cows, and selling milk and curd.

The childhood of Krishna was full of merrymaking and danger. He was attacked by many types of demons in the service of Kamsa: Pûtanâ, the nurse with poisoned breasts, whom Krishna sucked dry and left her dead; Sakata disguised as a cart, which Krishna kicked to pieces; Trinâvarta who was invisible in a whirlwind, whom Krishna weighted down and choked to death; and an almost endless assortment of demons, beasts, and snakes. Some of these he killed dramatically, others he subdued and then converted, like Kâliya, the giant water serpent on whose head he danced. He performed miracles such as lifting Mount Govardhana on his finger to protect the Yâdavas, the local villagers, from Indra's torrential rain, sent by Indra in retaliation because Krishna had encouraged the villagers to stop worshipping Indra. Thus Krishna earned one of his many names, Govinda, "one who lifted the mountain." When his foster mother sought to catch him as the butter thief—or, some versions said, for putting dirt into his mouth, others, for eating sweets—he simply opened his mouth and showed her the entire universe.

Râdha became his best female friend, though each of the Gopîs thought that she was his favorite. Krishna was always accompanied by his brother Balarâma, who had been brought to Gokula by the sage Garga. Their play *(lîlâ)* with the Gopîs during this period became the subject of an extensive literature on devotion and love. On the surface it was highly erotic, including pranks like stealing the clothes of the Gopîs and making them come before him and beg, and calling all the women into the forest for lovemaking, even multiplying himself at least on one occasion so that each of them could have their own Krishna. The Gopîs were even called the 16,008 wives of Krishna. But good mythology, like good theology, has many levels of meaning—and at the deepest level that kind of lovemaking has been seen as pointing to a devotional relationship that risks everything for a personal experience of Krishna's presence and grace: loving, total, dangerous, and so much more.

By way of balance, Krishna also lived as a student *(brahmachâri)* in the *âsrama* of the sage Sândipani—following the orthoprax Brâhmanical stages of life *(asrama-varna-dharma).* Ready to perform their divine mission, Krishna and Balarâma traveled to Mathurâ for the fateful encounter with Kamsa. There they killed Kamsa, and released Vasudeva and Devakî from prison.

Kamsa's death was said in some accounts to have been necessary to deny Râvana his most powerful ally for the Râma-Râvana war. However, unraveling the nested myths in the Râma myth cycle is another problem; Krishna's purpose for incarnation did not end with his cosmic victory of evil, personified in Kamsa, but was prolonged in a sagely way as chariot driver for Arjuna in the great Bharata war. Krishna helped Draupadî, joint wife of Arjuna and his brothers, when she was assaulted by Dushshâsana, son of Duryodhana, leader of the Kauravas. On the Kurukshetra battlefield Krishna advised Arjuna about his duty and even manifested himself as the Supreme. After the Pandavas won the great war and set up their rule, the Yâdava dynasty, to which Krishna belonged, declined and was finally destroyed by internal strife. Krishna's death was told from a number of points of view. The most widely accepted is that the real reason for his death was that his mission as an incarnation was over. So one day he was sitting on a branch in a tree. A hunter mistook the sole of his foot for a bird and shot him with a poisoned arrow. (His foot was the only spot not protected by the magical potion of Durvâsa.) So Krishna died and ascended to *svarga* (heaven) and merged again into Vishnu.

> *See also* Arjuna; Avatâra; Bala-Râma; Devakî; Draupadî; Durvâsa; Duryodhana;
> Kâliya; Kamsa; Râdhâ; Vishnu
> *For further reading:*
> P. Banerjee, *The Life of Krishna in Indian Art* (1978; reprint New Delhi: Publication Division Ministry of Information, 1994); Alf Hiltebeitel, *The Ritual of*

Battle (Ithaca, NY: SUNY Press, 1976; reprint 1990 with Wendy Doniger); John S. Hawley, *Krishna, the Butter Thief* (Princeton: Princeton University Press, 1983) and *At Play with Krishna* (Princeton: Princeton University Press, 1981); Milton Singer, ed., *Krishna: Myths, Rites, and Attitudes* (Chicago: University of Chicago Press, 1969).

KRITTIKÂS

Goddesses; the Pleiades, wives of the seven sages *(sapta-rishis)*

Six of the wives of the seven sages, known as the *mahârishis,* were suspected of committing adultery with Agni and were cursed to become the Krittikâs, star sisters of the Pleiades. Astrological symbolism resides in this myth, giving an idea of what was observable at that time in the heavens. Mythologically there was ambiguity about their becoming stars. Some versions implied that this fate was a reward for their nursing the creation of Śiva, as Subrahmanya, while other versions made it a punishment. Also the paternity of Skanda as Subrahmanya, the fierce warrior, was questioned, with some myths stating that Agni was his father instead of Śiva and the six Krittikâs were his mothers.

See also Agni; Kârttikeya; Sapta-rishis; Skanda; Subrahmanya

KSHÎRÂBDHI-MATHANAM

The myth of the Churning of the Milky Ocean

This is one of the richest Hindu myths. It is a creation myth and also a trickster myth, and it is nested in the Vishnu myth cycle as an *avatâra* (incarnation) myth. It has versions that are pan-Indian and versions that are sectarian (those used to prove the supremacy and ultimacy of Vishnu). When it functions as an origin myth, answering the question of how the gods *(devas)* became immortal, this myth also becomes a trickster myth—how the *devas* trick the demons *(asuras)* out of their share of the sacrifices and especially out of receiving the drink of immortality *(amrita* or *amritsa)*. There are many versions of this myth, as well as many uses of it in other myths, both in the form of references to it and in the form of reversals of its themes.

In the sixth *manvantara* (world cycle) of the current *kalpa* (eon), the *devas* were losing in their battles with the *asuras.* One account said that the god Indra had slighted a *brâhmin* sage named Durvâsa and from that day on the power of the gods declined. So the *devas* went to Brahmâ, who immediately—as was usually the case in the Vaishnava myth cycle—counseled them to go to Vishnu.

Vishnu told the gods to follow his instructions exactly. They would have to work with the demons, but in the end Vishnu would enhance their glory. So the *devas* convinced the *asuras* that they must work together in order to obtain the drink of immortality. They would need to churn it up from the Milky Ocean *(kshîra-sâgara).* First herbs were thrown in the clear waters. Mount Manthara was used as a churning staff, and the giant snake Vâsuki became the churning rope. The *devas* took Vâsuki's tail, while the *asuras* grabbed his head with its fiery breath. Vishnu became the support for the mountain as the turtle *avatâra* (Kûrma) and simultaneously took an invisible form and pressed down on the mountain from above. The gods and demons pulled back and forth with Vâsuki, stirring the ocean and bringing all manner of things into being: Kâmadhenu (the wish-granting cow), Vârunîdevî, Pârijâtam, the *apsaras,* Chandra-Soma (the moon), venom *(halâhala),* which was absorbed by the serpents *(nâgas),* Dhanvantari with the pot of amrita, and Mahâlakshmî. The avatâra Kûrma raised Mount Mandara when it started to sink. The demons grabbed the pot of amrita from the sage Dhanvantari and would have become immortal had they drunk it. But the demons were tricked out of their share when Vishnu appeared as Môhinî and mesmerized them with her feminine charm and beauty. She told the *asuras* that she was lonely and looking for a mate. Môhinî said that they should close their eyes and the one who opened them last would be the one she would marry. But Môhinî went immediately to Devaloka (heaven) and gave the amrita to the *devas.* And even though the *asuras* attacked, the *devas* were strengthened by the divine drink and won dominion over the three worlds.

> *See also* Amrita; Apsara; Avatâra; Candra; Dhanvantari; Halâhala; Kâmadhenu; Kûrma; Lakshmî; Vishnu

KUBERA

A dark spirit who became the wealthiest god (deva)

Kubera has been interpreted to be a *deva* and, as such, the god of wealth. There were several versions of his parentage. In the *Atharvaveda* Kubera was chief of the spirits of darkness and son of Vaishravana. In the *Mahâbhârata* Kubera was son of the grandfather *(prajâpati)* Pulastya, by his wife Idavidâ, and brother of Viśravas. However, in the *Purânas* his lineage, born of Viśravas by Ilibilâ, became fixed and he was king of the Yakshas (the "marvelous" or "mysterious" ones)—and thus an *asura* (demon). His half brother was Râvana, demon of *Râmâyana* fame. Yet Kubera is accepted among the gods and even prayed to at the end of all ritual sacrifices.

Kubera married Bhadrâ (auspicious) and their daughter was Mînâkshî (fish-eyed). As myths were conflated, Kubera acquired both celestial and terrestrial domains. He was the lord of riches, especially those within the earth, which he could move by his will from one place to another. He often brought gems and precious metals near the surface during the rule of righteous kings and hid them during times of wickedness. He was also regent of the north (a world protector, *Lokapâla*). Kubera received his mace from the fragments of the sun that the celestial architect, Viśvakarman, trimmed from the sun to reduce his brilliance, in order to help the sun's wife live with him. His celestial city was well known for its wealth, located north of Himâlaya. He ruled the island kingdom of Lanka before his half-brother Râvana drove him away, even stealing Kubera's aerial vehicle, called the Pushpakavimâna. Even though Kubera is preserved as god of wealth by the continuing use of a prayer to him in Brâhmanical ritual, Ganeśa overshadows him in the hearts of the majority of Hindus.

See also Ganeśa

KUBJÂ

An ugly widow

The myth of Kubjâ is embedded within that of Tilottamâ, an *apsara*. Kubjâ either gained liberation from her performance of auspicious rituals, especially the one known as the Mâgha bath, or was transformed into a beautiful woman by the embrace of Śrî Krishna. Kubjâ was the rebirth of the celestial damsel called Tilottamâ, or Kubjâ might be seen as the incarnation of Tilottamâ.

See also Tilottamâ

KUCELA

A poor brâhmin

Kucela was a fellow student with Krishna of the sage Sândîpani. They were close friends as students, but lost contact in the following years. Kucela could not provide for his large family, and all were on the verge of starvation. One day his wife sent Kucela to visit Krishna with only a small package of rice as a gift—their last food. Krishna accepted the rice and ate a handful. Perhaps Krishna forgot to provide a feast for Kucela as they became engrossed in their renewed friendship, and perhaps Kucela forgot his mission to seek help for his family. (The various versions are rich with different details.) But the visit came to an end, and Kucela was almost home when he realized that Krishna had not given him anything to take back to his family. However, when he reached the place where once his miserable hut was, Kucela found a palace. Krishna had abundantly provided for his every need. Thus, Kucela, the friend of Krishna, became known as Sudâman, "the one upon whom [Krishna] bestowed abundantly."

See also Krishna

KUMBHAKARNA

An asura (demon)

Kumbhakarna appeared in the *Râmâyana* in a line of rebirths that started in Brahmâ's court in heaven *(svarga)*. In that lifetime he had been Vijâya, one of a pair of twin doorkeepers who were cursed for not properly performing their duties. He was reborn as Hiranyakaśipu and killed by Vishnu in his Narasimha incarnation *(avatâra)*. Next he was reborn as Kumbhakarna, to be killed by Vishnu in his Râma *avatâra*.

Kumbhakarna was a son of Viśravas by his *râkshasa* (night-wandering demon) wife Keshinî. He was a full brother of Râvana. The brothers practiced such power austerities *(tapas)* that the gods became frightened. They had Sarasvatî (goddess of learning) dance on Kumbhakarna's tongue when he asked Brahmâ for a boon. Kumbhakarna was going to ask for annihilation of the *devas (nirdevatvam)*, but with Sarasvatî dancing on his tongue, he asked for sleep *(nidrâvatvam)*. So that was what Brahmâ gave him. Kumbhakarna slept for six months and then was only awake for a day. When the war was going poorly for Râvana, Kumbhakarna was awakened, readied for battle with two thousand pots of liquor, and sent against Sugrîva, the great monkey warrior. Kumbhakarna was able to defeat Sugrîva by pounding him into submission with a giant boulder, and then carried him into Lanka as a prisoner. He returned to the battle and met Râma in single combat. But after a great fight, Râma cut off his head.

Kumbhakarna's advice to Râvana during various phases of the war showed that he judged his brother's actions as wrong and yet did his duty as a younger brother. In Brâhmanical orthoprax morality Kumbhakarna had done his duty in that birth. He was reborn as Dantavaktra, a Dânava king of Karûsha, to be killed by Vishnu in his Krishna avatâra. Then he returned to Vaikuntha, the abode of Vishnu.

See also Hiranyakaśipu; Jâya; Râvana

KUNTÎ

Mother of the Pandavas and wife of King Pandu

Kuntî was the aunt of Shrî Krishna, mother of the five Pandavas and a sixth son Karna, and wife of King Pandu. Kuntî was a heroine of the *Mahâbhârata*. As a child Kuntî was given to a royal cousin, King Kuntibhoja, who was childless. She was given responsibility over religious arrangements in his palace. That was when she met and served the powerful *brâhmin* Durvâsa. In his gratitude for her devotion, Durvâsa gave her a magical incantation that had the power to manifest any god upon whom she was thinking and allow her to have a child by him. She could not contain her curiosity to see if it worked and chanted the *mantra* focusing of the sun god, Sûrya. How gentle Sûrya was, assuring her that she would not even lose her virginity by having a child with him. So they conceived Karna, and only with the help of her stepmother was she able to hide her pregnancy. When she gave birth to this exceedingly handsome baby, Karna, he was immediately placed in a box and sent afloat down the river Aśvâ, on into the Yamunâ, and then into the Gangâ. The box was pulled from the river by Adhiratha, charioteer of King Dhritarâshthra, and taken to his childless wife Râdhâ. So Karna was brought up by these foster parents in the country of Anga.

Some accounts said that Kuntî chose her own husband in a *svayamvara,* wedding of her own choosing, but others more logically stated that she was married to the pale old King Pandu, to strengthen military alliances. Pandu soon took a second wife, Mâdrî. Versions differ about Pandu's age and health and whether or not he was cursed for killing a *brâhmin* who was making love with his wife in the form of deer. According to that version, a death curse had been placed on him: if he made love with his wives he would die. In both versions, the result was the same: both wives were childless, and he tried to get his wives to have sons by some noble person. It was then that Kuntî remembered her boon from Durvâsa. With Pandu's blessing, Kuntî used the mantra three more times for herself, having Dharmaputra (Yuddhishthira) by Dharma-deva, Bhîma by Vâyu-deva, and Arjuna by Indra-deva. Pandu wanted his wife Mâdrî to have children as well, so Kuntî gave her the last use of the fivefold boon. Mâdrî wisely focused on the Aśvins and had twins by them. That winter in exile in the forest Pandu forgot about the curse, made love with Mâdrî, and instantly died. Both wives would have joined him on his funeral pyre *(sati),* but the priests insisted that one of them must live to care for the little baby boys. So Kuntî lived to raise both sets of sons, known as the five Pandavas, in the palace at Hastinâpura with her husband's brother, King Dhritarâshthra, his wives, and their hundred sons, the Kauravas.

Eventually this arrangement brought out too much rivalry between the cousins, and Kuntî and her sons, the Pandavas, moved to the Lac palace at Vâranâvata. When it was set aflame in an attempt to kill all of them, they escaped through a secret tunnel and went into hiding. Each time an attempt was made to reconcile the brothers with their cousins more conflicts, deceits, and suffering occurred. Through it all Kuntî tried to mediate between the Kauravas and the Pandavas. After the great Bhârata war Kuntî helped all the others in their grief over the enormous losses of so many of their kin. She then went with Dhritarâshthra and his wife Gândhârî into the forest on the banks of the Gangâ. There they practiced stern penances, taking food only once a month, until they all died in a forest fire. Kuntî, joined by Mâdrî and Pandu, then entered Devaloka (heaven).

See also Arjuna; Bhîma; Dhritarâshthra; Gândhârî; *Mahâbhârata;* Pandavas; Pandu

KÛRMA

Second incarnation of Vishnu as a tortoise

This is one of the richest myths in the Vishnu myth cycle. Its popularity makes it pan-Indian and not just sectarian, even though many versions attempt to prove the ultimacy of Vishnu and his supremacy over Śiva. When it is seen as an origin myth, answering the question of how the gods became immortal, this myth also includes a trickster myth, which tells how the gods tricked the demons out of their share of the sacrifices and especially out of receiving the drink of immortality (amrita, or amritsa). There are many versions of this myth, as well as many uses of it in other myths, both in the form of references to it and of variations upon its themes.

In the beginning the gods (devas) and the demons (asuras) decided that they must work together in order to obtain the drink of immortality. They needed to bring amrita into being from chaos, thus to bring it up from the primordial ocean. They would have to make a churn large enough to stir the possibilities of existence into being from the Milky Ocean. Vishnu incarnated as a turtle and dove to the bottom of the sea. Upon his back rested the famous Mount Mandara, which would be the churning stick. The serpent Vâsuki was used as the churning rope, and the gods and demons pulled back and forth, stirring the ocean and bringing all manner of things into being. Finally, the pot of amrita came to the surface in the hands of the sage Dhanvantari. The asuras took the divine ambrosia from him—and may have even been willing to share it. But the devas had a promise from Vishnu that the asuras would not be allowed to have a share. The demons were tricked out of their share of the drink of immortality by a manifestation of Vishnu as Môhinî, a temptress of unusual beauty. Seductively, Môhinî coaxed the asuras to allow her to divide it equally among them—but only after they took a purificatory bath. Their trust was misplaced, as Môhinî left with the amrita as soon as they went for their bath. And when the devas had fortified themselves with the divine nectar, they were a match for the asuras. The correct order (dharma) having been restored, Kûrma's purpose for incarnating had been accomplished, so he was able to merge back into Vishnu.

See also Amrita; Avatâra; Kshîrâbdhi-Mathanam; Môhinî; Vishnu

KURUKSHETRA

A place north of modern Delhi

Kurukshetra simply means "the field of the Kurus." The Kurus or Kauravas decended from Kuru, a king of the Lunar Dynasty. About eighty-five miles north-northeast of Delhi, Kurukshetra has been an important pilgrimage site (tîrtha) for at least twenty centuries. References in the Mahâbhârata to a fire altar *(vedi)* of Brahmâ would indicate that this area was considered the very heart of the Aryan or Bharata homeland. These plains also saw great historic battles, including those with the Mughals in the sixteenth through the eighteenth centuries.

See also Arjuna; Krishna; Mahâbhârata
For further reading:
Surinder Mohan Bhardwaj, *Hindu Places of Pilgrimage in India* (Berkeley: University of California Press, 1973).

LAKSHMANA
Son of Sumitrâ and Daśaratha

Lakshmana was the younger half-brother of Râma by the third and youngest wife of King Daśaratha of Ayodhyâ. But his affection for Râma was understood to have been the result of his previous lifetime—as an incarnation of Lord Vishnu's serpent, the one who floated as his bed on the cosmic ocean, Ananta (also called Śesha). Lakshmana could even be counted as a one-eighth incarnation of Vishnu. Lakshmana was the archetype of brotherly devotion, an example of pure human love and devotion *(bhakti)*.

Lakshmana married Ûrmilâ, with whom he had two sons. He left them behind in Ayodhyâ and followed Râma and Sîtâ into their forest exile of fourteen years. Lakshmana was heroic and loyal to Râma in every way. When a *râkshasî* (female night-wandering demon) named Sûrpanakhâ found Râma very attractive and wanted him as her husband, Râma rejected her. Furious she attacked the brothers, and Râma ordered Lakshmana to disfigure her. Lakshmana cut off her breasts and nose. Another account said that it was her nose and ears. Sûrpanakhâ went straight to her three brothers, who swore they would avenge her mutilation. The giant *râkshasas* led an army of fourteen thousand against Râma and Lakshmana and engaged them in a furious battle. However, the human brothers killed every one of them. Then Sûrpanakhâ told her really big brother, Râvana, and the war of revenge began with Sîtâ's abduction to Râvana's kingdom in Lanka.

After helping Râma defeat Râvana and all his forces and returning to Ayodhyâ, Lakshmana continued to help with Râma's divine rule. However, the purpose for the incarnation had been completed, and Yama (the god of death, also called Kâla, time) came disguised as a *brâhmin*. He demanded a private and uninterrupted audience with Râma. Râma assigned Lakshmana the task of keeping all out on pain of banishment. Old, meddlesome Durvâsa arrived and ordered Lakshmana to let him see the king immediately or he would curse Râma with the worst of calamities. Knowing that he would have to be banished for breaking what had been Râma's royal command, Lakshmana burst in and forced Râma to placate Durvâsa. Râma escaped Durvâsa's curse, but Lakshmana was forced into exile.

The ending of this incarnation had a stark version and a pleasant one. In one account, Râma became depressed without his brother. Râma ended his life by drowning in the Sarayû River at Gotâra and returned to Vishnu (Vaikuntha in one account; Vishnupâda ("Vishnu's feet") in another; some see them as the same). Lakshmana heard of Râma's death and drowned himself at the same place in the river. Another version stated that Lakshmana retired to the banks of the Sarayû River and practiced penance there. The gods showered flowers on him and transported him bodily to heaven—thus avoiding the problem of suicide.

See also Daśaratha; Durvâsa; Râma; *Râmâyana;* Râvana; Sîtâ

LAKSHMÎ
Goddess, wife of Vishnu

Lakshmî's multiple importance in Hindu mythology cannot be captured in a few paragraphs. Three perspectives will demonstrate the breadth of her roles and the changes in the ways in which she was perceived.

Linguistically and historically, *lakshmî* in the *Rigveda* was a word of feminine gender that quantified good fortune (the one of hundred thousands). Lakshmî became personified in the later *Vedas* as the correspondences *(bandhu)* with the priestly tradition found in the universe. In the *Śatapatha Brâhmana* she and Śrî were the two wives of the celestial father, Âditya. However, Âditya as father-creator disappeared when *âditya* became a term for a group of gods, the âdityas—the sons of Aditya. Throughout the Vedic period Lakshmî floated from one father to another: daughter of Prajâpati, Kshîrasâgarakanyakâ ("churning of the milky ocean daughter"), mother of Kâma—usually with a lotus in one hand *(padmâ).* By the time of the *Epics* Lakshmî had become a major goddess. She appeared in the sage Nârada's list of gods and goddesses whom he worshipped, and elsewhere she had become associated with Vishnu as his wife, or as one of his wives.

From this point on, the myths about Lakshmî were imbedded in theological perspectives. In goddess theology *(Śâkta)* Lakshmî was Devî, the mother and source of the universe, supreme energizing and creative energy of Vishnu. In Hindu polytheism Lakshmî was one of the many interesting goddesses with a myriad of stories about her many births and rebirths. In Vaishnava theology Lakshmî was wife of Vishnu—the Supreme, from whom all exists. Shaiva theology honored Lakshmî as Vishnu's wife in much the same way as Hindu polytheism. Thus, depending on the perspective, there were many variations of birth, or origin, myths, purpose, or savior, myths, and so on.

Lakshmî appears as Gajalakshmî, goddess with the elephants, giver of all that is good and bountiful in life. (TRIP)

Lakshmî's birth in the *Devî Bhâgavata Purâna* was from the Supreme Being's left side. Then she divided herself again into Lakshmî Devî and Râdhâ Devî, each wedding different aspects of Vishnu to herself. Then in each incarnation *(avatâra)* of Vishnu, according to the *Vishnu Purâna*, Lakshmî also incarnated: at the churning of the Milky Ocean as Padmâ, in the dwarf *avatâra* as Kamalâ or Padmâ, in the Paraśu-Râma incarnation as Dharanî, in the Râma *avatâra* as Sîtâ, in the Krishna *avatâra* as Rukminî. In all other descents, she was there as well. From this perspective Lakshmî's story would be found nested in the story of Vishnu's incarnations.

There were stories from perspectives that suggest that Lakshmî was appropriated by Śaivas. These fragments could be explained from any perspective, but they are worth mentioning to suggest her role in situations other than that of being Vishnu's wife. Lakshmî cursed Mahâvishnu to have his head fall off; she stayed in the court of Kubera (god of wealth) and also in the court of Brahmâ, and then as the goddess Śrî, saying that she was only Lakshmî, not Sacî (a wife of Indra), and that she had left Bali for Indra. The stories about Lakshmî courting kings may have been responsible for a division of Mahâlakshmî (Great Lakshmî) into two forms: a chaste and virtuous Vishnu-priyâ-Lakshmî and a flirtatious Râjya-Lakshmî. But a curse was used to explain why she lived with or was the wife of so many different gods.

As the goddess of wealth and plenitude, Lakshmî is worshipped in temples and homes in many forms, such as Gajalakshmî (a river goddess) or Dhana-lakshmî (giver Lakshmî). Her images almost always hold a lotus (padmâ) in one hand.

See also Avatâra; Devî; Vishnu

LANKA

A city; an island

In the *Râmâyana* the story is told that Brahmâ gave Lanka to Kubera, god of wealth. Celestial architects Viśvakarman and Maya together designed this celestial city and built it of gold. Its first location was on the top of Mount Trikûta, a peak of Mahâmeru (great Meru). However, in a fight between Vâyu, god of wind, and Vâsuki, king of the Nâgas, the entire peak, including the celestial city, was broken off and knocked into the sea, becoming Lanka.

Râvana defeated his half-brother Kubera and ruled Lanka for many years. When Râvana abducted Sîtâ, it was to his island kingdom that he brought her.

See also Kubera; Mahâmeru; Râma; Râvana; Vâsuki; Vâyu; Viśvakarman

LANKÂ-LAKSHMÎ

The doorkeeper at Râvana's palace

The *Kamba Râmâyana*'s account of Vijâya-Lakshmî and the story of the Jâya and Vijâya from the *Bhâgavata Purâna* are mirrored copies of each other. Lankâ-Lakshmî had been Vijâya-Lakshmî in her previous lifetime. As Vijâya-Lakshmî, she had been a negligent doorkeeper at Brahmâ's palace. So Brahmâ cursed her to be reborn as the doorkeeper of Râvana. Brahmâ told her that she would be released from the curse and would return to heaven by the touch of Vishnu. Some accounts take the mystery out of the story by giving away the entire ending: Hanuman, a partial incarnation of Vishnu, was destined to fulfil the condition of her release.

Thus, Hanuman arrived to Lanka and was barred entry by an enormous female warrior, Lankâ-Lakshmî, who let out a ferocious roar. Hanuman knocked her down with a single blow. Lankâ-Lakshmî politely asked his mission, learned of Râma, went to him, worshipped him, was blessed by Râma, returned to Satya-loka (the place of truth, heaven), and resumed her duties with a better attitude.

See also Hanuman; Râma

LIKHITA

A sage

In the *Mahâbhârata* Likhita and Śankha were brothers, with their *aśramas* (hermitages) next to each other on the banks of the Bâhudâ River. One day Likhita was hungry and went over to his brother's *aśrama* and began eating his vegetables. Śankha discovered the theft and took Likhita before the king. The king's law stated that a thief would be punished by cutting off the thief's hands. So King Sudyumna did just that. With blood flowing from each arm, Likhita stood before Śankha. The older *brâhmin* congratulated his brother for accepting his punishment and then told him to bathe in the Bâhudâ. Likhita did and his hands began growing back. He ran to Śankha, who told him that this was accomplished by the power of his (Śankha's) austerities *(tapas)*. Likhita questioned why his brother could not have purified him without having his hands cut off. Śankha answered that it was the duty *(dharma)* of the king to administer the law and that King Sudyumna had become great by so doing.

See also Dharma; Tapas

LÎLÂVATÎ

A prostitute

In the *Padma Purâna* Lîlâvatî (charming) was a prostitute in the *krita yuga* (first age, also called *satya yuga*). She went to another town looking for better clients. She noticed devotees celebrating a festival at the temple. When she inquired, Lîlâvatî learned that it was the celebration of the birthday of Râdhâ Devî and that anyone who observed the vow of devotional penance and fasting *(vrata)* that day would be absolved of all their sins. Lîlâvatî joined in the temple worship for the whole day. Shortly afterwards, she died of snake bite. Yama came to take her soul to hell for all her sins as a prostitute. Vishnu's helper also arrived in a chariot pulled by celestial swans *(hamsas)* and took her to heaven because of her one day of devotion.

    See also Bhakti

LINGA, LINGAM
A symbol of Śiva

There is scholarly agreement that there was worship of the male generative organ in the Indus Valley civilization. Both archeological remains and explicit references to "worshippers of the phallus" in the *Rigveda* support such an interpretation. However one interprets Śiva's origin—as from the Indus Valley, from tribal religion, within the Aryan clans, or any combination of these—use of the *linga* to represent Śiva was indisputable in the Epics and *Purânas.* Three myths will suffice: one of self-castration, another about an attempted curse, and then one about the consequence of a curse.

    In the *Śiva Purâna* Brahmâ, Vishnu, and Rudra (Śiva) were arguing over creation. When Brahmâ and Vishnu told Śiva that he was the lord of everything and for him to create as he wished, Śiva dove into the cosmic waters for more than a thousand celestial years. Brahmâ and Vishnu decided not to wait for creation any longer, so Vishnu gave Brahmâ enough energy *(śakti)* to bring everything into being. Just when Brahmâ had finished his creation, Śiva emerged from the water and angrily destroyed everything by fire. The frightened Brahmâ worshipped Śiva lavishly, whereupon the pleased Śiva granted Brahmâ a boon. Brahmâ asked that everything be restored. Śiva restored Brahmâ's creation, discovered that he had no use for all the creative energy he had stored up, and tore off his linga. The discarded linga extended deeper into the cosmic waters than Vishnu could dive and higher into the cosmos than Brahmâ could soar. So they instituted worship of the linga with heart and mind focused upon Śiva, because all desires would be fulfilled by Śiva.

    In the *Brahmânda Purâna* the seven great sages (sapta-rishis), primordial *mahârishis* (great sages) led by Bhrigu, were visited by Śiva in the pine forest on the slopes of Himâlaya. Despite all their asceticism and orthodox living they were unable to recognize the god of gods, Mahâdeva himself. He was smeared

Śiva sitting in front of the Śiva Linga in this common representation (TRIP)

with ash, naked, his *linga* decorated with red and white chalk, howling and dancing. He excited their wives, so the sages used all their ascetic powers (*siddhis*) to curse him—but to no avail. Their curses had been effective against all the other gods: Brahmâ's sacrifice was destroyed; Vishnu's incarnations were made miserable by Bhrigu's curse; Indra was castrated by Gautama's curse; the Vasus were imprisoned as embryos; Nahusha was cursed to be a serpent; the Milky Ocean was made undrinkable; Dharma-deva was cursed by Mândavya. So again they tried, cursing Śiva's *linga* to fall off. Even then they failed. But Śiva chose to disappear, cutting off his own *linga* and leaving the world without any light or energy. So the sages raced in panic to Brahmâ and learned that they had been dealing with the lord of the universe. They learned from Brahmâ how to propitiate him with an image of the *linga* as they worshipped and praised Śiva. Finally, Śiva revealed himself to them and taught them the supreme *yoga* so that they would be purified.

In the *Padma Purâna* the great sages wanted to know who was the supreme lord and deserved their worship. Bhrigu was selected to test each of the Trimûrti, the Hindu Triad. Bhrigu went to Kailâsa and demanded to see Śiva. But Nandi, Śiva's bull, rudely prevented him from going into Śiva's palace because Śiva was making love and was not to be disturbed by anyone. After many days of waiting, Bhrigu cursed Śiva: because he was so addicted to lovemaking, he would only be worshipped as a *linga* and *yoni* (female generative symbol). Bhrigu further declared that no twice-born (orthoprax Hindus of the upper three castes, but in this story, seemingly just *brâhmins*) would worship Śiva. Next Bhrigu traveled to Brahmaloka and again was not welcomed. Brahmâ sat on his lotus flower full of passion (*rajas*). So Bhrigu cursed him: Brahmâ would cease to be worshipped by anyone. Finally, Bhrigu went to the northern shore of the Milky Ocean and found Vishnu sleeping on his serpent, Ananta (eternity). When Vishnu did not wake up immediately, Bhrigu became angry at his lack of courtesy and kicked Vishnu. Îsvara awoke, saw Bhrigu, and welcomed him in the highest manner expected by a *brâhmin*—even thanking him for kicking him with feet whose dust caused good fortune. The proud *brâhmin* had finally found a god who was worthy of worship by *brâhmins*. So he returned to the great sages and reported that only Vishnu could be worshipped by the twice-born. Then he bragged about his curse: thanks to him, in the future Śiva would only be worshipped in a despicable form—the *linga*.

See also Bhrigu; Brahmâ; Sapta-Rishis, Śiva; Vishnu
For further reading:
Wendy Doniger O'Flaherty, *Siva: The Erotic Ascetic* (New York: Oxford University Press, 1973) and *Asceticism and Eroticism in the Mythology of Siva* (Delhi: Oxford University Press, 1973).

MÂDRÎ, MÂDRAVTÎ

One of the two wives of Pandu

Mâdrî was the second wife of King Pandu and was a mother of two of the five Pandava brothers. When she was lent a magical incantation by Kuntî (the king's first wife) that would allow her to have a child by any deity she focused on, Mâdrî concentrated upon the Aśvin twins, and twins were born to her, Nakula and Sahadeva. When Pandu died shortly after his wives gave birth to the five sons of gods, the Pandavas, Mâdrî joined him on his funeral pyre *(sati)*.

See also Kuntî; Pandavas; Pandu; Satî

MAGIC, BLESSINGS, CURSINGS

Many myths mention the use of magic directly. The myth of Bala, an *asura* (demon), mentioned that he knew and taught ninety-six kinds of magic to trouble the *devas* (divinities). Hanuman was said to practice the eight superhuman powers *(ashtha siddhis)*. The *asuras* had a life-restoring magic *(mritansañjîvanî)* that they had been using in their battles against the *devas*. It was this magic that necessitated giving the *devas amrita*, a potion that bestowed immortality, which was churned up from the Milky Ocean. Śîlavatî was a wife who, by practice of austerities *(tapas)*, was able to cast a spell that prevented the sun from rising.

Many terms are used in the myths for those who practice this art: for example, *mâyâvî* and *tapasvinî* (magician). The logic of ritual and private magic is discussed in chapter 1, "Renunciation, Sacrifice, and Magic."

See also Bala; *Kshîrâbdhi-mathanam*; Mâyâ; Siddhi; Tapas
For further reading:
Lee Siegel, *Net of Magic: Wonders and Deceptions in India* (Chicago: University of Chicago Press, 1991); Jan Gonda, *Change and Continuity in Indian Religion* (The Hague: Mouton, 1965); Paul D. Devanandan, *The Concept of Maya: An Essay in Historical Survey of the Hindu Theory of the World, with Special Reference to the Vedanta* (London: YMCA Publishing House, 1954); Teun Goudriaan, *Maya Divine and Human* (Delhi: Motilal Banarsidass, 1978).

MAHÂBALI

See BALI

MAHÂBHÂRATA

One of the two Epics; a scripture

The *Mahâbhârata* is an epic of enormous proportions—a hundred thousand verses, making it arguably the largest such poem in existence. It has tradition-

Battle scenes from the great or Mahâbhârata *war (TRIP)*

ally been said to have been dictated by the sage Vyâsa to his divine scribe, Ganeśa, who wrote it all down using his single tusk as the stylus. It is currently divided into eighteen parts, with two important appendices: the *Harivamsha* and the *Bhagavad Gîtâ*.

Although the epic may originally have been drawn from bardic material about warrior heroes, it was appropriated by an orthoprax Brâhmanical tradition that was eventually dominated by the Bhârgava priestly lineage. Even so, varied perspectives survive within its caste framework *(varna-aśrama-dharma)*. Although nested storytelling predominates, a simple account can be given of the basic events.

Two sons, Dhritarâshthra and Pandu, were born to King Vicitarvîrya. Dhritarâshthra was the elder, but because he was born blind, he was disqualified to succeed Vicitarvîrya. So Pandu became king and had five sons, the Pandavas. But shortly after their mysterious birth, he died. So Dhritarâshthra came to the throne, which set up a problem of who would succeed him as king: his eldest son Duryodhana or Pandu's eldest son Yudhishthira. His one hundred sons and the five Pandavas were raised, educated, and trained in the martial arts together. Duryodhana claimed succession and forced the Pandavas and their joint wife Draupadî into exile. But when Duryodhana took the throne, the Pandavas challenged his right. So to avoid war Dhritarâshthra divided the kingdom. But Yudhishthira lost their half in a gambling match, Draupadî was humiliated as Duryodhana's son claimed even her clothes, and the Pandavas were forced into a twelve-year exile, plus a year of living incognito. The twelve years of forest adventures nested stories within stories, followed by more adventures in the year living incognito.

The Pandavas returned to claim their half of the kingdom in the fourteenth year, but all this privation was for naught. Duryodhana would not honor the agreement to return their kingdom. The great eighteen-day war began. Just before combat was actually joined comes the episode recounted in the *Bhagavad Gîtâ:* Arjuna lamented fighting a war against so many of his friends and kin, and Krishna, his charioteer, answered that he must do his duty *(dharma)* and fight, but that he could avoid sin by renouncing the fruits of his actions (thus engaging in *nishkâma karma*—desireless action).

The Pandavas actually did win the war, but the emotional toll was so great that Yudhishthira abdicated and left the kingdom to a young relative. He and his brothers, their wife, Draupadî, and a dog set out for heaven, which was reached by going north into the Himâlayas. All died along the way, except Yudhishthira and his dog. When they finally reached heaven, the dog was refused entrance, and Yudhishthira would not go into heaven without him. The problem was solved when it was revealed that the dog was really Dharma-*deva*. Yudhishthira was shocked to find Duryodhana already in heaven and, worse, that he himself would have to be reborn to another lifetime on earth because of his attachments and lack of renunciation.

See also Arjuna; Dharma; Draupadî; Duryodhana; Kurukshetra; Pandavas

MAHÂDEVA
An epithet of Śiva
Mahâdeva means the great god. It is one of the many titles or epithets of Śiva.

See also Śiva

MAHÂMERU
Great Meru, a celestial mountain
On the celestial mountain were the nine heavenly cities of Brahmâ, Indra, Agni, Yama, Niritti, Varuna, Vâyu, Kubera, and Îsâna. The abode of Śiva, Kailâsa, was also placed on Mahâmeru in Śaiva texts. According to the *Mahâbhârata*, Mahâmeru was the king of mountains.

MAHÂVISHNU
See VISHNU

MAHISHA, MAHISHÂSURA
An asura (demon)
At the beginning of this creation, Kaśyâpa-prajâpati and Danu had two powerful sons who competed with the *devas* (gods), Rambha and Karambha. They practiced austerities *(tapas)* in order to defeat the gods, but in spite of this Karambha was killed by Indra. Rambha chose to use Brahmâ's boon for his ascetic practice to gain a son who would not be defeated by *devas* or *asuras*. The boon was granted, and the son was born to his wife, a *mahishî* (she-

buffalo) of great charm. Some versions stated that Rambha lost his caste because of this marriage. They moved to Pâtâla (the netherworld) before the son was born. A giant buffalo *(mahisha)* tried to steal Rambha's wife, and, in attempting to prevent the theft, Rambha was killed. Mahishî joined her husband on his funeral pyre *(sati)*. The young buffalo demon grew and eventually became the king of the *asuras*. Nobody could defeat Mahisha, as the son was called—because of his father's boon and an extension in the myth of *karma* from father to son.

Mahisha was intoxicated with pride and even forced the gods to worship him. Finally, they were led by Indra to ask a solution from Brahmâ, Vishnu, and Śiva. They decided upon war. A terrible battle occurred, but Mahisha just could not be killed. The gods had to rest. Then, after several centuries had passed, they gathered together and realized that Mahisha could not be killed by a male—and that would include the Trimûrti (Brahmâ, Vishnu, and Śiva). Mahisha could only be defeated by a woman. Most accounts credited the gods with combining all their powers to create a single being of light, a *devî* (goddess) of celestial beauty with eighteen arms named Durgâ. She rode her lion to the entrance way into heaven *(Devaloka)* and proclaimed that she would become the wife of anyone who could defeat her in armed combat. Mahisha fell in love and was determined to have her. He sent his seconds, then his army, and lastly himself. Finally, he changed into his ferocious form of the buffalo demon but Durgâ cut off his head with a discus *(Vishnu cakra)*. Thus Mahishâsura was killed by Durgâ, and peace and order were restored to the three realms.

In one major variant of the story, Kâlî sprang from Durgâ's forehead, personifying her anger, so that it would be Kâlî who killed Mahisha. And when the world again was threatened by evil, by the demons Śumbha and Niśumbha, Durgâ's avenging energy, Kâlî, destroyed them.

See also Devî; Durgâ; Kâlî

MAINÂKA
A mountain in the Harivamsa

There was a time when the mountains could fly. When they came to earth, they caused injury and suffering. Humans prayed to Indra, and he cut off the mountains' wings.

The mythic tradition used Mainâka in a variety of ways without much regard to an actual location. Mainâka was the son of Himâlaya and was rescued by his friend Vâyu, the wind god. Mainâka lived according to one account in the ocean. Thereby Mainâka helped Hanuman, the great monkey god and servant of Râma, cross the ocean on his way to Lanka to save Sîtâ. In another account

Mainâka was the mountain on which King Bhagîratha practiced the austerities *(tapas)* that convinced Śiva to bring the Gangâ to earth.

See also Bhagîratha; Hanuman; Indra; Vâyu

MAITRA-VARUNA
A sage with the patronym from Mitra and Varuna

This version of an episode involving King Nimi and the sage Vasishtha was given in the *Devî Bhâgavata*. Nimi and Vasishtha had cursed each other, and the result for Vasishtha was that he was alive but had no body. Vasishtha went to Brahmâ for advice and was told to merge with the brilliance of Mitra-Varuna (the composite sun deity). So Vasishtha went to Mitra-Varuna's *aśrama* (hermitage) and merged with that brilliance. When the *apsara* (celestial damsel) Urvaśî came to the *aśrama*, she excited Mitra-Varuna, whose seed was collected in a jar, and two sages were born when the seed ripened—the great sages, Agastya and Vasishtha.

See also Agasti; Mitra; Urvaśî

MAITREYÎ
A woman sage

Maitreyî was mentioned in the *Vedas* and *Purânas* as one of the wisest and most virtuous of women. Maitreyî was married to the great philosopher-sage Yâjñavalkya. She was noted as being especially learned in the scriptures. In one of the *Upanishads* Maitreyî engaged her husband in one of Hindu philosophy's great dialogues: about happiness as the most important experience in life.

See also Upanishad

MÂLINÎ
A Brahmin woman

This story has interesting implications about *karma* and rebirth. A *brâhmin* woman was mentioned in the *Skanda Purâna* for her bad character and equally bad deeds. Consequently, she was reborn as a dog. But during that lifetime she was able to observe a vow of purification *(Śukladvâdashi vrata)* and was reborn next as an *apsara* (celestial damsel)—the famed Urvaśî. It was Urvaśî who was attracted to Arjuna during his time as a dance instructor. It was also Urvaśî who was cursed by Mitra and Varuna for exciting them.

See also Arjuna; Subrahmanya; Urvaśî

MÂNASÂ-PUTRA, MÂNASA-PUTRA

Mind-born of Brahmâ

This title of child of mind was given to those who were born of the mind of Brahmâ, the creator. Lists of seven, nine, and ten are given. In most cases the *mânasâ-putras* are thought of as identical to the Prajâpatis, the progenitors of all beings in each creation. The list of nine included Bhrigu, Pulastya, Pulaha, Kratu, Angiras, Marîci, Daksha, Atri, and Vasishtha.

See also Prajâpati

MANDAKARNI (ALSO CALLED SATAKARNI)

A sage

Mandakarni did austerities *(tapas)* in a pond for ten thousand years. Indra became fearful that Mandakarni's *tapas* would be used to gain a boon that would upset the order of heaven, so he sent five celestial maidens *(apsaras)* to distract him. The five apsaras did distract Mandakarni. He built a palace near the pond and lived with the maidens for many years. The palace became famous for music and dance. Even Râma and Lakshmana visited *Pañcâpsaras* Palace (five celestials palace) during their exile in the forest. Mandakarni had no tapas left to threaten Indra any more.

See also Apsara; Tapas

MÂNDHÂTA

See YUVANÂSHVA

MANDODARÎ

Wife of Râvana, king of asuras (demons)

In her previous birth, Mandodarî had been a celestial damsel *(apsara)* named Madhurâ. Madhurâ went to Kailâsa to worship Śiva, having observed a special vow, the *Somavâra vrata*. When Madhurâ reached Kailâsa, Pârvatî, Śiva's wife, was not there. Madhurâ worshipped and praised Śiva. But they were attracted to each other and made love. When Pârvatî returned to Kailâsa, she saw Madhurâ's breast smeared with the ash from Śiva's body. Pârvatî went into a great fury and cursed Madhurâ to live as a frog for twelve years. Śiva was grief-struck. He consoled Madhurâ that after twelve years she would become a very beautiful woman and would be married to a great king. Madhurâ became a frog in a well.

Maya, an *asura* born to Kaśyâpa and Danu, was married to Hemâ, an apsara. They had two sons, Mâyavi and Dundubhi, but also wanted a daughter. For twelve years they prayed to Śiva for one. One day as Maya and Hemâ were worshipping Śiva, they heard a cry for help from the nearby well. They found a beautiful young woman in the well. They adopted her and named her Mandodarî.

Mandodarî was married to Râvana—certainly a great enough king. Mandodarî was very pious and noble. She tried to dissuade Râvana from tormenting Sîtâ, the wife of Râma, and warned him that his actions could prove to be fatal. Mandodarî was also described as one of the five ideal women in Hindu mythology *(pañcakanyâs)*.

See also Râvana; Sîtâ

MANGALA

The planet Mars

The *Skanda Purâna* says that Mangala (Mars) was born of the sweat of Śiva, which was produced on his forehead when he heard the news that his wife Satî had committed suicide at Daksha's sacrifice *(Dakshayâga)*. The planet Mars is worshipped as a deity.

See also Daksha; Satî; Śiva

MANTHARÂ

An evil servant

The maid of Queen Kaikeyî was reborn from a previous lifetime as a gandharvî (heavenly musician). Manthatâ's sins from that lifetime produced her condition as a hunchback in her birth as the queen's maid and advisor. Manthatâ planted the idea in Kaikeyi's mind to ask Daśaratha to send Śrî Râma to the forest for fourteen years and to enthrone her own son, Bharata, as the king.

See also Daśaratha; Kaikeyî; Râma; *Ramâyâna*

MANTRA

Sacred chant

During the Vedic period priests intoned verses, some spontaneous but most carefully crafted according to the strict rules that made Sanskrit so precise and difficult to use. These *mantras* became formulas, which were memorized to make sure that no error was made in pronunciation, grammar, phrasing, accent, pitch, and so on. Their use in Vedic religion is discussed in chapter 1, "The Vedic or Samhita Period." The logic of *mantra* usage in the evolution of Hindu mythology can also be see in chapter 1, "Renunciation, Sacrifice, and Magic."

See also Magic, Blessings, Cursings; Mâyâ; Om; Siddhis; Tapas

MANU, MANUS

The first man of each age; a creator

In the *Rigveda* there were references to Father Manu, implying that he was either a creator or a progenitor of the human race. In the *Satapatha Brâhmana* Manu was known as the first human, father of the race, first to kindle the sacrificial fire, and creator of the social order. There was also a story of Manu's instruction by a fish on how to build a boat. The fish then helped Manu survive a great flood. When he was safe, Manu gave thanks, and a woman, Idâ (or Ilâ), was created. With her as mother Manu produced the human race.

The Epics traced all royal lineages to Manu. One of his sons, Vikukshi, founded the solar race of kings at Ayodhyâ. Purûravas, son of Manu's daughter Idâ, founded the lunar race of kings at Pratisthana.

In the later *Purânas* there arose multiple Manus, a Manu, or first man, for each *Manvantara*. Manvantaras are approximately three hundred million years each, and the present one is the seventh Manvantara. The current Manu is Manu Vaivasvata. The six previous Manus were Svayambhuva, Svarocisa, Auttami, Tamasa, Raivata, and Cakshusa. There will be seven more—Savarni, Daksasavarni, Brahmasavarni, Dharmasavarni, Rudrasavarni, Raucya or Devasavarni, and Bhautya or Indrasavarni.

See also Manvantara

MANVANTARA

Manu-antara (age of Manu)

There are many different calculations about just how long a *manvantara* is—but all agree that it is in the millions of human years. A smaller figure sets the number of years at only 4,320,000, while a larger calculation came to 306,720,000 human years. Each day in the life of Brahmâ, or *kalpa*, consists of a thousand fourfold *Yugas* (*caturyugas* or *mahâyugas*). Each *manvantara* consists of seventy-one fourfold Yugas (*caturyugas*), or 306,720,000 human years. There are fourteen *manvantaras* or "ages of Manu." For more details and calculations based on the *Vishnu Purâna*, see the discussion in chapter 2.

See also Manu

MARÎCI

A Marut; a Prajâpati; a mahârishi

Brahmâ created Marîci, whose life remains clouded in some mystery. His greatness cannot be doubted, but some say that he was a Marut (one of a group of gods associated with Indra, thus gods of storms and battle). Others that he was a Prajâpati (progenitor or grandfather), or even one of the seven *mahârishis* (sapta-rishis), who were also the seven cosmic principles. In the *Brahmânda Purâna* his wife was Anasûyâ (without spite). According to the *Bhâgavata Purâna* Marîci (light) and Ûrnâ married and had six sons so powerful that they rivaled the creator. One day when they saw Brahmâ, they mocked him, saying that he was a father who had married his own daughter (Sarasvatî). Brahmâ cursed them to be born as demons. So these six had rebirths in two important incarnations of Vishnu as sons of demons—of Kâlanemi and then of Hiranyakaśipu—and one as humans, as sons of Vasudeva and Devakî.

In the *Mahâbhârata* Kaśyâpa-Prajâpati was only the son of Marîci, who was one of the six mind-born sons *(mânasâ-putras)* of Brâhma. The *Vâlmîki Râmâyana* added Kaśyâpa as the seventh and youngest sons of Brâhma and thus a brother of Marîci.

See also Maruts; Prajâpati

MÂRKANDEYA
A sage in the Bhâgavata Purâna

Mârkandeya had a miraculous birth and would never grow older than sixteen years old. His father was the sage Mrikandu, whose worship pleased Śiva. Appearing with a boon, Śiva asked Mrikandu whether he wanted a son who was

Mârkandeya was destined to die at sixteen but Śiva saved his devotee from Yama, lord of death. (TRIP)

brilliant but short-lived or dull with a long life. Mrikandu chose the brilliant son. Mârkandeya surpassed all his expectations in his knowledge of the *Vedas* and *Śâstras,* but the years passed all too quickly. When Mârkandeya learned that he would soon die, he began practicing severe austerities *(tapas).* When Yama's helpers came for Mârkandeya, they could not approach him because of the great heat from his tapas. So Yama came and threw his noose, which encircled both Mârkandeya and his idol of Śiva. Śiva angrily arose from the idol and killed Yama to save Mârkandeya, his devotee.

Mârkandeya practiced severe austerities through the first six *manvantaras.* Then in the seventh *manvantara* Indra tried everything to stop his devotions but could not. The *Purânas* state that Mârkandeya is still alive, sixteen years of age, and a great devotee *(bhakta).*

See also Bhakti; Śiva; Tapas

MARUTS

Celestial gods

The Maruts were said to be sons of Rudra, sons or brothers of Indra, sons of the ocean, and later sons of Kaśyâpa-prajâpati (a progenitor). In the *Rigveda* they were associated with Indra, god of war, and Vâyu, god of wind. Perhaps they were storm gods; certainly they helped in the fight against the ancient monster, Vritra. They seemed to know the art of chanting, as they could intone appropriate Vedic verses. Later their numbers increased from 27 to 180.

See also Indra; Vâyu; Vritra

MATSYA

Fish incarnation of Vishnu

There are many versions of the myth of Matsya in the *Purânas,* with many interesting paradoxes and twists in the story line. Even the names of principle characters change. But the essentials of the myth speak of an *avatâra* of Vishnu coming down to earth at the end of an age in order to save the world from spiritual darkness. Vishnu had to save both the first human being, the sage Satyavrata (who was to become the Manu, the first human, of the next or seventh *manvantara*) and save the *Vedas.*

So Vishnu incarnated as a tiny fish, and Satyavrata found him. When this tiny creature spoke to him, expressing its fear of being in the pond, the sage took him home in a water jar *(kamandalu).* The fish kept growing, so that Satyavrata had to move it to larger and larger bodies of water until he finally placed it in the ocean. Then he recognized the fish as Vishnu, lord of the universe. At that point

Matsya told Satyavrata of the imminent end of the age with its resulting dissolution *(pralaya)*, and told him to prepare by saving animals and plants. Satyavrata must also save the seven sages *(sapta-rishis)*. He gathered everything into a boat. When the flood began, Matsya appeared and threw them a rope, which, in some versions, was said to be the great serpent Ananta.

While pulling the boat, Matsya instructed the future Manu and the Rishis in the wisdom of the Vedas. This involved rescuing the Vedas, which had fallen from the mouth of Brahmâ when he fell asleep at the beginning of the involution.

The great demon Hayagrîva had been waiting for his chance to steal the Vedas for the demons *(asuras)*, and thus the entire next age would have been without the scriptures. Matsya defeated Hayagrîva and saved the Vedas for the world, as each incarnation of Vishnu has always done.

The details of this myth vary slightly in different *Purânas*. In one, the seventh Manu, Vaivasvata, was the hero saved from the deluge of destruction at the end of a cosmic cycle (a day of Brahmâ). Vishnu came as a small fish, which Vaivasvata Manu found and saved, only to be responsible for moving it to larger bodies of water as it grew. Finally only the ocean could hold Matsya. Then Manu realized that this marvelous fish must be Vishnu, lord of the universe, whom he worshipped. Matsya warned Manu of the flood and had him tie a ship to the fish's great horn. Thereby the ship was protected from the great storms until the flood subsided.

In the *Bhâgavata Purâna* the demon Hayagrîva stole the *Vedas* as Brahmâ ended the age and began his sleep. It was Vishnu as Matsya who saved the *Vedas*, the sage Satyavrata, the seven *rishis*, and a boatload of animals and seeds for plants, for the beginning of the next age. During the deluge of destruction (the night of Brahmâ), Vishnu as Matsya instructed Satyavrata and the sapta-rishis in the highest wisdom so that it would not be lost in the coming *kalpa*.

See also Avatâra; Manvantara; Sapta-rishis

MAYA

The celestial architect, a *daitya* (descendant of Diti, giants)
Maya built palaces for both *devas* (gods) and *asuras* (demons). But in some accounts he was the architect for the *asuras*, while Viśvakarman was the builder for the gods *(devas)*. His daughter, Mandodarî, married Râvana.

See also Mandodarî; Râvana; Viśvakarman

MÂYÂ

A concept; the creative power of god

There is no concept in Hindu religion, philosophy, and mythology that, when oversimplified, has led to more misunderstanding. The phrase "it is all illusion, *mâyâ*" reflects this kind of usage. In fact the concept of *mâyâ* is complex, and its meaning depends on the context; it is central to understanding Hindu mythology. The concept of *mâyâ* provides the supporting structure both for the magical effectiveness of the austerities and powers of Hindu mythology *and* for a fundamental rejection of any worldview that involved taking such illusions seriously. Other details about this contradictory usage of the concept of *mâyâ* are found in the last two sections of chapter 1.

Linguistically, *mâyâ* comes from the verbal root *ma*—"to measure," "to mete out," and by extension "to create" or "to construct." *Mâyâ* implied a power or a process of creation and the results of that process. Thus, in the *Rigveda* Varuna used *mâyâ* to construct the earth and give it order *(rita)*, and Indra used *mâyâ* to conquer Vritra, the monster who prevented the rains. By the time of the *Upanishads*, *mâyâ* was beginning to acquire at least five contexts of meaning with many possibilities for overlapping—ritual, metaphysical, epistemological, mythological, and magical. All agreed that *mâyâ* had to do with the enigmatic qualities of life and the consciousness of life. Metaphysically and epistemologically, *mâyâ* pointed to the process of mental creation and its correspondence to material creation. It entailed how we know, what we know, who knows—and so much more. This theoretical usage of *mâyâ* would allow for a contradiction or rejection of the practical usages of *mâyâ*—roughly corresponding to ritual, mythological, and magical approaches.

As discussed in chapter 1, the practical understanding of *mâyâ* (and *śhaktî*) as power rested on a "science" of observation and experimentation that supported their application in ritual and ascetic practices. Orthoprax priests had concluded that rituals worked when done precisely, as did incantations of *mantras* as prayers of praise or formulas of magical control. Further, this understanding of *mâyâ* as control of the mysteries of life concluded that austerities *(tapas)* led to the power to control nature, including the gods, or to acquire any object of desire, including heaven *(svarga)* or immortality. The mythological view of *mâyâ* is the most practical one: that there are practices (rituals, austerities, devotion, or a combination of these) that give mortals some control over the results of their action (connecting with *karma*) and hope for the future. Many, many myths mention the use of magic directly, and many terms are used in the myths for this art: for example, *mâyâvî* or *tapasvinî* (magician) and *indrajala* (magic or illusionism).

See the general discussion of these concepts in the last section of chapter 1, "Renunciation, Sacrifice, and Magic" and "Mâyâ as Illusion."

See also Magic, Blessings, Cursings; Śaktî; Tapas

For further reading:

Lee Siegel, *Net of Magic: Wonders and Deceptions in India* (Chicago: University of Chicago Press, 1991); Jan Gonda, *Change and Continuity in Indian Religion* (The Hague: Mouton, 1965); Paul D. Devanandan, *The Concept of Maya: An Essay in Historical Survey of the Hindu Theory of the World, with Special Reference to the Vedanta* (London: YMCA Publishing House, 1954); Teun Goudriaan, *Maya Divine and Human* (Delhi: Motilal Banarsidass, 1978).

MITRA

One of the twelve *âdityas*; a sun god

In the *Rigveda* Mitra's name was often associated with Varuna. One chapter *(Sukta)* in the *Rigveda* said that if Mitra and Varuna were prayed to, the result would be an abundance of rain. Mitra was also glorified as the god of night and as ruling the earth and sky, together with Varuna.

In the *Purânas* Mitra was a son of Kaśyâpa-prajâpati (a progenitor) and Âditya. By the time of the *Vishnu Purâna*, there were twelve âdityas. The other eleven were Vishnu, Sakra, Aryamâ, Dhâtâ, Tvashta, *Purusha*, Vivasvân, Savita, Varuna, Bhaga, and Amsa.

See also Âdityas; Varuna

MÔHINÎ

The feminine form of Vishnu

Môhinî appeared at the churning of the Milky Ocean, again for the birth of a river and a divine monkey, and then for the incarnation of a sage.

In order to prevent the *asuras* (demons) from obtaining their share of the divine nectar of immortality *(amrita)* that was produced from the churning of the Milky Ocean, Vishnu transformed into a beautiful women, Môhinî. The *asuras,* led by Jambha, were beguiled by her charm, surrendered the pot of amrita they had taken from the sage Dhanvantari to Môhinî to divide equally among them, and went to bathe at her request. Thus, by the double deception of shape-shifting and untruth, Vishnu saved the amrita for the *devas* (gods).

Śiva heard about this gender transformation and wanted to see this form of Vishnu. So Śiva persuaded Vishnu to appear again as Môhinî. Upon seeing her great beauty, Śiva became excited and made love to Môhinî. The sweat that was produced during their love play fell down and turned into a river called Gandakî, according to the *Skanda Purâna.*

Hanuman was also born from an encounter between Śiva and the feminine form of Vishnu as Môhinî. The semen of Śiva was deposited in the womb of Anjanâ by the seven Rishis *(sapta-rishis)*, according to the *Śiva Purâna.*

There is a recent myth associated with the union of Śiva and Môhinî that claims that Swami Ayyappa, a very popular deity in South India, was another off-spring of their union.

> *See also* Amrita; Añjana; Dhanvantari; Gandakî; Hanuman; *Kshîrâbdhi-Mathanam;*

MURUKAN
A Tamil god
Murukan was a Tamil god, who has been identified with Skanda, Śiva's son. Like Skanda, Murukan is a god of war and a god of love. He is always young, heroic, and handsome.

Murukan is the most widely worshipped of the gods in much of South India, especially Tamil Nadu. Three pilgrimage centers and six major festivals allow a mixture of folk, Tântric, and Brâhmanical traditions.

> *See also* Kârttikeya; Śiva; Skanda

NACIKETAS, NÂCIKETA
A young boy
Naciketas was born to the sage Vâjaśravas (also known as Âruni). Naciketas's dialogue with Yama (death) was made famous in the *Katha Upanishad.*

Vâjaśravas believed that he would gain heaven *(svarga)* by giving cattle as charity (or perhaps to the gods in sacrifice). The young Naciketas noticed that the cows were old and barren, so he doubted the efficacy of his father's offerings. Naciketas knew that his father had promised to give away everything, so he asked if his father would also give him away, and to whom. Vâjaśravas ignored his son, but his repeated question brought out an angry remark: that Naciketas would be given to Yama, the god of death. Naciketas took his father's words seriously and went to Yamaloka to see Yama.

When Naciketas reached the palace of Yama, the god was not there. Naciketas had to wait there for three days and nights without any food or drink. On the fourth day Yama came and was surprised to see the young Naciketas waiting for him. Yama, in one version, had offended a *brâhmin* by not giving him proper hospitality, so Yama offered Naciketas three boons (perhaps for each of the days he waited without food or drink). In another version it was Naciketas's own words and understanding that pleased Death and earned the boons.

Naciketas used the three boons wisely. He asked that his father should not be angry when he returned and would recognize him, that Yama would teach him the art of *Agnividya* ("knowledge of fire"—but this could mean far more than sacrificial rituals, it could have meant the secret of "inner fire"), and that Yama would tell him what was eternal after death. Yama tried to persuade Naciketas to accept only the first two boons granted. But when this failed, Yama promised riches or whatever the boy wanted—but Yama would not grant the third boon. Naciketas, however, was persistent and replied that Yama could keep the riches; all he wanted was to learn about the eternal. Yama finally agreed to tell Naciketas about that which is eternal—even after the death of the physical body.

Naciketas returned home a great sage.

See also Yama

NÂGA, NÂGAS

A class of serpents

The Nâgas were the race of serpents or snakes who were born from Kaśyâpa-prajâpati (a progenitor) by his wife Kadrû. Many had divine powers and were neutral as far as their relationship with the gods was concerned. It was their great power that made them threatening to humans.

When Bala-Râma, brother of Krishna, died, his spirit left his body through his mouth as a white serpent and was welcomed into the netherworld by the Nâga kingdom. Prince Candrângada was rescued by the Nâga king Takshâka and lived in his kingdom for a while, even marrying the Nâga princess Ulûpî.

Nevertheless, Nâgas were also dangerous, having absorbed the venom *(halâhala)* that was churned up from the Milky Ocean. Garuda, the sun eagle, was their natural enemy, eating them as his preferred food. Vâsuki, Kâliya, and Takshâka were among the most famous Nâgas.

In some lists Nâgas were classified as minor gods or *devas.*

See also Ananta; Âstika; Bala-Râma; Candrângada; Gavijâta; Janamejaya; Kâliya; Kaśyapa; Parîkshit; Takshâka; Vâsuki

NAHUSHA

A king

Even before his birth, Nahusha has been proclaimed as the one to kill the demon *(asura)* that attempted to violate Pârvatî's "wish-born" daughter, Aśokasundarî.

In the *Epics* and *Purânas* Pârvatî had been taken to the most beautiful garden in heaven by Śiva in the midst of their love play *(lîlâ).* Pârvatî saw the kalpa tree *(Kalpa vriksha),* the wish-fulfilling tree, and wished Aśokasundarî into being. Aśokasundarî grew into a beauty who became the object of desire of an *asura* named Hunda. He attempted to molest her but was cursed to be killed by Aśokasundarî's mortal husband-to-be, the yet-unborn Nahusha. Hunda then attempted to kill Nahusha in his mother's womb.

There was a birth in the *Tantras* that can be sometimes nested within the story of Nahusha. It involved a blessing from the sage Dattâtreya, who was served by King Âyus for a hundred years in order to obtain a son—Nahusha. King Âyus was given a magical fruit for his wife after he gave the sage meat and liquor in a skull. Queen Indumatî ate the fruit, and Nahusha was born. Hunda stole the baby boy, planning to eat him and so obtain the power of the fruit, but through a series of mistakes missed getting to eat the baby. Instead Nahusha was raised by the sage Vasishtha. Good old sage Nârada showed up to tell the grieving parents that their baby was fine and would return at the right time. Hunda tried to kill Nahusha many times, but all his attempts failed. Hunda was finally killed by Nahusha. Then, Nahusha married Aśokasundarî and to them was born the famous Yayâti, a future emperor. They also had a hundred beautiful daughters.

An additional Purânic story illustrated an old theme: that too much power and success could spell trouble. The great King Nahusha was needed in heaven to rule in Indra's absence. But Nahusha desired Indra's wife Indrânî and was cursed by the sage Agastya for his sin. Nahusha became a python in the very forest of the exiled Pandavas. Nahusha was released from the curse once he met them. Then he returned to Indra's heaven.

Nahusha's great-grandsons became the Yâdava dynasty, so important in the *Mahâbhârata*.

See also Agastya

NAKULA
The fourth of the Pandava brothers of Mahâbhârata fame
Nakula and his brother Sahadeva were born to King Pandu and his wife Mâdrî. However, their birth was not normal—a curse prevented Pandu from touching his wives on pain of death, and a magical incantation had allowed their mother to have twins by the Aśvins (the twin divine physicians). Some texts made them incarnations of the twin gods. (For more details about their birth see entry on Kuntî.)

Nakula, like Arjuna, was a great archer. To Nakula and Draupadî, the Pandavas joint wife, was born a son named Satânîka. Nakula had another son named Niramitra born to his second wife, Karenumatî. Karenumatî was the daughter of the king of Chedi. During a year of incognito stay in the kingdom of Virata, Nakula assumed the name Granthika and looked after the royal horses along with his brother Sahadeva.

Nakula defeated many great kings in the Mahâbhârata war. He even defeated his teacher, Dronacharya, but did not kill him, as he was a *brâhmin*. A few years after the Kurukshetra battle, the five Pandavas retired to the forest (their *mahâprasthâna*, great pillar). Nakula and Sahadeva died on the long journey that the brothers undertook to heaven, but they were able to go directly, returning in some versions to their original form as the Aśvin twins.

See also Drona; Kuntî; *Mahâbhârata*; Pandavas; Pandu

NALA

The king of Nishâda

King Nala of Nishâda, son of Virasena, and Damayantî were known as great lovers in the Purânic literature. They were foresters in their previous births—with the same name, Âhuka and Âhukâ. They were granted a boon by Śiva that they would be born in royal families in their following birth. According to *Śiva Purâna*, Śiva helped in their romance as the swan who flew from Nala to tell Damayantî about him.

See also Arayanna; Damayantî

NALAKUBERA

One of the two sons of Kubera

Nalakubera had a god, Kubera (god of wealth), as his father and his grandson was Viśravas—in his dark, or demonic, lineage. In a lineage that seemed to recognize more of Kubera's divinity, Nalakubera's grandfather *(prajâpati)* was Pulastya (a progenitor).

The demon Râvana was Nalakubera's uncle. Ravâna, the constant womanizer, raped Rambhâ, to whom Nalakubera was engaged. Rambhâ pleaded with Râvana that he was an uncle to her and should not do such an evil thing. But Râvana did anyway. Nalakubera was enraged and cursed Râvana: that his head would be split into pieces if he ever touched a woman again without her consent. This was the reason that Ravâna could not touch Sîtâ when he abducted her to get even with Râma.

Manigriva was the brother of Nalakubera. One day the two brothers were playing with celestial damsels *(apsaras)* in a pond, when the cranky old sage Nârada came by. When the damsels saw him, they put on their clothes and paid their respects to him. Unfortunately, Nalakubera and Manigriva could not see Nârada, and they continued playing in the buff. Nârada cursed them for their indecent behavior: they would become two trees in their next birth. They could be released from the curse by Śrî Krishna.

Nandi is Śiva's vâhana, his vehicle or mount. (TRIP)

In their next birth the two brothers became two trees in Ambâdi (Gokula) near the home of Śrî Krishna. One day as baby Krishna passed between the two trees, the two brothers received back their human forms.

See also Krishna; Kubera; Râma; Râvana; Sîtâ

NANDI
Bull of Śiva

Nandi was both a divine bull and a human manifestation of Śiva. One account stated that Kandikeshvara (the tawny-colored dwarf), or Adhikâra-Nandin, had lived a good and long life that was coming to an end. He prayed to Śiva for a longer life, and Śiva not only granted his request but placed Nandi, as he came to be called, over a portion of his dwarfs *(ganas)*. Adhikâra-Nandin was Nandi in his human form with the physical appearance of Śiva and stands at the entrance to many South Indian temples as a door guardian. There are several separate accounts of his birth. One had Adhikâra-Nandin springing from the right side of Vishnu as a gift to the *brâhmin* Sâlankâyana, whose austerities brought a son who looked exactly like Śiva. This was said to be Adhikâra-Nandin's forty-ninth rebirth. Another version stated that the *rishi* (sage) Nandi earned a boon from Śiva by his great austerities and it was his wish to become head of Śiva's ganas.

Nandi the eternal bull had a number of roles—all in relation to Lord Śiva. Nandi was Śiva's vehicle *(vahana)*, his chamberlain, the chief of his attendants (*ganas*, dwarves), the guardian of all the four-legged creatures. The *Vâyu Purâna* said that Nandi was the son of Kaśyâpa-Prajâpati and Surabhî. He married Suyashâ, daughter of the Maruts (who have become *ganas* in Śaivite mythology).

The bull Nandi is prominent at all Śaiva temples, usually facing the inner shrine *(garbha griha)*. He should be white as milk in color.

See also Śiva

NARA

A sage

Nara was one of the four sons of the god *(deva)* Dharma. Dharma-deva had been born from the breast of Brahmâ. Dharma-deva married the ten daughters of Daksha. His four sons were Nara, Nârâyana, Hari, and Krishna. Nara and Nârâyana became great ascetics, practicing severe penances. They stayed in the Badarika *âsrama* doing *tapas* (austerities) for a thousand years. Hari and Krishna became great *yogis*.

In the battle after the Churning of the Milky Ocean Nara and Nârâyana helped the *devas* defeat the *asuras* (demons). Indra entrusted Nara with the task of safeguarding the pot of nectar *(amrita)* won in that contest.

During the destruction of Daksha's sacrifice *(Daksha yâga)*, Śiva's trident went astray and sailed all the way to the *asrama* (hermitage) where Nara and Nârâyana were meditating. It hit Nârâyana in the chest. Nârâyana used the sound *Hum* to eject it and send it back to Śiva. When Śiva came to destroy the two sages, Nara created an ax from a piece of grass and stopped Śiva's destruction.

Once there was a contest with the *asura* king Prahlâda. Nara and Nârâyana both used their divine bows and arrows, but it was Nârâyana who finally defeated Prahlâda. And it was Prahlâda who realized that he had been in a context with Vishnu. A stanza in the *Mahâbhârata* said that Nara was one of the four incarnations of Vishnu in the *Manushya Yuga* of the *Svâyambhuva Manvantara* (first age of the first cosmic cycle).

According to the *Devî Bhâgavata* Nara and Nârâyana were reborn as Arjuna and Śrî Krishna in the *Dvâpara Yuga* (the third age of this cosmic cycle)—because of a curse of the sage Brighu.

See also Brighu; Daksha; Nârâyana; Tapas; Vishnu

NÂRADA

A celestial sage

After Brahmâ had created the seven sages *(sapta-rishis)* from his mind *(mânasâ-putras)*, he created Rudra (a storm god) from his anger, Nârada from his lap, Daksha (a progenitor) from his right thumb, and Vîranî from his left. The *Purânas* accounted for seven of his rebirths, including as a *gandharva* (celestial musician) named Uparbarhana, as emperor Drumilla's son Nârada, then again as Brahmâ's son Nârada (but ending that lifetime as a monkey), as the son of Daksha as Nârada, as a worm, and even as a woman sage and mother of sixty children. The *Purânas* were not able to construct a consistent notion of which *manvantaras* (cosmic cycle) these births occurred in. But with so many lifetimes and so little need for consistency, Nârada made an appearance in more different stories than perhaps any other figure in Hindu mythology.

A few good examples would include Nârada's frustrating Daksha-Prajâpati's attempt at creation by coition (of course Daksha cursed Nârada to forever be a wanderer), Nârada telling Citrasena about Śiva's desire to kill him so that Citrasena escaped death, Nârada telling Pârvatî about Śiva killing her son Vighneshvara who had prevented Śiva from entering the room where she was bathing, Nârada losing to Haritâśva in a musical contest, Nârada telling Râma about a *śûdra* named Jambuka who was doing ascetic practices even though he did not have a right to because of his caste, Nârada telling Kamsa that he was the product of the rape of his mother, and many more.

Nârada's treatment in the later *Purânas* fit into the pattern found there of projecting lust into the narrative of the great. Brahmâ cursed Nârada with sensuality, and Nârada cursed Brahmâ that his own lust would make him unworthy of worship. Nârada picked up a number of epithets that summarized his character: strife-maker *(kali-kâraka)*, monkey-faced *(kapi-vaktra)*, spy *(pishuna)*.

    See also Brahmâ; Citrasena; Daksha; Gandharvas; Haritâsva; Jambuka; Kamsa; Pârvatî

NARAKA, NARAKÂSURA

An asura (demon)

Hiranyâksha in the form of a boar had abducted the earth, Bhûmî, and taken her to Pâtâla, one of the netherworlds. On the way his tusks touched Bhûmî, and she became pregnant with Naraka. Vishnu came in the form of a boar, Varâha, and killed Hiranyâksha. Vishnu rescued Bhûmî and had pity on her baby *asura* son, Naraka. Vishnu gave him the divine weapon Nârâyanâstra and a boon that no one could kill him but Vishnu.

This is the formula for certain tragedy in the *Purânas*—but it was usually caused by the conceit of Brahmâ giving such a boon. Narakâsura used his boon well and caused a lot of suffering among the *devas* (gods) as he was growing up. The *Mahâbhârata* stated that Naraka raped Kasherû, daughter of Tvashthâ, then abducted 16,100 maidens and brought them to his harem. No one could defeat him. Finally Naraka was killed by Śrî Krishna, who was of course an incarnation of Vishnu.

    See also Bhûmî; Hiranyâksha; Krishna

NARASIMHA

An incarnation of Vishnu

Narasimha was the man-lion incarnation of Vishnu. He was the fourth of ten incarnations and was half man *(nara)* and half lion *(simha)*. An appearance of Lord Vishnu was needed to defeat each of the rebirths of the demon twins, Jâya and Vijâya, who sprang from a curse by Vishnu of his doorkeepers in heaven. Vishnu had already incarnated as a boar to take care of Hiranyâksha, and now he incarnated in a special way to kill Hiranyakaśipu.

To begin at the beginning, once again Brahmâ's vanity had allowed an *asura* to gain a boon *(vara)* of immortality. This demon, Hiranyakaśipu, was the brother of Hiranyâksha, whom Vishnu had had to kill to end the rule of evil in the previous age. Since immortality boons are always provisional, not absolute, Hiranyakaśipu asked that he might not be killed by any of the kinds of beings that he could imagine, nor killed in heaven or on earth, not inside or outside, not in the day or in the night. Once his austerities *(tapas)* and his praise of Brahmâ had won this boon, he became fearless and invincible. He and his hosts ended goodness, drove the gods *(devas)* out of heaven, and brought calamity to earth. How would goodness and right order *(dharma)* be restored and by whom?

These paradoxes were solved by Vishnu alone among the gods (proving him once again to be both the supreme god and the Absolute) when Vishnu took an incarnation that was a combination of beings—a man-lion. There was rich material in this myth for those who were devoted to Vishnu, since it was a striking example of the way he would come down in any age when evil began to reign. He killed the demonic powers that thwarted the divine order, and—in this instance—that prevented the demon's own son, Prahlâda, from worshipping Vishnu. So Vishnu manifested himself as Narasimha from a stone pillar in the twilight (neither day nor night), took Hiranyakaśipu upon his lap (so that he was neither in heaven nor on earth), and disemboweled the demon for his blasphemy. But Vishnu also did this for the good of Hiranyakaśipu—so that he could be blessed by the very touch of the Supreme and thereby be readied for another and better rebirth.

See also Avatâra; Hiranyakaśipu; Hiranyâksha; Jâya; Prahlâda; Tapas; Vishnu

NÂRÂYANA

Nârâyana was one of the four sons of the god *(deva)* Dharma. Dharma-deva had been born from the breast of Brahmâ. Dharma-deva married the ten daughters of Daksha. His four sons were Nara, Nârâyana, Hari, and Krishna. Nara and Nârâyana became great *Rishis* (sages) practicing severe penances. They stayed in the Badarika *âsrama* (hermitage) doing *tapas* (austerities) for a thousand years. Hari and Krishna became great *yogins*. Nârâyana shared many of the episodes of

Lord Nârâyana, an incarnation of Mahâvishnu, with his wife Lakshmî, goddess of wealth (TRIP)

his life with his brother Nara. Nârâyana and Nara's tapas heated up
Indra's throne, so he was determined
to bring their tapas to an end. Indra
arrived at their aśrama on his elephant Airâvata and roared that he
would give the sages a boon *(vara)*.
But they ignored him. Next Indra sent
frightening animals, and finally he
sent his best—an army of *apsaras*
(celestial damsels) and their attendants. The apsaras included Rambhâ,
Menakâ, and Ghritâcî. The sages
came out of their meditation and
enjoyed listening to the singing and
watching the dancing. Then Nârâyana
decided to teach Indra a lesson. He

Om or Aum, the most sacred mantra of Hinduism (TRIP)

slapped his thigh *(ûru)* and created a young woman more beautiful than all of
Indra's army of beauties. He named her Urvaśî (the one from a thigh). Indra's
beauties became afraid in the presence of such powerful sages. They apologized
and propitiated the sages, who sent them all away with Urvaśî as a gift to Indra.

See also Apsara; Nara; Urvaśî

OM OR AUM
The primal sound

In the Vedic period *Om* became the holiest invocation *(mantra)* in Hindu
mythology and religion. Om was a contraction of the vowels *a* and *u* and the
anusvâra m. In this one sound were encapsulated the conceptions about sound
(Vâc), about its effectiveness in the Vedic fire rituals, and about the vibratory
nature of the universe. Om was the name given to the one sound that contained
everything else *(ekakshara)*, the one thing that was not perishable *(akshara)*, and
it was the one sound that should begin and end every ritual *(pranava)*. By the
time of the *Upanishads* the magical power of *Om* in the sacrificial rituals carried over into the meditations of the seers *(rishis)*. It was said that the one who
knows that *Om* is the imperishable or who meditates on *Om* could attain
Brahman (the Absolute).

In the *Laws of Manu (Manuva Śâstra)* it was said that Prajâpati, the creator,
had taken the milk of three cows (the three *Vedas*) and created the three elements of *Om* (a, the first vowel; u, the last vowel; and the *anusvâra "m"* as the

last consonant). The *Purânas* extended this image of a triad to the divine triad: Brahmâ (the creator), Vishnu (the preserver), and Śiva (the destroyer).

See also Chanting; Mantra; Vâc

PÂNCAKANYÂ

The five ideal women

Literally, *pânca-kanyâ* means the five "girls" or "daughters," but it is used in Hindu mythology to refer to five heroines. The list does vary, especially as some of the heroines were defamed by the mythmakers of the Purânic period.

The five ideal women are role models for all Hindus. They are not perfect but they fulfill their *dharma* as mothers, sisters, wives, and occasionally leaders in their own right. They are most often listed as Ahalyâ, Draupadî, Mandodarî, Sîtâ, and Târâ.

See also Ahalyâ; Draupadî; Mandodarî; Sîtâ; Târâ

PÂÑCÂLÎ

One born in Pancâla

See DRAUPADÎ

PANDAVAS

The collective name of the five sons of King Pandu

Three sons were born to Pandu and his wife Kuntî, and two sons were born by his second wife Mâdrî. They were in the order of birth: Dharmaputra (Yudhishthira), Bhima, Arjuna, Nakula, and Sahadeva.

See also Arjuna; Bhima; Draupadî; Duryodhana; Krishna; Kuntî; Mâdrî; *Mahâbhârata*; Pandu; Yudhishthira

PANDU

Father of the Pandava brothers of the great Bhârata war

Pandu was born of the sage Vyâsa and Ambalikâ. The child was named Pandu because of his pale skin. It was a substitutionary parentage—one in which a king used a sage to have a child by his queen. (For more details see the entries on Dhritarâshthra and Vyâsa.)

One day Pandu was hunting in the forest. He saw two deer and shot one of them. But the deer was a sage named Kindama. He had changed into a deer to sport with his wife, and now Pandu's arrow had separated them. So before he died the sage cursed Pandu: he too would die if he ever touched his wife—and leave a widow just as he had left the sage's wife a widow with his careless shot.

After his two wives had become pregnant by divine intervention, Pandu and his wife Mâdrî were walking in the garden. Pandu felt an irresistible urge to embrace Mâdrî. At that moment, despite Mâdri's protest, he dropped over dead. Mâdrî and Kuntî prepared the funeral pyre, and Mâdrî was chosen to be the one to join her husband on the pyre *(sati)*. Kuntî raised all five of the sons that were born to the two mothers as the Pandava brothers.

See also Arjuna; Draupadî; Duryodhana; Krishna; Kuntî

PARÂSARA

A renowned sage

Parâsara was born to Śaktri and his wife Adrisyanti. Parâsara's father Śaktri was eaten by a rakshâsa (night-wandering demon) before he was born. So Parâsara grew up with an immense hatred for Rakshâsas. So this great sage of the sacrificial lore performed a mighty sacrifice *(yâga)* that began destroying all rakshâsas. Thousands died in the fire pit. His grandfather, the Mahârishi (great sage) Vasishtha, felt sorry for the rakshâsas and advised his grandson to abandon the *yâga*. Vasishtha said that anger burned up a lifetime of honorable deeds and austerities so it was best abandoned. Brahmâ was so pleased with Parâsara for obeying Vasishtha that he sent his son, the Mahârishi Pulastya, to tell Parâsara of the boon he would receive. When Vasishtha saw Pulastya, he honored him with the customary flowers and water *(arghya),* and then both of them blessed Parâsara. He was told that he would become the author of the *Purâna Samhitâ*.

Parâsara was the father of the sage Vyâsa, who was born to him by a fisherwoman called Satyavâtî. Some of the chapters *(suktâs)* in the first book *(mandala)* of the *Rigveda* were said to have been written by him. Parâsara became known as the founder of the most important of the lineages of teachers *(guru paramparâ)*.

See also Satyavâtî; Vyâsa

PARASU-RÂMA

(1) A well-known sage; (2) An avatâra (incarnation) of Vishnu

The story of "Ax Râma" (the literal meaning of Parasu-Râma) contains a chilling warning to the kings and rulers of India. *Brâhmins* could revolt against them if their rule was unjust or cruel.

The story proving the need for an incarnation of Vishnu began with the curse of a sage. The god *(deva)* Agni had gone to King Kârtavîryârjuna and asked for food. The king gave Agni permission to take as much food as he wanted, any time, anywhere. Agni went on a rampage, burning forests and mountains. A sage named Âpava lost his *asrama* (hermitage) in one of the forest fires and cursed the king: Vishnu would come to earth to end the arrogance of the warrior caste (*ksatriyas*).

So Vishnu was born as Parasu-Râma into the home of the *brâhmin* sage Jamdagni. He and his wife Renukâ already had four sons, so Parasu-Râma was their fifth. Parasu-Râma studied under his father and was his best student. One day Renukâ was late returning from fetching water from the river. In fact she had lost all track of time as she watched love play in the river—a reminder of the life she had lost when her royal father married her to a simple *brâhmin*. Jamdagni was angry and demanded an explanation. She told why she was late and implied that she had been tempted with unclean thoughts at the sight of lovemaking in the river. Her husband ordered each of his sons in turn to kill their mother. Finally, Parasu-Râma did as his father ordered. When his pleased father granted him a boon for his obedience, Parasu-Râma asked that his mother be restored to life.

Parasu-Râma trained in archery and did austerities *(tapas)* to Śiva. Some stories told how he helped Śiva defeat demons invading heaven. Finally Parasu-Râma was ready for his task.

King Kârtavîryârjuna came one day to the hermitage and asked for food and drink. Some accounts stated that Jamdagni provided a feast for him and his entourage with the miraculous products of his divine cow, Sushîlâ. Other accounts stated that King Kârtavîryârjuna came when Jamdagni was away and was fed by Renukâ. Either way, the king wanted the divine cow and stole it, then or subsequently. In each version Jamdagni was killed while Parasu-Râma and his brothers were away from the asrama. When Parasu-Râma returned, he found his mother beating her breast in agony. For each of the twenty-one times she hit herself Parasu-Râma went on to lead an attack on *ksatriya* kings. The lost cow was returned with her calf. Parasu-Râma went about South India killing men, women, and children to rid the earth of evil rulers. (His name became associated with the origin of the State of Kerala. In fact, a historical *brâhmin*'s story may have been incorporated into the myth of Parasu-Râma, an incarnation of Vishnu.)

Parasu-Râma, the fifth of ten incarnations of Vishnu, was born in the tretâ yuga—not this age, but the previous one. That was an age when *ksatriyas* did not follow their *dharma* to rule justly and to protect Vedic wisdom.

Another version of the reason for Vishnu's need to incarnate had an interesting twist. A King Arjuna (note the twist in the story when the villain has the name of one of Hindu mythology's greatest heroes) was a merciless tyrant. This

Arjuna had worshipped Brahmâ and obtained a boon that prevented any *kṣatriya* from taking his life. Thus, Vishnu had to incarnate as a brâhmin in order to reestablish divine order and proper rule.

See also Avatâra; Dharma; Jamdagni; Renukâ; Vishnu

PARÎKSHIT

A king

Parîkshit had a miraculous birth. At the very end of the war told of in the *Mahâbhârata,* one of the last surviving Kauravas launched the magical weapon of Brahmâ (a *Brahmashira*) to exterminate all of the Pandavas, but Arjuna had an equal weapon that he launched to defeat it. However, the future Parîkshit's pregnant mother was struck in the abdomen by the Kauravas' terrible weapon. She barely survived, and Parîkshit was killed in the womb. Krishna cursed the attacker for his evil deed. When Parîkshit was stillborn, his mother Uttarâ pleaded with Krishna to give life to the child even though it was three months premature. Krishna did, and Parîkshit came to life.

Parîkshit grew to manhood, married princess Mâdravatî, and by her had four sons. Because Yudhishthira abdicated rather than rule his destroyed kingdom, Parîkshit was enthroned as the King of Hastinapura, the grandson of Arjuna, and one of the last Pandavas of the *candra-vaṁśa* (lunar royal line).

Parîkshit loved hunting. One day after a long and tiring hunt in the forest, he came upon a hut and asked an old man for a drink. The old man, however, did not move. So the king threw a dead cobra on him. Still, the sage sat totally silent, not aware of his presence or that of the snake. The king returned to his palace. There are a number of variations at this point in the story. The sage's son, Śamîka (or Gavijâta or Śringi), was teased by other *brâhmin* boys or came home and discovered the perceived insult to his father. In any case, Śamîka was offended by the joke and put a death curse on King Parîkshit: he had only seven days to live.

In another variant the son of Nâgabhushana ("one having snakes as his ornament," i.e., Śiva), Gavijâta, was teased by companions that his father was really "one having dead snakes as his ornament." The son immediately cursed the one who had done this: he would be bitten by the king of snakes, Takshâka, and die within seven days. When he learned the circumstances, he went to the king and warned him of the curse so that there might be counter measures. But Parîkshit stated that he was ready to die when the time for death came.

In yet another variation Parîkshit had his engineers build a new palace on a pillar in the middle of the ocean with psychics and *yogis* protecting him. The giant serpent Takshâka made a final attempt on the seventh day. Disguised as an old priest, Takshâka met Dhanvantari, the physician of the gods, on his way to protect the king. After they became friends, Dhanvantari returned home. Takshâka changed his shape and entered an apple being taken to King Parîkshit. When the king picked up the apple, Takshâka changed into his true shape and size and killed Parîkshit instantly.

The king's son Janamejaya sought revenge and attempted to rid the earth of snakes by doing a great snake sacrifice *(Nâga yâga).* Parîkshit did not attain heaven *(svarga)* when he died, so the sage Nârada advised Janamejaya to do a sacrifice for the salvation of the spirit of his father *(ambâ-yâga).* The sacrifice required many *brâhmins,* who were all richly rewarded with gifts. Nârada announced at the end of the *yâga* that Parîkshit had attained a seat beside Devî in heaven.

See also Âstika; Janamejaya; Kakshasena; Nârada; Takshâka

PÂRVATÎ

A devî (goddess), daughter of Himâlaya, wife of Śiva

Pârvatî, goddess of the mountain, Himâlaya, primary wife of Śiva, mother of at least two of Śiva's sons, is by far the most complicated of Hindu goddesses. She is given differing and often contradictory natures by the three main perspectives of later mythology—Śâktas (those who worship the divine mother), Śaivas (those who worship Śiva as the Supreme), and Vaishnavas (those who worship Vishnu as the Supreme). Scholars often classify Pârvatî as a "cool," or orthodox, manifestation of Devî, yet she also has her own "hot" aspects.

Pârvatî is complex even as wife of Śiva and mother of two sons. Part of the tension derives from the ambiguous nature of Śiva—both an ascetic and a husband. Some myths attempted to preserve his asceticism even though he had sons. Some made a concession: he had to end his austerities *(tapas)* to provide a divine son by Pârvatî in order to conquer evil. Śiva was aroused from his meditation (or austerities—not always the same) by Kâma, the god of love, to marry Pârvatî. However, an ascetic should not be aroused by Kâma or actually consummate marriage, so Pârvatî's motherhood was often denied by Śaivite versions. In these versions, it was because these sons of Śiva were either Śiva's creations from his mind or by Pârvatî's own mind-creations, that Pârvatî acknowledged Ganeśa (originally named Vighneshvara) and Subrahmanya (also known as Skanda and Kârttikeya) as her sons. For more details on the many versions of the story of each of these two sons, see the individual entries. Yet, there were also several more children—another son and daughter, Andhaka and Aśokasundarî—again raising the question whether they were mind-born from one or the other parents. Many other sons of Śiva, such as the sage Durvâsa, were

Pârvatî, daughter of Himalaya, wife of Śiva, and one form of the Mother, Devî (TRIP)

accounted for alternately as manifestations. The idea of manifestation of the Supreme is less mythical, less anthropomorphic, and less problematical—and does not require a real wife or mother.

There are a number of accounts that are not ascetic in regard to paternity issues. Several semi-divine beings come from the love play (coition) of Śiva and Pârvatî: Andhaka (a demon) and Hanuman (a divine monkey). Pârvatî could be quite rambunctious in her love play. It was said in the *Vâlmîki Râmâyana* that Pârvatî and Śiva's love play rocked the foundations of the heavens and the earth, so both the gods and earth complained to Śiva. He stopped, but Pârvatî became angry. She cursed Bhûmî-devî (mother earth): she would become many forms and be the wife of many. Pârvatî also stated that, since Bhûmî had prevented her from having a son, Bhûmî-devî would have no more children. On another occasion Pârvatî cursed citraketu and his wife for laughing at her love play with Śiva, which they chanced to see.

While Śiva and Pârvatî were married and thus should have served as a divine model for the householder life, their relationship was not always desirable. Śiva was usually the problem. One day Śiva had behaved so badly, abusing the *devas* (gods) and his wife Pârvatî, that she decided to leave him. In order to prevent this, Śiva discarded that portion of himself that was making life miserable for everyone—to be born as a sage, Durvâsa.

Another time Śiva received a woman visitor named Madhurâ at Kailâsa while Pârvatî was away. Madhurâ came to worship Śiva but was rewarded with special favors. When Pârvatî returned to Kailâsa, she saw Madhurâ's breast smeared from the ash of Śiva's body. Pârvatî went into a fury and cursed Madhurâ. Śiva was not able to do anything.

When Pârvatî was first born as Satî, the daughter of Daksha, she wedded Śiva. This episode complicated Pârvatî's character beyond most mythmakers' abilities to restore clarity. Pârvatî would be the eternal wife of Śiva, yet it was Śiva's angry sweat as Bhadrakâlî (an aspect of Pârvatî), coming to protest Daksha's snub of Śiva as Satî (another manifestation of Pârvatî) and killing Daksha, Satî's father. Satî burned herself in Daksha's Brâhmanical fire sacrifice, becoming the paradigm for "widow-burning" *(sati)* as an act of purification.

When Śiva learned of his wife Satî's self-immolation in the sacrificial fire of her father Daksha, he loosened his matted hair in full anger. Out of this angry energy was born two attendants: Vîrabhadra and Bhadrakâlî. Bhadrakâlî was Pârvatî in another form. Śiva sent Vîrabhadra and Bhadrakâlî to kill Daksha. Even though Bhadrakâlî was Pârvatî's manifestation, her actions were seen in the myths as Śiva's *karma*, making him a *brâhmin*-killer. It was Śiva, not Pârvatî, who had to do penance.

Pârvatî seemed to need to be where the action was and sometimes got into trouble because of it. Pârvatî complained to Śiva that she had not been given a role in Vishnu's Râma incarnation. Therefore, Śiva caused her to lose consciousness of her true nature and be reborn as Lankâ-Lakshmî, a doorkeeper or guardian in Lanka for Râvana. She fought with Hanuman who knocked her unconscious with a blow from his left hand. When she regained consciousness, she remembered that she was Pârvatî as Bhadrakâlî. She thanked Hanuman and returned to Kailâsa and Śiva. Pârvatî's role in the Krishna incarnation was most dramatic. In order for Krishna to escape death at his birth by the hands of his evil uncle Kamsa, a baby girl was substituted. As Kamsa tried to kill her, Bhadrakâlî appeared in full glory and power.

Pârvatî is worshipped today in many forms, beginning with Kâlî in the Śaktî cult, Tântric forms like Candî, Câmundî, milder forms like Gaurî, Kârtyayanî, and so on. Candikâ was the furious aspect of the Goddess for those who interpret all her manifestations as those of the Supreme.

See also Devî; Ganeśa; Kâlî; Kârttikeya; Satî; Śiva; Subrahmanya

PAŚUPATI, PÂŚUPATI

An epithet

Paśupati was an epithet for a divinity that meant "lord of the creatures (paśu)" and "lord of cattle (pâśu)." In the early Vedic hymns this appellation pointed to Agni, the god of fire, whose divine heat *(tapas)* was creative and destructive *(rudra)*. Another figure, *Purusha* (the first man), was also praised as Paśupati. However, it was Rudra as the fire *(agni)* that kills that finally appropriated the epithet—or one should say Rudra-Śiva, since Śiva appropriated Rudra's entire mythology. In the *Śatapatha Brâhmana* Rudra accepted birth in order to punish Prajâpati, the creator, who had had incest with his daughter, and to become ruler of all creatures.

Rudra-Śiva was the divine herdsman, the five-faced lord of life, naked, teacher of the highest and most secret knowledge, possessing the five energizers *(prânas)*. Śaiva theology spoke of the three constituents of life—all interconnected, all necessary: Paśupati (lord), *paśu* (creature), *paśa* (reins, noose, controller of karma, of destiny).

See also Agni; Prajâpati; Rudra; Śiva

PITRIS

The ancestors

The *pitris* were first a class of demigods (not quite full *devas*, gods), as well as the "fathers" or "ancestor spirits." As a class of demigods they were connected with the ritualistic offerings to the spirits of the dead. One of the earliest concepts of an afterlife spoke of the way of the fathers *(pitri-yana)* as distinguished from the way of the gods *(deva-yana)*. *Pitri-yana* was associated with the moon, while *deva-yana* was the solar way.

Their origin had several explanations. In one version the *pitris* were created by the seven sages *(Sapta-Rishis)* who were created by Brahmâ. Another version stated that Brahmâ himself created the *pitris,* including three classes of embodied and four classes of disembodied spirits. The embodied *pitris* were called Agnishvattas, Barhishads, and Somapâs. The disembodied *pitris* were the individual deities Yama, Anala, Soma, and Aryaman.

In both household *(grihatya)* and public *(śrauta)* rituals, the lineage, even today, is mentioned back three generations—father, grandfather, and great-grandfather. The *pitris* are offered water and rice balls *(pandas).*

See also Brahmâ; Deva

PRAHLÂDA

A demon; a devotee of Vishnu

Prahlâda was the son of the *asura* Hiranyakaśipu. His father became emperor of the demons and attempted to have everyone worship him. However, his own son, Prahlâda, refused and continued to worship Vishnu. Prahlâda would have been killed if Vishnu had not incarnated in just the right way, as the man-lion Narasimha, to be able to kill Hiranyakaśipu. The killing was unusually bloody, with Narasimha ripping out Hiranyakaśipu's intestines and wearing them as a garland in a naked dance that lasted only a moment. Then Vishnu appeared to Prahlâda, blessed him, and disappeared.

After his father's death Prahlâda became emperor of the demons in Pâtâla (the netherworld). He gave up the administration of his kingdom in order to practice austerities *(tapas)* and worship Vishnu. His grandson Bali, though a great menace to the gods, was another famous *asura* devotee of Vishnu.

See also Bali; Hiranyakaśipu; Narasimha; Vishnu

PRAJÂPATI, PRAJÂPATIS

A creator god; the office of creators or grandfathers

Prajâpati was first a Vedic god *(deva)* of real importance, only to be reduced over the centuries to the function of a group (rank) of gods. Prajâpati literally means the lord of creatures, of living beings. During the period of the *Brahmanas* he was the supreme being and father of the gods. He may have had his own cults. But his supremacy was taken over by Brahmâ, who was seen as creating Prajâpati to be his (Brahmâ's) agent of creation. Later still, the myths tell of other Prajâpatis also being created by Brahmâ to carry out all the aspects of creation. However, as Vishnu and Śiva rose to supremacy, Brahmâ came to be seen as their agent, subcontracting creation to first seven, then ten, and finally twenty-one or more Prajâpatis, of whom Brahmâ was seen as one.

The twenty-one Prajâpatis who created the rest of the world were Brahmâ, Rudra, Manu, Daksha, Bhrigu, Dharma, Tapa, Yama, Marîci, Angiras, Atri, Pulastya, Pulaha, Kratu, Vasishtha, Parameshti, Sûrya, Chandra, Kardama, Krodha, and Vikrita.

Besides what was going on in theistic mythology with its personal creators, there was a philosophical school of thought that found the divine to be beyond name and form *(nâma-rupa)* as an impersonal Absolute *(Brahman)*, that "created" only in the sense that all phenomena were seen as a fundamentally unreal projection *(mâyâ)* from the Absolute. This change in theology restructured cosmology and gave primacy to an asceticism of renunciation rather than an asceticism for powers and rewards.

However, the mythological viewpoint continued into the present. The Prajâpatis or grandfathers continued as the re-creators after each destruction or partial destruction of the universe. Their continuing proliferation constituted Hindu mythology's fundamental rejection of viewpoints that the cosmos is illusion.

> *See also* Brahmâ; Brahman; Magic, Blessings, Cursing; Mâyâ; chapter 2
> *For further reading:*
> Mircea Eliade, *A History of Religious Ideas,* vol. 1 (Chicago: University of Chicago Preess, 1978); J. F. Staal, *Agni: The Vedic Ritual of the Fire Altar,* vol. 1 (Berkeley: University of California Press, 1983); Jan Gonda "The Popular Prajapati," *History of Religions* 22 (1982): 129–149; David M. Knipe, "Prajapati," in the *Encyclopedia of Religion,* Vol. 11.

PRAKRITÎ

(1) Matter; (2) A goddess

Prakritî was a term meaning nature, origin, or progress, which was used to express one of the foundational ideas of India's earliest philosophical system, Samkhya (or Sankhya). In Samkhya *prakritî* was the category of matter or materiality. Hindu mythology simplified Samkhya's complexity and even personified Prakritî as a goddess *(devî).*

However, before *prakritî* was personified, the early Vedic hymns linked matter with other notions of creation or origin such as the first man, or first being *(purusha)* in *Rigveda* 10.90, the father of beings or creatures (Prajâpati), and even the large, or great, self *(mahan atman)*. By the fifth century of the common era, these associations developed into a theory of evolution in mature Samkhya thought.

Prakritî was understood as unconscious and its opposite, *purusha,* as conscious. While Samkhya built the universe—that whole—from its two foundational constituents, other philosophical schools attacked these views as dualistic, and, therefore, incapable of getting behind these two to the One. From their point of view, the two fundamental constituents were themselves created by the One *(Brahman)* or the one Supreme, as Devî, Vishnu, or Śiva.

See also Brahman; Devî; Prajâpati; *Purusha*
For further reading:
Edeltraud Harzer, "Prakriti," in *Encyclopedia of Religion,* vol.11; J. A. B. van Buitenen's three-part article "Studies in Samkhya," *Journal of the American Oriental Society* 76 (July-September 1956): 153–157, 77 (January-March 1957): 15–25, and 77 (April-June 1957): 88–107; J. A. B. van Buitenen, "The Large Atman," *History of Religions* 4 (1964); Gerald James Larson and Ram Shankar Bhattacharya, *Samkhya: A Dualist Tradition in Indian Philosophy,* vol. 3 of *Encyclopedia of Indian Philosophies,* edited by Karl H. Potter (Delhi: Motilal Banarsidass, 1970).

PRALAYA

A concept

Pralaya ("dissolution") generally meant the destruction of one creation before the next. Chapter 2 deals with Hindu conceptions of time and of multiple creations.

The *Agni Purâna* mentioned four kinds of *pralaya:* a daily destruction *(nityapralaya),* the destruction at the end of a *kalpa* or a day of Brahmâ *(Brâhmapralaya),* the destruction at the end of a thousand *catur-yugas (Prâkritapralaya),* and the final destruction and dissolution of the individual self *(âtman)* and absorption into the Supreme Self *(âtyantika-pralaya).*

See also Catur-Yuga; chapter 2 on time
For further reading:
Hermann Jacobi, "Ages of the World," in *Encyclopaedia of Religion and Ethics,* vol. 1; Mircea Eliade, "Time and Eternity in Indian Thought," in *Papers from the Eranos Yearbooks,* vol. 3, *Man and Time,* edited by Joseph Campbell (New York: Pantheon, 1957; reprinted Princeton: Princeton University Press, 1982); Wendy Doniger O'Flaherty, "Pralaya," in *Encyclopedia of Religion,* Vol. 11.

PRÂNA, PRÂNAS

A concept

Prâna means "breath" or "life" and by extension could mean "energy" or "life force." There was one hymn in the *Atharvaveda* in which Prâna was personified as a *deva* (god). It was, however, as life force that *prâna* appeared in Hindu mythology.

In the practice of *yoga* (especially *hatha yoga*) the five primary breaths (*prânas* or *vâyus*) and the five secondary ones (*upaprâna*) circulated in the vital pathways (*nadis*). These breaths were controlled (in the practice called *prânayâma*) to gain mastery over the senses. This mastery over the senses was central to practicing austerities *(tapas)* and thus accumulating merit *(punya)* so that one might receive a boon *(vara)*. Many myths mention *prânayâma* as the method being used by a demon or a sage in order to gain a boon from a god.

See also Tapas; Yoga

PURÂNAS

The heart of Hindu mythological literature

Purâna means "ancient" and thus this body of literature claimed to be authoritative, especially for the *kali yuga* (the present age). Scholars date their composition in three periods (300–500; 500–1000; 1000–1800). *Purânas* deal with both philosophical and existential issues, mostly presented through a poetic narrative. The five topics covered in the *Purânas* are primary and secondary creations or re-creations, genealogies of gods, kings, and heroes, and the cycles of time and history. There are eighteen major *Purânas* and eighteen minor *Purânas*. Some of the main *Purânas* are the *Bhâgavata Purâna, Agni Purâna, Skanda Purâna, Vishnu Purâna,* and *Padma Purâna*.

See also chapter 1, "The Purânic Period (c. 300–1800 C.E.)"

For further reading:

Caterina Conio, "Puranas," *Encyclopedia of Religion*, Vol.12, with a listing of some English translations on p. 89; The All-India Kashiraj Trust series has completed the *Vâmana Purana,* the *Kurma Purana,* and the *Varâha Purana;* the Motilal series "Ancient Indian Tradition and Mythology" (1977) continues to publish translations of major *Purânas;* R. C. Hazra, *Studies in the Puranic Records on Hindu Rites and Customs* (1940; reprint, Delhi: Motilal Banarsidass, 1975); Achut Dattatraya Pusalker, *Studies in the Epics and Puranas* (Bombay: Bharatiya Vidya Bhavan, 1955).

PURUSHA

The cosmic person

Purusha meant "man" and later by extension "soul" or "consciousness." It was utilized both in Hindu mythology and philosophy—often in quite divergent ways. In the various philosophical-theological schools *(darśanas)*, *purusha* shared contexts with *âtman* (self), *brahman* (Absolute), *kshetrajñâ* (the knower of the field). In the great creation hymn of the *Rigveda* (10.90), *purusha* was clearly the first one, linked to its desire for and actual materialization *(prakriti)*. In the later Vedic period, especially the *Upanishads*, *purusha* is pure consciousness *(cit)* and pure self *(âtman)* alone without materiality *(prakriti)*. The universal self or Absolute *(brahman)* came to replace *purusha* completely.

In mythology *purusha* became a synonym for Brahmâ, the creator, and then for the supreme being, either Vishnu or Śiva.

See also Brahmâ; Brahman; Prakriti
For further reading:
Edeltraud Harzer, "Purusa," in *Encyclopedia of Religion*, vol. 12, pp. 106–107; Gerald James Larson and Ram Shankar Bhattacharya, *Samkhya: A Dualist Tradition in Indian Philosophy*, vol. 3 of *Encyclopedia of Indian Philosophies*, edited by Karl H. Potter (Barnaras: Motilal Banarsidass, 1970).

PURIFICATION

See Shuddhi

PÛSHAN

Early Vedic god; an epithet of Sûrya, the Rigvedic sun god

Pûshan was the son of Sûrya, the sun, or an *âditya*, a son of Kaśyâpa (a progenitor) and Aditi. He was reduced in later mythology to a guardian of the roads, to toothlessness, and to an eater of gruel.

Pûshan was an early Vedic god *(deva)* who was connected with Bhaga (god of inheritance). At the earliest level Pûshan was a god of fertility, associated with semen and with the offering of *soma* (the divine nectar). His name implied that he was a nourishing god, and there seemed to be an early cult conducted by those who worshipped him because he was believed to make them prosper.

Pûshan's deeds and epithets came to be appropriated by Sûrya. Before he faded from importance after the Vedic period, his guarding of the roads implied his protection on the final road to heaven *(svarga)*.

See also Âdityas; Deva; Sûrya

RÂDHÂ

The consort of Śrî Krishna

Râdhâ is one of the most popular figures in Hindu mythology and is even understood by some to be a manifestation of the Supreme. Râdhâ has many personas and a complex mythology. Râdhâ is the young, innocent maiden coming into the forest at night in response to Krishna's magical flute. Râdhâ is the favorite wife of Krishna (an incarnation of Vishnu) from his many wives among the cowherds of Vrindâvana (Gokula). And Râdhâ is the wife of Adhiratha (or Kalâvati) and the foster mother of Karna (the divine son of Kuntî and Sûrya). Which of Râdhâ's many faces appears in a story is said to be caused by the listener to her myths—she takes the aspects of the listeners' own *mâyâ* and is born from their projec-

Râdhâ, gopi and favorite of Krishna (TRIP)

tions—carnal for the carnally minded, innocent as a virgin for the pure, and so on.

Râdhâ began to emerge toward the end of the epic period. Songs to Râdhâ may have come from a cow-herding community in northern India, the Abhirs. And it was poetry and song, not mythology per se, that fueled her amazing rise to supreme importance in Hindu mythology. Although some poems and songs extolled her as a shy maiden, most presupposed that she was married. As her association with Krishna grew, Vaishnava theologians accounted for the fact that she belonged to another man *(parakiya)* in several ways: Râdhâ was the incarnation of Lakshmî; Râdhâ, like Krishna's other lovers, was eternally married to him, incarnating in this lifetime to be near him.

Râdhâ could be seen in some myths as the personification of loving devotion to the Supreme *(prema bhakti).* However, Râdhâ also began to appropriate the characteristics and attributes of Lakshmî and even Durgâ: power *(śhaktî),* nature *(prakritî),* creation *(mâyâ).* Râdhâ assumed the role of Lakshmî, wife of Vishnu, as the intercessor between God (appearing as Krishna) and humanity.

In spite of all her religious importance, however, Râdhâ's complete surrender to love of Krishna in every mood, rehearsed constantly for each generation in songs, plays, art, and now films, has made her stories eternal.

See also Bhakti; Krishna; Lakshmî; Vishnu

For further reading:

John Stratton Hawley and Donna Marie Wulff, eds., *The Divine Consort: Radha and the Goddesses of India* (Berkeley: University of California Press, 1982); A. K. Majumdar, "A Note on the Development of the Radha Cult," *Annals of the Bhandarkar Oriental Research Institute* 36 (1955); Barbara Stoler-Miller, "Radha: Consort of Krsna's Vernal Passion," *Journal of the American Oriental Society* 95 (October-December 1975) and *Love of the Dark Lord* (New York: Columbia University Press, 1977); Friedhelm Hardy, *Viraha-Bhakti: The Early History of Krsna Devotion in South India* (Delhi: Oxford University Press, 1983); Donna Marie Wulff, *Drama as a Mode of Religious Realization: The Vidagdhamadhava of Rupa Gosvami* (Chico, CA: Scholars Press, 1984); John Hawley, *At Play with Krishna: Pilgrimage Dramas from Brindâvan* (Princeton: Princeton University Press, 1981) and *Sur Das: Poet, Singer, Saint* (Seattle: University of Washington Press, 1984).

RÂHU

An asura (demon)

Râhu can be seen as the earliest Vedic astrological pre-science embedded in a story—the ascending and descending nodes created as the moon's orbit intersects the ecliptic plane of the earth, used in predicting solar and lunar eclipses.

Mythologically, Râhu was one of the great demons *(daityas)* at the Churning of the Milky Ocean. Râhu managed to change his shape and drink from the pot of immortality-giving nectar *(amrita)*. The sun (Sûrya) and moon (Candra) discovered what he had done and informed Vishnu, who immediately cut off his head. The upper part, the ascending node, was Râhu, while the lower part of his body was Ketu, the descending node, the dragon's tail. Râhu would forever attack the sun and moon as they came near, swallowing each of them—only to have them fall out of his severed neck. Some versions gave him a chariot with eight black horses, racing back and forth across the heavens to attack each of his old enemies.

The *Purânas* stated that Râhu was the son of Kaśyapa (a progenitor) by his wife Simhikâ, therefore, a *daitya*. Râhu was worshipped as one of the nine planets *(navagraha)* in temples.

See also Amrita, Candra; Ketu; *Kshîrâbdhi-Mathanam*; Sûrya; Vishnu

RÂKSHASA

One of a class of *asuras* (demons)

Râkshasas were often described as a subset of the *asuras*. Other subsets were *yakshas* and *daityas.* The word *râkshasa* came from the root *raksh,* meaning to guard. They may have originally been guardians, as one myth indicated that when Brahmâ created the waters, he created *râkshasas* to guard them. Individual *râkshasas* were often good but prone to getting cursed by the gods. Râvana was sufficiently evil to make up for any who were not. Their origin was variously explained as being created from the foot of Brahmâ, or from the paternity of one of two grandfathers *(prajâpatis)*—Pulastya or Kaśyâpa.

Râkshasas were given many epithets that suggest that heroes or incarnations would be needed to kill them: killers, offering thieves, cannibals, nightstalkers, blood-drinkers, and the like.

See also Brahmâ; Kaśyâpa; Prajâpati; Râvana

RÂMA
The seventh incarnation of Vishnu

The Râma myth cycle is especially complex because there are so many literary and oral versions, each language of India having its own variations, as well as expressions in art, dance, drama, and film or video. Since Râma was an incarnation of Vishnu, his story is nested within the Vishnu myth cycle, requiring stories about the need for another incarnation and its outcome. Some of the power of the basic story can be suggested by the fact that it traveled all the way to the island of Bali (then considered a part of greater India), to be performed there to this day.

While the variations are complex, the plot would be simple without nested stories about previous births and rebirths. Râma was the elder son of King Daśaratha by his first wife Kausalyâ. Râma was a one-half incarnation of Vishnu, being conceived from a half portion of divine pudding, given by Vishnu. Daśaratha's other wives, Kaikeyî and Sumithrâ, received the other half and also conceived sons. (For more details see entry on Daśaratha.) Daśaratha prepared to crown Râma as king or as king-regent, but his second wife Kaikeyî demanded that she be granted now boons she had won long ago. (See entry on Kaikeyî for more details.) Râma helped his father with the decision to grant her the boons, so that he could fulfil his duty *(svadharma).* Thus Râma, his brother Lakshmana, and his wife Sîtâ went into exile, according to the wish of his stepmother.

After about ten years of exile in the forest, the three moved, on the advice of the sage Agastya, into a region where there were dangerous *râkshasas* (demons). One of them, Sûrpanakhâ, saw Râma and fell in love. What happened next, Râma's rejection of her and Sûrpanakhâ's mutilation at the hands of the brothers, provoked her older brother Râvana to seek revenge. (For more details see Lakshmana.) Râvana abducted Sîtâ, though fortunately prevented by a curse

Śrî Râma, divine king and an avatâra of Vishnu (TRIP)

from raping her as he had done to so many women, including his nephew's wife. Râvana took Sîtâ to Lanka. Râma won the aid of Hanuman and Sugrîva and their monkey armies. (Was this a disguised reference to South Indians, Dravidians, helping Râma?) Hanuman built a causeway or bridge from the Indian subcontinent to Lanka, and Râvana was finally defeated. Technically, the reason for Vishnu's incarnation was complete. However, the myth's significance for modern India continued, with Râma's return to Ayodhyâ and setting up of his divine rule there. (In 1992 and 2002 Ayodhyâ was the focus of communal killings in the hundreds provoked by a desire to set up another period of ideal Hindu rule from Râma's birthplace and capital.)

Râma's rule restored virtue and order *(dharma)* and brought a golden age. Nevertheless, several incidents marred this perfect period. Râma did not support Sîtâ powerfully against the charge that she was polluted after she had lived in the house (or palace) of another man. Sîtâ was forced to perform a fire ritual to prove her purity, then banished anyway into the ever dangerous forests for most of her life, or in some versions, the rest of it.

This ending has been revised constantly because it is central to the theme of the relationship between the perfect king and the perfect wife. This conflicted aspect of the myth cycle has been reworked in numerous ways in order to attempt to overcome some of the ambiguities. The following is generally agreed: Sîtâ was blameless, an ideal wife. She followed her husband to the forest and waited for Râma to come and rescue her in Lanka without yielding to Râvana's temptations. She was both courageous and faithful in every way. After her rescue and Râvana's death, her life took a sad turn. Râma abandoned the pregnant Sîtâ because of the verdict of the people of his country: that Sîtâ must not be pure after having stayed in Lanka for such a long time. In many versions of the myth, public opinion led Râma to denounce Sîtâ.

There are several endings to this myth. One brings Sîtâ back to the throne; another has her returning to her mother, the earth. They begin in much the same way. After abandoning Sîtâ, Râma ruled the country for many years. Once his sons by Sîtâ, Lava and Kusa, came to visit him. They pleaded that he take their mother back. They, along with their mother, were being looked after by the sage Vâlmîki. Râma accepted Sîtâ back and restored her to the palace as his queen. The latest versions—with this correction—end happily here. However, the earlier versions had a different ending. After her return to the palace, the murmuring of the people began again: she was not chaste (pure) enough to be the wife of Râma. And Râma abandoned Sîtâ again. This time she chose to return to the earth, her mother (Bhû-devî). The earth split apart and took her—entering back into the furrow from which she was born.

Râma did not live long after Sîtâ's death. He drowned himself in the river Sarayu. (Or, it was also said that he went through water purification to heaven.) Râma and Sîtâ returned to Vaikuntha and were merged into Vishnu and Lakshmî.

See also Avatâra; Lakshmî; Râkshasa; *Râmâyana*; Râvana; Sîtâ; Vishnu
For further reading:
Velcheru Narayana Rao, "Rama," in *Encyclopedia of Religion,* vol. 12; Robert P. Goldman, trans., *The Ramayana of Valmiki,* vol. 1, *Balakanda* (Princeton: Princeton University Press, 1984); W. Douglas P. Hill, trans., *The Holy Lake of the Acts of Rama* (1952, reprint, Oxford: Oxford University Press, 1971); H. Daniel Smith, *Reading the Ramayana: A Bibliographic Guide for Students and College Teachers* (Syracuse, NY: H. Daniel Smith, 1983).

RÂMÂYANA
An Epic
The *Râmâyana* is one of the two great *Epics* of Hindu mythological literature. The other is the *Mahâbhârata*. The *Râmâyana* was said to have been authored by the sage Vâlmîki. The *Râmâyana* dealt with the story of Śrî Râma and Sîtâ.

The *Râmâyana* is divided into two sections, the first with six books *(kandas)* and the second with one. The first and seventh books are believed by most scholars to have been added later to the original. The traditional view in India, however, is that the whole was created by Vâlmîki, even though there were three recensions, none of which contain more than two-thirds that is common to the others. Tradition places its action in the *treta yuga,* or second age of this era. That means that the events of Râma's life preceded those of Krishna's, that he made his appearance as an *avatâra* (incarnation) of Vishnu before Krishna. Scholars have noted much borrowing of themes and mythic solutions from stories about quite different figures or characters.

The *Râmâyana* gathered folk tales of a local prince Râma of Kosala who had been sung about for centuries by martial bards. He was a perfect warrior. The literary retellings of the Râma myth by the poets—Vâlmîki, Bhasa, Kalidasa, and

In the epic Râmâyana Hanuman serves Râma with pure devotion. (TRIP)

Bhavabhuti—were more secular than religious, more heroic than ascetic, and all quite tragic. By about the twelfth century the vernacular and regional poets like Ramayanas and Tulsidas had transformed not only Râma into the supreme lord but all elements including Râvana into loving devotion *(prema bhakti)*. Everything had become an allegory of devotion, harmony, and bliss.

> *See also* Avatâra; Hanuman; Lakshmana; Lakshmî; Râkshasa; Râma; Râvana; Sîtâ; Vishnu
>
> *For further reading:*
> Velcheru Narayana Rao, "Ramayana," *Encyclopedia of Religion*, vol. 12; Robert P. Goldman, trans., *The Ramayana of Valmiki* (Princeton: Princeton University Press, 1984); V. Raghavan, ed., *The Ramayana Tradition in Asia* (New Delhi: Sahitya Akademi, 1980); H. Daniel Smith, *Reading the Ramayana: A Bibliographic Guide for Students and College Teachers* (Syracuse, NY: H. Daniel Smith, 1983).

RÂVANA

A râkshasa (demon)

Râvana was born as the son of Viśravas. Dasânana is another name of Râvana, and it means one who has ten heads. Râvana's character changed dramatically in the many retellings of his actions as the central antagonist of Râma in the *Râmâyana*. At one extreme Râvana was the consummate expression of evil and at the other an obedient devotee of Râma (Tulsidas' version).

It is the story of Râvana as a ten-headed, shape-shifting abductor of Sîtâ that all India has loved century after century. They have loved the Râvana who kept getting cursed by the sages because of his evil actions. Râvana became the most well-known râkshasa in Hindu mythological literature, since his life was connected with Râma. Râvana's previous lives were as Jâya and Hiranyâksha. He was reborn to carry on his program of evil as Śiśupâla.

See also Hanuman; Hiranyâksha; Jâya; Râkshasa; Râma; *Râmâyana;* Śiśupâla; Sîtâ

RENUKÂ

A princess who married a sage

Renukâ's story has many troubling elements. She was a princess (and thus a *kṣatriya*) married to the *brâhmin* Jamdagni. She gave birth to an *avatâra* (incarnation) of Vishnu, Parasu-Râma, whom her husband commanded to kill her. She was brought back to life. In one version she was raped by King Kârtavîryârjuna, who stole her divine cow Sushîlâ and then had her husband killed. Then she sent her son, the youngest with the ax (Parasu-Râma), on twenty-one military expeditions to slaughter as many *kṣatriyas* as possible. Renukâ jumped into the funeral pyre *(sati)* of her husband and died.

See also Jamadagni; Parasu-Râma; Sati; Satyavâti

RIGVEDA

The oldest Hindu scripture

The *Rigveda* precedes all other Hindu scriptures in age and sacredness. The name *Rigveda* is a compound of *rik* (verses of "praise") and *veda* (book of "knowledge," or "wisdom"). It comes to us in such a highly crafted language (*Samskrita,* Sanskrit) that it was believed to have been received by the Seven Sages (*sapta-rishis*) whose students would memorize each word, each cadence, each intonation.

Internal evidence suggests that it was composed by quite a few sages, who gave their names to individual hymns and collections, or chapters (*śuktas*). These were organized into ten books *(mandalas)*. One recension consisted of 10,472 verses *(riks)* and 1017 hymns *(śuktas)*. These were all handed down orally, memorized exactly by each generation for more than a thousand—perhaps two thousand—years until finally written down.

Rigvedic hymns praised Indra, Agni, Soma, Sûrya, Brahmâ, Purusha, Prakritî, Varuna, Mitra, Ushas, and (briefly) Vishnu. The hymns presupposed very ancient stories or myths but did not spell them out; in spite of that, they

The Rigveda is one of the oldest continuously used scriptures in the world and Hinduism's most sacred. (TRIP)

contain a treasury of mythic themes, which were shaped and reshaped over the succeeding periods. There are several theological-philosophical hymns, such as the *Purusha Śukta* and the *Nâsadiya Śukta,* that suggest a high level of reflexive thought, reminding the student of Hindu mythology to look for multiple meanings in the same passage—metaphor, allegory, nonliteral allusions. This flexibility of Vedic thought encouraged later Hindu mythmakers to elaborate, conflate, and exchange quite freely the gods' life stories and personal characteristics, timelines, epithets, achievements, and failings.

See also Agni; Brahmâ; Deva; Indra; Mitra; Prakriti; *Purusha;* Soma; Sûrya; Ushas; Varuna

RISHI

One of a class of teachers

The term *rishi* means "a seer," or "one who is foresighted." In the mythology the term *rishi* is interchangeable with *sage,* or may even be used for a distinguished priest (*brâhmin*). Another related term would be *guru* (teacher). The seven sages (*sapta-rishis*) were also known as the *mahârishis*—the seven. Some disciples of modern sages appropriate the ancient title of *mahârishi* for their teacher, but properly it refers to those seven who preserve the divine scriptures, the *Vedas*, at the beginning of each age.

See also Sapta-rishis

RISHYAŚRINGA
A brâhmin

Rishyaśringa received his strange name, "deer-horned," because his mother was a doe. It happened this way: the sage Vibhândaka had been living a strict celibate life at his *aśrama* (hermitage) deep in the forest. One day he saw the beautiful *apsara* (celestial damsel) named Urvaśî. He lost his seed in the pond by which he was meditating, and a doe immediately drank it. She became pregnant and eventually gave birth to Rishyaśringa. He was a normal human except for a horn in his forehead—some version place a rack on his head. Rishyaśringa was brought up by Vibhândaka at the *aśrama* without any other contact with humans.

The kingdom of Anga was suffering from a drought. The royal sages told their King Lomapâda that only a *brâhmin* who had not seen a woman could end the draught. His men finally found such a person—Rishyaśringa. So the king sent "professional" women to bring him back to his palace. With some effort they brought him to the king, who promptly married Rishyaśringa to his daughter Sântâ. The king sent rich gifts to appease the father, but Vibhândaka ignored them and came to curse the king. However, upon arriving Vibhândaka realized that his son had married the princess, so Vibhândaka told Rishyaśringa that he could remain there until he completed the rain sacrifice *(yâja)* and had a son. Both missions were accomplished, and Rishyaśringa returned to the forest.

In Vâlmîki's *Râmâyana*, Rishyaśringa was the royal sage at the court of King Lomapâda when the childless King Daśaratha of Ayodhyâ asked for help. Rishyaśringa was sent to Ayodhyâ and did the fire ritual called *Putrakâmeshthi.* From the sacrificial fire came a monster with a pot of pudding. The being gave King Daśaratha the magical potion, which the king in turn gave to his three wives. The result was the birth of Râma, Bharata, Lakshmana, and Śatrughna.

See also Apsara; Daśaratha; Magic, Blessings, Cursings; Mâyâ; Râma; Urvaśî

RITA
A concept

Rita was a concept in the *Rigveda* that was associated with cosmic order, as well as truth and justice. Rita can be said to be a Vedic version of the later concept of *dharma*. Linguists point out rita's kinship to the Avestan word *asha* and Varuna's place in ancient Persian religion as the *ahura* (kin to *asura*, but used to mean god, not demon) whose all-seeing eye brought truth and justice. In the *Rigveda*, Varuna was also an *asura* whose all-seeing eye brought truth and justice—and was never viewed as a demon.

In the *Mahâbhârata*, however, Rita was personified as one of the eleven Rudras (storm gods). Except for this minor reference, *rita*'s meaning and usage was appropriated by the term *dharma*.

> *See also* Dharma; Rudras
> *For further reading:*
> William K. Mahony, "RTA," *Encyclopedia of Religion*, vol. 12; Edward Washburn
>   Hopkins, *Ethics of India* (New Haven: Yale University Press, 1924); F. Max
>   Müller, *The Six Systems of Indian Philosophy* (Banaras: Chowkhamba, reprint
>   1962); Cromwell Crawford, *The Evolution of Hindu Ethical Ideals* (Honolulu:
>   University of Hawaii Press, rev. ed. 1982).

RUDRA

A Vedic god; a tântric form of Śiva

Rudra was a Vedic god *(deva)* long before Śiva would have been accepted as Brâhmanical, or orthopraxic. However, the name Rudra was eventually appropriated for Śiva, as a designation of a manifestation of Śiva that was both dangerous and just within the boundaries of respectability. Even before this process was complete, another—that of turning a Vedic god into a class of gods—had taken place. The Rudras, however, demand their own entry.

In the hymns of the *Rigveda*, Rudra was the howler, the roarer, and the terrible. He was a storm god, either associated with the Maruts (warrior lords) or their father. His epithets were *hara* (the remover), *îshâna* (master, or the ruling one), *Mahâdeva* (the great god), and *Śiva* (auspicious). Some of these epithets could be applied to other Vedic gods such as the Maruts, but all were appropriated by Śiva later.

Rigvedic stories of Rudra portrayed him as a wild god, shooting arrows without much cause at both gods and men. Rudra only had four hymns offered to him and, forgotten by the *devas* as they divided the sacrificial offering, only received the leftovers. One story told of him as the fiery hunter-warrior, attacking the creator Prajâpati because of his incest with his daughter Ushas, goddess of the dawn. Prajâpati made him lord of the creatures *(Paśupati)* to appease him. A related episode—substituting Brahmâ for Prajâpati—found Rudra collecting seed that Brahmâ had lost after becoming excited by *apsaras* (celestial damsels) who were attending a Vedic sacrifice. Brahmâ had offered his seed to the sacrificial fire (an identification of Rudra with Agni, the fire god) and from that offering three sages were born—Angiras, Marîci, and Bhrigu.

During the next periods Rudra received several versions of his birth, or creation. Most versions told that Rudra was created by Brahmâ out of his own anger. He was also portrayed as a son of Kaśyapa and Surabhî, or Kaśyapa and Aditi, or even as an androgyne that was divided into male Rudras and female Rudrânî.

All of this changed in the *Purânas*. Since Rudra had been called Śiva (auspicious) in the *Vedas*, Śiva appropriated every aspect of Rudra. Rudra was the manifestation of Śiva's anger—at Daksha's sacrifice or at the sacrifice in which the *devas* forgot to give Rudra (Śiva) a share. At Daksha's sacrifice Śiva's anger far exceeded that of Rudra when he had been denied a share, before the myth was appropriated to Śiva. Rudra plucked out eyes of the gods (as he did with Bhaga, a Vedic god) or disfigured them, but then restored things later. However, Śiva as Rudra (or in some versions as two demonic figures) killed Daksha, a *brâhmin*, or plucked off Brahmâ's head. Thus, Śiva committed the greatest sacrilege against *dharma*—killing a priest. Rudra, as Śiva's darker and angrier nature, came to be associated with this warning to orthodox priests—not to become too arrogant, for Śiva's wrath might manifest itself as the dark hunter-killer. The Kapalikas were a sect of Śaivism who carried the skull, just as Śiva carried Brahmâ's for his twelve years of penance, and they were warrior-ascetics, dangerous and fierce.

Rudra's wife was Prisnî (water bag), an association with his aspect as a storm god who brought fertilizing rains.

Most recently, Rudra has been worshipped as the Tântric form of Śiva.

See also Brahmâ; Daksha; Prajâpati; Śiva
For further reading:
Wendy Doniger O'Flaherty, *The Origins of Evil in Hindu Mythology* (Berkeley: University of California Press, 1976), *Śiva: The Erotic Ascetic* (Oxford: Oxford University Press, 1973), and *Hindu Myths* (New York: Penguin Books, 1975); Sukumari Bhattacharji, "Rudra," *Encyclopedia of Religion*, vol. 12, p. 481–482; David N. Lorenzen, *The Kapalikas and Kalamukhas: Two Lost Saivite Sects* (Berkeley: University of California Press, 1972).

RUDRAS

A troublesome class of gods, storm gods

There are different versions of the number and names of the Rudras. A popular version was that the Rudras were born to Aditi. That would make them *âdityas* (demigods). In the *Purânas* there were more than eleven Rudras—and they differed in name and number. The eleven Rudras mentioned in the *Mahâbhârata* are Mrigavyâdha, Nirrti, Ahirbudhnya, Pinaki, Sarpa, Ajaikapat, Dahana, Îśvara, Kapâli, Bharga, and Sthanu. In the *Vishnu Purâna* the names of the eleven Rudras are Hara, Bahurupa, Tryambaka, Aparajita, Vrishâkapi, Sambhu, Kapardi, Raivata, Mrigavyadha, Sarva, and Kapâli. Some of these names later became part of the incarnations of Vishnu or the manifestations of Śiva. Hanuman was called the eleventh Rudra by several *Purânas*.

> *See also* Rudra; Śiva; Vishnu

RUKMINÎ

The most important wife of Śrî Krishna

Rukminî was the wife of the more mortal version of Krishna. She and Krishna were in love, but her brother Rukmi opposed the marriage. He hated Krishna and arranged a marriage of his sister to King Śiśupâla. All the kings of the region came to the wedding celebration, including Krishna, who had been told through a messenger by Rukminî that she loved him and wanted him to come and take her away. Krishna secretly left his army some distance from the city, came to the wedding alone, and promptly stole Rukminî. Śiśupâla, Rukmi, and their allies gave chase, but were surprised and defeated by Krishna's army. This version ignores the popular stories of Krishna's favorite as Râdha and of his dalliance with the cowherds, the Gopîs. Rukminî was his favorite of five wives, and all joined him in his funeral pyre at his death.

Rukminî's connection with Devî (as Lakshmî) was added in the *Purânas*. Devî incarnated first as the daughter of Bhrigu, then at the churning of the Milky Ocean, again when Vishnu was *Âditya* she was Lakshmî of the lotus, when Vishnu was Paraśu-rama (Râma with the ax) she was Bhîmî, when he was Râma she was Sîtâ, and finally when Vishnu was Krishna she was Rukminî. This Purânic version then had to be reconciled with the story of Râdha.

> *See also* Krishna; Râdha

ŚABARÎ

A woman forester

The story of Śabarî is famous because of her innocent love of Śrî Râma. However, this love story is embedded in a rebirth story.

Śabarî was Mâlinî in her previous life. She was the daughter of a *gandharva* king, although she was called an *apsara* (celestial damsel) by some versions of the story. Mâlinî was married to an old *brâhmin* who neglected her in all of his austerities. So she took a woodcutter as her lover. When the sage Vîtihotra learned what was happening, he cursed Mâlinî to be reborn as a hunter-woman. After much pleading, Mâlinî was able to get Vîtihotra to reduce the curse: Râma would be able to absolve her, and she could regain her previous birth as an apsara.

Mâlinî was instantly reborn as Śabarî, the hunter-woman. Śabarî discovered an ascetic *(muni)* named Matanga, whom she served and from whom she gained knowledge *(brahmanjñâ)*. One day Râma and Lakshmana came, and she showed them great respect. She even tasted each fruit that she served to them to make sure that they were good enough for her guests. Then Śabarî told Râma and Lakshmana where to find Sugrîva, son of the sun and monkey ally who would help them free Sîtâ. She was instantly transformed into a gandharva maiden (or *apsara* in some versions). A gandharva prince appeared in a chariot on the divine plane. It was Vîtihotra—now a gandharva. They saluted Râma and went to the abode of the gandharvas.

See also Gandharvas; Mâyâ; Râma

ŚAKTÎ

A concept (feminine); the Goddess
Śaktî is a term for the concept of energy (and as such a feminine noun), and it can be said to have been personified as Divine Energy, or the Mother Goddess, the source of energy. The concept is linked to the power of the austerities *(tapas)*, creative and supernatural powers *(siddhis)*, and the power of the sacrifice *(mâyâ)*. Śaivites claimed it as a property of Śiva, his creative energy *(śhaktî)*. Thus, it could be personified as his wife, Devî. And Śaktî was one of Devî's names and one of her manifestations. However, from a Śakta (a devotee of Śaktî as Supreme) perspective, Śaktî was and is the cosmic energy of the Supreme Mother. And to illustrate this emphatically, Śaktas state that Śiva without *śaktî* is only *śava*, corpse. (Removing the feminine "i" ending in the Sanskrit and derivative languages literally changes the first syllable of Śiva's name from *Śi* to *Śa*, and thus his name becomes Śava.) Thus, it is Mother's energy that transforms the corpse *(śava)* to a god *(Śiva)*.

See also Devî; Mâyâ; Śiva; Tapas

ŚAKUNTALÂ

An *apsara* (celestial damsel)
Śakuntalâ's story is one of the favorite love stories of India, told in quite different ways by two great poets—Vyâsa and Kalidâsa (both c.400–500). Śakuntalâ was the daughter of a sage and an apsara, and her son became an emperor.

Śakuntalâ's mother, the famous apsara Menakâ, was sent by Indra to stop the threat that the sage Viśvâmitra's austerities *(tapas)* posed to his rule of heaven *(svarga)*. Menakâ was successful, diverted the sage from his ascetic practice, used up his energy *(śaktî)*, and became pregnant. However, as soon as she delivered, Menakâ left the child beside the Mâlinî River and went back to Indra's heaven. The sage Kanva found the baby being tended by birds *(śakuntas)* and took her back to his *aśrama* (hermitage), where he raised her. She grew into a beautiful young woman. One day when Kanva was away from the aśrama King Dushyanta arrived, tired from hunting and hungry. But not too tired. He fell in love with Śakuntalâ and married her in the *gândarva* way (by their own word and action). After several days he returned to his palace with the promise that he would send for her. But he forgot. The great poets diverged in the reasons they gave for this forgetfulness. Vyâsa's solution has the least complications—the king just forgot and was reminded by a voice from heaven when mother and son arrived at his palace many years later.

Kâlidâsa's version blamed this forgetfulness on a curse from the rascal sage Durvâsa, whom Śakuntalâ failed to serve properly when he came to the aśrama. However, in this version she did have the king's signet ring, but she lost it in a river. She and her grown son Bharata were rejected by King Dushyanta, who probably had heard paternity claims before. Eventually, a fish was caught with the ring, and the ring made its way to the king, who then remembered giving it to a young girl. Dushyanta finally found Śakuntalâ and Bharata, and Bharata eventually inherited his father's throne and became the great emperor who gives his name to modern India (according to Kâlidasa's version).

See also Anasûyâ; Bharata; Durvâsa; Dushyanta; Kanva; Tapas

SAMJÑÂ
Wife of Sûrya, the Sun

Samjñâ was the daughter of Viśvakarma, the divine architect. When she became the wife of Sûrya, she could not stand his heat, so she practiced austerities *(tapas)* in order to create a substitute. Finally, after having three children—Manu (the first man), Yama (god of death), and Yamî (goddess of the Yamunâ River)—by Sûrya, she had acquired enough power *(siddhis)* to create Châyâ, her own shadow self. Samjñâ had many years of peace (and coolness). Châyâ and Sûrya had three children—Śanaishcara, Manu (not one of the Manus), and Tapatî. Châyâ had done fairly well at raising all six children, but one day she cursed Yama. Because a mother would never curse her own son, Sûrya knew that she was not really Yama's mother. He decided to meditate and realized that Samjñâ had taken the form of a mare. So Sûrya took the form of a stallion and from their love play came the *Asvin* twins named Nâsatya and Dasra. They also had another handsome son named Revanta.

The *Bhavishya Purâna* differed in details about the children of each of Sûrya's wives. A daughter of Châyâ in this account was named Tapatî (daughter of heat, *tapas*). Tapatî married King Samvarana after quite a romantic story and give birth to the emperor Kuru, from whom came the Kaurava line.

See also Châyâ; Siddhi; Tapas

SAMNYÂSIN, SAMNYÂSA
The renunciate stage of life

The four life stages *(asrama-dharma)* are viewed by many scholars as joining the Vedic model of three life stages of the Aryas ("the noble ones," who were twice-born) with a fourth stage, that of renunciation, which developed outside of the Aryan or Brâhmanical tradition. The renunciation movement spanned such diverse movements as Buddhist and Jains, Ajivikas and indigenous ascetics *(munis, yogis,* and the like), as well as some anti-Brâhmanical Aryas, those who produced the earliest elements of the *Upanishads.* But the genius of the Brâhmanical tradition was its ability to embrace what could be embraced and push aside the rest. *Yogis* and *munis* were brought into the Brâhmanical tradition as ascetics by having them affirm the *Vedas* as authoritative *(sruti)* and allowing the disciplines of *yoga* to be interpreted as internalized Vedic sacrifices. A system of caste and stages of life *(varna-asrama-dharma)* became obligatory for all. Those who had become liberated from rebirth while still in the flesh *(jivan-muktas)* were the only ones who were not subject to this system.

Thus, the renunciation of all social ties *(samnyâsa, sannyâsa)* by the renouncer *(samnyâsin, sannyâsi)* was paradoxically made the fourth stage of Brâhmanical society. It was a brilliant way of both legitimating the activities and lives of the renunciates and marginalizing them politically. All that was important was left in place: priests would still be the intermediaries in public rituals and in temple worship, the caste system would remain just as it was, and ascetics would serve as models of giving up everything but the bare essentials for survival. Any attempt on the part of the samnyâsins to acquire wealth, property, or even worldly power would be self-refuting.

Samnyâsis were homeless, dead to the world and worldly obligations. Technically, only *brâhmins* (some sources said the three upper classes) were eligible to renounce worldly obligations—and only after they had completed the earlier stages of student, householder, and forest dweller. A grown son would thus be left as head of the household and the one responsible for the annual rituals *(samskâras)* to tend the ancestor spirits *(pitris).*

See also Brahmacâri; Catur-Varna; Dharma; Upanishad
For further reading:
Louis Dumont, "World Renunciation in Indian Religions," *Contributions to Indian Sociology* 4 (1960): 33–62; G. S. Ghurye, *Indian Sâdhus,* 2d ed. (Bombay: Popular Prakshan, 1964); David M. Miller and Dorothy C. Wertz, *Hindu Monastic Life: The Monks and Monasteries of Bhubaneswar* (Montreal: McGill-Queen's University Press, 1976); Patrick Olivelle, "Samnyasa," in *Encyclopedia of Religion,* vol. 13 and *Renunciation in Hinduism: A Mediaeval Debate,* 2 vols. (Vienna: Institute of Indology, University of Vienna, 1986-87).

SAMSÂRA

A concept

Samsâra has the essential meaning of the cycle of rebirths or simply rebirth. Samsâra is one of the key concepts in understanding the reason Hindu mythology can be so complex—figures changing genders from one lifetime to the next, rebirths in lifetimes with different names but carrying from a previous lifetime the results of actions not then completed, and teams of characters being reborn in new relationships or even in reversals of roles from previous lifetimes.

Rebirth was not a notion found in the early Vedic myths. There was a Vedic idea of redeath *(punar mrityu).* Eventually redeath became rebirth *(punar avritti):* the idea became prevalent that something would return to another life. But what returned and with how much memory of previous existences was the very essence of later mythology.

See also Dharma; Karma
For further reading:
Brian K. Smith, "Samsara," *Encyclopedia of Religion,* vol. 13, p. 56; Wendy Doniger O'Flaherty, ed., *Karma and Rebirth in Classical Indian Traditions* (Berkeley: University of California Press, 1980); Noble Ross Reat, "Karma and Rebirth in the Upanisads and Buddhism," *Numen* 24 (December 1977); Ronald W. Neufeldt, ed., *Karma and Rebirth: Post Classical Developments* (New York: SUNY Press, 1986).

SAÑJAYA

A sage and minister of King Dhritarâshthra

In the *Bhagavad Gîtâ* Sañjaya is one of its four characters—the other being Arjuna, Krishna, and King Dhritarâshthra. The idea of boon-granting *(vara)* had become so common by the time of the late epic literature that a sage like Vyâsa

Sandstone figure of Câmundâ, the fierce, protective eight-armed mother, from Orissa, eastern India, ninth century. (The British Museum/Heritage-Images)

can give someone, Sañjaya, the power *(siddhi)* of clairvoyance and clairaudience (distance sight and hearing). This power was called the divine eye *(divya-drishti).* Through this power, Sañjaya was able to give blind King Dhritarâshthra a full account of what was happening on the plains of Kurukshetra in the great Bharata war. He even narrated the entire *Bhagavad Gîtâ,* with its conversation between Krishna and Arjuna, to the king as that conversation was happening miles away.

See also Arjuna; *Bhagavad Gîtâ;* Dhritarâshthra; Krishna; *Mahâbhârata;* Siddhi

SAPTA-MÂTRÎS, SAPTA-MÂTRIKÂS

Seven mothers

The collective name of the seven divine mothers—seven *(saptan)* mothers *(mâtrîs* or *mâtrikâs)*—has been associated with Śiva both in mythology and iconography. The Brâhmanical view in the *Mahâbhârata* depicted them as destructive female energies responsible for ill fortune and disease and especially attracted to harming children. The mothers were assimilated into both the Śiva myth cycle and that of Devî, the Great Mother. Aspects of the mothers are appropriated by Kâlî and Durgâ, while Câmundî (or Câmundâ) simply became a dangerous manifestation of Devî.

In the episode of the demon Andhaka coming to Kailâsa to steal Pârvatî, Śiva wounded him with an arrow, but from the squirting blood arose thousands of secondary Andhakas. So, Śiva created a *Śaktî* named Yôgêshvarî, while the other gods created the seven *mâtrîs,* named Brahmânî, Vaishnavî, Mâhesvarî, Kaumârî, Vârâhî, Indrânî, and Câmundî. The *Varâha Purâna* stated that there are eight *Mâtrikâs*—counting Yôgêshvarî in the group. It stated that they were personifications of evil (in the form of desire, anger, covetousness, pride, illusion, fault-finding, gossip, and envy). In the *Kûrma Purâna* Śiva sent Bhairava (his own fierce energy or his son) and the Mâtrikâs to hell (Pâtâla).

Iconographically, the *sapta-mâtrikâs* appear at the base of many important Śaivite cave and temple sculptures—such as Ellora, Belur, and Kumbhakonam.

See also Andhaka; Deva; Devî; Śiva

SAPTA-NÂGAS

The collective name of the seven divine serpents

The Sapta-Nâgas were Ananta, Takshâka, Karka, Padma, Mahâpadma, Sankhaka, and Gulika. Iconographically, they all wear the sacred thread of a *brâhmin,* have an extended hood, and may have multiple heads.

See also Ananta; Nâga; Takshâka

SAPTA-RISHIS

The collective name of the seven most important sages

There were seven Sages *(sapta-rishis)* at the beginning of the era, the current *manvantara.* The *sapta-rishis* were Marîci, Angiras, Atri, Pulastya, Vasishtha, Pulaha, and Kratu.

There are other lists of the seven sages, such as Vasishtha, Atri, Kaśyapa, Viśvâmitra, Gautama, Jamadagni, and Bharadvâja. They were the witnesses of the many creations. They were the ones who heard the eternal *Vedas* and vouch for their integrity in every age. The seven are also called the *mahârishis,* the great sages.

However, the difference between lists has led some Hindu authorities to say that the *sapta-rishis* may vary from *manvantara* to *manvantara.*

In one myth the *sapta-rishis* were rescued by Vishnu in his fish incarnation (as Matsya) along with the *Vedas* so they would help in the renewal of the universe.

See also Chapter 2 on Time; *Manvantara;* Matsya; Rishi

SARASVATÎ

A goddess

Sarasvatî is a goddess of primary importance. She is accepted by Hindus as the goddess of learning, the arts, and scholarship. However, Sarasvatî's nature is far more complex and her mythology more interesting than is widely known.

Sarasvatî, whose name means "flowing" and "watery," has been associated with an ancient river that was quite important in the Vedic period but eventually dried up because of a desertification that was occurring in the region. During the early Vedic period Sarasvatî was associated with Agni, as one of the three flames of his fiery tongue (along with Ilâ and Bharatî) or as his wife. In the multiple traditions reflected in the earliest Vedic hymns, Sarasvatî next became the partner of Indra and then the Aśvins, the twin physicians of the *devas* (gods). Sarasvatî healed with her purifying waters, and her banks were particularly sacred for the Brâhmanical animal sacrifices of that period. Ram and ewe were her favorite offering. In a time of intertribal warfare she granted absolution from the worst of Aryan crimes, brâhmanicide *(brahma-hatyâ).*

From the earliest hymns Sarasvatî was associated with knowledge and learning, and in the *Yayurveda* she was identified with Vâc, goddess of sacred sound. In the *Brâhmanas* Sarasvatî had become the wife of Brahmâ, at a time when his cult was the strongest—before Buddhists and Jains made Brahmâ the chief target of their anti-Vedic, anti-*deva* message. But Sarasvatî survived these attacks, even finding a place of honor in these heterodox and heteroprax traditions.

Sarasvatî, goddess of music, literature, and learning, was wife of Brahmâ but increased in popularity and importance. (TRIP)

In the *Purânas* Sarasvatî was made the daughter of Brahmâ, being born from his face, and charged him either with lust or incest in his desire of her. Brahmâ grew heads in each direction because he could not keep his eyes off Sarasvatî. When Brahmâ was totally discredited, Sarasvatî became the spouse of Vishnu— or for most Hindus, a goddess without a husband, worshipped separately, clad in white and sitting on a white lotus—and on the tip of the tongue of students and scholars who worshipped her. Her vina (lute), a manuscript, a white lotus, and a rosary or a water vessel adorned her hands. At her side was her vehicle *(vahana)*, a swan *(hamsa)* or (rarely) a ram.

In the *Mahâbhârata* Sarasvatî had a son named Sarasvata, whom she kept alive during a twelve-year drought by feeding him her fish. He had the strength to keep the *Vedas* alive when other *brâhmins* became too weak to remember them.

Several *Purânas* described the constant quarreling of the three wives of Vishnu: Sarasvatî, Lakshmî, and Gangâ. Finally Vishnu gave two away—Sarasvatî to Brahmâ and Gangâ to Śiva.

Currently, Sarasvatî is especially celebrated on the ninth day of the Navaratri festival (also called Durgâ Puja) with rice and barley offerings. Invocations to her call her by several other names: Gayatrî and Sâvitrî.

See also Brahmâ; Sâvitrî; Vâc
For further reading:
Donna Marie Wulff, "Sarasvati," *Encyclopedia of Religion*, vol. 13; Jan Gonda, *Pusan and Sarasvati* (Amsterdam: North-Holland Publishing, 1985); T. A. Gopinatha Rao, *Elements of Hindu Iconography*, 4 vols. (1914–1916, reprint New York: Paragon, 1968); Jitendra Banerjea, *The Development of Hindu Iconography*, 2d ed. (Calcutta: University of Calcutta, 1956).

ŚÂSTRAS

A set of law codes

The *Śâstras* (precepts, rules) are a class of texts that cover religion as well as law, medicine, and the (pre-) science of that period. They were classified as tradition *(smriti)*, ranking below the *Vedas* in sacredness. They have some mythological material, but it is their insight into the context of duty *(dharma)* according to the goals *(vargas)*, stages of life *(aśramas)*, and castes *(varnas)* that constitute their great value for mythology.

Before the *Śâstras* there were three, rather than four, life goals, expressed as the three goals of life *(trivargas):* social responsibility *(dharma)*, material responsibility *(artha)*, and responsible pleasure *(kâma)*. As such, these three goals of life represented Brâhmanical ideals and together constituted the summum bonum of

Aryan culture. Only after Buddhist and Jain asceticism were ingeniously accommodated by a fourth goal, liberation *(moksha)*, and a fourth stage of life, renunciation *(samnyâsa)*, was the life-affirming ethic of Brâhmanism altered and made inclusive of ascetic ideals. And that is the situation reflected in the *Sâstras.*

The most important of the law codes *(Dharma Sâstras)* for Hindu mythology were the "Laws of Manu" *(Mânava Dharma Shâstra)*. They described ritual duties *(samskâras)*, as well as the four goals *(catur-vargas)* and the four castes *(catur-varnas)*. The *Kâma Sutra* of Vatsyayana, also considered a *Sâstra*, revealed how responsible pleasure was taught to the wealthy citizen *(nagaraka)* and how life was to be lived to its fullest. The acquisition of power and wealth, along with the experience of maximum pleasure, was thought to be compatible with earning heaven *(svarga)*—a point of view reflected in so many nonascetic myths.

> *See also* Dharma; Samnyâsa; Varna
> *For further reading:*
> P. V. Kane, *History of Dharmasastra*, 5 vols. (Poona: Bhandarkar Oriental Research Institute, 1930–1962); J. D. M. Derrett, *Dharmasastra and Juridical Literature* (Wiesbaden: Harrassowitz, 1973); *The Manusmrti*, volume 25 of the *Sacred Books of the East*, ed. by Georg Bühler, 1886; Patrick Olivelle, trans., *Dharmasûtras: The Law Codes of Ancient India* (Oxford: Oxford University Press, 1999); Ludo Rocher, "Sastra Literature," *Encyclopedia of Religion*, vol. 13; Ludwik Sternbach, *Bibliography on Dharma and Artha in Ancient and Mediaeval India* (Wiesbaden: Harrassowitz, 1973).

SATAKARNI
See MANDAKARNI

SATÎ
(1) A concept; a practice

Satî literally meant "good one," or, since it had a feminine ending, "good woman." It was extended to mean "pure one," especially a wife who had purified herself in the funeral pyre of their husband. By the modern era *satî* (suttee in nineteenth-century literature) came to mean "widow burning" (which reformers like Rammohan Roy called "widow murder"). A number of myths presented *satî* as a natural response of the wife to the death of her husband. Such a death would be in conflict with prohibitions of suicide in the law codes. Whether or not these matter-of-fact accounts of wives leaping into their husbands' funeral pyres were a glorification of the practice of *satî* in the mythology is open to question, as well as whether or not one gained heaven *(svarga)* or achieved liberation *(moksha)* through the practice. The aged parents of Śravana jumped into their son's funeral pyre: but there was no judgment as to whether or not that could be called a *satî* for both or either of them. There are a number of temples where *satî* used to be performed in Rajasthan.

> *See also* Aurva; Daksha; Kuntî;
> Mahisha; Renukâ; Rukminî; Sîtâ

(2) The wife of Śiva

Satî (goddess of purity, or faithfulness) was the daughter of Daksha (god of ritual skill), one of the *âdityas*. When Satî came of age, Daksha organized a *svayamvâra* in order for Satî to choose her own husband. All of the gods were invited except Śiva. As she circled the gods, Satî thought only of Śiva. And as

The satî marks of Mahârâja Manu Singh's widows commemorate where they threw themselves on his funeral pyre in 1843 rather than being captured. (TRIP)

she placed the garland that indicated her choice of a husband, Śiva manifested with the garland around his neck. Daksha had to accept Śiva as his son-in-law. Later Śiva showed Daksha no respect, when Daksha entered the hall and Śiva did not rise. Their enmity grew.

The culmination came when Daksha invited all the gods except Śiva to a sacrificial feast. Śiva told Satî that he was not bothered by the slight. But Satî went to her father's celebration and ended her life in protest of her father's rejection of Śiva. One version stated that she burned herself in the heat *(tapas)* of her own *yoga*. Another had her committing suicide in the Brâhmanical fire pit so sacred to orthoprax Vedic religion. (Although later myths used her act as an example of *satî* in the sense of widow burning, she was not a widow throwing herself upon the funeral pyre of her deceased husband.) For a different ending, see the entry on Śiva.

Śiva was so upset that he picked up her corpse and danced with her on his shoulders. The dancing was about to destroy the universe. Therefore Vishnu hacked up Satî's body with throws of his discus. The number of pieces that fell to the earth varies—5, 51, 52, 72, 108—in any case, each piece became a *tîrtha* (a place of pilgrimage). A thousand places claimed to be where one of her parts fell, and each had one or more parts preserved in its temple. Kâmarupa in Assam claimed that her most private part, her *yoni*, fell there, so Satî is worshipped there in her yoni form. The Daksha Mahâdeva temple in Hardwar claims to be the site of the sacrifice *(yajñâ)*.

See also Daksha; Śiva; Tîrtha-yatra
For further reading:
John Stratton Hawley, ed., *Sati, the Blessing and the Curse: The Burning of Wives in India* (Oxford : Oxford University Press, 1994); Julia Leslie, *The Perfect Wife* (Oxford: Oxford University Press, 1989); Meena Menon, Geeta Seshu, and Sujata Anandan, *Trial by Fire: A Report on Roop Kanwar's Death* (Bombay: Bombay Union of Journalists, 1987); Wendy Doniger O'Flaherty, *Asceticism and Eroticism in the Mythology of Siva* (Delhi: Oxford University Press, 1973), reprinted as *Siva: The Erotic Ascetic* (Delhi: Oxford University Press, 1973); Rammohun Roy, "Second Conference between an Advocate for and an Opponent of the Practice of Burning Widows Alive," *The English Works of Rammohun Roy*, edited by Kalidas Nag and Debyajyoti Burman (Calcutta: Sadharan Brahmo Samaj, 1945–1948), part 3.

SATYAVÂTÎ

Mother of the sage Vyâsa

Satyavâtî was the mother of the great sage Vyâsa. However, her story is quite interesting, as well as complicated because of all the nested elements. She was born of a fish who had been cursed, given to a king but returned because of her smell, named three times, and impregnated by a sage, who gave her a famous child but returned her virginity.

Satyavâtî's mother was a nymph *(devastrî)* named Adrikâ who had been turned into a fish by the curse of a *brâhmin*. One day the semen of King Uparicaravasu happened to fall in the river Gangâ, and Adrikâ swallowed it. She became pregnant. Later she was caught by a fisherman who found two human babies in the stomach of the fish, a boy and a girl. The two babies were presented to King Uparicaravasu. He accepted the son, but gave the girl child back to the fisherman because of her smell. That smell earned her the name Matsyagandhî (the one who smells like a fish). The fisherman brought up the girl as his daughter, giving her the name Kâlî ("black [girl]"), because she was so dark.

One day the fisherman was ferrying a sage across the Gangâ, when the *brâhmin* became attracted to Matsyagandhî (Kâlî). He created an artificial fog, made love to her, changed her smell to musk, and instantly a son was born. He blessed her so that she was still a virgin. The *brâhmin* Parâshara left immediately. Kâlî raised her son as Krishna ("dark [boy]"), as he was also dark. Later he received the name Vyâsa. Vyâsa went to the forest to practice austerities *(tapas)* soon after his birth.

Another day a king was hunting beside the Gangâ and caught the wonderful scent of musk. He found its source inside the fisherman's cottage and made this fisherwoman his second wife, renamed Satyavâtî. She bore him two sons. King Śantanu's first son, Bhîshma, chose celibacy. One of Satyavâtî's sons died in infancy and the other, Vicitravîrya only lived long enough to marry. But he too died, leaving his wives, Ambikâ and Ambâlikâ, without children and the kingdom with an heir. Satyavâtî arranged for her earlier son, Vyâsa, to provide the kingdom with an heir. (For further details see Ambikâ.) Ambâlikâ gave birth to Pandu, and Ambikâ gave birth to Dhritarâshthra. Pandu had five divine sons, while the other had one hundred sons who were their enemies in the Mahâbhârata war. When Pandu died, his grandmother Satyavâtî retreated to the forest with Ambikâ and Ambâlikâ. There the three women practiced austerities *(tapas)* and devotion *(bhakti)* and attained heaven *(svarga).*

See also Dhritarâshthra; Jamdagni; *Mahâbhârata;* Pandavas; Pandu

SÂVITRÎ

(1) Holy verse in the *Vedas;* (2) Wife of Satyavân

The Sâvitrî is also called the Gâyatrî. It is recited each morning and evening by millions of Hindus. The Sâvitrî is addressed to Sâvitrî (the generator) who in the earliest Vedic lore may have been one of the attributes of the great sun god, Sûrya. The Sâvitrî was also personified in the later *Vedas* as the goddess Sâvitrî, wife of Brahmâ, and mother of the *Vedas.* Sâvitrî was a princess, born to King Aśvapati of Madra and his wife Mâlati. When Sâvitrî reached the right age for marriage, she and the ministers of her father set out in search of the right person to marry. She found Satyavân, the son of King Dyumatsena of Salva. Sâvitrî fell in love with him and married him. Satyavân was a gem of a person. Their life seemed perfect. Nârada, the sage with all the bad news, appeared and told Sâvitrî and her father that Satyavân would live only one more year.

Sâvitrî was grief-stricken to hear this news. However, she continued to live with Satyavân and loved him deeply. At the end of one year, Yama, the god of death, came to take the spirit of Satyavân. Sâvitrî begged Yama for her husband's life. Her request was denied. Yama took Satyavân's life. Because of the power of her fidelity, Sâvitrî was able to follow Yama to Yamaloka (the realm of death). Yama tried to dissuade her, but she was determined to return with her husband alive or lose her own life. Yama could not take Sâvitrî's life, since her time had not yet arrived. Finally, Yama had to yield to Sâvitrî's wish and give back Satyavân's life. Satyavân and Sâvitrî lived for a long time thereafter.

See also Nârada; Yama

SIDDHI, SIDDHIS
A concept

Siddhi is a central concept of Hindu mythology; the term means "power" or "supernatural ability." The siddhis, often listed as eight, could be acquired by austerities *(tapas)*.

These supernatural abilities included the ability to obtain anything *(prâpti)*, having an irresistible will *(prâkâmya)*, the ability to subdue anything to one's own will *(vashitva)*, and having a sweet mouth *(madhupratîka)*. Invisibility, the ability to walk through barriers, teleportation, clairvoyance, and clairaudience also appear in the myths.

There are terms that were used in the myths that link the person who acquired powers by austerities with magic: for example, *mâyâvî* and *tapasvinî* (both meaning roughly "magician"). The practice to acquire magical powers was called *siddha-sâdhana* (discipline). The logic of ritual and private magic is discussed in chapter 1.

See also Magic, Blessings, Cursings; Mâyâ; Tapas

ŚIKHANDÎ
A daughter born to King Drupada, an ally of the Kauravas

Śikhandî's story had its beginning in another life. Wrongs done in that life carried into the next, with a vow to kill the warrior who had wronged her. In that previous birth she was Ambâ, the eldest daughter of the King of Kâshî. She was engaged to marry King Salva, when she and her two sisters, Ambikâ and Ambalikâ, were abducted by Bhîshma. The three sisters were to be given to Bhîshma's timid half-brother, King Vicitarvîrya. Ambâ objected and was returned to Kâshî. However, King Salva had no desire to marry one whose chastity could be questioned. Humiliated, Ambâ went to Hastinapura and demanded that Bhîshma marry her. Bhîshma refused, saying that he had taken a lifelong vow of celibacy.

Ruined, Ambâ went to the forest to do austerities *(tapas)* in order to get revenge. She received a boon to be reborn as Śikhandî in order to kill Bhîshma.

Because of his own austerities and his asceticism as a *brahmachâri*, Bhîshma was almost invulnerable as a warrior. Śikhandî either fought in disguise as a man or, according to one version, was a hermaphrodite warrior. In the final battle with Bhîshma, Śikhandî was the material cause of his death. Aśvatthâma, one of the Kaurava warriors, killed her in turn.

See also Brahmacâri; Dhritarâshthra; *Mahâbhârata*; Tapas

ŚIŚUPÂLA

Śiśupâla was the third rebirth of Jâya for his failure to carry out his duty *(dharma)* as a doorkeeper *(dvârapâlâka)* of Lord Vishnu at Vaikuntha. He was cursed because of that failure, and he played a role in three incarnations of Vishnu. His twin brother Vijâya shared in the original deed and caused an equal amount of trouble.

The first two rebirths of Jâya were as Hiranyakaśipu and Râvana. Finally, as Śiśupâla he received the grace of Krishna. Śiśupâla was a *kśatriya*, born to King Damaghosha and Queen Cedi. He was a little unusual as a baby, having three eyes and four hands, and braying like an ass. When the parents attempted to abandon him, a disembodied voice predicted that his third eye and extra hands would fall off as soon as he sat in the lap of the person who would kill him. The king kept putting him in every great warrior's lap, until in the lap of his uncle Krishna it happened as predicted. Śiśupâla grew into an enemy worthy of a divine opponent, since Krishna had carried away Rukminî, his intended bride. Finally, Krishna did kill him at Yudhishthira's great horse sacrifice at the end of the Mahâbhârata war. Because he had spent so many lifetimes focused single-mindedly in his hatred on Vishnu, Śiśupâla was absorbed into the grace of the Supreme. Thus, the cycle of rebirths was finally ended, and the grace of Vishnu was finally granted.

See also Avatâra; Hiranyakaśipu; Hiranyâksha; Jâya; *Mahâbhârata*; Râvana; Vishnu

SÎTÂ

A wife of Śrî Râma; an incarnation of the goddess Lakshmî

Sîtâ was born from the earth when it was ploughed. Thus the earth, Bhû Devî, was her mother. Sîtâ was brought up by King Janaka as his daughter. According to many *Purânas*, Sîtâ was the incarnation of Lakshmî, wife of Vishnu.

Râma wed Sîtâ after winning the marriage contest—lifting and shooting an arrow from the divine bow of Śiva. Sîtâ was a devoted wife and always followed the footsteps and words of Râma. In spite of his warning, she even followed Râma to the forest when he was banished.

One version of the many adventures in the forest includes the temptation of Râma by a *râkshasa* princess named Śurpanakhâ. But when Râma shunned her, saying that he only loved Sîtâ, Śurpanakhâ attempted to kill Sîtâ. Laxmana, who had joined his brother in exile, defended Sîtâ and cut off Śurpanakhâ's nose and ears. She vowed revenge and went back to her brother in Lanka, King Râvana. He in turn vowed to abduct Sîtâ to punish Râma. With the help of his uncle Marîci, who changed his shape into a golden deer and led Râma away from his cottage in the forest, Râvana successfully abducted Sîtâ. Here is how it happened: one day in the forest Sîtâ happened to see a golden deer. She had an intense desire to touch the deer, and she asked Râma to catch it for her. The golden deer was Marîci, the uncle of Ravana, disguised, for râkshasas were shape-shifters. Râma chased the deer for Sîtâ, but it lured him far away. Râma finally understood that this was a trick. He shot an arrow, but while the deer was dying, it cried out in the voice of Râma, calling for the help of Lakshmana. Sîtâ followed Lakshmana in search of Râma. At that moment Râvana appeared, disguised as a sage, and abducted Sîtâ. Râvana, the great demon king, flew away with her to Lanka in his flying machine, called the Pushpaka-vimâna ("flower vehicle," first owned by the god Kubera).

The *Râmâyana* tells of the heroic deeds of Râma and his allies as they tried to rescue Sîtâ. But the rescue took a very long time, while Sîtâ was forced to undergo many trials, her endurance of which made her the example of the perfect wife. Sîtâ was finally rescued from Lanka by Râma with the help of Hanuman and others. Râvana—the demon of many rebirths, starting with Jâya—was killed by Śrî Râma.

Some versions have Sîtâ returning as queen to a life of luxury and happiness. But others tell a tale of sorrow and agony. Râma banished Sîtâ to the forest in deference to the people of his country. The people of Ayodhyâ questioned Sîtâ's chastity, as she lived in Lanka with the evil demon for so long. Meanwhile, Sîtâ gave birth to two sons, Lava and Kusa, at the *aśrama* (hermitage) of Vâlmîki, who looked after her and raised the boys. Râma finally met his sons, who could not be defeated by his army, and brought them and their mother Sîtâ back to the palace. But again, Sîtâ was put to tests to prove her chastity to the people of Ayodhyâ. This time she did not wait for the verdict of Râma. She committed suicide, or *sati*. Some versions have her mother, the earth, opening and taking Sîtâ back into her abode.

Râma did not live very long after Sîtâ's death. He drowned himself in the river Sarayu. (It could be said that he went through water purification to heaven.) Râma and Sîtâ returned to Vaikuntha and were rejoined as Vishnu and Lakshmî.

Sîtâ was famous as one of the five ideal women *(pañcakanayâ)* in Hindu mythology. Her story is a story of sacrifice and sorrow endured in order to help her husband keep both her *dharma* (ordained duty) and his.

> *See also* Avatâra; Hanuman; Lakshmî; Pañcakanayâ; Râkshasa; Râma; Râvana; Vishnu
>
> *For further reading:*
> Wendy Doniger O'Flaherty, *Women, Androgynes, and Other Mythical Beasts* (Chicago: University of Chicago Press, 1980); David R. Kinsley, *Hindu Goddesses: Visions of the Feminine in the Hindu Religious Tradition* (Berkeley: University of California Press, 1986).

ŚIVA

A god; the Supreme Lord of the universe

If the mention of the word *Śiva* (auspicious) in the *Vedas* is considered to refer to Lord Śiva, Śiva spans all periods of Hindu mythology. No matter when he enters Hindu mythology, Śiva is among the two or three most important gods—either as one of the later Hindu Triad, as the highest of the many gods (*devas*), or as the Absolute itself (*Brahman*).

One might think of layer upon layer of stories about Śiva. Viewed from the present, the mythologies are intertwined and very complex. If each layer is viewed separately within the period of its development, there were different versions of the same story—some seeming to contradict the others.

Śiva not only had an independent mythology but also influenced the evolutionary patterns of the minor gods of later myths. Śiva was the father of two significant minor gods named Gaṇeśa and Skanda, or Kârtikeya. The influence of Gaṇeśa was reflected in the life of any Hindu in the regard for this deity as the remover of all obstacles.

In early Vedic texts mighty Rudra, the wrathful one and a god of storms, was referred to as *Śiva*, the auspicious one. However, in the next period Śiva appeared in the Epics as a god of supreme status, probably elevated from tribal origins. Then in the later Purânic texts he was given the popular epithet *Maheśvara-Śankara-Śiva*—the first element meaning "the great god" and the second and third meaning "the auspicious one." The transformation from the Vedic Rudra and Purusha to the Purânic Śiva (and later to the Tântric Bhairava) might also indicate the merging of early myths into the later Śaivite traditions, demonstrating the process of religious institutionalization of mythology. Finally the *Śiva Purâna* attributed all the three cosmic functions of creation, preservation, and destruction to the three forms of *Sadâ-Śiva* (the always auspicious one). That replaced the post-Vedic version of the Hindu Triad (in which Śiva was the destroyer of that which was created by Brahmâ and preserved by Vishnu) with a Śiva who was the Absolute. Since, as it is told in the *Kûrma Purâna*, he was the lord of destruction and began and ended creation, he was also the master of death, *Mrityunjaya*, and time, *Mahâkâla*. There were also myths in *Mârkandeya Purâna* propounding the nature of Śiva as exceeding the powers of Yama, the god of death. Śiva stood distinct among the Hindu gods for his complex and yet paradoxically unique features. He was an ascetic and detached from the attractions of life, yet at the same time the only god symbolically represented with sexual imagery. Though he was an ascetic he was worshipped (all over India) symbolically in the form of the *linga* (phallus), which was a sign of the ordinary life of householders and of procreation. What was interesting was that sexual imagery itself was used in order to transcend the innuendoes of the same—by its very use

Śiva as Mahâyogi is the master ascetic. (TRIP)

the imagery became nonsexual. Through worshipping the *linga* one went beyond the ordinary experiences of procreation. (Scattered over the map of India are twelve temples dedicated to the worship of the *jyotirlingâs,* "fire lingas," the consecrated symbolic image of Śiva in the form of the phallus.) This interesting feature of the symbolism of a supreme god like Śiva was justified, according to the many variants of a myth about a curse from the sage Brighu upon Śiva: Śiva would be the only god not worshipped by his face.

Śiva was the master of dance, and the only one of the gods who could plunge into motionless yogic *tapas* (ascetic practices) and meditation. Though himself was a resident of the graveyard *(smasâna vâsi)* and the lord of ghosts and goblins, he was the bestower of wealth and prosperity *(Śankara).*

As the king or lord of dance *(Natarâja),* Śiva perfected dance, relating power *(tândava natana)* and grace *(lasya natana)* manifested through the physical body and affecting the cosmic body of the universe. Symbolically, Śiva as Natarâja represented the intricate process of causation and the profound philosophical ideas associated with it. The ash-smeared, ferocious, and angry Śiva danced alone in the graveyard, burning down all that was created. His *tândava natana* marked the destruction and return of what had been created to an original state of equilibrium. A story connected with the *tândava* of Śiva was that of the *Daksha yâga,* of Sati's jumping into the fire altar, after being humiliated by her father Daksha. Śiva danced in the most ferocious way and destroyed the entire setting of the *yâga* (sacrifice). He himself, not able to bear the throes of the pain he felt over his wife's ending her life, ended the manifested universe to find solitude.

While the *tândava* dance of Śiva was always associated with his dancing alone in the absence of his female counterpart, the *lasya natana* was of more aesthetic significance. It involved the gentle moods of Śiva and Parvati, his wife (or second wife in some accounts). The *lasya natana* of the divine couple was depicted in popular iconography as the *ardha narîśvara* or half male (right side), half female (left side). This was the dance of peace, love, and creation. Both *tândava* and *lasya* constitiued the cosmic dance of Śiva.

Śiva was not only the king of dance and abode of auspiciousness *(Śivam)* that resulted in the epitome of that which was beautiful *(sundaram)* but also the origin of truth *(satyam).* He was the one god who encompassed the three seemingly contradictory planes of truth: beauty and wisdom and power. Therefore, one saw him as the great ascetic, the great dancer, and the great Yogi.

Śiva was the first teacher of humankind, according to one myth, told in the *Dakshina murti Stotra.* He presented the wisdom of immortality to mortals. He took the form of a young teacher facing northwards, the *Dakshina murti* (one who faces north). And, quite appropriately, the mode of teaching was silence.

Another notable feature throughout the development of myths about Śiva was his third eye and its nature. Śiva was the god of yogic powers. Śiva granted the light of wisdom through his third eye or turned the object of his wrath into ashes by the fire emanating from it. From the stories about his third eye came the popular epithets of *Kshiraprasâdi* (one who is compassionate to bless) and *Kshiprakopi* (one who is wrathful). He was worshipped on the day of Śivarâtri by the *panchâkshari mantra Śiva,* the five-syllable mantra *aum namah Śivaya,* and by the thousand and eight epithets describing his glories.

Iconographically, the linga was the most universal symbol of Śiva as the generative principle of the universe. However, there were numerous forms of Śiva that the artist captured to reflect the contrasting features of the mythology.

Temples to Śiva were often located at places celebrated in the scriptures or by local myths and legends. For example, the Elephanta cave temples carry out an extraordinary mythic program, telling of Śiva and Parvati's *lîlâ* (love play) in a cosmic game of dice symbolizing the creation and involution of time and space, causality, life and death, age after age.

> *See also* Âdi; Anasûyâ; Andhaka; Ani-Mândavya; Anjanâ; Âstika; Bâli; Bhadra-kâlî; Bhaga; Bhagîratha; Bhairava; Bhrigu; Bhûmî; Candaka; Candrângada; Citraketu; Daksha; Damayantî; Dattâtreya; Devasenâ; Devî; Durvâsa; Ekavîra; Ganapati; Gandakî; Ganeśa; Gangâ; Ghantâ-karna; Gunasharman; Kârttikeya; Linga; Pârvatî; Rudra; Skanda
>
> *For further reading:*
> Wendy Doniger O'Flaherty, *Asceticism and Eroticism in the Mythology of Siva* (Delhi: Oxford University Press, 1973), reprinted as *Siva: The Erotic Ascetic* (Delhi: Oxford University Press, 1973); David Dean Shulman and Don Handelman, *God Inside Out: Siva's Game of Dice* (Oxford: Oxford University Press, 1997); Anne-Marie Gaston, *Siva in Dance, Myth, and Iconography* (Oxford: Oxford University Press, 1982).

SKANDA

Son of Śiva and god of war

Skanda was the six-headed son of Śiva, god of war. Skanda can be seen as either sharing his function with Kârttikeya, Guha, Kurmâra, and Subrahmanya or as absorbing them as epithets. Śiva's son had been the son of Agni, god of fire, in earlier mythology. In the *Mahâbhârata* there were several versions of Agni's paternity of Skanda. In one account of the story of Agni and the frog damsel, Agni had been hiding in the ocean and finally agreed to father Skanda. In another version Agni as the sacrificial fire warmed the wives of the Seven Sages *(saptarishis)* and managed to get six of them pregnant. (For more details see the entries on Krittikâs, Kârttikeya, and Subrahmanya.) In the standard version Agni's role was appropriated by Śiva; it was his sperm that impregnated the sage's wives, having first gone into the sacrificial fire. In both cases, the son is the six-headed warrior. His names preserve some of the main aspect of his mythology: Skanda (fall [of Śiva's seed]), Kârttikeya (son of the Krittikâs, the Pleiades), Guha (reared in a secret place), Kurmâra (youth), and Subrahmanya ("favorable to priests").

> *See also* Kârttikeya; Krittikâs; Pârvatî; Śiva; Subrahmanya

Skanda, the scarlet-hued form of the youthful god of war (TRIP)

SOMA

(1) A deva (god); (2) a plant and the Vedic drink made from it; (3) the moon

This entry will focus on Soma as the plant and Vedic drink. For more information about Soma as a *deva* and as the moon, see the entry on Candra. In the Vedic period Candra, the moon, and Soma, the entheogenic (religious experience–inducing) plant, were connected by associations *(bandhus)* in the early hymns.

Mythologically, Soma emerged from the Milky Ocean in a pot, a process made possible by the Kûrma incarnation of Vishnu and Vishnu's shape and gender shifting as Môhinî. Soma was the drink or nectar of immortality *(amrita)*, fought over by gods and demons, but eventually brought from heaven by an eagle *(syena)*, later said to have been Garuda (vehicle of the god Sûrya).

Ritually, *soma* was at the very center of Vedic ceremonies, offering sustenance and energy to the *devas* and ecstasy to *brâhmins*. The bird delivering *soma* was associated with the *gâyatrî*, Vedic religion's most sacred *mantra*, the verse with three eight-syllable *padas* (feet). Some hymns gave the impression that *soma* was purchased from a rustic dealer who was paid and ceremonially

Soma, an ancient solar deity (the moon) and the drink of immortality, possibly from the pressings of a poisonous mushroom (TRIP)

driven away, reenacting the primordial combat between gods and demons or the conflict of the demons with the later guardians of soma, the *gandhârvas*.

Soma and Agni were linked in this cult of ecstasy. Soma was "king," and Agni took Soma to the *devas*. Often the hymns referred to them as combined or symbolically united.

Soma was not fermented or distilled. Priests pressed or extracted soma by pressing stalks between stones into a wooden bowl. They used wool to filter the juice and may have mixed it with clarified butter (ghee). The most famous soma rituals were the consecration of the king (*Rajasuya*), the horse sacrifice (*asvamedha*), the "drink of power" ritual (*Vajapeya*), and various fire rituals (*Agnistoma*). The gods had come to depend on earthly priests to pour soma into the ritual fire and on Agni to bring their shares to heaven (*svarga*). Buddhists ridiculed this belief, saying that if they believed that Agni could take something to heaven, they should jump into the fire themselves.

Many scholars think that the real *soma* could not be easily obtained in the lower altitudes and hot climate away from the Himâlayas, and a few centuries before the time of the Buddha *soma* was only a memory in the rituals. Consequently, the priests' ritual ability and the rituals themselves became all important. The belief in the power of ritual (*mâyâ*) rose, along with the belief in the power of austerities (*tapas*).

There were several psychedelic, hallucinogenic, or entheogenic cults in the ancient world, many associated with divine mushrooms: Avestan *haoma*, Greek ambrosia and nectar, Chinese *ling-chih*, a mushroom of immortality. *Soma* is viewed as such an entheogenic or psychedelic, principally on the work of Wasson and O'Flaherty. It is not universally accepted that *soma* was the mushroom fly agaric since this mushroom could only be found at 4,000 feet above sea level or higher. However, this very fact would account for its scarcity and finally its loss.

Certainly at its peak *soma* was central to Vedic rituals, as many hymns in the *Rigveda* and the entire *Samaveda* dedicated to it attest.

See also Kshîrâbdhi-Mathanam; Magic, Blessings, Cursings; Mâyâ
For further reading:

S. S. Bhawe, *The Soma-Hymns of the Rigveda* (Baroda, 1957–1962); Ralph T. H. Griffith, ed. and trans., *Hymns of the Rgveda*, 4th ed, 2 vols. (reprint Banaras, 1963) and *The Hymns of the Samaveda* (1893; 4th ed., Varanasi, 1963); Wendy Doniger O'Flaherty, *The Rig Veda: An Anthology* (Harmondsworth, UK: Penguin Books Ltd., 1982); R. Gordon Wasson, *Soma: Divine Mushroom of Immortality* (New York: Harcourt Brace Jovanovich, 1968) and "The Soma of the Rig Veda: What Was It?" *JAOS* 91, no. 2 (1971); John Brough, "Soma and Amanita Muscaria," *Bulletin of the School of Oriental and African Studies* 34 (1971); William K. Mahony, "Soma," *Encyclopedia of Religion*, vol. 13.

ŚRÎ RÂMA

See RÂMA.

ŚRÎ KRISHNA

See KRISHNA.

SUBRAHMANYA

Son of Śiva

Subrahmanya means literally "favorable to priests," often used as an invocation to the *devas* (gods) in Vedic *soma* sacrifices. Subrahmanya was also the designation for one of three assistants to the Vedic Udgâtri priest. However, this beautiful Sanskrit compound was simply appropriated in the *Purânas* to name Śiva's most frightening creation, a son born to destroy a demon before he was a week old. The story of Agni's rape of the wives of the sages was also appropriated but reconstructed in such a confusing way that they were not Subrahmanya's mothers but merely his nurses.

The need for such a warrior son is accounted for in a story that began back at the beginning of this *kalpa*, when Vajrânga's wife had been abused by Indra and Brahmâ. Vajrânga did the necessary austerities to gain a boon to allow his son to avenge this abuse, a son more powerful than Indra and not to be killed by anyone more than a week old. Târaka, the *asura* (demon), was that son, developing into a conqueror of the three worlds.

The *devas* pleaded with Śiva to solve the problem. So he and his favorite wife Pârvatî began making love to produce a son to take care of the problem. But their thousand-year play *(lîlâ)* began to shake the foundations of the universe. The *devas*, including the goddess Bhîmî (earth), begged them to quit. Śiva stopped immediately, but then lost his seed onto the earth, overflowing forests and mountains. Bhîmî complained, and the gods had Agni consume the seed with his fire. Pârvatî became angry and cursed Bhîmî for causing her not to get a son by Śiva. The curse was that Bhîmî would have many forms, be a wife to many, and not enjoy the happiness of having children. (For details about other versions of this myth, see the entries on Skanda and Kârttikeya.)

Śiva's semen was carried to the Gangâ and then deposited on the Udaya mountain in the Shara grass. Thus, Subrahmanya was born and began crying. The six Krittikâs or divine stars, formerly the six wives who had been raped by Agni, descended to the crying infant. When he saw them, Subrahmanya developed six heads so that he could be breast-fed by each one of them. Śiva came and crowned his enormous infant the commander-in-chief of his forces. Finally, before he was more than a week old, he led his army against the armies of Târaka-asura, Mahisha, Bâna who was the son of Mahâbali, and numerous other great demons. Subrahmanya killed the otherwise unkillable Târaka-asura, and other demons were killed as well.

Another story was told to give the reason that Subrahmanya took the vow of celibacy. Pârvatî loved her new child so much that she petted him constantly. So Subrahmanya became obsessed with his desire for physical pleasures. He became a menace to all the goddess in heaven, raping them at will. Finally, Pârvatî called Subrahmanya and gave an image of herself to him, telling him to see every woman as his divine mother. Thus, Subrahmanya was able to become celibate.

See also Kârttikeya; Krittikâs; Pârvatî; Śiva; Skanda

ŚUDDHI

A concept

The concept of purification *(śuddhi)* is linked to pollution *(mala)* and the ways it is removed: ritually, physically, or even by divine grace. Central to the Vedic sacrifices was the notion that blood sacrifices would atone for wrong-doing and remove a form of purification called *agniśuddhi.* Śiva was not invited to Daksha's fire ritual, and that snub implied he was impure. Śiva's impurity may have been by birth—his very caste status *(varna)* was questioned by the Brâhmanical tradition, according to which Śiva was a tribal or Dravidian deity and thus suffered caste pollution. A myth about pollution from touch told of how Candrasharman, a *brâhmin,* had killed his teacher, yet he was still worried about further pollution from touching or eating with sinners who were lower caste. If he broke caste rules *(varna-dharma),* it involved more karmic demerits *(apunya)* and the possibility of a bad rebirth.

Many went on pilgrimages *(yatras)* to sacred sites or "river crossings" *(tîrthas)* in order to fulfill vows *(varas)* to remove various kinds of pollution. Other methods for removing pollution were the reciting of chants *(mantrayâna)* and worship *(puja).* Purification has remained a central concern in the mythology and in everyday life of modern Hindus.

See also Karma; Tîrtha-yatra; Varna

ŚUKRA

Master of magic, teacher of the asuras (demons)

In the *Epics* Śukra was the son or grandson of Bhrigu, the powerful magician who almost killed Agni. Śukra was also known as Kâvya. Śukra became the greatest master of magic of his age, but he served the *asuras.* The *devas* (gods) sent sage Kaca to learn how he had made the *asuras* invincible. (For more details see the main entry on Kaca.) Devayânî was Śukra's daughter and had a prominent role in that story.

The *Purânas* made Śukra an example of sensual excess. Śukra constantly used up his austerities *(tapas)* and the powers *(siddhis)* he had acquired by his *tapas,* plunging into years of abandoned living. It began when he was a boy. His father Bhrigu went into deep meditation *(nirvikalpa-samâdhi)* for a thousand years. Śukra became bored and with the power of his mind followed the lovely *apsara* (celestial maiden) Vishvâcî into Indraloka, Indra's heaven. Several other celestial maidens were showing him around when he discovered Vishvâcî. They immediately fell in love. Śukra made the whole place dark, so that the maidens left Vishvâcî and him alone. They made love for eight fourfold *yugas (catur-yugas).* Finally, he had used up all his virtue *(tapas)* and fell from heaven. His shriveled-up soul eventually took rebirth as a *brâhmin's* son, and during that life he was a *muni* (ascetic, magician). But again he used up his *tapas* when he fell in love with a doe (who was really a cursed apsara) and had a son by her. He forgot his practices and his religious duties and died of snakebite. So it went lifetime after lifetime—some austerities and then yielding to carnal temptations.

Finally, Bhrigu awoke from his meditation. His dead son's emaciated body lay beside him. Yama told him what had happened through all of his son's rebirths while Bhrigu was practicing his own *tapas.* Yama decided to bring Śukra back to life as Bhrigu's son.

Śukra became the preceptor of the *asuras,* instructing them in austerities and rituals to keep them strong. He had some run-ins with Śiva—some negative, some positive. Once he stole Kubera's wealth, Śiva swallowed him. In Śiva's fiery belly, Śukra worshipped Śiva and was discharged. Later, he worshipped Śiva more earnestly and was given the *mantra* for restoring life *(mritasañjîvanî mantra)*. It was this knowledge that the *devas* sent Kaca to learn and bring back to them. Kaca seduced his *guru*'s daughter but succeeded in his mission.

In his old age Śukra observed the third stage of life *(vânaprastha,* forest dweller) and attained heaven *(svarga)*.

See also Bhrigu; Devayânî; Kaca; Magic, Blessings, Cursings; Mâyâ; Siddhi; Tapas

SÛRYA

The sun god

Sûrya was a primary deity of the Aryans at the time of the earliest hymns of the *Rigveda.* The solar cult saw the sun as the most obvious symbol of life, consciousness, and divinity. For some time within each of the first three periods of Hindu mythology, Sûrya was acknowledged as the creator, the principle of life, the Supreme, or supreme ruler of all. Afterwards Sûrya underwent the process so familiar in Hindu mythology—appropriation of his powers and attributes by other deities, subordination to other deities, and finally attacks on his very character.

In the *Cândogya Upanishad* Sûrya was at the threshold between the unmanifest spheres above that were self-born *(svayambhû)* and those below that were manifest. Elsewhere Sûrya was praised as creator, self-born, and both manifest and unmanifest. As late as the *Mahâbhârata* Sûrya was the gateway to the way of the gods *(devayâna).* Some *Purânas* said that Sûrya was the cause of all, worthy of praise, and the supreme light, and that Sûrya dwells in humans and humans in Sûrya.

All this praise was not just poetic license. The worship of Sûrya as the Supreme had some support until the middle ages, and even then a small reawakening took place in the attempted building of the Sun Temple at Konarak—a temple that was not completed or consecrated because of the Muslim conquest of one of the last kingdoms in north India.

Despite this worship, stories that show Sûrya in a subordinate position or his qualities assimilated by other deities better reflect mainstream Hindu mythology. Sûrya was also known by names such as Âditya (and when he became one of twelve sons of Kaśyâpa and Aditi, Sûrya was an *âditya*), Vivasvân, Sâvitrî, and Savitur. He joined solar deities who were now personified as demigods of the Purânic pantheon. He acquired a golden chariot with one wheel (making the chariot orbit the sky) drawn by seven horses. (The Konarak temple must have showed his chariot with twelve wheels for the twelve months before it was destroyed.) His charioteer was Aruna, whose brother Garuda, the sun eagle, was most often his vehicle *(vahana).* (For more details, see the entries on Aruna and Garuda.) The *Purânas* gave him two, four, or at the most seven wives.

His principle (Purânic) wife was Samjñâ (knowledge); the others were Châyâ (shade), Prabhâ (light), Râjñî (queen), Savarnâ (colors), Svâti (self-being), and Mahâvîrya (great courage). His children suggest his complete fall from supremacy and loss of divine character: three from Samjñâ (Manu, Yama, and Yamunâ or Yamî) plus the Aśvins when he and his wife mated as horses, three from Châyâ, three from his other divine wives—and, if Ushas is taken as his daughter, incest with her—and liaisons with mortal women and animals, fathering at least Karna, dark warrior of the *Mahâbhârata,* and Sugrîva, the monkey king. The 108 names of Sûrya had long been forgotten by the time of the *Purânas*—the ones that, if remembered, brought entrance through his gate to heaven. Sûrya was henceforth seen in Buddhist, Jain, Shaiva, and Vaishnava iconography bowing with upraised hands in praise of some being truly wise or supreme, who was depicted as his superior, from whom he needed knowledge or grace.

His last roles in the Purânic myths were as the food of Râhu (swallowed with each solar eclipse), the one too busy to fight Râvana, and the giver of a boon here and there. The Gâyatrî *mantra* that is still chanted to the rising sun remains as an artifact of Sûrya's once great place in Hindu mythology.

See also Âdityas; Aruna; Châyâ; Garuda; Karna; Manu; Samjñâ; Sâvitrî; Ushas; Yama; Yamunâ

TAKSHÂKA

A mighty serpent

The grandfather of this *kalpa,* Kaśyapa-prajâpati, founded the kingdom of serpents with his wife Kadrû. Takshâka was one of her seven greatest children, the septa-nâgas. Takshâka and her most righteous children were cursed to be reborn on earth and to be burned alive as their punishment for not obeying their mother.

The story goes like this: Kadrû had become involved in a wager with another wife of Kaśyapa, Vinatâ. They bet on the color of the tail of the divine horse Uccaishshravas, each wagering her own service to the other. In order to win, Kadrû commanded her snake children to hang on the tail of the horse to make it black. Takshâka refused to support this deceit, was cursed, and became the leader of the good serpents on earth.

However, life on earth and power seemed to bring arrogance. Takshâka was central in the myth of the biting death of King Parîkshit. And the story continued with Parîkshit's son Janamejaya holding a snake sacrifice *(sarpasatra)* to rid the earth of serpents, especially Takshâka. However, Takshâka hid beside the creator Brahmâ. The high priest Uttanka, who was presiding at the sacrifice, searched for the king of snakes psychically and saw Takshâka beside Brahmâ.

The priest was furious and decided to bring Brahmâ and his throne along with Takshâka into the fire. The magic worked so well that that they were all pulled down from heaven and were within moments of being consumed in the flames. Exactly at that instance the *brâhmin* Âstîka arrived and was paid full respect by King Janamejaya. That included offering to fulfill any wish that Âstîka might have. Âstîka asked for an immediate end to the sarpasatra, and Janamejaya kept his word to the *brâhmin* and ended the sacrifice.

Takshâka was not always a danger to kings. He saved King Candrângada from drowning and hosted him in his watery kingdom. Takshâka on occasion helped Brahmâ or Indra, but just as often found his interest at odds with that of a god or hero—for example, when he crossed Arjuna and Arjuna killed Takshâka's favorite wife.

Takshâka's watery kingdom seemed to overlap with Pâtâla (hell) in some of the Purânic myths. Takshâka was there to welcome Balabhadra-Râma (Balarâma) when he died and reached Pâtâla.

See also Ananta; Âstika; Candrângada; Gavijâta; Janamejaya; Kaśyapa; Nâgas; Parîkshit; Sapta-Nâgas; Vâsuki

TÂLADHVAJA

A king and the husband of a sage

The story of Tâladhvaja was retold to solve a variety of problems—above all, how a sage could remain an ascetic when he had changed genders to marry a king. The solution in the *Devî Purâna* was a kind of popular use of Advaitan philosophy in a myth: using a popular understanding that life is *mâyâ,* an illusion or dream. King Tâladhvaja's story was nested in one about the sage who made the most appearances in other people's stories—the great sage Nârada.

In order for Nârada to experience the relative value of attachments in life, Vishnu gave him the experience of a lifetime as a householder—better yet, as a mother. Vishnu asked Nârada to take a bath, so Nârada left his lute *(vina)* and deerskin robe on the shore. When he emerged from the river, he had become Saubhâgyasundarî, a lovely young woman. It so happened that King Tâladhvaja arrived at just that moment and engaged Saubhâgyasundarî in conversation and then in marriage. He took her back to his palace, and after twelve years of honeymooning, she began to give him children. Years passed, and Saubhâgyasundarî was the matriarch of a huge family of children and grandchildren. However, war broke out with an adjoining kingdom. King Tâladhvaja was defeated and fled the battlefield. Saubhâgyasundarî arrived there to find all of her sons and grandsons slain. As she wept, Vishnu appeared and instructed her in the meaning of life. Finally, Vishnu asked Saubhâgyasundarî to bathe in the river. And when she emerged from the river, she had become the old sage Nârada again.

Meanwhile, King Tâladhvaja had arrived to see his wife go into the river for a bath and suddenly become an old sage. Tâladhvaja could not be consoled by Nârada. Vishnu appeared and told Tâladhvaja that human attachments are only an illusion *(mâyâ)*. So Tâladhvaja gave up his kingdom, practiced austerities, and attained liberation *(moksha)*.

The ending allowed two interpretations: a relatively real experience *(visishita-advaita)* of Nârada as the wife of Tâladhvaja or an illusory one *(mâyâvâda)*. This ending thus illustrates one of the strengths of mythology—it does not have to be fully rationalized or be made philosophically perfect.

See also Mâyâ; Nârada

TANTRA, TANTRISM

A religious sect or practice

Tantra has had many meanings: a class of literature (the *Tantras*), practices that are non-Vedic *(tantrika)*, one of the religious sects of Hinduism. There is no single word in Sanskrit for Tantrism as a religious perspective, even though its additions to the Hindu tradition make it quite distinctive. Tantrism can be seen in the point of view of Hindu mythology. It is a practical path, with techniques for acquiring magical or supernatural powers *(siddhis)*. It is the entire cosmos as unified; there is no absolute division between pure and impure. What an orthodox Hindu would find polluting, the Tantrika would use as an avenue for purification or, more likely, to develop *siddhis*. The five Ms *(pañca-makâras)*, so called because each began with m—*madya* (wine), *matsya* (fish), *mâmsa* (meat), *mudrâ* (an aphrodisiac), *maithuna* (sexual union)—were used to develop *siddhis*, the Tantrika hoping eventually to gain liberation *(moksha)* by these very practices. Physical pleasure *(kâma, maithuna)* could lead to happiness *(bhukti, ânanda)* in this world and the next, and one could even become free in this lifetime *(jîvanmukti)*. This whole practice was based upon energy *(shaktî)* that was pure or could be purified.

The Tantrika lived in a unified world in which anything could be done because everything was divine or could be made divine. The Tantrika was armed with prayers *(mantras)*, rituals, gestures *(mudras)*, symbols *(yantras)*, postures *(asanas)*, divinities, and even demons for protection and for growth. In fact, the frightening deities and demons were something in which the Tantrika specialized. Transforming the dark into light, the polluted into the pure, was at the heart of their practice. This approach was almost always controversial and supposed to be secret—only discussed among the initiated with a master. It was a path of small groups, not a mass movement.

The main divisions of Tantrism were along the same line as sectarianism Hinduism: Vaishnava, Śaiva, and Śākta. There were also worshippers of the sun or Sûrya (Sauras) and Ganeśa (Ganapatyas) who were also Tantrikas. Further distinctions were made as to the three currents *(srotas)*—right *(dakshina),* left *(vama),* and accepted *(siddanta).*

See also Durgâ; Kâlî; Lakshmî; Râdha
For further reading:
André Padoux, "Tantrism, An Overview" and "Hindu Tantrism," in *Encyclopedia of Religion*, vol. 14; Arthur Avalon (J. Woodroffe), *The Serpent Power*, 7th ed. (Madras: Ganesh and Co., 1953); Edward C. Dimock, Jr., *The Place of the Hidden Moon* (Chicago: University of Chicago Press, 1966); Sanjukta Gupta, Dirk Jan Hoens, and Teun Goudriaan, *Hindu Tantrism* (Leiden: E. J. Brill, 1979).

TAPA

A god with five fathers

Tapa was a *deva* (god) who was born of the *tapas* (austerities) of five sages: Kaśyâpa, Vasishtha, Prânaka, Cyavana, and Trivarcas. Hence, he was also known by the name Pânca-janya (one born of five). He can be said to be the personification of *tapas.* However, the *Mahâbhârata* added that Tapa had his own sons: Purandara, Ushman, Prajâpati Manu, Shambhu, and Âvasathya—all obscure enough. To these sons were added the five *urjaskaras*, five sons of sacrifice, and the his final son—Parishrânta, the exhausted sun. Tapa's mother was not mentioned.

See also Kaśyapa; Tapas

TAPAS

A concept

Tapas, a central term in Hindu mythology, literally means "heat." It served as a metaphor for the heat generated in ascetic and esoteric practices. Austerities that generated *tapas,* often themselves called *tapas,* were not always ascetic in spirit. Most myths link *tapas* with powers *(siddhis):* one practiced *tapas* in order to gain *siddhis.* The demons *(asuras)* often quit any aspect of their practice that was ascetic (fasting, yoga, meditation, worship) as soon as they acquired the *siddhi* they sought (immortality, invincibility, and the like). Often Brahmâ, and sometimes Indra or other *devas,* granted a boon *(vara)* for a particular power *(siddhi)* as a reward for a particular form of austerity *(tapas).* In this latter conception *tapas* was analogous to Vedic sacrifice, providing the *devas* with something they wanted so that they would grant a human desire. Besides *siddhis*, these desires could even include the reward of heaven *(svarga)*. Myths about the way the *asuras* would practice *tapas* that flattered Brahmâ suggested that repeating a chant *(mantra)* of praise *(japa)* for a thousand years either pleased Brahmâ or obligated him to grant the desired boon. When tapas was equated with purification rituals, it was linked to the notion of penance. However, stories of people becoming purified by penance in order to have the siddhi to make war with invincibility only emphasize the connection of tapas to magic *(mâyâ)*.

See also Mâyâ, Siddhi
For further reading:
Chauncey J. Blair, *Heat in the Rig Veda and the Atharva Veda* (New Haven: Princeton University Press, 1961); David M. Knipe, "Tapas," *Encyclopedia of Religion*, vol. 14 and *Image of Fire: Vedic Experiences of Heat* (Delhi: Motilal Banarsidass, 1975); Mircea Eliade, *A History of Religious Ideas*, vol. 1 (Chicago: University of Chicago Press, 1978) and *Yoga: Immortality and Freedom*, 2d ed. (Princeton: Princeton University Press, 1969); Wendy Doniger O'Flaherty, *Asceticism and Eroticism in the Mythology of Siva* (London: Oxford University Press, 1973).

TÂRÂ

One of the five perfect women
The story of Târâ illustrates the Purânic mentality of defaming its heroes and heroines, since some accounts make her a willing participant in adultery and others exonerate her and present her as one of the *pañcakanayâ*, five perfect women.

Târâ was married to the great sage Brihaspati and was unusually beautiful. Consequently Târâ was abducted by Soma (or Candra, the moon), and that resulted in a war known as Târaka-maya. Rudra and the demons *(asuras)* were on one side with Soma, and Brihaspati and the gods *(devas)*, led by Indra, were on the other. Brahmâ finally restored Târâ to her husband. However, she was with child. Both Soma and Brihaspati claimed the child, who was named Budha (the planet Mercury). Finally, Târâ said that the child was fathered by Soma.

See also Brihaspati; Candra; Pañcakanayâ; Soma

TILOTTAMÂ

An apsara

Tilottamâ was an example of robotics, according to the modern Hindu idea that every form of knowledge, including modern science, can be found in the *Vedas* and *Purânas*. Tilottamâ had to be made from all the elements of beauty, animate and inanimate, to make a woman who would enchant two demons *(asuras)*. Tilottamâ was put together by the divine architect, Viśvakarman. Brahmâ had made his usual mistake and granted invincibility to the *asuras* Sunda and Upasunda. They needed to be tricked into fighting each other, as that was the only loophole in the boon. Therefore, Brahmâ instructed Viśvakarman to make Tilottamâ. Before she went to earth she worshipped the *devas* (gods) by the custom of circling them (circumambulation, or *pradakshuna*). Śiva was so enamored by Tilottamâ that he created a face on each side of his head so that he could always see her. And Indra instantly produced a thousand eyes for the same purpose.

Sunda and Upasunda had conquered the three worlds and sent the *devas* away in terror, but now they met their match. They both fell in love with Tilottamâ and fought to the death for her, killing each other. However, the story does not end there. The *Padma Purâna* corrected the *Mahâbhârata*'s story of the creation of Tilottamâ by Viśvakarman. It told the story that an ugly widow named Kubjâ spent eight years doing auspicious ceremonies that culminated in a purification bath *(Mâgha pûjâ)*. Kubjâ was reborn as Tilottamâ. Her austerities led to the return of the proper order in heaven.

See also Tapas; Viśvakarman

TÎRTHA-YATRA

A practice

A *yatra* was a pilgrimage, or visit, to a river crossing, or ford *(tîrtha)*. Thus the term *tîrtha-yatra* came into usage. Over the centuries it came to mean a visit to any holy place, a pilgrimage to a sacred region (such as the plain where the *Mahâbhârata* battle was fought), to a temple city (such as Melkote), or to a river (such as the Gangâ or the Yamunâ).

Some have seen in the practice the influence of Dravidian or Indus Valley ritualistic bathing and a continuation of early purification practices. However, there may be something more interesting. Vedic literature mentioned Brâhmanical rituals *(Agni yagas)* being performed at river fords *(tîrthas)* wherever Aryan culture had become dominant in an area. Add to that the need for large amounts of water when warriors were killed to perform their death rituals, as in the myth of King Asamañjasa's sons: they were killed, but no rituals could be done for lack of water. King Bhagîratha was able to get Śiva to bring the heavenly Gangâ to earth, and the death rituals were finally done. Combine the clues, and the fords may well have marked battle sites and the places where the sacred ashes of warriors rested, showing how Aryan culture had been spread and lands pacified.

A full-blown cult of pilgrimage was already in evidence in the *Mahâbhârata*. Surinder M. Bhardwaj's classic study of pilgrimage sites *(tîrthas)* showed a clockwise journey, starting at Pushkara in Rajasthan, and then visiting ancient Mahakala (Ujjain), Dwaravati (Dwarkar), Kurukshetra, Varanasi, Gaya, and so on, hoping to end at Prayaga (Allahabad). The literary references to boatmen have meaning when there are great rivers to cross and no bridges. Two kinds of stories about the sacred guided the pilgrim—those of local significance and those of a pan-cultural nature. It was Bhardwaj's thesis that pilgrimage defined an Aryan consciousness. It circumscribed those areas where the fire rituals were done, where vows could be fulfilled, where worship to Brâhmanical deities could be done.

Tîrtha-yatra was one way of acquiring merit *(punya)*. It was another type of austerity. It was an inexpensive substitute for Brâhmanical sacrifices. But the routes traced carefully by Bhardwaj showed no interest in land that had not been sanctified by Aryan conquest. Vast regions were not visited. Where there was no myth about a divine activity, there was no interest in a journey into that region.

By the modern period *tîrthas* are classified in a number of ways: mythically (divine, demonic, sagely, human), religious (sectarian or pan-Hindu), cultural (regional or pan-Indian), liturgical (water for purification or temples for worship), geographic (battle sites, forests, mountains), and so on.

Myth and pilgrimage are linked in the most fundamental ways: myth locates where the pilgrim can experience the sacred. Modern Hindus choose from 1,800 *tîrthas* to nurture religious needs and longings. However, there is an innovation of visiting the four corners of India: Badrinath in the north nestled in the Himâlayas, Puri in the east, Ramesvaram in the south, and Dvarka in the west. There seems always to be the desire to go to Benares (Varanasi) and return home with sacred water from the Gangâ. Finally, pilgrimage is further encouraged by festivals and fairs so rich in number and variety that they alone could possibly keep the myths alive. Each place has its special myths, festivals, and observances. And all of this activity of visiting sacred sites *(tîrthas)* is believed to gain merit, a better rebirth, and eventually liberation.

See also Kurukshetra; *Mahâbhârata*
For further reading:
Agehananda Bharati, "Pilgrimage in the Indian Tradition," *History of Religions* 3 (Summer 1963); Surinder M. Bhardwaj, "Hindu Pilgrimage," *Encyclopedia of Religion*, vol. 11 and *Hindu Places of Pilgrimage in India: A Study in Cultural Geography* (Berkeley: University of California Press, 1973).

TRITA

A deva (god)

Trita was a Vedic god whose name meant "the third." His main importance comes from sharing the same achievements with Indra. Some scholars say that he was Indra's double, but a more likely interpretation is that Trita was already fading from prominence by the time of the Vedic hymns. That is, Trita represented an earlier mythology. He was known in the earliest Avestan (Persian) mythology. Indra was given Trita's heroic deeds: the slaying of the monsters Vritra, Vala, and Viśvarûpa, son of Tvashthri.

One story in the *Rigveda* told how Ekata (first), Dvita (second), and Trita (third) went to draw water. The two threw Trita in the well and sealed it with a wheel. Trita composed a hymn (*Rigveda* 9.34.4) and prepared a *soma* sacrifice (*yâga*) in the well. (It may be a type of Cain and Abel story of brother[s]'s envy and attempted murder, but it is only a fragment.)

See also Indra; Tvashthri; Vritra

TVASHTHRI

God of craftsmanship

Tvashthri, literally the shaper, was the son of Kaśyapa and Aditi. Alain Daniélou called him the personification of one of the six minor principles of Vedic culture: craftsmanship. The hymns in the *Rigveda* made him function something like later concepts such as *śaktî* (divine energy) and life force *(prâna)*, except that Tvashthri was the very divine craftsman at work in the womb, forming the offspring of all species, determining their beauty and strength. By the time of the *Brâhmanas* Tvashthri had become the agent in crafting into being whatever was manifested. He made Indra's mighty thunderbolt *(vajra)* from the bone of the sage Dadhîci. However, his son Viśvarûpa was a rival of Indra, and some accounts said that Indra killed him.

Some versions maintained that there were two different Tvashthris: one the divine craftsman and another an *âditya* (celestial god).

See also Âdityas; Dadhîci; *Purusha*; Viśvakarman

ÛMÂ

A goddess

Ûmâ was a goddess whose name meant "light." She was the wife of Śiva and was also known by the name of Pârvatî in one of her births.

See also Devî; Pârvatî; Śiva

UPANISHAD

A scripture from the last of the four divisions of the Vedas

The meaning of *upanishad* is "to sit near attentively." They usually consisted of a metaphysical discussion between the sage and a disciple. There are 108 *Upanishads* traditionally, although only a dozen, the so-called major *Upanishads*, are in every list. Minor *Upanishads* are still being written.

In the early Vedic period, before the *Upanishads* were recognized as authoritative, there was a three-fold division of the *Vedas:* the *Samhita* (collection of hymns), *Brâhmanas* (commentaries), and *Âranyakas* (forest texts). The *Upanishads* formed the last *(anta)* part of the *Vedas*, also called Vedânta (from *veda* and *anta*).

The *Vedas* were the earliest Indian scripture and have always had the greatest authority. However, that does not mean that if a story or a figure is not mentioned in the *Vedas*, it is considered untrue or without authority. In fact, there were a number of ways of resolving such a problem. First, it could be said to be additional revelation and therefore compatible. Or, it could be new (that is, not mentioned in the *Vedas*) and a necessary supplement, given the declining spirituality of each of the four *yugas*. New revelations were needed for the *kali yuga*, the one we are in now. Many more ways were available to allow for discrepancies and even contradictions to the *Vedas* in later Purânic and Tântric mythology.

One major *Upanishad*, the *Isha*, presented a woman sage teaching the *devas* (gods) about the Absolute (Brahman). Some of the important *Upanishads* are the *Taittirîya Upanishad, Mândukya Upanishad,* and the *Brihadâranyaka Upanishad.* The *Brihadâranyaka Upanishad* is the longest *Upanishad.* The *Upanishads* are known as one of the foundational pillars *(prasthânatreya,* "three pillars") of Indian thought. Because of their deeply philosophical and meditational approach, the *Upanishads* provide few myths—and only several names of sages with some ideals like union *(samadhi)* with the Absolute *(Brahman).*

See also Brahman; Vedas

For further reading:

Surendranath Dasgupta, *A History of Indian Philosophy,* vol. 1 (1922; reprint, Cambridge: Cambridge University Press, 1961); Paul Deussen, *The Philosophy of the Upanishads* (1905), 2d ed., trans. A. S. Geden (reprint New York: Dover Publications, 1966); Robert Ernest Hume, *The Thirteen Principal Upanishads,* 2d rev. ed. (Oxford: Oxford University Press, 1949); Arthur Berriedale Keith, *The Religion and Philosophy of the Veda and Upanishads,* 2 vols. (Cambridge, MA: Harvard University Press, 1925); William K. Mahony, "Upanisads," *Encyclopedia of Religion,* vol. 15; Sarvepalli Radhakrishnan, *The Principal Upanisads* (London: Allen and Unwin, 1953).

URVAŚÎ

An apsara (celestial nymph)

Urvaśî's story is unusual. She was an *apsara*, but instead of being born or created in heaven she was born from the thigh of a mortal. She resulted from a conflict between Indra and her father, the sage Nârâyana. It happened in this way. Nârâyana and Nara, sons of Dharma and grandsons of Brahmâ, were heating up the throne of Indra with their powerful austerities *(tapas)*. Indra tried three ways to stop their acquisition of power: boons, fear of his show of power, and the temptation of his celestial beauties. The first two had absolutely no effect, but possibly because of spring the sages opened their eyes to see all the famous apsaras from Menakâ to Ghritâcî and 10,080 maidservants. To teach Indra a lesson, Nârâyana slapped his thigh *(ûru)*, and from it was born "the one born of a thigh" *(urvaśî)*. She was first in beauty of all the *apsaras*. Other beautiful women were also created, and all given to Indra. He apologized to the sages and left with his celestials as well as the new gifts. Once in Indra's heaven, Urvaśî became eleventh among the singers and dancers.

Later, either Brahmâ (in the *Devî Bhâgavata*) or Mitrâvarunas (in the *Bhâgavata Purâna*) cursed Urvaśî to be born on earth. Urvaśî had heard of a handsome king named Purûravas, found him, fell in love, and married but with three conditions. Even with all his other beauties Indra soon missed Urvaśî and sent his *gandharvas* to bring her back. Somehow they knew that she had promised to stay with King Purûravas only if he tended her two lambs, let her eat only ghee (clarified butter, food of the gods), and did not allow her to see him nude. So the gandharvas waited until they were at play in the bedroom. They stole the lambs, and when the king jumped from the bed to save them, the gandharvas lit the sky with a bolt of lightning. King Purûravas was caught without any clothes. He raced after the lambs and soon found them. However, when he returned, Urvaśî had left. Purûravas wasted away searching for his lovely Urvaśî. Years later he found her at Kurukshetra, site of many a pilgrimage. Her famous words are committed to memory by every Indian schoolchild in their vernacular, or better yet in Sanskrit: "Women are like wolves. Don't have an alliance with them, O King! Kings should not put their faith in women and thieves." (Of course, this was not quite the way the great medieval poet Kâlidâsa described their story in his *Vikramorvasî*, one of the great love poems and dramas of India. But that is another story.)

See also Apsara; Brahmâ; Gandharvas; Indra; Kurukshetra; Nârâyana

USHÂ

Daughter of Bânâsura and wife of Aniruddha

Ushâ was a *daitya* (demon) princess, daughter of Bâna and granddaughter of Bali, both great *asura* (demon) rulers. Ushâ dreamed of the man she would wish to marry. Citralekhâ, a woman with this special *siddhi* (power), drew a picture of Aniruddha, grandson of Krishna, according to Ushâ's dream. Then, Citralekhâ brought Aniruddha to the palace with her magic. When Aniruddha was brought to Ushâ's room and saw his own picture, he fell in love with Ushâ.

Bâna or his preceptor immediately sensed Aniruddha's presence and sent the palace guards to kill him. Aniruddha was able to defeat them, but he was taken prisoner by magic and bound in serpents with the help of Śiva and Skanda, Śiva's son and god of war.

Krishna and Aniruddha's father, Pradyumna, rescued him, bringing both Aniruddha and his bride Ushâ back to their palace in Dvârakâ.

This little story has great popular appeal. One even finds it alluded to or added as a scene within modern Indian films or video serials.

See also Citralekhâ

USHAS

A goddess

In Vedic mythology Ushas was the goddess of dawn and the herald of all that was connected with the advent of the sun, Sûrya, supreme ruler of the heavens.

She announced Sûrya, who brought along with her, light to make the pastures fertile, horses, chariots, wealth, and plenitude. The mighty sun god seemed unapproachable to the Vedic worshipper because of his formidable luminance; Sûrya could not be directly viewed by ordinary mortal eyes. Ushas was approachable in the light of early morning devotion and would lead mortals to the all-powerful sun god. Bringing forth Sûrya, she was invoked as the eye of the gods (*Rigveda* 7.77.3: *devânâm chakshuh . . . vahanti*).

She was ever the young woman and the immortal divine one who bestowed material wealth upon the Aryans. She was described as the mother of plenitude (*Rigveda* 7.77.2: *gavâm mâta*), beautiful and ever young, yet also the one who ages humankind. The cool rays of Ushas, the beautiful mother, had the power to direct and channel the mighty powers of the sun god.

Even in the Vedic hymns her lineage was traced back to two different origins. The first made her the daughter of a somewhat obscure sky god named Diva (also called Vivasvân). This lineage seemed to be the most common in the hymns to her and made her the sister of the solar deities known as the *âdityas* (*Rigveda* 7.77.6), including the mighty Varuna.

However, the second lineage involved a complex problem in Vedic mythology: the mode of creation. According to it, Ushas was said to be the daughter of Prajâpati, father of all beings. He represented a monotheistic direction in later Vedic mythology, where he rivaled the Vedic Triad of Sûrya, Indra, and Agni, rulers of the three realms. A careful reading of the hymns revealed that he created Ushas in an unspecified way, perhaps by word or division of himself, but not with a mate—for he, Prajâpati, was the origin of everything. He then mated with her, and she became the mother of all things. Some scholars miss the unique solution of the Vedic poets in this myth. It need not be written off as incest; it can be seen as a mythopoeic solution for creation, in which a feminine solar deity was the mother of creation. Yet, in the second lineage she was still referred to as the sister of the âdityas, showing an inability on the part of the poets to fully draw out the implications of her relationship to the âdityas—since they had become her children.

Ushas was related to other female goddesses and gods in the Vedic period like Vâc (goddess of speech), Prâna (god of breath), and Manâh (goddess of mind). Ushas was the bestower of material wealth in all its forms. Even though she was immortal, she did not give immortality to mortals. There seemed to be a developing religious or spiritual hierarchy in her gifts of material prosperity and pleasure contrasting with those of the later Vedic goddesses who gave higher knowledge, power, and wisdom. Her gifts were this-worldly. Vâc, especially, prefigured a still later goddess, Sarasvatî, who ruled the realm of knowledge of specific sciences and arts—in fact, who was the repository of all conceivable knowledge.

Ushas is still significant in contemporary India. She is acknowledged and worshipped through the Gâyatrî *mantra*, the spiritual armor of Hindu *brâhmins* and *brahmachâris* (celibate individuals) throughout India. This *mantra*, used as a morning (and often evening) devotion, has been recited by the most orthodox for three thousands years.

See also Âdityas; Agni; Devî; Indra; Mantra; Prajâpati; Prâna; Sarasvatî; Sûrya; Vâc; Varuna

VÂC

A goddess

Vâc means "word" and "song," as well as being the name of an early Vedic goddess. Vâc refers to both speech and speech-consciousness. Vâc enters into the seers *(rishis)*.

A Rigvedic hymn to Vâc stated that all actions and powers were grounded in speech. It was the primordial energy out of which all existence originated and in which it subsisted. At the same time it claimed that *Vâc* extended beyond the heavens and the earth. This was an example of an associative process that the hymnists were using what were called *bandhus* (links)—a logic that connected processes with divinities.

Speech was recognized as the first expression of truth. The sage Dirghatamas proclaimed, "From her [Vâc] flows the oceans; through her the four regions exist; from her the ground *[akshara]* of the *Veda* flows; on her the entire universe stands." Then he stated that only the manifested forms of speech can be known; the deepest levels remain hidden. He further added that prayer is the highest heaven in which speech dwells. Through prayer—the fundamental mode of speech-consciousness—the individual mind tried to resonate with the cosmic mind in Vedic hymns.

The *yâjña* (sacrificial) performances were based on the psychology of speech-consciousness. Through the liturgical, performative knowledge of sacrificial celebration, the limitations of ordinary existence and the grounding of human existence in the more fundamental levels of consciousness were recognized and experienced.

In the *Brâhmanas* Vâc was equated with Sarasvatî, the goddess of wisdom and the arts. In the *Upanishads* Vâc was created from the self *(atman)*. However, the tendency to pull down the gods and goddesses reigned in the *Purânas*, and her reputation was besmirched. As Vâc-Sarasvatî, she was the mind-daughter of Brahmâ. So the *Matsya* and *Śiva Purânas* implicated her in the sin of incest with her father, Brahmâ. Virâtrûpa Agni (Brahmâ's son as half a male) mated with his sister Vâc, and their offspring became the year.

In Śaivite cosmology, Śiva manifested the cosmos in five stages: joy *(ânanda)*, knowledge *(vijñâna)*, thought *(mana)*, life-breath *(prâna)*, and physical life *(bhûta)*. Bhûta divided into speech *(vâc)* and food *(anna)*. Thus, Vâc was subordinated to Śiva as the true creator, and speech became just one of the principles involved in the origin of the universe.

See also Brahmâ; Sarasvatî; Śiva

VADHRIMATÎ

A princess mentioned in the Rigveda

Princess Vadhrimatî was married to a hermaphrodite. With the blessings of the Aśvin brothers she received a son named Hiranyahasta.

The story came from a time when gods had sons with princesses. In a slightly different version Vadhrimatî was married to a eunuch. Despondent that she could not have a child, Vadhrimatî prayed to the Aśvini-devas, the divine twins, the physicians of the *devas* (gods); they happily fulfilled her desire. Hiranyahasta grew up a sage, possibly even a *brâhmin*, since he married the daughter of sage Matarisvan. Another version said he married a princess, the daughter of King Madirâshva.

See also Aśvins; Varna

VAIKUNTHA
The abode of Vishnu

Vaikuntha was the celestial abode of Vishnu. Vaikuntha literally means the "place of no hindrance." In the *Purânas,* it was located variously—in heaven *(svarga),* north of the heavenly mountains (Himâlaya), even on Mount Meru (Mahâmeru), the axis of the earth. Most commonly Vaikuntha was located on the southern slopes of Mahâmeru. It had streets of gold, buildings of jewels, and was graced by the celestial Gangâ. For some sources it was identical with Goloka, the heaven of Krishna.

See also Gangâ; Vishnu. For more on Hindu cosmology see chapter 1.

VAIVASVATA MANU
The Manu of the seventh Manvantara, the current age

Vaivasvata Manu is the "first man" of the current *manvantara* (age or era). In the *Rigveda* there were references to Father Manu, implying that he was either a creator or a progenitor of the human race, but this reference seemed to refer to the sun god Sûrya. In the *Satapatha Brahmana* Manu was known as the first human, father of the race, first to kindle the sacrificial fire, and creator of the social order. There was also a story of Manu's instruction by a fish *(matsya)* to build a boat. The fish then helped Manu survive a great flood. When he was saved, Manu gave thanks, and a woman, Idâ (or Ilâ), was created. With her as mother Manu produced the human race.

The *Epics* traced all royal lineages to Manu. One of his sons, Vikukshi, founded the solar race *(sûrya-vamsa)* of kings at Ayodhyâ. Purûravas, son of Manu's daughter Idâ, founded the lunar race *(candra-vamśa)* of kings at Pratisthana.

The later *Purânas* tell of multiple Manus, a Manu, or first man, for each *manvantara. Manvantaras* were approximately three hundred million years each, and the present one is the seventh *manvantara.* The current Manu is Vaivasvata Manu. The six previous Manus were Svayambhuva, Svarocisa, Auttami, Tamasa, Raivata, and Cakshusa. There will be seven more: Savarni, Daksasavarni, Brahmasavarni, Dharmasavarni, Rudrasavarni, Raucya (or Devasavarni), and Bhautya (or Indrasavarni). The Manus are discussed in chapter 2 in the section on mythic time.

See also Agastya; Manu; Manvantara; Pârvatî; Śiva

VÂLMÎKI

A very famous sage and the author of the Râmâyana

There are no authentic records about Vâlmîki's parentage. The popular version considered him to be the tenth son of Varuna, god of the sea.

Vâlmîki was considered to be the first poet. There is an interesting story about the earlier part of Vâlmîki's life. He began this life as a hunter named Ratnâkra who looked after his family in the forest by hunting for animals—but also by robbing travelers. One day he happened to see the *saptarishis* (seven sages), who warned him about the consequences of his sins and predicted that no one would share the consequences with him. This striking truth awakened Ratnâkara. He went home and asked his wife whether she would share the consequences of his sins. His wife said that one enjoys the fruits of one's own actions and these cannot be shared with anybody. This revelation of the saptarishis changed Ratnâkara.

When Ratnâkara met the saptarishis again, he began to chant the name of Râma according to their advice. Many years went by as he practiced austerities *(tapas).* The body of Ratnâkra was covered with termites. Finally, the saptarishis came back on the same road. They called to Vâlmîki for him to come out of his tapas. They named him Vâlmîki because he came out of a termite's nest *(valmika).*

Vâlmîki was living in his *âsrama* (hermitage) by the river Tâmasâ. One day he saw a hunter who shot a bird from a tree with an arrow. It was one of a pair. The surviving bird was flying around in agony. This tragic scene inspired Vâlmîki to write his first verse.

See also Sapta-rishis; Varuna

VÂMANA

The fifth of the ten incarnations of Vishnu

Vâmana was the dwarf incarnation *(avatâra)* of Vishnu. The myth utilized the device of deceit, or outwitting the opponent, even though the struggle was between the supreme god Vishnu and a demon *(asura)* named Bali. Although an avatâra was required to restore the proper order and return righteousness to the world, Bali exhibited such high ethical qualities that some may be confused about which party was the example of righteousness.

Bali (also known as Mahâbali) had obtained a boon *(vara)* of invincibility and (conditional) immortality from Brahmâ, so he could not be conquered by the gods *(devas)* unless he was cursed by his teacher *(guru)* Śukracharya. Śukra had greater knowledge of the *Vedas* than the chief priest of the gods, his mastery of magic was greater, and the austerities *(tapas)* performed by the *asuras* exceeded those of the gods *(devas)*. Thus, Bali was able to lead the *asuras* to victory after victory over their rivals.

The *devas*, led by Indra (who in the myths from the Epic Period onwards was weak and easily defeated by the demons because he did not properly keep the rules of *dharma*), turned to Brahmâ. As always (in a Vishnu myth cycle), Brahmâ the creator must send the gods to Vishnu, the Supreme. It was Vishnu who decided whether there was a special need to end the time of disorder and restore dharma. His goal during this time was to send King Bali to the netherworld *(pâtâla)* and to help Indra regain his position as head of the *devas* and ruler of heaven *(svarga)*. However, Bâli was not a perfect villain and the myth had some moral ambiguities that remained unsolved.

Vishnu incarnated as a *brâhmin* boy into the family of Aditi and her husband, the sage Kaśyapa. In earlier myths, they were the cosmic parents of the gods. Yet in this myth, it was Aditi's *tapas* that allowed Vâmana to be born as her son. As a dwarf *(vâmana) brâhmin*, he went to the court of Bali. Although misshapen, he was still honored as a priest. His feet were washed by King Bali before his court, and he was asked to name a request. Vâmana asked only for the land that he could encompass in three steps. Bâli wished to be more generous and asked Vâmana to name something more worthy. However, when Vâmana kept asking for the same thing, the king's sage Śukra guessed that this must be Vishnu in disguise and warned his disciple, the king. King Bali had such a high code of ethics that he would not withdraw the boon. And to the horror of all, the dwarf grew into a giant whose three strides encompassed all of creation. His teacher cursed Bali because he would not heed his teacher's warning. Thus, the very condition that would break Bali's boon of invincibility was fulfilled.

Garuda, the cosmic eagle and now Vishnu's vehicle *(vâhana)*, swooped down from the heavens, bound Bali, and took him for judgment to Vishnu. Some versions even have his ancestor—Prahlâda, the *asura* hero of the Narasimha *avatâra*—appearing to plead for Bali. In any case, Vishnu recognized the honor and merit of Bali and granted him entry into his abode, a realm higher even than the heaven of the gods.

See also Aditi; Avatâra; Garuda; Kaśyapa; Prahlâda; Śukra; Vishnu

VARÂHA
Third of the ten incarnations of Vishnu, as Varâha, the wild boar

In the *Padma Purâna* the world order had again been disrupted. The fierce *asura* (demon) Hiranyâksha had gained a boon *(vara)* of invincibility. With his provisional immortality, he stormed around the three regions of the universe wanting to fight and kill the gods. He became bored when he could do no more evil, so he dragged Bhîmî-devî, the earth, to the bottom of the cosmic ocean. Svayambhuva-Manu and Śatarupâ, the future parents of humanity, and the gods asked Brahmâ what could be done. From his meditation a tiny boar was produced out of his nose. The boar quickly grew to an enormous size and then dove into the depths of the cosmic ocean. It was the ever troublesome Sage Nârada who revealed to Hiranyâksha that Vishnu had left heaven. Although Hiranyâksha found Varâha, his taunts could not start a fight. Varâha first brought Bhîmî to the surface and restored the earth to its proper place. Then he turned to the task of delivering the world from its current threat of evil, which was always the task of each *avatâra* (incarnation). Varâha disposed of Hiranyâksha in a mighty battle.

See also Avatâra; Bhîma; Hiranyâksha; Nârada

VARNA
A concept

Varna means "color"; it refers to a ideal system of four classes or groupings of society—the so-called caste system. Both these *idealized* classes and the current *jati* (birth) system of several thousand endogamous groups are translated by the word caste, which probably came into English from Portuguese. Surprisingly, the *real* caste system of *jati* and its world of marriage and occupation laws are not referenced in Hindu mythology. It is the ideal caste system of the four *varnas* that is noticed: the *brâhmana (brâhmins)*, the priests; the *râjanya (kṣatriyas)*, a ruling or warrior group; the *vaiśya*, artisans or merchants, and the *śûdra*, servants or workers.

In the modern era reformers Svâmî Vivekânanda (often called Father of Renaissance Hinduism) and philosopher (and later president of India) S. Radhakrishnan talked about the ideal of interrelated support each group should give to the others for their mutual uplift spiritually, socially, and culturally. This type of support would explain how in the myths groups of persons were connected in their *karma* from one lifetime to the next as they jointly worked out their spiritual lessons.

Hindu mythology may be looking at the ideal of varna from another perspective. Many myths offer nonorthodox conceptions: *kṣatriyas* changing to *brâhmins* by their own austerities; *brâhmins* who are evil, who maim or kill their enemies, who lie and deceive, who do not know the *Vedas*; all types of intercaste marriage; and *brâhmins* who eat meat. Perhaps these departures from the ideal reflect the very theme of the myths—that this age is the *kali yuga*, when *dharma* has been forgotten, especially *varna-dharma*.

See also Dharma

For further reading:

A. L. Basham, *The Wonder That Was India*, rev. ed. (New York: Grove Press, 1963); Louis Dumont, *Homo Hierarchicus: An Essay on the Caste System*, translated by Mark Sainsbury (Chicago: University of Chicago Press, 1970); Morton Klass, "Varna and Jati," *Encyclopedia of Religion*, vol. 15 and *Caste: The Emergence of the South Asian Social System* (Philadelphia: ISHI, 1980).

VARUNA

A god (deva)

Varuna was one of the oldest of the Vedic deities. Varuna may have been part of the first triad of gods known in the Vedic period—along with Mitra and Aryaman. A little later but still within the early Vedic period, they were replaced by Agni, Indra, and Sûrya.

Varuna was both an *asura* (demon) and a *deva*, leading to the notion that Varuna, ancient lord of justice *(rita)* and truth *(satya)*, had a violent streak. There were accusations in the later myths that this violence was why Indra took away Varuna's power.

In the early *Vedas* Varuna was the king of the earth and the sky, and the creator. He was also associated with Mitra, the ruler of the night—though in later Vedic hymns we find him as the chief of the *âdityas*, thus an *asura*, and contrasted to Mitra, a *deva* and a ruler of the day.

Later when Indra took over the rulership of heaven, Varuna became the god of oceans, who rode on a *makara*, his fish or water monster vehicle. This phase was especially elaborated in the *Purânas*. He was presented as the father of Brahmâ, who created the whole world, and also of the sage Vasishtha, one of the seven Rishis *(sapta-rishis)*. Like the more famous god of death and justice, Yama, one of the attributes of Varuna was a noose *(nagapâsa)* by which he tied the guilty, a remembrance of his role of judge of the just and the unjust.

See also Indra; Rita; Sûrya; Vedas

VÂSUKI

A mighty serpent, and the eldest son of Kadrû and Kasyapa

Vâsuki served as the churning rope when the wondrous objects, including the nectar of immortality *(amrita)*, were brought up from the Milky Ocean.

See also Kshîrâbdhi-Mathanam; Nâga; Sapta-nâgas

VÂYU

A deva (god)

Vâyu was the Vedic wind god. He fought alongside Indra and the Maruts (gods of storm) in defeating Vritra, the storm demon who held back the celestial waters. He was a charioteer of enormous power. Vâyu would be connected in the *Upanishads* with breath of life *(prâna)*. By the time of the *Purânas*, however, Vâyu was reduced to one of the eight Dikpâlakas (guardians of the directions) of the universe.

See also Vritra

VEDAS

The Scripture

Veda means "knowledge," but specifically refers to the eternal wisdom of the four collections of hymns, sacrificial rituals, and other sacred texts that are called the *Vedas.* Along with the four

Vâyu, the wind, shown riding his vâhana, the antelope (TRIP)

collections (the *Samhitas*, the *Brahmanas*, the *Âranyakas*, and the *Upanishads*), two more bodies of literature, the *Sutras* and the *Vedângas*, are sometimes included in the *Vedas.* The *Vedas* are said not to be composed by human hand *(apaurusheya).* Tradition teaches that they have always existed, and myth accounts for the preservation and reappearance of the Vedas after each dissolution of the universe. The seven seers *(sapta-rishis)* in most accounts, the Manu of the age (who might also be a *mahârishi*), or an *avatâra* (incarnation) like the boar (Vâmana) incarnation of Vishnu makes sure that the inerrant *Vedas* come into an age. But the myths show an anxiety about how they are preserved as an evil time sets in, or when demons have stolen the *Vedas* and an *avatâra* is required to restore them.

Even so, many believe that the *Vedas* contain all knowledge *(veda)* past and future. All science has been discovered in some previous age, and there is evidence of the gods or demons using airplanes to cross the sky, as does Râvana when he captures Sîtâ, and using missiles and nuclear weapons against each other, as does Indra when he launches his *vajra* (divine weapon, formerly a lightening bolt) or Râma his "arrows."

The Aryans resisted all forms of writing for several millennia even after they had come in contact with it, depending instead on their educational system and memory techniques *(pathas, vikritis)*. An oral scriptural tradition and its reverent transmission was believed to be more reliable than writing, because writing could be altered, while a collective memory could not. The *Vedas* were therefore known as *śruti*, "that which is heard." There were several schools *(śakhas)* and subschools *(caranas)* that kept alive variations within the tradition.

Scholars have argued that internal examination of the Vedic corpus indicates a time when the Aryans knew of but had not yet migrated to what is now northeastern Pakistan and northwestern India. They called this region Saptasindhu (the seven rivers' land). They shared an ancestry with their pre-Avestan cousins who later inhabited what is now Iran. The early part of the Vedic or Samhita period (c. 1500–900 B.C.E.) appears to have been a time when the warriors *(kśatriyas)* were highest in esteem and power and the priests *(brâhmins)* were charismatic prayers and ritualists. The later Vedic period was a time of religious transformation, with several triads of gods rising to and then losing supremacy (the last triad of the period being Agni, Indra, and Sûrya), Varuna's rapid decline, the loss of the entheogen ("god-experience"–inducing plant) *soma* from actual ritual use sometime before the end of the *Brâhmana* and *Aranyâka* period (c. 900–c. 600 B.C.E.), and the rise of the godling *(âditya)* Vishnu and a non-Aryan god of the cremation ground, Śiva, to supremacy over the Vedic pantheon. (There are major entries on each of the aspects of Vedic religion.)

Within the *Samhitas* (collections) is a fourth section known as the *Atharvaveda* that is quite unlike the rest in tone and content. The other three sections were often referred to as the three *(triyi) Vedas*, excluding or assigning lesser authority to the *Atharvaveda*. It was filled with magic, both positive and negative, ranging from *mantras* and potions for fertility to death prayers. In fact the notion of knowing *brahman*, in the sense of power, was what the *Atharva* priests claimed, as over against the rituals and sacrifices of Vedic *brâhmins*. They knew the power *(brahman)* and the magic *(mâyâ)* that could control both gods and sacrifice. Although their practice does not come unaltered into later periods, their influence on Hindu mythology and its practices to acquire magic powers *(siddhis)* has not been fully accounted for. Their magical practices were called the *pañca* (five) *kalpas* (sacred precepts).

The period when the *Brâhmana* and *Âranyaka* literature were created closed with a priesthood that was asserting its primacy over the other castes *(varnas)*, confident that its "science" of sacrificial rituals and Vedic chanting *(mantrayâna)* could control the universe and optimistic that it knew how to pre-pare Aryans for a life beyond the grave.

The Upanishadic literature was not included as part of the Vedic corpus for centuries after its composition. Its outlook challenged the hereditary nature of the Brahmanical priesthood, its sacrificial religion, its knowledge of that One by which everything was known *(Brahman),* and its notion of the afterlife. Once this challenge was integrated into a new worldview, the fourfold *Vedas* would become authorative, orthodox, and orthopraxic for what would eventually be-come Hinduism. But many would maintain that Vedic authority was a symbol and Hindu mythology of the *Purânas* was the reality.

> *See also* Agni; Indra; Magic, Blessings, Cursings; Mâyâ; Rigveda; Siddhis; Sûrya; Tapas; Upanishad
>
> *For further reading:*
>
> R. N. Dandekar, "Vedas," *Encyclopedia of Religion,* vol.15; Wendy Doniger O'Fla-herty, *Rigveda* (New York: Penguin, 1981); Jan Gonda, *Vedic Literature* (Wies-baden: Harrassowitz, 1975).

VEDIC GODS

See Chart on Vedic Gods in Appendix

VISHNU

One of the three major gods of modern Hinduism

Vishnu rose from a minor role as a solar deity in the *Rigveda* to one of the Hindu Triad with Brahmâ and Śiva to the Absolute of the universe in Vaishnavism. Vishnu's willingness to incarnate in time of need to restore righteousness *(dharma)* was the inspiring theme that made him both absolute and a compas-sionate giver of grace *(prasâda).*

Vishnu in the *Rigveda* was but a minor godling, whose solar activity of mov-ing through the three regions of the universe may well have been another's func-tion. He was Indra's friend and ally. When Indra slew the boar who stole the property of the *asuras* (demons), Vishnu carried away the dead beast, leaving the stolen property for the gods. Mentioned several times in the hymns of the *Rigveda,* Vishnu's role expanded rapidly in each succeeding age. In the *Brah-manas* Vishnu shared in the operation of the sacrificial ritual and appropriated a role in the triad of Agni-Indra-Sûrya, joined by Brahmâ and Śiva. By the Purânic period, especially the *Bhâgavata Purâna,* Vishnu created the creator Brahmâ and either used Śiva or sent his own *avatâras* (incarnations) to function both as sav-iors and destroyers. (There are additional entries on some of the ten *avatâras—* Matsya, Kûrma, Varâha, Narasimha, Vâmana, Paraśu-Râma, Râma, Krishna,

Vishnu, the preserver, who incarnates in time of need to bring righteousness back to earth (TRIP)

Buddha, and Kalkin—and some of the manifestations.) Perhaps the most unusual myth about Vishnu was his manifestation as Môhinî at the Churning of the Ocean where Vishnu appears as a beautiful goddess to deceive the *asuras* (demons) and allow the *devas* (gods) to acquire *soma* (the drink of immortality).

During the period before each re-creation of the universe Vishnu would rest upon his serpent bed formed by Ananta (also known as Śesha) on the Milky Ocean. The abode of Vishnu was called Vaikuntha. Vishnu was always blessed with wonderful opponents—Bali, Hiranyâksha, Hiranyakaśipu, Râvana, and many others. Each necessitated a manifestation of power or grace, and that was freely given.

Just as in the literature, among the pilgrimage sites *(tîrthas)* Vishnu's sacred geography appropriated almost all of the sites of Indra and Brahmâ, until no other god, not even Śiva, had more sites of worship.

Iconographically, Vishnu usually has four arms (although there could be many more), a dark blue complexion, and royal headgear. In his hands are the conch, discus, mace, and lotus. Upon his chest is the miraculous jewel called the Kaustubha (treasure of the ocean) and a curl of hair known as Śrî-vatsa (beloved of Śrî, or fortune). His vehicle is Garuda, the sun eagle, taken from Sûrya. His wife (or wives) are Śrî (fortune) and Lakshmî (thousands, or good fortune). Many see her as one, Śrî-Lakshmî, even when two images represent her presence. There were other wives during his various incarnations, such as Bhîmî (earth) and Rukminî, principal wife of Krishna.

Vishnu's epithets demonstrate that his followers understand his many revelations as transcendent, as an incarnation *(avatâra)*, as an emanation *(vyuha)* like Vasudeva or Aniruddha, as divine immanence and inner ruler, and as an idol for worship *(murti)*.

> *See also* Avatâra (and also Kalki, Matsya, Narasimha, Paraśu-Râma, Râma, Vâmana, Varâha); Bhîma; Krishna; Kûrma; Lakshmî; Môhinî; Shrî; Tîrthas; Vaikuntha
>
> *For further reading:*
>
> Jan Gonda, "Visnu," *Encyclopedia of Religion,* vol.15; Milton Singer, ed., *Krishna: Myths, Rites, and Attitudes* (Honolulu: University of Hawaii Press, 1966); Heinrich Zimmer, edited by Joseph Campbell, *Myths and Symbols in Indian Art and Civilization* (1946; reprint, Princeton: Princeton University Press, 1972); Jan Gonda, *Visnuism and Sivaism: A Comparison* (London: Athlone, 1970).

VIŚVAKARMAN, VIŚVAKARMA

The celestial architect

Viśvakarman (omnificent) may originally have been an epithet for any powerful god, but it was used in the *Rigveda* most often for Indra and Sûrya. There are two

Rigvedic hymns to *Viśvakarman* praising him as the all-seeing god, the one who names the gods, and that one beyond the comprehension of mortals. He was said to be the sacrifice and the one to whom the sacrifice is given. The *Nirukta* added that Viśvakarma, son of Bhuvana, held a *sarva-medha* (total sacrifice) offering something of everything and ending with himself.

In the *Epics* and *Purânas* this Viśvakarman was reduced in status and personified as one with creative power, the heavenly architect. He could even be called a Prajâpati, when the term came to refer to any creative being. Viśvakarman was described as having the powers and the very office of Tvashthri, a reference that is too vague to suggest anything more than the fearsome Tvashthri has been reduced to an office. Viśvakarman became the great builder of celestial palaces and kingdoms, as well as constructing the magical weapons of the gods. The *Râmâyana* has him building Lanka for the demon Râvana and then generating the ape Nala who builds the bridge to Lanka for Hanuman's invasion of Lanka.

Some Purânic accounts make Viśvakarman the son of the eighth Vasu (attendants of Indra), Prabhâsa. Others say that Viśvakarman married Yogasiddhâ, a wonderfully beautiful and virtuous woman, with whom he had a daughter, Samjñâ. When Samjñâ found her husband, Sûrya, too bright and hot, Viśvakarman put the sun on a lathe and trimmed away an eighth. From what fell from his lathe Viśvakarman forged the discus of Vishnu and the trident of Śiva as well as weapons for the rest of the gods, including Kubera, god of wealth, and Kârttikeya, god of war.

In the *Vâmana Purâna* Viśvakarma became the mean father who cursed his beautiful daughter, Citrângadâ. He in turn was cursed by the sage Ritadhvaja to be reborn a monkey. (The treatment of Viśvakarman [Viśvakarma] demonstrates just how authoritative the *Vedas* are when Vedic gods are so easily reduced to mean fathers.)

See also Citrângadâ; Tapas; Tvashthri

VIŚVÂMITRA
A famous sage
Viśvâmitra was already important in the *Rigveda* as a sage and composer of many hymns in book *(mandala)* three. However, his lineage shifted with the sources so much that one later authority stated that he was the son of both King Kushika and King Gâdhi. Viśvâmitra (universal friend) was able to raise himself from *kṣatriya* caste to *brâhmin* by his austerities *(tapas)*. He was still, however, made to submit to his *brâhmin* rival Vasishtha in later mythology to show the submission of *kṣatriyas* to *brâhmins*. This rivalry became so exaggerated in the later

literature that Viśvâmitra and Vasishtha were depicted as hating each other so much as to murder each other's sons and, according to one low moment in these stories, eating each other's sons. Such a portrayal ignored their status as *mahā-rishis* (also *sapta-rishis*) in this current *manvantara,* the seventh cycle of creation, and therefore models of Vedic virtues. The later mythmakers simply were so prone to debase their subjects with sin and weakness that they lost sight of how these figures had been portrayed in earlier periods.

In an Epic account Viśvâmitra became the object of the *apsara* (celestial damsel) Menakâ's seduction. Viśvâmitra had begun to accomplish too much in his austerities and was a threat to Indra's rule of heaven. So Indra sent Menakâ, and she successfully diverted the sage from his *tapas.* They had a girl who was later named Śakuntalâ (one raised by the birds), after they abandoned her and Śakuntalâ was found and raised by the sage Kanva. The story of King Dushyanta's discovery of the young beauty Śakuntalâ and his impregnating her and abandoning her is found in her entry.

Viśvâmitra's rivalry with the chief priest of King Harishcandra of Ayodhyâ involved many episodes and prior causes. Vasishtha had counseled King Harishcandra to exile his son Satyavrata. However, the king repented this deed and gave over his throne to Vasishtha while he practiced austerities. The kingdom experienced a twelve-year drought during this time. Viśvâmitra had left his family to practice austerities, and they were starving. The young prince Satyavrata took pity on them and provided them with fresh meat from his hunt each day. One day there was no game so he killed Vasishtha's cow. To make matters worse, the cow was Kâmadhenu, the wish-granting cow given by the gods. When Vasishtha learned what had happened, he turned Satyavrata into the shape of an outcaste *(candâla)* and cursed him with the name Triśanku (three sins). When his father King Dushyanta died, Triśanku became king, but asked to go bodily to heaven. Vasishtha and Viśvâmitra fought over this, but Viśvâmitra was able to perform this miracle even against the opposition of the *devas* (gods).

Viśvâmitra also got the better of Vasishtha in their next contest, which involved King Harishcandra, son of Triśanku. Harishcandra had no children by his one hundred wives, so upon the advice of his chief priest Vasishtha and against Viśvâmitra's warning, he became involved with the sacrificial rituals to the god Varuna. However, Varuna's price for granting children was that the first one be sacrificed to him. After many years of postponing this human sacrifice, finally the day came. Śunahśepha, the young prince who was to be the victim, having just received the sacred thread, had been secretly trained with a magical *mantra* that would win over Varuna. This training had been given by Viśvâmitra. Śunahśepha chanted the *varunamantra* as he was tied to the slaughter-stone, and Varuna appeared, granting the boy his freedom and the king a cure from the disease that had come to him for not performing the sacrifice. Śunaḥśepha was given to Viśvâmitra, according to the logic that since his teaching had given Śunaḥśepha his life, Viśvâmitra was the prince's father.

Viśvâmitra was given many other roles. He had another relationship with an *apsara* named Rambhâ. He appeared as an advisor of King Râma and his brother Lakshmana. In the *Mârkandeya Purâna* Viśvâmitra's feud with Vasishtha reached the point that they each cursed the other to become birds. However, their fighting continued with such fury that Brahmâ changed them back into sages and forced them to reconcile their differences.

See also Ambarîsha; Dushyanta; Hariscandra; Kalmâshapâda; Kâmadhenu; Kanva; Sapta-rishis

VRINDÂVANA

Home of Krishna

Vrindâvana was both the mythical land of Krishna's youth and an actual geographic area between modern Delhi and Agra. Vrindâvana's meaning of "sacred basil grove" referred to the ancient forest that once graced that region. The modern town lies on the western bank of the Yamunâ River. (See main entry under Kâlindî.)

It was to Vrindâvana that the cowherds of Gokula retreated when King Kamsa's violence toward Krishna became too much for them to bear. It was in Vrindâvana the Krishna and his older brother Balarâma grew, played, teased, and generally lived an idyllic life—with only an occasional interruption from a demon or demoness bent on killing them.

This region (Vraja, or Braj) became self-aware in the sixteenth century when the Krishna cult of Bengal connected myth and devotion by pilgrimage to the very places mentioned in the stories and established actual sites for devotees to visit. Caitanya directed his disciples, the Gaudiya Vaishnavas, to purify long forgotten sites and renew worship there. The six great Gosvamis (cow monks—referring to the cowherd period of the Krishna myth) did just that and had *mahârâjas* of Râjesthan build splendid temples to Krishna.

Now this entire region is rich with pilgrimage sites, and during the months of the monsoon pilgrims walk and play where Krishna and Râdhâ did, hear the many dramas and performances, and worship in the many temples along the route.

See also Krishna

For further reading:

G. Archer, *The Loves of Krishna in Indian Painting and Poetry* (London: Allan and Unwin, 1957); David L. Haberman, "Vrndavana," *Encyclopedia of Religion,* vol.15; William Norvin Hein, *The Miracle Plays of Mathura* (New Haven: Yale University Press, 1972); John Stratton Hawley, *At Play with Krishna: Pilgrimage Dramas from Brindavan* (Princeton: Princeton University Press, 1981).

VRITRA

A mighty asura (demon)

In the *Rigveda* Vritra was a monster whose name meant the one who "held back," "restrained," or "enveloped." Killing Vritra was Indra's crowning moment. Vritra enveloped a celestial mountain and held back its waters, but Indra's action released the waters, bring the fertilizing rains and prosperity to the Aryans, even providing soma for gods and men. He did this with his thunderbolt, implying that he was a nature god of rain and storm, but also a war god who brought victory and bounty. He accomplished his victory over Vritra by both his strength as a warrior and his magic as a priest. Since Vritra also used magic in the single combat against Indra, he was later said to be a *brâhmin*—thus in the later versions making Indra a *brâhmin*-killer. Also later, it was a *brâhmin* who provided his own thigh bone to make the divine weapon, Indra's thunderbolt *(vajra)*—the sage Dadhîci. Alternately, Indra was reduced in the Purânic literature to so little of his former power that he had to be joined by other gods to conquer Vritra, or even to receive his ability to conquer Vritra from Śiva or Vishnu.

There was a rebirth story in the later *Purânas* that explained Vritra's origin. He came from a curse by Pârvatî. Citraketu had received a boon that allowed him to fly with his wife. He both misused it and laughed at Śiva's wife, Pârvatî. She and Śiva were playing in Kailâsa and Citraketu thought their love play was humorous. However, Pârvatî did not think much of being spied upon and cursed Citraketu to be reborn as Vritra-asura.

The killing of Vritra and his cohorts is one of the many places where Vedic myths can be compared with Indo-European mythology. This theme—the killing of the dragon—has many versions. It involves a particularly ancient myth of creation by dismemberment, fertility motifs that require sacrifice, and the sin or pollution of these acts, which can only be purified by the rituals known by the wise of the community.

See also Citraketu; Dadhîci; Indra; Soma
For further reading:

Georges Dumézil, *The Destiny of the Warrior,* trans. by Alf Hiltebeitel (Chicago: University of Chicago Press, 1970); Wendy Doniger O'Flaherty, *Hindu Myths* (1972; reprint New York: Penguin Books, 1982) and *The Origins of Evil in Hindu Mythology* (Berkeley: University of California Press, 1976); Sukumari Bhattacharji, *The Indian Theogony* (Cambridge: Cambridge University Press,

1970); Alain Daniélou, *The Myths and Gods of India* (Rochester, VT: Inner Traditions International, 1991), originally published as *Hindu Polytheism* (New York: Bollingen, 1964); Joseph Campbell, *The Hero with a Thousand Faces* (New York: Bollingen Foundation, 1949).

VYÂSA

The most famous sage in Hindu mythology

Vyâsa is more properly referred to as Veda Vyâsa since the name was a common one, meaning "arranger," or editor. Veda Vyâsa was said to have edited the four *Vedas* and authored the *Purânas* and the *Mahâbhârata.* Accomplishing all that would require a human who lived several thousand years, so scholars do place the story of his achievements as those of one man in the area of mythology.

Vyâsa was born to the *brâhmin* ascetic Parâsara and Matsyagandhî, the fisher-woman. (See main entry under Satyavâtî.) Parâsara married Matsyagandhî *gandharva* style in a fog while crossing the Vamunâ River and left her immediately. Vyâsa was born on an island *(dvîpa)* and dark of complexion *(krishna),* so that he was also known by Krishna Dvaipâyana. Although he was an ascetic like his father, he was asked to father sons by his dead stepmother's wives, resulting in the famous kings Dhritarâshthra and Pandu.

Vyâsa had another son who never entered a womb. Nârada had found him somewhat depressed and thought that the cause was Vyâsa's desire for a son. So Vyâsa began a severe penance near Mount Mahâmeru. But Indra was threatened and sent Ghritâcî, the *apsara* (celestial damsel), to stop him. She changed into a beautiful parrot who had five colors. Vyâsa became infatuated with the parrot *(śuka)* and discharged his seed on some of the firewood. As the wood was placed in the fire, a divine son was created. Vyâsa named him Śuka after the parrot. Śuka grew into a householder sage and helped Vyâsa put together a great educational institution at his *aśrama* (hermitage). However, when Śuka left and attained divinity, Vyâsa became quite unstable, wandering about calling out his son's name ("parrot, parrot"). Śuka appeared as a vision and consoled his father. Later the sage lost all his disciples. In his next birth Vyâsa was reborn as Apântaratamas, continuing his rebirths and proving that even a sage like Veda Vyâsa needed more than his great works to win release *(moksha).*

See also Dhritarâshthra; Ghritâcî; Nârada; Pandu; Parâsara; Satyavâtî

YÂJÑA

Ritual of sacrifice

Yâjña or sacrifice was practiced from the earliest period of the *Vedas.* At first it referred to the external fire sacrifices and oblations that constituted the principal way in which Aryans related to their gods. Offerings were made to the fire *(agni)* of clarified butter *(ghî* or *ghee)*, wood, spices, grains, *soma* (the ambrosia of immortality), and even animal sacrifices. Later sacrifices became vegetarian with the exception of Tântrics and Śaktas.

Yâjña as internal sacrifice was articulated as early as the *Upanishads* by equating the external fire with the internal heat *(tapas)* of mediation and, by further extension, the austerities *(tapas, sadhanâs)* in order to acquire boons and powers *(siddhis)*. *Yâjña* is always associated with fire, both the physical fire that carries the offerings to heaven for the enjoyment of the gods or Agni, god of fire, as the divine messenger who transports prayers and offerings to their divine objects.

See also Aurva; Bhrigu; Garuda; Hamsa; Hayagrîva; Idâ; Ilâ; Janamejaya

YAMA

A god

Yama came to be the god of death in later mythology, but he had wide range of roles in the earlier mythology. In the *Rigveda* Yama was one of the first pair. As such he was referred to as the first mortal (later being called the first human). His twin sister Yamî wanted him as her partner, but he refused. Later mythology charged him with incest. In the earliest mythology he was the son of Vivasvat, an early solar deity. Later he was assimilated into Dharma, god of social order, and made one of the guardians of the four corners of the earth (Lokapâlas). Yama was personi- fied in the *Katha Upanishad*, and his talk with the youth

Yama, lord of death, riding his vâhana, the water buffalo (TRIP)

Naciketas about the nature of death and its mystery portrayed him as a great philosopher-teacher.

During his evolution in later mythology Yama became more sinister, the feared god of death. His two dogs, Syama and Sabala, came for souls, no longer leading them to *Devayâna* (way of the gods) or *Pitryâna* (way of the departed ancestor spirits), but to a stopover in *Pâtâla* (hell). Pâtâla too had changed from a comfortable abode of the dead to a realm of punishment populated with all sorts of dreadful creatures: *rakshâsas* (blood-thirsty demons), *yakshas* (tree spirits), *ganas* (dwarves), and *angirasas* (a class of ghosts), as well as souls of the dead. Yama became associated with time as a killer (Kâla) and death (Mriti), and thereby with the lord of the cremation ground, Śiva.

See also Dharma; Kâla; Śiva; Upanishad

YAMUNÂ

A river

See main entry under Kâlindî. This is an alternative name for the river Kâlindî of Purânic fame. The river goddess of Kâlindî was also the wife of Śrî Krishna.

YOGA, YOGAS

A system of thought and practice

The word *yoga* is frequently used in Indian philosophy. It means "union" and connotes uniting the individual self with the higher Self. The *Bhagavad Gîtâ* defined yoga as "skillfulness in action" and "steadiness of mind." Yoga as a system of Indian thought was founded by Patanjali, probably of the second century B.C.E.

Around the time of the *Bhagavad Gîtâ* Indian philosophers and theologians began to classify religious or spiritual experience according to three or four types, which they called ways *(margas)* or disciplines *(yogas)*. Devotion *(bhakti)* appeared in both classifications of religious types. Devotion was the way (marga) or practice (yoga) known as *bhakti marga* or *bhakti yoga*. Two other types appeared in both lists: *karma yoga* (the way of works, or ritualism) and *jñâna yoga* (the way of knowledge). The fourth type, *râja yoga* (the royal way), influenced the way *jñâna yoga* was interpreted. In a list of three religious types, *jñâna yoga* and *râja yoga* referred to mysticism—knowledge of the Absolute. Thus, both were essentially mystical paths, leading to knowledge of the Absolute. The distinctive *yoga* of cognitive, spiritual study *(jñâna)* that produced far more than the six traditional philosophies *(darsanas)* was lost.

When four religious types are recognized, *râja yoga* is mysticism and *jñâna yoga* is a rational, philosophical path of knowledge, meaning, and purpose.

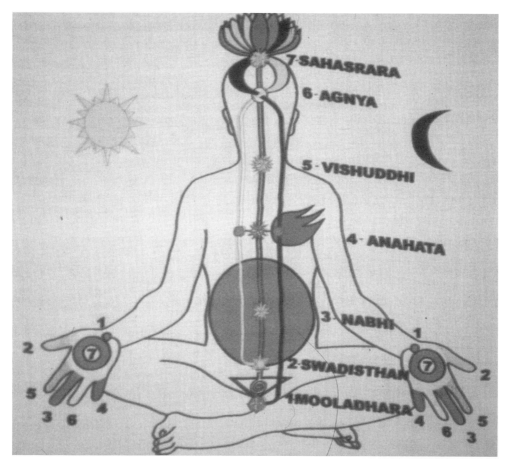

Yoga is one of the surest practices to tapas, the austerities that gain siddhis, the powers so sought in Hindu myths. (TRIP)

Among these paths or spiritual disciplines, *bhakti* is the most accepting and appreciative of mythology and its uses, while the *jñâna yoga* of Hindu rationalism was unsympathetic and even hostile toward mythology. Rational Hinduism's modern manifestation, the Brahmo Samaj, is consistent with those philosophers of the past who rejected idols and myths. Mystical practice (*râja* and/or *jñâna yoga*) entails renunciation of everything, including worship, images, and myths.

See also Bhagavad Gîtâ; Bhakti
For further reading:

David N. Lorenzen, "Hathayoga," *Encyclopedia of Religion,* vol. 6; Shashibhusan Dasgupta, *Obscure Religious Cults,* 3d ed. (Calcutta: Firma K. L. Mukhopadhyay, 1969); Mircea Eliade, *Yoga: Immortality and Freedom,* 2d ed. (Princeton: Princeton University Press, 1969); John Woodroffe (Arthur Avalon), *The Serpent Power,* 7th ed. (1919, reprint New York: Dover, 1964).

YUVANÂŚVA

A king who got pregnant

Yuvanâśva was a king who had a hundred wives but no children. In the *Vishnu* and *Bhâgavata Purânas* Yuvanâśva went into the forest to seek help from ascetics. Yuvanâśva found a group of *brâhmins* who promised him sons if he did a special ritual sacrifice, the *Indradaivata yâga.* It involved collecting energy from their *mantras* in a jug of water as the rituals were performed each day. One day Yuvanâśva was thirsty and made the mistake of drinking from the jug of water that was storing the *mantras* to bring him children. Yuvanâśva became pregnant and after ten lunar months gave birth to a child. Mândhâta (or Mâdhâtṛi) was born from the pregnancy of his father, Yuvanâśva. But the ministers of his kingdom advised that he abandon the child in the forest. Although that was done, Mândhâta was nourished by sucking milk from his own toe—an idea credited to Indra, whose *mantra* had produced the child. When Mândhâta reached manhood, he became a great and powerful king. There were many allusions in other stories to his virtue and wisdom.

APPENDIX: CHART ON THE VEDIC GODS

"Vedic" and "Gods" are used in a broad sense, the way they are used in most of Hindu mythology.

Pre-Aryan [Indus Valley] Period
"Proto-Śiva"
Theriomorphic (animal) symbols

Vedic or Samhita Period
A dyad: Dyuas (sky), Prithvî (earth)
The "first" Triad: Sûrya, Indra, Agni
A myriad of "nature" gods and goddesses
    Some of the major *devas*: Aśvins, Mitra, Soma, Vâyu
    Some of the goddesses: Ushas, Vâc
    Some of the minor gods: Vishnu, Rudra, Maruts
    Some of the demons: Varuna (a good *asura*), Vritra

Brâhmana and Âranyaka Period
Subordination and ordering of Vedic gods to sacrificial and sacramental
    system of Brâhmins.
Thirty-three *devas,* enumerated as eight *vasus,* eleven *rudras,* and twelve
    âdityas—with two gods unnamed.
An increasing number of *asuras* (demons)

Upanishadic Period
Monotheistic beings or principles *(Prajâpati)*
Panentheistic unities *(Prâna, Brahman)*
Dualities *(Purusha-Prakritî)*

Theistic or Sectarian Gods (from the Epic, Puranic, and Tantric Periods)
The Competing Supreme Gods:
    Vishnu and the ten *avatâras*
        Wive (s): Parvâtî, Lakshmî, Śrî
        ten (or more) *avatâras*
    Śiva and his manifestations
        Wive(s): Satî, Umâ, Lalitâ, Kâmeśvarî
    Devî and her manifestations
        Durgâ, Kâlî, Umâ, Śakti, and potentially any feminine aspect of the
            divine

The "second" Triad: Brahmâ, Vishnu, Śiva
    The twenty-one Prajâpatis who created the rest of the world were
        Brahmâ, Rudra, Manu, Daksha, Bhrigu, Dharma, Tapa, Yama, Marichi,
        Añgiras, Atri, Pulastya, Pulaha, Kratu, Vasishta, Parameshti, Sûrya,
        Chandra, Kardama, Krodha, and Vikrita.
    The seven sages: The *sapta-rishis* were Marichi, Añgiras, Atri, Pulastya,
        Vasishtha, Pulaha, and Kratu.
A myriad of minor gods:
    Ganapati (Ganeśa), Subrahmanya, Kâma
    All the early major Vedic gods: Sûrya, Indra, Agni, Varuna
A myriad of demigods and demons:
    Apsaras, gandharvas, pitris, daityas, dânavas, nagas, râkshasas, piśâcas,
        pretas

4

SELECTED PRINT AND
NONPRINT RESOURCES

Because Hindu mythology is living, active, and still developing, categories that work well for dead mythologies falter. Fortunately, Hindus have been tolerant and forgiving about how these categories often distort our understanding. Books suggested could easily fit in more than one category (under both myth and religion, for example).

When one began a study in a new area of interest such as Hindu mythology, learning how to gain access to the various kinds of resources and evaluating their worth used to be a serious hurdle. Now, on the other hand, finding current and available resources has never been easier. Evaluating their worth is still difficult, because it is relative to one's interest. American Hindu parents (members of what is called the Hindu Diaspora) might have several extra criteria in mind depending on their personal religious perspective, their desire to find books representing an insider rather than an outsider point of view, and so on. A college professor on comparative world literature would have another set of criteria in mind for choosing a text or set of readings on Hindu mythology. Thus, the first task is to determine one's needs and interests.

So much has changed with electronic access to bibliographic lists that a review of some of the basics seems to be in order.

Fallacy #1. Only books are valuable reference and research tools.

It is true that reference and research tools are more likely to be refereed by scholars and edited for publishers and are more reliable than nonprint materials. However, most North American libraries are organized with both print and nonprint materials. Knowing how to use both types of materials and how they work together is important. In the section of this chapter on nonprint resources, specific materials are referenced, and at the same time solid research strategies are suggested to help one find what is available from the Internet—either by using one's computer or that of a library. By following these suggestions you will be able to locate digital resources that complement your print materials and are appropriate to your needs.

Fallacy #2. A good bibliography will meet the needs of teachers, parents, and children.

Needs and interests vary widely. My undergraduate students need one bibliography, my graduate students another. However, my three granddaughters would not appreciate one book on either list. For those who want a book on Hindu mythology for their third grader for a school assignment, the choices will be much different than for parents looking for a book to read to or along with the child. Research tools are more useful here than a list, as new books are published each month. Currently, a set of resources for evaluating children's books is *The Horn Book Guide* and *Horn Book Magazine* (www.hbook.com). These provide reviews of children's and young adult books. The guide reviews, rates, and indexes practically every hardcover trade children's book and is helpful for parents and teachers. Public library databases and commercial search engines (such as http://www.amazon.com and http://www.google.com) also work well for parents and teachers searching for what is available.

For the sake of providing examples, I will list a few children's books on Hindu mythology that have received good reviews and that were available commercially at the moment of this writing: *The Broken Tusk: Stories of the Hindu God Ganesha* (recommended for ages 10–12) by Uma Krishnaswami (North Haven, CT: Linet Books, 1996); *The Butter Thief* (for ages 4–8) by Chris Murray (Kim Murray, illustrator), (Los Angeles, CA: Bhaktivedanta Book Trust, 1996); and *Demons, Gods and Holy Men from Indian Myths and Legends* by Shahrukh Husain (Durga Prasad Das, illustrator), (New York: Peter Bedrick Books, 1979).

Another resource on the availability of children's books on Hindu mythology is *Hinduism Today*, a monthly magazine, which also has an online presence (www.HinduismToday.kauai.hi.us). However, the online version does not have the advertisements for children's books that are carried in the published addition. Occasional reviews of books are published online.

With some reservations about passing along this information, I will mention Hindu comic books. Absurd as such a choice might seem, one would be choosing the way many children in India have learned about Hindu myths and legends. One series, by Amar Chitra Katha (www.amarchitrakatha.com), has over 180 titles. They are currently distributed by Navrang, Inc. (www.navrang.com), but distributors change. Another comic book publisher is Chaturang Katha (which does not have a web presence at this writing). Both Amar Chitra Katha and Chaturang Katha were distributed by India Book House and Penguin Books India (www.penguinbooksindia.com). Again, that has changed. If one is looking for children's books on South Asia on the Web, Asia Book House (www.asia-bookhouse.com) and Pilgrims Books of Kathmandu (www.pilgrimsbooks.com) are good sources.

Fallacy #3. Published addresses on the World Wide Web should work [forever].

The Internet changes constantly (an old Buddhist insight about life), so one must adapt every search idea or learn to find what has evolved or survived. The public library and commercial search engines such as the one offered by Amazon.com (http://www.amazon.com) will help most popular readers who are new to Hindu mythology. Web sites in the next section should help also (as long as they survive). Scholarly Web sites tend to last slightly longer than individual and commercial sites (but scholars die, move on to a new university, and some even "password" or hide their sites when they become too popular).

For some recommendations on sites that are likely to survive for some time see the section on the Wide World Web below.

Fallacy #4. Books by believers should only be read by believers.

The Himalayan Academy, the Bhaktivedanta Society, and many other devout Hindu organizations are publishing many good books. The perspective of such books may be much narrower than a scholarly one, but often the readability is very high. They are especially good for those who are involved in interfaith dialogue. These books can be found with public library and Web search engines (such as www.google.com). A few examples from the time of this writing are *Loving Ganesa* by Satguru Sivaya Subramuniyaswami Subramuniya (Kapaa, HI: Himalayan Academy Publications, 2000); *Dancing With Siva: Hinduism's Contemporary Catechism* by the same author (Kapaa, HI: Himalayan Academy Publications, 1997); and the many writings of A. C. Bhaktivedanta Swami Prabhupâda (popularly known as the founder of the Hare Krishnas) on Bhakti Yoga and Hindu scriptures such as the *Bhâgavata Purâna* and the *Bhâgavad Gîtâ.*

Fallacy #5. Only scholars can use Sanskrit dictionaries.

An amazing resource, which should be used by every student of Hindu mythology and religion, is a set of online Sanskrit dictionaries that makes it possible for a serious student to look up any term and study its varying meanings as it is located in different texts and contexts. At first, the beginner will have to work with English searches. However, with a little practice many nonspecialists can learn to enter Sanskrit transliterations with Roman letters. Go to <http://www.uni-koeln.de/phil-fak/indologie/tamil/mwd_search.html> and work with the Cologne Digital Sanskrit Lexicon. (For further discussion see entry discussing the dictionary below.)

The bibliography that follows will be helpful for readers who are seeking scholarly materials that are sufficiently reliable to serve as a foundation for their study. If one becomes a serious student of Hindu mythology, then Sanskrit is a must. And if one continues, then regional Indian languages must be added as well, for local Hindu mythologies. Only English language materials lie within the scope of this working bibliography.

PRINT RESOURCES

Encyclopedias and Dictionaries

Dowson, John. *A Classical Dictionary of Hindu Mythology and Religion, Geography, History, and Literature.* 11th edition. London: Routledge & K. Paul, 1968.

This dictionary is widely available and is fairly reliable, despite its age.

Eliade, Mircea, ed. *The Encyclopedia of Religion.* London: Macmillan, 1981. 15 volumes.

A CD-ROM version was completed in 1993. This encyclopedia is the beginning point for most studies, providing a way to learn what was known and largely accepted for most of the twentieth century. It contains over 150 chapter-size articles on topics directly pertaining to Hindu mythology, plus many more on more general topics about Hindu scripture, belief, community, and practice.

Hastings, James, et al., eds. *Encyclopedia of Religion and Ethics.* New York: Charles Scribner's Sons, 1908–1929. 13 volumes.

Dated and largely replaced by Eliade's *Encyclopedia of Religion.* Currently, a few articles are available from an ongoing project to digitize the work at <http://www.dabar.org/Religion/Hastings/TOC.htm> by Daniel J. Dyke.

Hopkins, E. Washburn. *Epic Mythology.* Delhi: Motilal Banarsidass, 1974, 1986. First published in Strassburg in 1915 as part of the *Encyclopedia of Indo-Aryan Research.*

Although quite old and in places hard to read, it has valuable material on the *Mahâbhârata* and *Râmâyana* that can be extracted.

Knappert, Jan. *Indian Mythology: An Encyclopedia of Myth and Legend.* London: Diamond Books, 1995.

This is a popular dictionary of concise entries on Indian myths by a professional writer who has also written on Islamic and Indonesian myths.

Klostermaier, Klaus K. *A Concise Encyclopedia of Hinduism.* Oxford: Oneworld, 1998.

Excellent resource by top scholar featuring concise entries.

Mani, Valtam. *Purânic Encyclopaedia: A Comprehensive Dictionary with special reference to the Epic and Puranic Literature.* Delhi: Motilal Bararsidass, 1975.

This is a remarkably thorough work on the Purânas and is invaluable for more comprehensive studies of Hindu mythology. For advanced students and scholars.

Shukla, H. L. *Semiotica Indica: Encyclopaedic Dictionary of Body-Language in Indian Art and Culture.* 2 vols. New Delhi: Aryan Books International, 1994.

There is no other resource quite like it for precise, contextualized language and its relation to general culture, art, dance, and religion. For advanced students and scholars.

Smith, H. Daniel, and M. Narasimhachary. *Handbook of Hindu Gods, Goddesses and Saints Popular in Contemporary South India.* 2d edition. Delhi: Sundeep Prakashan, 1997.

This volume is a very important regional study. It is especially useful in locating Tamil gods and correlating them with their Sanskrit equivalents. However, this volume is much more. It demonstrates that the southern theistic traditions are ancient and must be studied for themselves alongside projects that are constructing a pan-Indian mythology from northern (Sanskrit) sources.

Stutley, Margaret, and James Stutley. *Harper's Dictionary of Hinduism: Its Mythology, Folklore, Philosophy, Literature and History.* New York: Harper and Row. 1977.

A carefully crafted resource useful in any research library.

Walker, Benjamin. *The Hindu World.* 2 vols. Delhi: Munshiram Manoharlal, 1983. First published by George Allen and Unwin, 1956.

This volume will be on the shelf in almost every college library. It is comprehensive in scope and reflects extensive scholarship. However, there are normative judgments that imply a moralizing that may limit its future value.

Hindu Mythology (and Hindu Theology)

Bhardwaj, Surinder Mohan. *Hindu Places of Pilgrimage in India: A Study in Cultural Geography.* Berkeley: University of California Press, 1973 (paperback reprint 1983).

This is an important study of Hindu sacred space as it relates to myth and religion. The multidisciplinary approach is able to demonstrate how places increased and declined in importance as pilgrimage sites, documenting the findings with religious texts, pilgrim travel guides, gazetteers, and pilgrim registers.

Bhattacharji, Sukumari. *The Indian Theogony; A Comparative Study of Indian*

Mythology from The Vedas to The Puranas. Cambridge: Cambridge University Press, 1970.

A comprehensive analysis of the origin of the gods and goddesses through the major periods of Indian religious history.

Buck, William. *Ramayana.* Berkeley: University of California Press, 1976.

This book is a retelling of the story line of the poet Vâlmîki's *Râmâyana* that has been well received by both Sanskritists and literary critics. It has the depth of a translation but freely collects, compresses, and interprets episodes for another culture and time. Recommended as an introduction for almost any level of audience.

Calasso, Roberto. *Ka: Stories of the Mind and Gods of India.* New York: Albert A. Knopf, 1998.

This is a reader's book—well written, even poetic. It is complex, scholarly, and innovative. It has been called the first of a new type of approach to Hindu mythology. Recommended for an intermediate level of study.

Campbell, Joseph. *The Masks of God: Oriental Mythology.* New York: Viking, 1962.

Dated but enduring, *Masks* combines storytelling and Freudian analysis. Part two treats Indian mythology and will be an introduction for many brought back to Campbell by his public television programs.

Chaturvedi, B. K. *Gods and Goddesses of India.* Vol. 1, *Ganesh;* vol. 2, *Brahma;* vol. 3, *Vishnu;* vol. 4, *Shiv;* vol. 5, *Saraswati;* vol. 6, *Lakshmi;* vol. 7, *Durga;* vol. 8, *Hanuman.* Delhi: Books for All. 1996.

What is lacking in sophistication and scholarly distance is overcome by comprehensive inclusion of devotional materials.

Coomaraswamy, Ananda K., and Sister Nivedita. *Myths of the Hindus and Buddhists.* New York: Dover, 1967. First published 1913.

So old in approach and literary style, yet it remains a classic of rare beauty for its joy in telling the stories.

Crooke, William. *The Popular Religion and Folk-Lore Of Northern India.* New Delhi: Munshiram Manoharlal, 1896.

Use with care, as material needs to be cross-checked for reliability.

Daniélou, Alain. *The Myth and Gods of India: The Classic Work on Hindu Polytheism from the Princeton Bollingen series.* Rochester, VT: Inner Traditions

International, 1985, 1991. Originally published as *Hindu Polytheism.* New York: Bollingen, 1964.

An important work from one of the leading French Indologists, this volume relates deities to social concepts. At once reductive and profound, it is a study for those well grounded in Indian culture and religion.

Dehejia, Vidya, ed. *The Legend of Rama: Artistic Visions.* Bombay: Marg, 1994.

This beautiful publication combines brilliant colored reproductions representing the range of art dedicated to illustrating the *Râmâyana* with excellent articles from a variety of scholarly disciplines.

Gray, Louis Herbert. *The Mythology of All Races.* 1916; reprint New York: Cooper Square Publishers, 1964.

This volume is found in many public libraries. It is dated and should only be used with care.

Gupta, Shakti M. *From Daityas to Devatas in Hindu Mythology.* Bombay: Somaiya, 1973.

This reference work describes the different classes of gods and goddesses along with their stories.

Hospital, Clifford. *The Righteous Demon: A Study of Bali.* Vancouver: University of British Columbia Press, 1984.

This is a scholarly study of the *asura* (demon) Bali that provides an excellent entrée into more recent studies of Hindu mythology.

Ions, Veronica. *Indian Mythology.* London: Hamlyn, 1967.

This is a quite popular treatment of Indian mythology that is likely to be found in many public libraries. It is profusely illustrated with brief explanations.

Kinsley, David R. *The Sword and the Flute: Kali and Krsna, Dark Visions of the Terrible and the Sublime in Hindu Mythology.* Berkeley: University of California Press, 1975.

This small volume is quite accessible for students, while maintaining a high level of scholarship. It explores the visions of Kâlî and Krishna and presents them in quite personal terms. An excellent book for classroom use.

Kirk, James A. *Stories of the Hindus: An Introduction through Texts and Interpretation.* New York: Macmillan, 1972.

Twenty-eight stories are told, with enough commentary so that the volume works well as an introduction to Hindu mythology or religion.

Kripal, Jeffrey J. *Kâlî's Child: The Mystical and the Erotic in the Life and Teachings of Ramakrishna.* Chicago: University of Chicago Press, 1995.

An advanced study and quite extraordinary book about the Hindu saint Ramakrishna, addressing controversial issues by weaving mythology, history, and literary analysis together.

Kosambi, D. D. *Myth and Reality: Studies in the Formation of Indian Culture.* Bombay: Popular Prakashan, 1962, 1983.

Too advanced for many, this study analyzes the foundations and development of Indian mythology, culture, history, religion, and philosophy.

Littleton, C. Scott. *The New Comparative Mythology: An Anthropological Assessment of the Theories of Georges Dumézil.* Berkeley: University of California Press, 1966

Recommended for advanced work in mythology and methodology.

Mackenzie, Donald Alexander. *Indian Myth and Legend.* Gresham, 1913.

Available in some public libraries. Use with care and cross-check material carefully.

Macdonell, Arthur Anthony. *Vedic Mythology.* 1898; reprint Delhi: Motilal Banarsidass, 1981; New York: Gordon, 1974.

A reprint of a work from a venerable Sanskritist that is still useful, though dated.

Narayan, R. K. *Gods, Demons, and Others.* New York: Viking, 1964.

A popular retelling of myths by a noted Indian novelist.

O'Flaherty, Wendy Doniger. *Asceticism and Eroticism in the Mythology of Siva.* Delhi: Oxford University Press, 1973. Also printed as *Siva: The Erotic Ascetic.* New York: Oxford University Press, 1973.

This is a classic. It is for advanced students of Hindu mythology and for those with an aptitude for studies that are both complex and rewarding.

———. *Hindu Myths: A Sourcebook Translated from the Sanskrit.* Penguin Books, 1975.

Far more than its title indicates, this is a college textbook for serious, mature students. Playful, irreverent, scholarly—no one else could have accomplished so much. It will remain a classic in the category of sourcebooks.

———. *The Origins of Evil in Hindu Mythology.* Berkeley: University of California Press, 1976.

This is another of Wendy Doniger O'Flaherty's masterful studies. Her translations of Sanskrit sources are the solid foundation upon which she builds great palaces of insight and understanding.

———. *Women, Androgynes, and Other Mythical Beasts.* University of Chicago Press, 1980.

A must-read for advanced studies in Hindu mythology and feminist studies.

Rao, T. A. Gopinatha. *Elements of Hindu Iconography.* 2 vols. Delhi: Motilal Banarsidass, 1985. Originally published in 1914.

This is still a standard for scholarship on Hindu iconography, although written as an act of devotion. Four parts totaling nearly 1,200 pages were published by Paragon in 1968; often advertised as written by Gopinatha Rao, T. A.

Shearer, Alistair. *The Hindu Vision: Forms of the Formless.* London: Thames and Hudson, 1993.

This is a popular level work—likely to be found in public libraries—on Hinduism, explaining its core beliefs, art, and iconography.

Shulman, David Dean. *Tamil Temple Myths: Sacrifice and Divine Marriage in the South Indian Saiva Tradition.* Princeton: Princeton University Press, 1980.

This is an important regional study. It marked the attention finally paid to the non-Sanskrit-speaking south, whose traditions were as rich and varied as those of their cousins in the north and whose heritage is just as well preserved.

———. *The Hungry God: Hindu Tales of Filicide and Devotion.* Chicago: University of Chicago Press, 1996.

A study for mature students with a solid background in South Asian studies and Hinduism.

———. *The King and the Clown in South Indian Myth and Poetry.* Princeton: Princeton University Press, 1985.

This is a rich and rewarding study about Tamil myth and poetry.

Shulman, David Dean, and Don Handelman. *God Inside Out: Siva's Game of Dice.* Oxford: Oxford University Press, 1997.

This study of art and myth probes the multiple meanings of the dice game between Śiva and Pârvatî in the mythology and iconographic program of the Elephanta and Ellora cave temples.

Ward, William. *A View of the History, Literature, and Mythology of the Hindoos: Including a Minute Description of their Manners and Customs, and Translations from Their Principal Works.* Port Washington, NY: Kennikat, 1970.

Originally published in four volumes from 1817–1820, this is an example of a missionary's view of Hindu mythology during the time of the campaign to abolish *sati* (called by Westerners *suttee,* or widow burning). It is an historical document of a period and its conceptions and misconceptions. The Kennikat reprint has made this view widely available at public libraries.

Hinduism

Baird, Robert, ed. *Karma and Rebirth in Modern India.* The Hague: Mouton, 1985.

A study for advanced readers about the variety of interpretations of *karma* and rebirth from the nineteenth century.

Bary, William Theodore de, ed. *Sources of Indian Tradition.* 2 vols. New York: Columbia University Press, 1958.

Still an excellent resource to give the student of Hinduism an idea about the extent and complexity of scripture in India.

Basham, A. L. *The Origins and Development of Classical Hinduism.* Boston: Beacon, 1989.

Kenneth Zysk, one of Basham's students, crafted this volume from Basham's lecture notes. It is a good introduction to Hinduism, but it does not have the power and influence of Basham's classic history, *The Wonder That Was India.*

Bhardwaj, Surinder Mohan. *Hindu Places of Pilgrimage in India.* Berkeley: University of California Press, 1973.

A ground-breaking study of pilgrimage sites and their significance in providing a process by which a pan-Indian tradition could be perceived despite all its variety.

Dimock, Edward C., Jr. *The Place of the Hidden Moon: Erotic Mysticism in the Vaisnava-sahajiyâ Cult of Bengal.* Chicago: University of Chicago Press, 1966.

This text links the myth cycles of Vishnu, Krishna, and Radhâ with the ritual and devotional elements of Bengali Vaishnavism. It is scholarly and highly recommended for the intermediate student of Hindu religion and mythology.

Dimock, Edward C., Jr., ed. and trans. *The Thief of Love: Bengali Tales of Court and Village.* Chicago: University of Chicago Press, 1963.

This volume situates itself in the study of regional (in this case Bengali) medieval literature. But it is much more. It demonstrates the overlap in medieval India of literature, religion, and mythology.

Flood, Gavin. *An Introduction to Hinduism.* Cambridge: Cambridge University Press, 1996.

This introduction for college students attempts to present both sides of every issue in the study of Hinduism. For example, in the discussion about the origin of the Aryans both "the invasion" and "the indigenous origin" hypotheses are thoroughly discussed, and no conclusion is drawn.

Fuller, C. J. *The Camphor Flame: Popular Hinduism and Society in India.* Princeton: Princeton University Press, 1992.

This was written as a textbook for the university classroom. It is a solid study, sociological in its basic approach and rich in detail.

Haberman, David L. *Journey through the Twelve Forests: An Encounter with Krishna.* Oxford: Oxford University Press, 1994.

The study combines an account of the Ban Yatra, the pilgrimage to the sacred sites around Krishna's birthplace, with an analysis of related myths, history, and religion. It is an excellent introduction to the study of Krishna.

Hawley, John Stratton, and Mark Juergensmeyer, eds. *Songs of the Saints of India.* Oxford: Oxford University Press, 1988.

This anthology serves to introduce poets and singers who represent a medieval devotional tradition that translates the myths into religious fervor. Ravidas, Kabir, Nanak, Surda, Mirabai, and Tulsidas embody a mythic world of gods and grace.

Jamison, Stephanie W. *Sacrificed Wife, Sacrificer's Wife: Women, Ritual and Hospitality in Ancient India.* Oxford: Oxford University Press, 1996.

This exploration of the conceptual model for the role of women in ancient India combines history, religious studies, feminist studies, and mythology. This study may serve as an example of the excellent work being done in this area.

Kakar, Sudhir. *Shamans, Mystics and Doctors.* Boston: Beacon, 1983.

For intermediate students, this study explores the social dynamics of Indian religion from a psychoanalytic perspective.

Klostermaier, Klaus K. *A Survey of Hinduism.* 2d ed. Albany: State University of New York Press, 1994.

For my money this is the best introductory text about Hinduism. Written by one of the top scholars in his field, this study is comprehensive in its concise chapters, and it is possible to get through all of it in one semester.

Neville, Robert C., ed. vol. 1, *The Human Condition;* vol. 2, *Ultimate Realities;* vol. 3, *Religious Truth.* Albany: State University of New York Press, 2001.

These three volumes were done by a team of comparativists and area specialists; a chapter in each volume covers Hinduism. It is highly recommended for the advanced student in Hindu studies.

Neufeldt, Ronald W., ed. *Karma and Rebirth: Post Classical Developments.* Albany: State University of New York Press, 1986.

This volume surveys the reform, modernist, and traditionalist approaches and their understandings of *karma* and rebirth. For intermediate or advanced students of Hinduism.

O'Flaherty, Wendy Doniger, ed. *Karma and Rebirth in Classical Indian Traditions.* Berkeley: University of California Press, 1980.

This volume covers both orthodox and heterodox, or, as scholars call them, orthoprax and heteroprax traditions, in the early and classical periods of Indian history. For intermediate or advanced students of Hinduism.

———. *Asceticism and Eroticism in the Mythology of Siva.* Delhi: Oxford University Press, 1973. Published in India as *Siva: The Erotic Ascetic.* New York: Oxford University Press, 1973.

This is a scholarly study of Śiva as a paradox of ascetic and erotic practice. For mature students of Hindu mythology.

Sax, William S., ed. *The Gods at Play: Lîlâ in South Asia.* New York: Oxford University Press, 1995.

Twelve scholars combine their research and disciplinary perspectives to study *lîlâ* (divine play) in many contexts, as it reveals much about myth, religion, and culture in India.

Singer, Milton, ed. *Krishna: Myths, Rites, and Attitudes.* Chicago: University of Chicago Press, 1966.

This collection of eight essays demonstrates the richness of devotion to Krishna and its mythological connections. It is scholarly in perspective and can best be utilized by students with a good background in Hindu religion and mythology.

Sivaraman, Krishna, ed. *Hindu Spirituality.* Vol. 1, *Vedas through Vedanta.* New York: Crossroad, 1989.

This volume illustrates a wide range of spiritualities under the rubric of

Hindu or Hinduism. There is a richness of detail and perspective that illustrates the overlap between Hindu mythologies and Hindu spiritualities.

Smith, Brian K. *Classifying the Universe: The Ancient Indian Varna System and the Origins of Caste.* New York: Oxford University Press, 1994.

For advanced students who would like to struggle with twelve differing cosmogonic solutions.

Texts in Translation

This list makes no attempt to be adequate for two reasons: the scriptural and literary tradition is so vast, and the number of translations so great. The bibliography in Wendy O'Flaherty's *Hindu Myths* and *Origins of Evil in Hindu Mythology* (see above) are excellent. New translations are published and carefully reviewed each year in scholarly journals, so the list is expanding rapidly. There are several sites on the Internet that attempt to be current on Hindu scripture in translation (see below). The four books listed simply happen to be both well done and readily available.

Dimmitt, Cornelia. *Classical Hindu Mythology: A Reader In The Sanskrit Purānas.* Philadelphia, PA: Temple University Press, 1978.

Representative and well done.

O'Flaherty, Wendy Doniger, ed. and trans. *The Rig Veda: An Anthology.* London: Penguin, 1981.

A work by University of Chicago giant and standard setter.

Olivelle, Patrick, trans. *Dharmasûtras: The Law Codes of Ancient India.* Oxford: Oxford University Press, 1999.

——. *Upanisads.* Oxford: Oxford University Press, 1996.

Reliable and readable translations that should work well in the classroom.

History

Basham, A. L. *The Wonder That Was India: A Survey of the Culture of the Indian Sub-Continent before the Coming of the Muslims.* New York: Grove, 1954.

This classic just will not die. It is such a monument of scholarship, historically and culturally, that the offense of implying that "the wonder" ended with the arrival of the Muslims can be ignored. It is still the best introduction to ancient India for most people.

Chatterji, Suniti Kumar, ed. *The Cultural Heritage of India.* Rev. ed. 5 vols. Calcutta: Ramakrishna Mission Institute of Culture, 1978. Originally published in three volumes in 1937.

> Five volumes of massive size and rich scholarship cover Indian history, scripture (literature), philosophies, religions, including the literature in each language. Each volume reaches about eight hundred pages. A must for any good research library.

Hawley, John Stratton, ed. *Sati: The Blessing and the Curse.* New York: Oxford University Press, 1994.

> This volume contains a collection of scholarly essays on the problem of understanding *sati* (widow burning); the collection encompasses history, mythology, religion, feminist studies, and much more. More publications appear each year, but this volume may serve to represent international and intercultural studies of high quality and value.

Majumdar, R. C., ed. *History and Culture of the Indian People.* 2d ed. 5 vols. Bombay: Bharatiya Vidya Bhavan, 1964–1969. Originally published in 1951.

> Enormous in scope but a must-read for any serious student of India.

Woodruff, Philip. *The Men Who Ruled India: The Founders.* New York: Schocken, 1953.

> This study attempts to make a fundamental contribution to the history of British imperialism. It is representative of the issue of colonialism that is raging in South Asian studies currently.

Material Culture: Art, Architecture

This section on material culture will list the books most likely (at the moment of writing) to be in a public library. Annotations for these reference materials will be omitted because of space. Since books on material culture are more expensive to publish, the Internet and nonprint media like CD-ROM and DVD are beginning to offer an increasing variety of resources. In the nonprint section the Electronic Cultural Atlas Initiative (ECAI), as well as other resources, will be discussed.

Banerjea, Jitendra Nath. *The Development of Hindu Iconography.* M. Manoharlal, 1974.

Banerjee, P. *The Life of Krishna in Indian Art.* Delhi: Publications Division, Ministry of Information and Broadcasting, Government of India, 1978, 1994. Originally published by Magha in 1915.

Begley, Wayne E. *Visnu's Flaming Wheel: The Iconography of the Sudarsana-Cakra.* New York University Press for the College Art Association of America, 1973.

Collins, Charles Dillard. *The Iconography and Ritual of Siva at Elephanta.* Albany: State University of New York Press, 1988.

Gaston, Anne-Marie. *Siva in Dance, Myth, and Iconography.* Oxford: Oxford University Press, 1982.

Huntington, Susan L. *The Art of Ancient India: Buddhist, Hindu, Jain.* New York: Weatherhill, 1985.

Rao, T. A. Gopinatha. *Elements of Hindu Iconography.* 2 vols. Delhi: Motilal Banarsidass, 1985. Originally published in 1914. (Often advertised or listed as Gopinatha Rao, T. A.)

Rowland, Benjamin. *The Art and Architecture of India: Buddhist, Hindu, Jain.* London: Penguin, 1967. Originally printed in 1953.

Sahai, Bhagwant. *Iconography of Minor Hindu and Buddhist Deities.* New Delhi: Abhinav, 1975.

Stutley, Margaret. *The Illustrated Dictionary of Hindu Iconography.* London: Routledge and Kegan Paul, 1985.

Zimmer, Heinrich Robert. *The Art of Indian Asia, its Mythology and Transformations.* New York: Pantheon 1955.

———. *Myths and symbols in Indian art and civilization.* Princeton, NJ: Princeton University Press, 1972.

SELECTED NONPRINT RESOURCES

Video and Film

India produces more film and video than any other country for its billion people. Only a tiny fraction of these productions have much international appeal. Two recently published encyclopedias have attempted to classify this enormous output, but they are already almost out of date: *The Encyclopaedia of Indian Cinema* by Ashish Rajadhyaksha and Paul Willemen (London: British Film Institute, 1999) and "India" by Radha Subramanyan in *The International Movie Industry*, edited by Gorham Kindem (Carbondale: Southern Illinois University Press, 2000).

One online resource that is stable and expanding is the WWW Virtual Library's section on Indian Film <http://www.india.com.ar/india213.html>. Currently there are 122 Web sites on Indian film studies, including sites on actors and actresses and sites on specific directors like the internationally known Satyajit Ray.

A connected academic resource is South Asia Resource Access on the Internet (SARAI) at <http://www.columbia.edu/cu/lweb/indiv/southasia/cuvl/video.html>. Its affiliate members are important, and each is listed below:

- Contemporary Documentary Films on South Asia (available from the Center for South Asia, University of Wisconsin) (http://www.wisc.edu/southasia/films/).

  The Center for South Asia has produced a number of excellent videos that were designed for the classroom.
- Documentary Films & Videos on South Asian Religion (Geoffrey Samuel, 1994. Via Coombspapers archives, Australian National University) <ftp://coombs.anu.edu.au/coombspapers/subj-bibl-clearinghouse/sth-asia-relig-films-videos.txt>

  This is an important resource and one to watch for new additions.

  Films by Anand Patwardhan (Biju Matthew, Rider University) <www1.rider.edu/~webcis/mathew/anand.html>

Valuable resource.

- Film South Asia (Himal South Asia) <http://himalassociation.org/fsa/>

  "A biennial festival of documentary films on South Asian subjects, which brings together the best the Subcontinent has to offer in nonfiction film." Site includes a very useful Clearinghouse of South Asian Documentaries, with a large searchable database of films.
- Indian Video Collection at University of Virginia Library <http://www.lib.virginia.edu/clemons/ivid/indianvideo.html>
- Film and Video Lending Library (University of Virginia South Asian Studies Center) <gopher://minerva.acc.virginia.edu:70/0/pubs/soasia/filmsall.csa>

  Beneficial to see the holdings of a major university collection.
- Newstrack: index to the Indian monthly news video journal, 1988–1994 (compiled by Philip McEldowney, University of Virginia) http://www.lib.virginia.edu/area-studies/SouthAsia/SAvideos/nwsTrack.html

  Dependent on the work of a single professor; very valuable.
- South & South East Asia Videos at the Media Resource Center, University of California, Berkeley http://www.lib.berkeley.edu/MRC/SSEAsiaVid.html

  Beneficial to see the holdings of a major university collection.
- South and Southeast Asian Film and Video Archive (University of Wisconsin, Madison) <http://www.library.wisc.edu/databases/SEAvideo/>

  The videos from this archive are available on Interlibrary Loan.
- South Asia Feature Films and Documentaries at University of Virginia

Library <http://www.lib.virginia.edu/area-studies/SouthAsia/SAvideos/ saClemVi.html>
- Taxi-vala: documentary video by Vivek Renjen Bald <http://www.users. interport.net/~vbald/taxivala.html>
   Site contains reviews, background, and links to contact the filmmaker.
- Videotapes on South Asia (University of Hawaii) <http://www2.hawaii. edu/~asiaref/sasia/savideos.html>

Films for the Humanities and Sciences <http://www.films.com> has a section on Religion and Philosophy, but a search did not net anything on Hinduism. However, their search engine revealed that they had 34 films on India for sale. They also are a clearinghouse for BBC, Discovery Channel, and other sources for documentaries.

Many commercial films have mythic themes, and some might be of interest. More films have become available in video stores for rental. A search of Blockbuster (www.blockbuster.com) yielded 120 videos with "India" in the title. However, they had no subject or theme category, so specific titles had to be used. The films that struck me as possibly useful include *Bandit Queen* (1994) with Seema Biswas; *Kama Sutra: A Tale of Love* (1996) with Indira Varma (R rated); and Richard Attenborough's *Gandhi* (1982) with Ben Kingsley. A search for the director Satyajit Ray netted 34 videos, 10 of which were available, including *Pather Panchali* (1955) and *The World of Apu* (1959).

Filmakers Library <http://www.filmakers.com> features award-winning Indian commercial films and videos. Their current list of Indian films contained nothing on Hindu myths per se. However, 2 of the 21 were promising: "Tales of Pabuji: A Rajasthani Tradition" and "Valley of The Gods: Worship in Katmandu." (For descriptions go to their Web site.)

The Hartley Film Foundation <http://www.hartleyvideos.org> has two good introductory films on religion in India, "India and the Infinite" and "Hinduism: Song of God."

CD-ROM and DVD

There are a number of CD-ROMs on either Hindu religion or mythology in English in India. I reviewed some when I was in Bangalore a few years ago that were Vaishnava in perspective. However, they are not being distributed in North America and do not have an Internet presence at the time of this publication. I think this situation will change rapidly, so one needs a search strategy rather than a list that will go out-of-date quickly. Tools mentioned previously include Google (www.google.com), Amazon.com (www.amazon.com), Yahoo (www. yahoo.com), and other popular commercial search engines. Hinduism Today contains advertisements for CDs but these do not appear in the electronic version on the Internet (www.HinduismToday.kauai.hi.us).

Web sites on Hindu Mythology

There is no problem in finding a few thousand Web sites that contain materials (writing and graphics) about Hindu mythology. The quality and entertainment value of some are quite high. If one expects to find scholarly, refereed materials with both scope and depth at this point in time, one may only find that level of material in "passworded" university professors' Web sites. Without the password this material will not be accessible. That being said, there are some useful materials available. But remember the warning at the beginning of the chapter: change is constant, and this is particularly true of Web sites; they come and go.

A list of the best Web sites is far less valuable than knowing what kind of materials are currently available and how one goes about finding them.

Spelling

It is unlikely that you will be able to search in Sanskrit (Devanâgarî) on the Internet for some years to come (assuming that you would want to try). So you will have to take into account the many ways Hindu mythological terms are spelled (depending on how the Sanskrit letters are transliterated, or how speech is transcribed). For example, "Siva" for Śiva will net many finds, but so will "Shiva." "Krishna" for Kṛṣṇa is the most used English spelling, but even "Krsna" will net some results. If the person is Hindi-speaking, they might also use "Krishn" or "Krsn," since the final *a* is dropped even when Sanskrit words are brought over into Hindi. The word *citra* (painting) is a very popular name and begins many Sanskrit compounds. However, its pronunciation invites the spelling as *chitra*, which approximates its pronunciation. There is also a real *ch* in Sanskrit, but it was often designated as *chh* in the past. Not everyone has switched to *c* and *ch* rather than *ch* and *chh*.

Commercial vs. Scholarly Sites

If you do not mind being lured to a site in order for them to "give you a cookie" (to obtain information about your visit and possibly your email address), then commercial sites with some graphics and text abound. They will grow even more attractive and plentiful in the future. All you need to do is search from your browser on a current search engine and thousands of sites will magically appear.

Scholarly sites are harder to find. General search engines (except for Google) seldom list them, unless at the very end of a search. Many commercially motivated search engines give special preference to sites that advertise, and so commercial sites emerge at the beginning of your search. Of course, if you want to buy a book on Hindu mythology, then it will please you that your search is tracked and you receive the appropriate news about what is available from Amazon.com or some other firm. (See the discussion at the beginning of this chapter about finding children's books.)

Online Sanskrit Dictionaries

Cologne Digital Sanskrit Lexicon. <http://www.uni-koeln.de/phil-fak/indologie/tamil/mwd_search.html>

> At present the Cologne Digital Sanskrit Lexicon contains the Monier-Williams *Sanskrit-English Dictionary*, with approximately 160,000 main entries. You can search for one of the Sanskrit main entries under either Sanskrit or English for a definition, and grammatical and any other information listed in Monier-Williams. The transliteration for Sanskrit input requires some special learning but it is well worth it.

Capeller's Sanskrit-English Dictionary. <http://www.uni-koeln.de/phil-fak/indologie/tamil/cap_search.html>

> At present the digital version of *Cappeller's Sanskrit Dictionary* (1891) contains approximately 50,000 main entries.

South Asian WWW Virtual Library

This network has linked approximately 4,000 scholarly sites on South Asia and continues to grow very rapidly. It is the brainchild of Australian librarian Matthew Ciolek. For scholars and serious students of India this is the portal to academic use on the Internet. One may access this vast network via the WWW Virtual Library <http://vlib.org/> and through its specific address for India at <http://www.india.com.ar/india2.html>. An enormous world opens, organized into "General Info" about India <http://www.india.com.ar/india201.html>, "Art and Culture" <http://www.india.com.ar/india202.html>, then skipping to "History" <http://www.india.com.ar/india207.html>, "Images" <http://www.india.com.ar/india209.html>, "Movies" <http://www.india.com.ar/india213.html>, "Religion" <http://www.india.com.ar/india222.html>, and "Indian Search Engine" <http://www.india.com.ar/india233.html>. There is no separate category on Hindu mythology at this point.

Electronic Cultural Atlas Initiative (ECAI)

This is a collaborative project of enormous scope whose purpose is to combine academic disciplines using the ECAI TimeMap to study any point on the globe digitally and visually, from multiple points of view. It is the brainchild of Lew Lancaster at the University of California, Berkeley. At the point of this writing some three hundred affiliated projects are available for viewing and study. The access address is <http://ecai.org>. Selection of projects on South Asia <http://ecai.org/Projects/index.html> links one via a database to the available projects, ranging from the "Digital South Asia Library" <http://dsal.uchicago.edu> at the University of Chicago (which must be explored in detail for its digital resources, including dictionaries, maps, and so on) to the "Virtual Village" (http://www.colleges.org/~village/) of Arampur. Some sites are yet to be completed, and others are only in the planning stage, but this collaboration promises to usher in a new kind of learning.

The Wabash Center Internet Guide: Hinduism

The Hinduism portion of the "Wabash Center Internet Guide" is quite extensive and very useful. Charles K. Bellinger created the guide with funding from the Lilly Foundation. Its main address is www.wabashcenter.wabash.edu/Internet/front.htm and the access point to Hinduism is <http://www.wabash-center.wabash.edu/Internet/hinduism.htm>. This selection opens on "Syllabi and Teaching Resources," followed by "Electronic Texts," "Electronic Journals," "Websites" (quite selective and well chosen), "Bibliographies," and "Listserv Discussion Groups." Although this site is housed in a Christian seminary context, it reflects work that is generally informed and nonideological. Several sites are worth highlighting.

Harappa: Glimpses of South Asia before 1947. <http://www.harappa.com/welcome.html>

   This site features images, movies, and sounds relating to Indian culture, as well as informative essays.

History of India. <http://www.historyofindia.com>

   This site provides a timeline of Indian history, with pictures.

Exploring Ancient World Cultures: India. <http://eawc.evansville.edu/inpage.htm>

   Provides the historical background for the development of Hinduism.

The Hindu Universe. <http://www.hindunet.org/home.shtml>

   This is a major site, which organizes material under subject headings and also provides a search feature. Headings include Arts, Customs, Worship, Interfaith Relations, Scriptures, and so forth. Maintained by the Hindu Students Council.

American Academy of Religion Syllabus Initiative

The American Academy of Religion has begun a project of collecting course syllabi <http://www.aarweb.org/syllabus/>. It contains a syllabus on films and video <http://www.aarweb.org/syllabus/films.asp>. It revealed 61 syllabi about Hinduism. These are a few samples:

"Hindu Myth, Image, and Pilgrimage." <http://www.courses.fas.harvard.edu/~lac18/>

A course by Diana L. Eck at Harvard University

"Ramayana as Literature, Performance, Ideology." <http://www.aarweb.org/syllabus/syllabi/l/lutgendorf/lutgendorfRAM.pdf>

A course by Philip Lutgendorf at University of Iowa

"Mahabharata as Literature, Performance, Ideology." <http://www.aarweb.org/syllabus/syllabi/l/lutgendorf/index.htm>

A course by Philip Lutgendorf at University of Iowa

"The Goddesses of India." <http://www.aarweb.org/syllabus/syllabi/l/lutgendorf/Goddesses_in_India.pdf>

A course by Philip Lutgendorf at the University of Iowa

"A Research Guide for Core 166." <http://www.exlibris.colgate.edu/curricular/Spring_02/CORE166India.html>

Another syllabus, not part of the AAR Syllabus project, that might be invaluable for teachers. It was developed by Rebecca Hewitt at Colgate for a basic course on India.

Miscellaneous Sites (Largely Personal and Commercial)

These selections from approximately a hundred thousand possibilities may serve to represent general sites on the Web. They range from works of individual pleasure and dedication to ideological sites that have a point of view or seek legitimization. If the site fits your need, then it is appropriate. If not, then it represents the chaos and clutter that populates the Wide World Web.

Angelfire. <http://www.angelfire.com/ca/Hinduism/>

This is a general site about Hinduism ranging from reincarnation and other Hindu concepts to scripture and practice. Figures such as Vivekananda and organizations such as the Arya Samaj are presented in a popular style.

Hare Krishna. <http://www.shamantaka.org/index.html>

This page is the gateway to the Hare Krishna movement. It is rich with information about this Vaishnava tradition, its philosophy, and practice.

Hindu Tantric Home Page. <http://www.hubcom.com/tantric>

This is a very thorough site that provides an introduction to the Tantric tradition, along with many primary texts and a bibliography. Maintained by Mike McGee.

Hindu Women. <http://www.hinduwomen.org>

Gender issues are discussed from goddesses to marriage problems, worship to fashion. News articles mix information with visuals on women's lives. A good site for information about women's issues and news.

Kamat's Potpourri. <http://www.kamat.com/kalranga/hindu/>

An unusually large collection of material on Hindu mythology. Especially good collection of images of the gods and goddesses.

List of India-Related Web Sites. <http://www.apnic.net/mailing-lists/s-asia-it/9905/msg00015.html>

Asia Pacific Network Information Center (APNIC), Brisbane, Australia.

Self-description: "Compiled with an aim of promoting India-related content in cyberspace." The site contains a total of 266 entries, such as Indian Search Engine, Links To Other Sites, Music, Culture, and History.

Mohan's Hindu Image Gallery. <http://www.hindugallery.com>

A fairly large collection of images of Hindu deities. The page also includes links to similar sites. Maintained by Mohan Ayyar.

Siamese Dream. <http://www.siamese-dream.com/reference/reference.html>

A commercial Web site that currently provides a free reference service: self-described as "an introduction to the main concepts of Hindu thought; the main gods and goddesses; and some of the major literary works."

Snowcrest. <http://www.snowcrest.net/dougbnt/hindu.html>

This site has a range of resources, including scriptures such as the *Bhagavad Gîtâ*, excerpts from the *Rigveda*, selections from the *Upanishads*, and Tantric texts. There are pages on Vedic culture and history and links to similar sites and newspapers. It is a commercial site.

No listing can be complete; that is the nature of ever-expanding scholarship. And this representative selection does not even list all the books in my own library, many of which are just too specialized to suggest to the general reader. I can only hope that this list will help point readers to the *wonder that is India* (making present Basham's famous phrase of tribute).

GLOSSARY

abhaya freedom from fear

âcârya a religious teacher

adharma breach of duty

Aditi the mother of the gods, wife of Kaśyapa

âdityas sons of Aditi, the gods *(devas)*

adrishta the unseen

advaita non-duality, literally "not dual"

Advaita Vedanta nondualistic *darśana* (often translated philosophy); monism; championed by Shankara

agnyâdhâna fire sacrifice; consecration of fire

ahimsa "non-murder," or nonviolence; noninjury

aiśvarya desire for power; sovereignty, supremacy, power; superhuman power

amrita drink of immortality

amrita-kalasha the magic of no-death

ânanda bliss; joy; sign of *mukti* or *moksha* (liberation and enlightenment)

Ananta "infinite"; name of the great serpent that served as Vishnu's bed

Anjanâ mother of Hanuman

apunya vice, "sin"

ardha half

Âranyakas forest texts of the *Vedas*

Arjuna a disciple of Krishna, and the hero of the *Mahâbhârata*

arîti a prayer

Ârya, Âryan "noble ones," twice-born, descendants of Indo-European clans

aśrama stages of life: student, householder, semi-retiree, and world-renouncer; hermitage

aśrama-dharma law code of the four stages of life

Ashthâvakra a deformed sage

ashtha siddhis eight superhuman powers

aśva a horse

aśva-medha   horse sacrifice

Aśvins   twins; the celestial physicians

Atman   the real Self; the true perceiver, eternal subject, infinite, immortal, perfect, and free; that which is one with the Absolute (*Brâhman*)

Aum   the all, the absolute, the sacred syllable *(OM)*

avatâra   an incarnation of the divine

avidyâ   ignorance

Bali   a demon king

bhakta   a devotionalist; one who practices devotion to a god or goddess

bhakti   devotion, worship paid to a god or goddess

Bhagavad Gîtâ   "The Song of the Lord," dialogues between Krishna and Arjuna

Bhairava   "terrible," one of the forms of Śiva

bhakti yoga   the *yoga*, or practice, of devotion

Bhû   earth, land; a goddess who personifies the earth

bodhi   supreme knowledge

Brahmâ   the creator

Brâhman   the Absolute

brâhmin, brâhman, brâhmana   member of the priestly caste

Brahmânda   egg of Brahmâ, the cosmic egg, the universe

brahmacarya   stage of the student; control of sexual impulses

Brahmo Samaj   "Society of God" founded by Rammohan Roy, great reformer and opponent of *satî* (suttee, or widow burning); Roy is often called the father of modern India.

buddhi   wisdom, reason

cakra   a wheel, a vortex of energy

Candra   the moon

catur   four

Catur Veda   four Vedas

catur varnas   four castes

catur yugas   four yugas, a kalpa

catur yogas   the four yogas: *jñâna* (rational), *bhakti* (devotional), *karma* (actional), and *râjâ* (mystical)

ciranjiva   immortality

Dadhîca   a sage who gave his thigh bone to be made into the thunderbolt weapon *(vajra)* that slew Vritra

daitya   demon sons of Diti

Daksha   a grandfather *(prajâpati)*; father of Sîtâ and father-in-law of Śiva

darśana   "taking the view" of a holy place or a holy person; also a "philosophy"

deva   a god, one of the general class of divine beings

devata   a divine being, a godling

Devadâsi   a temple prostitute; literally "a servant of god"

Devaloka   heaven; the place of the gods

Devî   a goddess; the Goddess

dharma   righteousness; proper social behavior; social duty; proper way of acting

Dhenu   a cow

dhyâna   meditation, contemplation

Dravidians   indigenous people; Indus Valley people

duhkha   pain, grief

eka, ekam   one, "the One"

gana   dwarfs, Śiva's's attendants

Ganapati   lord of the army of *ganas*; god of luck and wisdom; Ganeśa

gandharvas   heavenly musicians

Ganeśa   elephant-headed son of Śiva

garbha   egg, embryo

Garuda   an eagle, vehicle of Vishnu

go   a cow

gotra   family, race; lineage; orders of created beings

guru   teacher; spiritual guide

gurubhais   brothers or disciples of the same *guru*, or teacher

hamsa   a swan

Hanuman   a monkey chief, son of Anjana and Vâyu

heteroprax   other or "alien" practice

Himâlaya   "abode of snow"; father of Pârvatî, wife of Śiva

himsa   murder, violence

Hiranyagarbha   "golden egg," golden womb

Hiranyakaśipu   a demon king, killed by Vishnu

Indra   god of storm and battle, king of the gods

indrajala   magic, illusionism

îśvara   the lord; god

japa   repetition of a divine name or of a mantra

jâtî   "birth," or social group within which one must marry if one is an orthodox Hindu; there are several thousands of *jatis* within the four castes, or *varnas*

Jambudvîpa   our earth island known as "rose-apple tree" island

jîva   an individual soul; life force of the individual

jîvan-mukta   one who has been liberated in this lifetime

jñâna   knowledge and truth

jñâna yoga   the spiritual path of knowledge

jñâna   one who follows *jñâna*, the cognitional path

Kailâsa   the Himalayan or heavenly home of Śiva

kâla   time

Kâlî   "the black one," fearful aspect of Devî or Pârvatî

kali yuga   dark age; present time; pleasure-loving age

kalpa   age, eon

Kâma   desire for material pleasures; the god of passion

Kâmadhenu   the heavenly cow

kapala   the skull, ritual object in some Tântric sacrifices

karma   law of cause and effect; morality; ethics

karmaphala   the result of an action

karma yoga   discipline or practice of unselfish activity; doing everything for God's sake

Kârttikeya   the god of war, son of Śiva (also Skanda)

Kaustubha   the jewel of Vishnu's chest

Krishna, Kṛṣṇa   divine charioteer for Arjuna; eighth incarnation of Lord Vishnu

kśatriya   member of the caste of princes and warriors

Kûrma   a tortoise; an *avatâra* of Vishnu

Lakshmî   goddess of beauty and luck

lâya   absorption or destruction of universe

lîlâ   divine play

linga, lingam   phallus; emblem of Śiva

loka   a world, region

mritasañjîvinî   the magic art of restoring someone to life

maha   great, mighty

Mahâdeva   "the great god," Śiva

mahat   cosmic consciousness

Maheśvarâ   Śiva ("the great lord")

maithuna   Tântric term for sacramental intercourse

mandala   circle; a "chapter" of the Rigveda

Mandara   mountain used by the gods to stir the cosmic ocean

mantra   sacred chant of "seed" sound, verse of scripture, or formula

Manu   first man of each age, father of the human race

manvantaras   world cycles, each ruled over by a new Manu

mânasa-bhâva   "mind born"—usually of Brahmâ

marga   a spiritual path

Matsya   a fish; fish incarnation of Vishnu

mâyâ   power; magic; illusion; the transitory world of phenomena, understood as concealing the reality of the Absolute

mâyâvî   "one with magical power," magician

monism   *Advaita Vedânta*, as nondualism

moksha   freedom; emancipation of the soul from rebirth

mritasañjîvinî   life-restoring magic

mukti   liberation; real freedom; state of nonaddiction

nâga   snake, serpent

Nara   "man"; the sage associated with incarnation of *Nârâyana*

Narasimha   the man-lion; fourth incarnation of Vishnu

Nârâyana   the supporter of life, Vishnu

Natarâja   Lord of the dance, a name of Śiva

nimitta   causality, effective cause

nirguna brâhman   the Absolute beyond all qualities or modifications

ojas   concentrated psychic power

Om   *Aum,* the sacred syllable

orthoprax   practice that is other; alien practice

padma   a lotus

pañcakanyâs   the five ideal women

paramâtma   the supreme spirit

Parasu-Râma, Parasurâma   Rama with the Ax; sixth incarnation of Vishnu

Pâtâla   the netherworld

Paśupati   Lord of cattle

Prahlâda   a demon and also a devotee of Vishnu

Prajâpati   Lord of created beings

prajâpatis   progenitors, grandfathers; creators of the *gotras* or orders of being

prajñâ   wisdom, knowledge

Prakritî   eternal nature

pralaya   destruction, dissolution of this *kalpa*

prâna   breath, energy, life; the five energizers or breaths of Rudra

pitri   spirit, soul after death

pûjâ   worship, in such forms as prayer and offerings

pundit   teacher—of anything from grammar to literature, sacred or erotic

punya   virtue, merit, good

purusha   "the man," the spirit or soul

râja   a ruler, king

râja yoga   "royal" *yoga,* or practice of mystical states; mysticism; the yoga of mastery over the mind

Râma   divine king; seventh incarnation of the Vishnu

Râvana   a demon king from Lanka who abducted the wife of Râma

rik   verse, merging with *Veda* to become *Rigveda*

rishi   sage or seer; traditionally seven great seers [*mahârishis* or *sapta-rishis*]

Rudra   early Vedic god; later a form of Śiva

sâdhanas   disciplines, some quite severe, such as fasting, trance-states, sexual abstinence

saguna brâhman   the Absolute modified by human or finite conception and imagination, "with *gunas* (attributes)"

samâdhî   trance; state of perfection, freedom, bliss

Samhitas   collections that included the *Rigveda*

samsâra   transmigration of the life force or soul; the sea of change and rebirth

samnyâsa   state of renunciation; freedom from addiction; bliss; God-realization

samnyâsin, sannyasin   someone in the fourth and highest *aśrama* (stage of life); the state of renunciation; world-renouncer

Sarasvatî   goddess of speech and learning

Satî   wife of Śiva; mother of Kârttikeya and Ganapati; daughter of Daksha

satî   good and virtuous wife; immolation of wife in funeral pyre of husband

śaktî   "power" and energy of universe; the Divine Mother; the Goddess

Śâktism   worship of *Śaktî* as the Supreme

Śankara   seventh-century philosopher and Shaivite priest who championed the *darśana* of Advaita Vedanta

Śâstras   religious texts of the middle ages of India, mainly devotional

śava   a corpse

Śesha   the serpent of eternity, having one thousand heads

Śiva   third member of Hindu divine triad, the destroyer; the Supreme; the "auspicious one"

śrâddha   faith and trust; Vedic offering to a priest

Śrî   wife of Vishnu, the goddess ("prosperity"); another name for Lakshmî

śruti   "that which is heard," the *Vedas*

smritî   "remembrance, memory, tradition"; the lesser scriptures

siddhi   a psychic (or occult) power, miraculous abilities

simha   a lion

Sîtâ   the wife of Rama, "furrow"

Skanda   son of Śiva, god of war (also Kârttikeya)

Soma   the divine plant; another name for Candra, the moon god

srishthi   creation or re-creation

sthiti   evolution

śûdras   the caste of servants and laborers

Sûrya   the sun god

sutra   a "thread"; one of a class of scriptures

svadharma   own duty

svarga   heaven

tândava   violent dance of Śiva done at Satî's death

tantra   meditation; secret discipline or practice

Tantras   treatises on ritual and esoteric practices

tapas   austerity, purification; magical means

tapasya   renunciaton

tîrtha   pilgrimage site; ford

triśanku   three sins of killing a *brâhmin*, a woman, or a cow

Trivikrama   "the three stepper"; fifth incarnation of Vishnu, who filled the earth, heaven, and hell with his three steps *(krama)*

Umâ   Śiva's wife; another name for Pârvatî

Upanishads   the philosophical section of the *Vedas*; from *upa* (near), *ni* (down), and *sad* (to sit)—thus the act of sitting down by one's *guru* to receive instruction

Vâc   goddess of speech, personification of the *Vedas*

Vaikuntha   abode of Vishnu, heaven

Vaishnava   a worshipper of Vishnu

vajra   thunderbolt, weapon of Indra

vâhana   a vehicle of a god or goddess

Vâmana   Vishnu's fifth incarnation, the dwarf

vara   boon

varna   "color" or caste; the four *varnas* are Brâhman, Kśatriya, Vaiśya, and Śûdra

Vâsuki   a name of Śesha, the cosmic serpent

Vâyu   god of wind

Vedas   the most sacred scriptures of Hinduism, veneration of which is essential to being a Hindu

vidya   knowledge, science

vijñâna   learning, knowledge; all-knowingness, comprehension

vikalpa   imagination, fancy; uncertainty, doubt

vikshepa   confusion

vira   brave; a hero

Virocana   a demon prince; "illuminating one"

Vishnu, Viṣṇu   member of the divine triad, the preserver; "all-pervader," "preserver"

vivarta   projection, illusion

viveka   discrimination

yâga   a sacrifice

yajya   ritual, worship, sacrificial rite

yâjña   a sacrifice

Yama   the god of death

yoga   union, from *yuj*, to yoke, join, concentrate upon

yogi, yogin   one who practices *yoga*

yuga   a world age

yuga   the four *ages:* the *satya yuga*, the *treta yuga*, the *dvapara yuga*, and the *kali yuga*

INDEX

ABOUT THE AUTHOR

George M. Williams was awarded a Ph.D. from the University of Iowa in 1972, specializing in religion in modern India. Williams taught for one year at Newton College of the Sacred Heart, Boston, before going to California State University, Chico, in the fall of 1972, joining their newly formed Department of Religious Studies.

His major interest for the past two decades has been in religions that liberate and in liberal religion. This interest has been furthered by his participation in the International Association for Religious Freedom and has led to two honorary doctorates: In May 1994 Starr King School for the Ministry awarded Williams with the Litterarum Humanarum Doctor, and in October 1996 Williams was presented the award of Doctor Honoris Causa from the United Protestant Seminary of Cluj [Kolozsvar], Romania.

A specialist on Svâmî Vivekânanda and the Hindu Renaissance, Williams helped found the section on Hinduism in the American Academy of Religion. He also served on the Electronic Publishing Committee of the academy and was its projects director for a number of years. In both 1997 and 1998 Williams held the Shree Muherjee Chair at National Institute of Advanced Studies, National Science Campus, Bangalore. While there he worked on projects involving preservation, digital archiving, translation, and preparation of a comprehensive database of the *Bhagavad Gita* and other sacred texts. In 1998 he held workshops for archivists and librarians from all over India on use of the Internet for research and publication, CD-ROM publication, and digital archiving.

In 2001 Williams completed a two year project: the digitizing and archiving of the works of Raja Rammohan Roy, the great reformer of Hinduism and the founder of the Brahmo Samaj. His goal is to finish a number of books and videos that will advance the notions of liberating spirituality.